The Wandering Years

The author

THE WANDERING YEARS

Diaries: 1922-1939

CECIL BEATON

WITH PHOTOGRAPHS

LITTLE, BROWN AND COMPANY

Boston   Toronto

And tell of time, what gifts for thee he bears.
What griefs and laughter through the wandering years.
                                                    Euripides, Bacchae

THE WANDERING YEARS

Diaries: 1922-1939

CECIL BEATON

WITH PHOTOGRAPHS

LITTLE, BROWN AND COMPANY

Boston   Toronto

To the Memory of
my Father

And tell of time, what gifts for thee he bears.
What griefs and laughter through the wandering years.
                                        Euripides, Bacchae

Contents

CONTENTS

Illustrations

A*

*All the photographs were taken by the author except
No. 26 (by Paramount), No. 32 (Press photograph),
No. 38 (by Nurse Alice Collard). The group No. 16
appeared in* English Vogue *The portrait on the cover
is a detail from a painting by Christian Bérard.*

Introduction

It isn't easy to make public the private record of a lifetime. Of all forms of writing, diaries are the most personal; their publication cannot but invoke question or criticism.

Most mysterious is why people write them. Someone once commented to me, 'I always mistrust people who keep diaries.' I winced and was set to wondering. Had I scribbled hundreds of volumes out of boredom, loneliness, frustration or the need for self-assertion?

Perhaps; but my obsession also stemmed from those same obscure motives that have impelled me to take snapshots all my life. Even as a child I felt haunted by a sense of the elusive. And when I grew up, *carpe diem* became my watchword. I exposed thousands of films, wrote hundreds of thousands of words in a futile attempt to preserve the fleeting moment like a fly in amber.

Hence perhaps the existence of these pages. They are winnowed from an exhaustive record in which anything and everything was set down. But does that justify their publication especially when the most private events are described? I shall inevitably be charged with over-zealous candour. Why, my critics will ask, didn't I hide the diaries under the floorboards?

Reply is not easy. There is, of course, the precedent of other diarists who published journals in their own lifetime. But they have been men of letters, adventurers, generals or statesmen. My province is more frivolous, as my critics never cease to remind me. But perhaps for that very reason I may unwittingly have captured fragments of a social scene that might be shared and give a certain nostalgic amusement to others.

If I am at times too candid, it is not by design but because indiscretion is almost unavoidable: individual idiosyncracies are more dangerous to deal with than the events of a military campaign or an intrigue in Arabia. In any case, the reader will find I have spared myself no more than others. I find it painful to reveal myself as I was. This is scarcely a flattering self-portrait. Yet truth begins with one's self. No attempt has been made to touch up those extracts in which I appear in a particularly unsympathetic light: for they, too, help to give a picture of the time. I hope, however, that the reader will bear in mind the social circumstances that formed me. In term's of today's more relaxed manners and disregard of conventions, the opinions or attitudes of a young Englishman of thirty years ago must inevitably seem preposterous.

But I must not protest too much. Let the diaries speak for themselves. Their content remains unaltered, though from time to time I have fused a number of entries to form a single recollection of a person or a place. Readers may complain that too much space has been given to a description of an unimportant occasion, whereas some other event that must have been of consequence to me has been indicated in a couple of lines or entirely ignored. But surely this is the very nature of most diaries? In any event they are apt to give a lop-sided impression, since the writer generally does most of his work when feeling melancholy, lonely or down on his luck. Hence the general picture is often self-pitying, or gloomily introspective.

I have tried to fill in the more serious lacunae with narrative comments—not so much to give an autobiographical form to the volume as to explain certain extracts that might otherwise be obscure or in need of a longer context. The story told here begins at Cambridge and ends with the outbreak of the Second World War.

CECIL BEATON

Part I

Cambridge

1922

After three escapist years at Harrow School, where my fledgeling interests were ex-curricular, and any signs of intelligence were seen only out of class, my father was faced with the problem of what to do with me. Most of my contemporaries now knew what they wanted to be in life; but at the age of eighteen I showed no particular aptitude for any known career. I had acquired somewhat of a reputation, and a certain amount of scandalous disapproval, for being able to make people laugh, and was considered sophisticated for my age. Yet I was, in many ways, remarkably undeveloped. It is true that I had been the art master's prize pupil, with a knack for water-colour sketches, and a derivative flair for caricature and theatre design; but I, myself, had little confidence in these talents. In fact, secretly I was as anxious about my future as my father must have been.

It was therefore a welcome reprieve when my parents decided that my education should be continued at a university. Most parents already knew to what university, and to which college their offspring were to go. But my father was delightfully casual about such things, and one

I

Saturday afternoon, at the thirteenth hour, set off at the wheel of the family Renault for Cambridge. Here he interviewed a Mr Armitage of St John's college. It is only now, so many years later, that I understand what a remarkably generous and loving parent I was fortunate enough to have. Perhaps too close a proximity prevented his children from seeing him as the wistful and rather whimsical person he was; and with the years he wore a sad expression that may have been the result of feeling unappreciated. When, however, he came across some stranger who reacted to his charm or his wit, his whole being changed, and he shone brilliantly. My father had been all his life an enthusiastic cricketer and was, in fact, renowned as a wicket-keeper.

Mr Armitage immediately recognised my father's charm, straightforwardness of manner, and simplicity of character, and he enjoyed the cricket talk. After the interview, it was arranged that, although the college was full, I should have rooms in Bridge Street and could 'go up' at the beginning of the next term and remain on, provided I could pass a special examination to be taken on arrival.

Neither of my parents was particularly interested in the arts or in their manifestations. My mother certainly had an innate taste and sense of design and proportion, which I have consulted all through my life. My father, as a young man, was an amateur actor in the days when the amateur theatre had a certain status; and he often delighted, and at the same time embarrassed, us by his imitations of the actors of his day. But it must have been baffling for this straight-sailing couple to discover that the eldest of their four children was turning out to be so different from all that was expected.

Even as a child, I preferred to sit silent and self-conscious among the grown-ups while other children played rounders or rolled in the mud. I displayed not the slightest interest in cricket, or how to throw a ball with a twist on it, and now I was showing dissatisfaction with home life, as well as signs of outrageous snobbishness. I was full of inner yearnings, growing my hair 'like a piano-tuner', and developing other ridiculous aspects of aestheticism.

My ambition to break out of the anonymity of a nice, ordinary, middle-class family certainly manifested itself in other tiresome outward forms; one of which was the pleasure I took in surprising, or even shocking people by the inimitable way in which I adorned myself. Thus, it is not at all unexpected that, on the first occasion here recorded, I should purposely have allowed myself to be caught wearing a peculiar assortment of garments, before changing into a conventional suit, by the

2

Victorian Mrs Perry, the only bona fide actress, albeit retired, my parents knew. Mrs Perry was the extremely respectable widow of a Folkestone doctor, with whom my family had made friends when holidaying one summer. Although Mrs Perry was an aggressive person-ality, and enjoyed every opportunity to take the centre of the stage, she had never been celebrated in the professional theatre. Yet to our somewhat conventional family house in Hyde Park Street she brought a distant exciting flicker of the footlights.

*October 4th 1922, 3 Hyde Park Street, London, and
47 Bridge Street, Cambridge*

When I woke this morning, I had only one thought in mind: I wanted Cambridge to be a success. I wanted it so much that I was late for breakfast, and had a terrible rush with the packing. I filled two huge trunks with books, albums, and photographic equipment, and got very hot doing so.

For no known reason I was wearing an evening jacket, red shoes, black and white trousers, and a huge blue cravat. I cannot think what impression I made on old asthmatic Mrs Perry arriving for lunch with my mother; she caught sight of me before there was an opportunity to change. But then Mrs Perry was once an actress and therefore less likely to be surprised than most of my parents' friends; not that she looked like an actress in her black bombazine and bonnet—more like an old Victorian land-lady, or Queen Victoria herself—and I am sure that putty face with the shiny warts had never been covered with grease paint.

At lunch she boomed away, breathily, in her rich fruit-cake voice about her uncle (Leigh Hunt) and Shelley, and it made one realise what a long way back she goes into history. However, when she started to hold forth about her daughter Elfie, and how she was going to be given the part of an understudy, lunch seemed to go on for ever. One big course followed another, while Mrs Perry held the limelight.

After much excitement and further packing in all sorts and sizes of extra boxes, I finally got off in a taxi. Not much bother at the station but I had to pay eight shillings for excess luggage.

In the train I read Mrs Pat's *Memoirs*, but my cold was bad. I sniffed a horrid lot, then just sat back looking out of the window. It was a cold, rainy day, with a grey and white sky. There were

3

stretches of jade-green fields, of grey, feathery trees. The cool, calm scene seemed to make me think clearly. I felt depressed at the prospect of the maths exam, and other terrible things: having to live among awful heartiness, and in filthy rooms smelling of onions, decorated with landlady's horrors.

I wanted in future to see everything as it really was. I wanted to have a little more grit. The man sitting in front of me had large, fat lips and a huge nose. He was ugly, but he looked as though *he* had grit; for some reason, that was what *I* wanted. Could I, in the event of another war, possibly go in the trenches and fight as others had done before me? I wanted to do that and more: I wanted to ride bikes and fight. I often despise people who do these things, but I wanted to be *able* to do them.

Sitting in the train with my gloves on, I thought of what I'd be like after Cambridge; and if I'd be there long, and if this diary would be interesting. Somehow I wished that I'd had my photograph taken on my first day of this new ordeal. It might be interesting later, though at the moment I'm tired of myself. I always seem so terribly the same, doing such stupidly petty things as telephoning and writing letters and having meals and going to theatres. I'm also tired of my appearance. I always look the same—the same hands, the same thin figure and a face without too much expression in it.

I drove here in a taxi, wondering if my rooms would be miles from anywhere, or if they'd be even worse than expected. The luggage was brought up. I tipped until the change ran out. My rooms were shown me by a cheerful, sensible man whom I liked. Then an old fellow came grumbling up the stairs, and the landlord gave him a shilling on my behalf—very kind.

My quarters turned out to be quaint, with old, sloping ceilings and floors, with white walls and black beams. At least I could make something of them. I was pleased. And when the housekeeper and the maid seemed 'all right', I lost the last of my depression.

After unpacking, I went out to see Armitage at St John's. He seemed delightfully vague and suggested I come back on Friday after I'd had my exam. I'm fortunate to be up here at all, without having passed the exam, but I really feel that I'm up here on the strength of my father's charm. I then bought a cap and gown, terrified of looking ridiculous in it—which I did.

The landlord (I believe his name is Haynes) brought up a Mr Sutcliffe, another 'new boy' of St John's, who has rooms beneath mine. We went to Hall together, but as he had his own friend I kept rather apart. It was a large dinner, and I fed my rotten cold according to the old wives' rule, and I talked to a red-headed youth, evidently from the north.

Afterwards, I came back to these digs quite happy, meaning to write diary, do some maths, despatch letters and go to bed early. But I had a visitor. It was Bobbie Heath, from Harrow, who charmingly decided to call. He liked my rooms and my dressing-gown very much. I showed him my drawings. He thought I was improving. It is nice to show one's drawings to people who appreciate them. Everyone at home is too casual about my efforts. He then switched to showing me some of his photographs, but I was by then too tired to be enthusiastic. At last he hobbled down the narrow stairs.

I'm too tired to write to Kyrle[1] now, but I'll write tomorrow. Gordon[2] will be here by then; also Boy[3], which will be splendid.

My bedroom is countrified. I had rather hoped for something more prosperous, but I suppose this is paradise compared to other quarters. There is no fireplace in the sitting-room—a pity when my friends come to eat food round the polished table.

Tomorrow the exam. I have an awful sinking feeling. It will be terrible writing to my father in America to say I've failed.

October 5th

I shan't hate Cambridge after all. In fact it ought to be quite fun: lots of people wander about, looking lost and bored. I daresay Oxford would be no nicer. Certainly they must have landladies there, and china cats, but perhaps nothing as horrid as the Market Square, or the road down by the Red Lion: that road is always crowded; people get knocked down by cars, there's an awful noise of bicycle bells and it smells with pipes in everybody's face.

My rooms are growing on me. But how shall I furnish them?

[1] The late Kyrle Leng, a friend of aesthetic interests and great charm, at this time up at Oxford.
[2] The late Gordon Fell-Clark, a contemporary at Heath Mount, Hampstead, and at Harrow School.
[3] Edward le Bas RA, also a contemporary at Harrow.

It will have to be cottagey. What pictures can I put on the walls? I'm tired of ballet pictures. I think Pamela Bianco's[1] illustrations would be suitable in black frames and large mounts. Or some Georges Barbier: I might write to Kyrle and find out what books Georges Barbier illustrated.

Generally, I stay awake for ages when I sleep in a new room. But last night, in spite of a hard pillow and no air coming through the little window, I fell asleep almost at once. When I woke early this morning, the bedroom with its sloping eaves looked romantic by dawn darkness. I lay for a while in delightful semi-consciousness, thinking about the day's business: that damned exam had to be got through, and so many other things. I had a big breakfast, though it felt odd to breakfast without newspapers.

I bought a compass and met Bobbie Heath on my way to the exam hall. My cold bothered me rather much. I don't know how I've done on the exam; it's impossible to tell. I was sure I'd passed last time, and hadn't.

At five o'clock I met Gordon. I was pleased to see Gordon. We had tea at Fuller's, Gordon very full of his successes with girls and said he was unofficially engaged. He looks just the same as at Harrow—perhaps a little coarser, also sunburnt in places.

When Gordon left to unpack I went to Bobbie's rooms. His sitting room has glorious dark oak panelling, also height, shape and tall windows. There were peonies and Canterbury Bells in huge pots, and a polished table where we sat and had more tea in an apple-green tea service. We laughed; we talked long as we ate strawberries and cream. I envied the oldness and the comfort of it all: the chandelier, the books, the Pera cigarettes. A terribly *gauche* youth came in. Bobbie has a way of making friends with awful people. He doesn't like them, but he's always friendly with them. I wish I were. I can't stand talking to people I don't like. Naturally they hate me for being so priggish. It would be better if I were more like Bobbie. I thought Bobbie looked like a young edition of Barrie's Lob. Or was he the host in *Shall We Join the Ladies*?

After dinner in Hall, a nice, red-haired Scot brought me my cap, which I had left under the bench. I went to the cinema

---

[1] A child prodigy whose recent exhibition of drawings had created a great stir at the Leicester Galleries.

with Bobbie. I was disappointed with Rod LaRoque, but saw Gordon there and talked to him all through the film.

It was a quarter past ten when I got back. At first I thought I was locked out. I was very disturbed, but the door had only got jammed. The housekeeper on the stairs said she thought curfew was at ten o'clock. 'Surely not, surely it must be twelve!' What a bore if I had to be in by ten every night.

I got into bed and read *Macbeth*. At twelve o'clock, sleepy and cold, I pulled aside the curtains to peep out on the jumbled roofs and windows—a view which in sunlight looks like a back street of what I imagine Venice to be like. It was raining fast. I could hear the rain against the old roof.

October 6th

It's jolly good of my father to send me up here. It must cost him a lot, and he's very generous about an allowance. I don't have to worry about money, so long as I'm not unreasonably extravagant. I feel so independent and original. I must buy lots of things for this sitting-room: emerald green curtains, green cushions and green china. I must also get some of those tall, twisted wooden candlesticks!

There is a little pot in here that one puts in front of the gas stove to take away the fumes. On it is written: 'Lost time can never be found.'

I thought about that pot as I lay warmly in bed for a long time after I ought to have got up. Then I put lotion on my hair, dressed properly and enjoyed a slack morning. No exam, no rushing off to tutors. I wrote a long letter to Modom,[1] scribbled diary and rubbed my fingers a lot, as chilblains are starting.

This afternoon I read *Macbeth* for about two hours, being very pleased when the murder of Duncan was found out. I have wonderful ideas for that scene with Lady Macbeth in black and dark grey.

After Shakespeare, I read *The Times* and saw the announcement of the Du Maurier dance. I was annoyed at missing it. Tea by myself. A little bored, I went out to find Boy's rooms. I met James Player, looking squashed: the poor thing couldn't

[1] My mother's sister, Madame Suarez, Aunt Jessie, who married Colonel Pedro Suarez, Bolivian Minister in London. She was now a widow living in reduced circumstances.

get up here, so he's trying for next year. Also saw Joe Harmsworth, terribly fat in a brilliant blue suit. He, too, is not up here, so I really am lucky. Joe told me Boy and Tris[1] were out golfing.

I went to be interviewed by Armitage. Outside John's I met Robert Leng. It was good to bump into a brother of Kyrle—even Robert. Robert seemed quite awake. I arranged to meet him tomorrow evening.

It turned out one had to wear cap and gown when visiting Armitage. By the time I returned properly dressed, five people had arrived before me. Ten more came and we waited in his rooms.

Armitage was late, of course. He is always rushed from seeing too many people. We talked about the work I should do if I'd got through maths. He said the English tripos would be fun. The work sounded amusing; I wanted to do it, if I was clever enough. Armitage said I would get into a nice set of people if I did do it, and would be able to join the Marlowe Society. This pleased me immensely.

Dinner in Hall was dull. I didn't know anyone. On the way back to my rooms, a figure met me in the darkness. It was Boy, looking ludicrous in cap and gown. We roared with laughter.

Boy enthused about my rooms, saying how lucky I was that they were so central, and how awful his were. I showed him my paintings (which *I* liked) and we talked quickly about people and artists—Augustus John, Orpen (a heated discussion), Epstein. I said I hated Aubrey Beardsley.

Boy entertained me with an imitation of his landlady sporting a black eye and holding her heart when she saw the huge mantelshelf had been removed. Then he left.

I think Boy will be good at oil painting. I was surprised to find out how much less cheap his taste has become since Harrow. He now admires Botticelli! It's rather exciting.

How amicable everyone is here. Even the people I used to hate and turn my back on now come up and shake hands. The most weird types have spoken to me. Fenwick, who reviled me at Harrow, came and sat next me at the cinema. I suppose *I'll* have to become friendly with the world too!

[1] C. T. Bennett, a former Captain of cricket at Harrow School.

October 7th

There were tomatoes with bacon at breakfast. I had a lot to do, as I was to meet Boy at eleven o'clock. I wrote diary and applied hair lotion.

Boy's rooms were a pleasant surprise! Two tall windows, and some not bad pictures on the walls—but what a jumble of oils, prints and etchings. I admired some designs he had done for covers of music scores. Really, Boy has improved. This morning he wore wonderful new greyers and a double-breasted waist-coat. A pity about his suede shoes though.

We went off to buy things. Boy was extravagant (but then, he can afford to be, and I envy him that). He forked out for a wonderful print of the Mona Lisa in an elaborate frame, and a book of Beardsley drawings with which I wasn't best pleased. I bought a surplice, and a box of figs and some cheap but pretty flowers, huge dahlias and Michaelmas daisies.

After lunch, I scoured the whole of Cambridge for a jade-green china service. At last an intelligent woman promised to get me a set, only there'd be a fortnight's delay. In the mean-while, she has lent me a willow pattern. I then succumbed and bought a Biblical vase. The colour is too sombre, but I had to get something for the flowers stuck in my washing jug.

I met Gordon for tea at the King's Parade Café. Everyone stared, everyone seemed to be listening to our conversation. We retreated to his digs, which are typically landlady's taste. After paying a king's ransom in tips for nice rooms, he has been stuck with plush and china cats. We played his gramophone, which wasn't much fun.

During dinner at Hall, I felt relieved to find someone I could talk to. Langton-May is another old Harrovian, but I never knew him well at school: he was so shy. Now he seems witty and grown-up in his ideas, and encourages me to be clever. He suggested that people are more friendly here out of in-sincerity. If we hated certain people at school, it was because of being bottled up: one got sick of seeing too much of them. But at Cambridge there are so many people one can afford to be amicable without worrying about having to see them again and again.

I opened the box of figs. I love their dull skin and dull red insides.

October 8th (Sunday)

I started Locke's new novel *The Tale of Triona*. Then Robert arrived punctually, and we went off on a sightseeing tour of Cambridge.

We took the weeping-willow path by the river at the back of Trinity. He called it the 'Vacs' or something. We wore ourselves out seeing too many beautiful things, including King's chapel like carved lace and Christopher Wren courts and Inigo Jones façades. Best of all the bridges. I liked the silvery stone one at Clare College.

We went to the Fitzwilliam Museum. There's a hideous thing of Bernard Shaw by Augustus John. Quite apart from the fact that it doesn't even resemble G.B.S., the colour is puking. John's etchings and drawings are infinitely better.

We found proof that Rupert Brooke had been at Cambridge. After reading the *Memoir* so many times, I somehow thought he'd gone to Oxford! But here was a photograph of the poet himself: calf-faced with long silken hair. There was the original manuscript of *Grantchester* in funny, sloping handwriting. At the top of the poem was written: 'Poem to be entitled The Sentimental Exile.' Now that I think of it, I do remember something about the Marlowe Society in Brooke's *Memoir*. How thrilling that such an amusing person should have been here, and not at Oxford.

I couldn't find Langton-May at Hall for dinner, and took any place. While we stood in silence waiting for grace to be said, the fair boy next to me suddenly began to quiver all over with laughter. He couldn't control himself. I felt sorry for him, as I know how awful it is not to be able to stop laughing. Later, he explained that the chorus of senile and beavered elders lined up in front of their carved chairs struck him as farcical caricatures of old age. What an odd sense of humour he'd got. To me, they were awe-inspiring embodiments of profound wisdom and scholarship, with their bald heads, parchment skin and wisps of white beard. One in particular might have been painted by Tintoretto: he had a straight nose and deep, hollow eyes with huge pouches under them.

Robert told me people at Oxford throw bread about in Hall: I can't imagine Kyrle doing it.

October 9th

This morning I was determined to face up to the geyser in the bathroom. It proved a complicated ten minutes, putting matches to the wrong places and turning on the gas instead of the water. Nevertheless, I had a bath.

After breakfast I wrote, then hung up a tie rack in my bedroom. When I looked out of the window, I was aghast to find the patina of my back street in Venice being spoilt. A red-headed boy had climbed up a ladder and now stood covering everything with bright pink paint. There was no way of stopping him, so goodbye Venice.

I bought the papers. How sad to read of poor Marie Lloyd's death. Everyone is dying. I was looking forward to seeing her in the music halls next holidays, with her cockney gusto, low-cut evening dress, diamonds and teeth. It's too tragic.

Boy came to take me for a tour in his motor-car. He looked at Venice being spoilt while I put on my new coat, a reddish tie and no hat.

It is pretty round Cambridge. We decided we must come out and sketch together. Boy drove well, and very fast. We talked very fast, too. I did envy him, having the car and being so clever with it. I can't even ride a bike! There were lots of things to see: black and white cottages with ragged roofs, flat fields and high sky looking like pictures by Arnesby Brown.[1] Also a funeral: two huge masses of flowers, and a procession of people in black. They seemed so unreal with all the green around them. Their black clothes were so black, and the flowers looked so white. (Poor Marie Lloyd!) We branched off on another road in order not to disturb them.

On the way back we went to Grantchester and looked at the orchard where Rupert Brooke wrote poetry at ten to three. But what a horrid little house. I really shouldn't have cared whether there *was* honey for tea.

We had tea in Boy's room, and he showed me some of his drawings. I liked one of Othello in scanty clothing murdering his wife.

Reminder: Never relight your cigar.

I wish I could find the really best people at Cambridge, if

[1] A painter whose canvasses I had admired at the Academy. Inevitably they consisted of a small strip of ploughed field beneath an enormous square of empty sky.

there are any. There must be some like Kyrle—clever, interesting, artistic, not absurd or dull. But somehow I'm rather shy. And I hate the way people stare at me. I can't think why they do it. I'm not fantastically dressed or odd looking.[1] Yet it's a fact: they *do* stare.

I long to join the dramatic clubs—the ADC and the Marlowe Society. I should like to work on a play. If I worked really hard, I could do it all myself—all the costumes and curtains and rehearsals. I could even learn to climb ladders and fix lights.

October 10th

Robert came to tell me that he'd been to the Senate House and seen *I had passed my exam*. Could it be true? I thought maths would baffle me forever. Now I'd never have to pull my hair out again when I thought of it. I'd never have to waste months of good time at that filthy tutor's, doing work I despised. Oh, what joy! Robert didn't stay long to share it. When he left, I threw myself on the bed and bellowed with triumph. All morning long, whenever I looked in the glass I saw a broad grin on my face. I sprinted out to send telegrams and postcards. If I could have whistled, I would have done so now. I didn't mind feeling idiotic when the man behind the counter read my messages. They were all flippant. To my tutor I wrote: 'You dear old soul, you've passed me.' To the Beaton family: 'Stupendous miracle; let the world rejoice; living marvel, etc.'

After lunch I stayed indoors, reading *Marius the Epicurean*. Telegrams of congratulations came from Aunt Jessie and from Nancy and Baba.[2]

Soon after five I went to see my supervisor. His rooms were very select: pale grey, white and orange, with Medici prints of Dutch paintings in polished ebony frames on the walls. Mr Bennett seemed fond of Herrick, also of Donne's sermons— and of giving me a list of lectures I have to attend! Shakespeare, the seventeenth-century dramatists, poetry; and I can go and hear Walter de la Mare if I wish.

Afterwards, came back and finished *Macbeth* for the third

---

[1] Since I was possibly wearing fur gauntlet gloves, a cloth of gold tie, scarlet jersey and flowing 'Oxford Bags', perhaps it is reasonable to suppose that I was noticeable.
[2] My sisters.

time. Acted the sleep-walking scene. What a part for a boy in
Elizabethan times!

Went to see Armitage. He was astounded that I had passed
maths, but said I should take up Art instead of French. At one
moment he looked at me and said, 'You *are* a queer fish!' I
felt he was a damnably rude fish! Anyhow, I like him. I also
know that he likes me. As he put it, 'I want you to make good,'
a phrase I particularly dislike.'

Armitage said he liked my papa for being a kind man and a
sportsman—a rare combination. Armitage sees hundreds of
parents in his position, also many famous people; but he has
hardly ever seen anyone who impressed him as much as my papa.
In fact, Daddy impressed him so much that he offered me a glass
of champagne, but I refused.

At five minutes to twelve I bolted back to my rooms, ate
three macaroons and was very cold in bed.

October 13th

I feel such a useless fool. I would like to be able to drive a car,
fish, row, paddle a canoe, hunt and shoot.

October 14th

At lunch today Boy ate enormously, especially of the Bismarck
herrings. Then we went to Ely and saw the cathedral. I was
annoyed at not being able to admire it. But we both liked the
Bishop's Palace, a wonderful old Jacobean thing with warm
colours and fantail doves circling around.

Boy brought me home and I read letters—the first from
Mummie since she left for America. They were written in the
middle of the Atlantic. It had been a terrifically rough crossing:
even the bandsmen were too seasick to appear.

I started to read *Sinister Street*. It's shaming not to have read
it before; and, if I don't do so immediately, it will be too late.
Compton Mackenzie has such a sense of humour.

October 16th

Lecture on Chaucer. Mr Wyatt was quite interesting. He evidently
knows his subject—not always the case with the masters at
Harrow.

After Chaucer, I went to see Mr Bullough about Art. I should imagine he is only half English. There was a little bronze statue on the mantelpiece (it could have been Hermes) and a large print of a lot of Velazquez topers making merry: *The Triumph of Bacchus*. Mr Bullough gave me a list of art lectures to attend on Wednesdays and Fridays in the Museum of Classical Archaeology.

Gordon made me buy a Cambridge Pocket Diary. He says they are useful. I always write my engagements down on odd bits of paper and promptly lose them.

I decided to buy a bright red tie, which annoyed one shop assistant. I said, 'Is this all you have? A rotten selection.'

He said, 'Well, we don't get any demand. *No one* wears a red tie nowadays.'

I said, 'That's exactly why I want one.' Two other shops and found nothing suitable. I'll have to send to Oxford for one!

I am writing this while eating lumps of crisp, crusty bread with butter and anchovy paste.

October 17th

Lecture at nine on literature in Pepys' lifetime. It would have been dull if I hadn't been attacked by a wasp. Everyone shouted to kill it.

I killed the wasp and had my hair cut. The more fool I, I never realised how short the man was trimming it.

Soon after tea I had to see Mr Bennett. He unmuddled me about my work. It appeared that I had gone to the wrong lecture on Thursday. I wondered what the Middle Ages had to do with Shakespeare!

October 18th

Lecture by a Mr Attwater, on poets of the seventeenth and eighteenth centuries. Lots of epigrams flying around. Mr Attwater is dark, fairly young, and looks as though he spent his life in a rugger scrum. He read poems and although nothing to do with the subject enlightened us about the decadence of the naughty Nineties.

As it was raining, I popped into the Fitzwilliam Museum to

see the Lady with the Yellow Shawl. I don't know why I admire
Augustus John; I criticise almost every picture of his that I see.
But each new Gainsborough seems better than the last. I spent
a long time looking at his two young children with Beggar's
Opera clothes.

At five-thirty Mr Bullough lectured on art and aesthetics.
He was splendid. He talked about the theory of art, and said that
beauty can be defined. I like Mr Bullough, though his neck is
much too thin and long. I believe he is half Italian.

October 19th

Now that my hair is cut short, my head seems such an awful
shape—like a donkey, all long and square. I'm such a damned
fool: I never realised how much the barber was shaving off. I
did the same thing last season, just when I was going to six
dances a week. When I complained to my mother, she said, 'I'm
sick of you worrying about your hair. There's every chance of it
growing again. You're getting very conceited.'

Boy came in at ten-thirty to motor me to London. He said,
'Do come to lunch. It will be dull if you don't. When no one
else is there, the family never has anything to say.' In the Seven
Sisters road he was talking so fast that he didn't notice a cross-
roads, nor the policeman who held up his hand. Right across the
road we went, at thirty miles an hour. A little black car jerked
out from the far side of a huge tram; and of course we had a
collision. The trouble was soon over, with very little damage.

We drove to a motor shop, left the car to be put right and
taxied to meet Boy's family at *Les Gobelins*. Mrs le Bas was in
brown, and *could* speak. In fact she was vociferous about Boy's
bad driving. Once he ran into a horse and they all had hysterics
when the huge thing fell right on top of the car, almost squash-
ing them. Gwen, always prettier than a flower, had huge ear-
rings; Molly looked deliciously absurd in the biggest hat that
I've ever seen. Lunch was fairly amusing. Molly said that once a
photographer had told her to laugh; and when she did he immediately shouted 'Stop it!' The le Bas were off to see José Collins
in the *Last Waltz*. José has recently married Lord Robert Innes-
Kerr, which prompted me to tell about the waiter in the small
Soho restaurant where José gobbles her pre-matinée lunches.

The waiter was heard to shout in a bored voice down the hatch: 'Another double-portion of tripe and onions for Lady Robert!' Boy and I went out to do some shopping. I bought wine glasses at Waring's and Pera cigarettes. Then we went to the Medici print place in Grafton Street, staying there a great time. Boy was extravagant as usual: he bought two Botticelli prints, Primavera and The Birth of Venus, at two pounds ten each! I brought Boy to H.P. street for tea. Loins opened the door for us, unaccountably wearing outrageous white clothes. Modom, in black and pearls, appeared blinking and surprised at the top of the stairs.

We talked very quickly while I put on the *Scheherazade* record. During the tomato sandwiches, Baba appeared. I couldn't help laughing at her: her hair had grown too long at the back, and she was wearing an awful grey woolly over her blue and white dress. Then Nancy came in her hair scraped off her forehead. I told her to go and have a shampoo, and she looked rather annoyed. Baba said, 'What a sight Angela Duveen is looking nowadays, without her tortoise-shell glasses.' I said, 'It's a pity; they held her face together.' We unwrapped the Botticellis, but Modom can never get farther than Murillo. Before starting back to Cambridge in the mended car, Modom insisted on a stirrup cup, and brought out a prized '75 port.

October 20th

Lunch today with Cooper, a gangling albino with whom a half-hearted friendship is maintained because his mother is a friend of my aunt Cada.[1] The meal was a morbid affair altogether. The knives and forks were cheap and tinny, the tablecloth not too clean, the food bad curry with apricots and biscuits. The cigarettes gaspers.

I decided that it might be all right to listen to Cooper on the telephone. But when one *sees* him he is hideous, and makes everything round him equally hideous. He regaled me with tales of how he lived for a fortnight in Whitechapel with a brown paper parcel as luggage: he's interested in social problems. Fortunately, his mother is artistic and his father enormously rich, so their house is wonderful. He showed me pictures which had

[1] Mrs Chattock.

16

appeared in *The Ideal Home*. What a waste that a youth who cares nothing for comfort or beauty should have all that money!

October 21st

I drew a bit too much during Mr Bennett's lecture on Shakespeare and didn't pay sufficient attention.

I passed the Market Square. Tomatoes, flowers, red sweets, the brass and the crowd—everything reminded me of *Petrouchka*. I went to Bowes and Bowes and looked at Aubrey Beardsley's books to see if I couldn't admire him after all. I made up my mind to buy the Pamela Bianco edition of drawings with accompanying Walter de la Mare poems, but at Eliza Johnson's they hadn't got it. Another shop did produce a copy, which to my delight was reduced to ten-and-six.

Lunch was spent looking through this new acquisition. What a remarkable creature Pamela Bianco must be: a child of twelve, doing spindly, wiry drawings with an archaic boldness combined with the feeling of a Florentine painter of the Renaissance. I am so pleased with my purchase.

A VISIT TO OXFORD

October 22nd (Sunday)

Robert Blundell had warned me to be ready early if I wanted to motor with him to Oxford. Eight o'clock seemed cruel on a Sunday morning, and I was so rushed I ate no breakfast whatsoever.

Robert, in a huge, cocoa-coloured overcoat and caramel muffler, came twisting up the stairs smoking an Egyptian cigarette. He delayed our departure, telling me how he'd driven to London last evening (without an *absit*) to see the Duncan sisters.

At last we started off in the open car. It was sunny and cold. We didn't go very fast—averaged about thirty miles an hour. I like Robert: he's quiet and unhurried, wise and uncritical. He is so sensible that he has the effect of making even me feel sensible too. The first twenty miles seemed long, but after Bedford the fields flew past. We whizzed through St Neots to Bicester. We talked in deep, grave voices, never glibly but seldom for long on the same subject. We talked about Ethel Levey and revue actresses, Colonel Repington's diaries, Mrs Asquith, signet rings and dogs.

When at last we reached the ugly outskirts of Oxford, I was aching and stiff from the cold wind. I spotted the Rothenstein boy and he directed Robert to Kyrle's rooms in the High Street. As I creaked out of the motor, my legs felt like ice and could hardly support me. Robert said when he would pick me up, then drove off. While I waited for the doorbell to be answered, I felt like an actor listening for his cue, yet uncertain of what he will say onstage. I followed someone up to Kyrle's rooms.

It was a somnambulist's arrival. Vaguely I noticed Kyrle's blue coat and red waistcoat, and—someone sitting on a sofa. The stranger wore a green tie, making me wonder where I'd seen him before. It was Victor Butler; and I'd seen him at Harrow. He had dropped in unexpectedly to see Kyrle. I sat with my back to Kyrle, in front of the fire, feeling acutely self-conscious and generally miserable. I couldn't utter a word. Victor Butler talked intelligently and Kyrle laughed raucously.

At last Victor left and I began to thaw, though still not quite at ease. I could have kicked myself for being so gauche. After all Kyrle and I had spent weeks together in Wales, when we slept out of doors, went fishing, rode a motor bicycle, got punctures and climbed up mountains. I stumbled about, making inadequate comments about Kyrle's room and furniture. He has some pieces of pure Hepplewhite and Sheraton, not the muck I accumulate. Neither does Kyrle go in for rubbishy chrysanthemums from the local market. He had a pot of lilies on top of a bookcase; and by a lamp were the tallest roses I've ever seen, also some green orchids. Kyrle's books and pictures are good: many first editions, lots of Kay Nielsens and a lithograph by Hartley.

Bob Gathorne-Hardy, Kyrle's room-mate, came in to say lunch was ready in his room. His appearance was almost comic: pink and white complexion, nose and mouth much too small for the rest of the face. He seemed brilliant, talking hard all the time. Perhaps he felt he had to, as I was so silent. Kyrle told me afterwards that Bob always makes ceaseless conversation. Be that as it may, he gabbled so quickly in a deep throaty bass I could hardly hear anything he was saying (that's an exaggeration). It added to my confusion.

After lunch we went back to Kyrle's room. But soon the

C.B. at 47 Bridge Street, Cambridge

Church parade: Nancy, Baba, my Mother, Aunt Jessie and C.B. outside Hyde Park Street

scout came in looking rather bewildered, and announced that there were two more courses to follow! We could not go back. We'd already had an enormous lunch: eggs scrambled with button mushrooms, chicken and a *soufflé*.

During coffee, Bob held forth on Restoration comedies. In a breezy, off-hand and I must say unsparing manner, he described all the plot complications. I was shocked but secretly delighted by the ease and charm with which he used four and even six letter words.

Quite unexpectedly, eight people burst into the room. Kyrle introduced everyone rather badly, making me feel still less at ease.

What an extraordinary crowd. Bob's brother, Eddie G.-H., looked like Andrew Aguecheek—uncommonly tall, vellum complexion, tortoise-shell glasses, long hair, a bemused expression about his eyes and mouth. He had a deep crumbling voice, outshone his brother in lewdness as he talked about seductions and affairs. Eddie spends three thousand a year on old books, at Claridge's and the races.

Then there was Billy Smith (son of W.H.) in bright new brown leather shoes, his hair cut so short at the neck and sides that it seemed shaved. Eddie Sackville-West looked like a bird in a tight suit, carrying a black stick in its claw. Lord David Cecil talked even more quickly than Bob. He, too, wore a perpetual smile on his pale face. His eyes had cushions of amusement underneath them, but they looked at you with the slow appreciation of a cow. His movements, by contrast, were staccato and unexpected. He dashed about the room, seized a hair brush in the middle of a sentence, went on talking while he puffed his hair out until he looked, as he said, 'like the barber in Happy Families'.

Kyrle took me aside and protested that he was furious at the intrusion. He then looked even more miserable when we glanced through the window and saw another half-dozen undergraduates walking arm in arm towards his rooms. In burst Teddy Hogg, together with handsome, blue-eyed, stuttering Eardley Knowles and others whose names I barely or never heard, including three or four peers. One I think, was Lord Cavendish Bentinck; another Lord Sudeley.

What a gabble! Everyone talked at once. I'd never seen anything like them before, and *en masse* they seemed overwhelming.

I gaped like a cod; I listened like a foreigner. Bob G.-H. said to someone, 'Hermia Wormsley ought to be ravished. In fact, it would do a lot of people good to be ravished.' Lord David Cecil, evidently showing off, interjected an extremely witty remark. Everyone roared with laughter, but as he rattled on so quickly I could hardly catch a word.

In the midst of things, Kyrle announced that he and I were going out. There followed a lull of silence as we left, but the babble began again before we descended the stairs. Outside, Kyrle said none of them minded what he said or did.

We walked arm in arm to see Magdalen. I didn't pay much attention to the surroundings, being too intent on trying to re-establish our former intimacy. By now we were walking in Addison's Walk, then went into Magdalen Chapel.

When I told Kyrle about the Pamela Bianco book, he replied that he'd known her at Harlech! I was impressed.

We went to the Ashmolean, where Kyrle had arranged for me to see the Uccello. The Stag Hunt in the Forest By Night is his favourite picture. Its detail, colour, form and perspective are indeed perfect.

Meandering again, we passed Eddie Sackville-West's and went in. Princess Bibesco and Puffin Asquith were there, so we did not break up the party. Puffin has a huge head of wiry, fuzzy hair. He talked in such spasmodic jerks I could hardly understand him. Elizabeth B. far from being the magpie beauty the news-papers write of, looked like a large oyster, and was just as silent.

When we returned to Kyrle's rooms, there were still a few people left. But they soon decided to go for a motor drive with Eddie G.-H., who reappeared wearing a pea-soup coloured cap and driving a hired Overland. The crowd borrowed Kyrle's coats and mufflers, and from the balcony we watched them roar off.

It was good to be left in peace. We talked at random, with our old ease. We ate bread and butter and listened to Schumann records. We looked at albums of photographs. I lingered over a picture of an Elizabethan house and garden. 'Whose house is this?' 'A woman who lives near here at Garsington: Lady Ottoline Morrell,' Kyrle answered. 'Isn't she the scarecrow that Augustus John painted? Doesn't she have magenta cheeks, beetroot hair and two protruding teeth? Oh, I long to meet her!'

'You will,' said Kyrle. 'You'll like one another. In fact,' he laughed and lines appeared round his eyes, 'she's rather like you!'

All too soon Robert was outside with his car. Motoring through the darkness I offered some frank impressions of Oxford while Robert pricked up his ears. I said, 'People at Oxford do give the impression of being very much more sexual than at Cambridge! They are ravishing Hermia Wormsley and heaven knows who else.' We stopped in Bedford to dine. I was glad Robert allowed me to pay, as I would have felt awkward if he hadn't.

When I got back to my rooms, I found a note saying I had been elected a member of the ADC. Perhaps Cambridge won't be so bad now.

October 23rd

Everyone had gathered in a huge mass for the St John's college group photograph. I was cheered by all for being so late. Then the usual fuss that goes on when a group is being taken: silly little men ran up and down waving fingers, telling so-and-so to lower his head as the sun caught his glasses, while such-and-such must stiffen his chest. Stupid people burst out laughing just as the snipper was snipped; and the usual roar of mirth when the snipper *had* been snipped.

We proceeded to the Fellows' anteroom, where we 'formed up' to march to the Senate House and sign our names in the Cambridge register. Luckily for me, we queued in alphabetical order.

When we arrived in this absurd crocodile, there were quite a number of youths from Trinity still waiting to sign. They leant against benches and walls in an exasperated manner. The Worth-ington-Evans boy swore like a duchess. He had had to wait for over an hour. I suggested that, for the occasion at any rate, he should drop the hyphen.

Only six people were ahead of me to sign. The formality proved ceremonious. Three men shout out your name. You walk forward. Two little boys offer pens, one of which is chosen. It is dipped in ink and you scribble your name in a huge book. With five hundred people staring, you walk very sedately into the open air, a proud member of Cambridge University.

Armistice Day

A huge, surging crowd had gathered in the Market Square for the Two Minute Silence. Then a maroon went bang. Everyone became still and silent, as though turned to stone. I stood apart in the middle of the road and looked down at the wet ground. A piece of bright emerald cabbage lay in the gutter. I thought of Claude[1] with his sleek pale face and hair, his interest in Bakst, his own drawings done with a needle sharp pencil, and how he'd gone off to the mud and horror of the trenches.

I remembered the first Armistice Day. I was in my bedroom at Temple Court,[2] brushing my hair. The maroons went off. My mother and I went mad with joy. I had a funny feeling inside me and lumps in my throat. I beat the lunch gong and ran two miles to John Barnes[3] and bought enormous Union Jacks to hang from the windows. At Piccadilly Circus that evening, the delirious mob surged like a sea through which the buses moved slowly like ocean liners in a storm.

I was brought back to Cambridge and the present day by two maroons going off at the end of Silence. Dogs barked. A woman with a pale, fat face and red hair said, 'Did you see that poor soul with her children? She was weeping. Her husband had been killed.' But the crowd was already intent on its marketing, buying and smiling at the stalls.

November 15th (Saturday)

We had drunk four bottles of champagne between the three of us. It was a good thing that Tris suggested we leave the Smoking Concert. I could hardly stand up. Out in the cold air I realised I was quite tight. Boy seemed in even higher spirits and let forth hyena-like yells of laughter. Tris was sober, so I held on to Tris. We came to my rooms and stood by the outer door. Boy and sober Tris began to bawl in unison, 'Mr Biggs! Mr Biggs!'

I laughed, half terrified. Mr Biggs[4] came rushing out. I murmured something about my friends being vivacious tonight, then

---

[1] My cousin Claude Chattock killed near Arras in 1916, aged twenty-three.

[2] Temple Court, Templewood Avenue, Hampstead, the neo-georgian house in which my childhood was spent.

[3] The local Harrod's.

[4] My landlord's partner.

walked with difficulty to my sitting room at the bottom of the yard. I sat laughing on the sofa. Mr Biggs came in all red and awkward and half-smiling. He asked if I was all right. 'Yes'— and to prove I wasn't tight, I opened my sitting room door, managed to walk gingerly the length of the yard, then only fumbling a bit, to unlock the door to go up to my bedroom. Mr Biggs watched.

Somehow I navigated the winding stairs, remembering what Hamar Bagnall had said one day my first term: 'These are awful rooms to come back to when you're blotto.' I stared in the glass to see what I looked like when drunk. It was much the same face, only white and shiny. I staggered a bit, sat on the bed and watched the walls going round and round. I didn't laugh much now. I felt ill. I tried to make myself be sick in a jug, which I was. It was all terribly sordid. What a good thing I hadn't been sick outside with Tris and Boy! or at the Cottrells! I wondered if Boy was being sick.

In bed the whirling sensation accelerated. I got up again and threw the contents of the jug out of the window. Then I rinsed the jug, dashing more and more water out of the window. I washed things: I sprayed eau-de-Cologne all over the room, but still I could smell sickness. I felt like Macbeth after the murder.

November 16th

Early this morning, I got a whole lot more water and threw it out of the window, in a panic about the mess on the tiles outside. I washed the jug and a towel. I had my bath. More eau-de-Cologne everywhere, and I came down to breakfast.

Mr Biggs visited me later. He looked like the cat that ate the mouse, 'I've got a complaint about you. Mr Turner said he had to get up in the middle of the night to shut his window, as such terrible things were coming through it. This morning there was puke all over the floor and the window sill.'

No good hiding the truth. I begged him to tell Mr Turner how ashamed I was, and that it was the first time I'd ever been tight.

Mr Biggs said, 'Well, next time don't bother to toss it out of the window. Just leave it there!'

Thursday, undated

Spent the morning being annoyed with *Tell England*. Then off to Stanley's for lunch, carrying lots of coats over my arm.

Stanley was terrifically hearty to begin with. He said he had heard Oxford was a hotbed of intrigue, with plots and notes left on pillows: 'Why has your attitude changed towards me?' I exclaimed, 'Why, it must be like Harrow all over again; only more lewd!'

Then Boy arrived and we sat down to eat some shredded sole. Stanley puts away the most enormous amount, indulging in the old Yorkshire habit of having cheese with his meat. Boy said he had had cheese and jam tart at our house and liked it. I explained it was an American habit my parents had picked up, as was marmalade and ham for breakfast.

Stanley can at times be terribly vulgar. Yet, after Boy left, he became interesting. We had the most marvellous conversation about poetry. Stan said everyone was a poet really, and rhyme and metre meant nothing. He said poetry was romance, just as beauty was romance. Stanley went on and on about women. He said, 'The female body is the most beautiful thing, so balanced in the hips and curves. It's the same with the aeroplanes I draw.' He told me about Monica Moulting and how he took her into a wood and made her listen to the trees growing, and how he could sit and look at her back for hours.

December 6th

Went to Hills and Saunders to see the pictures of the ADC's *Troilus and Cressida* scenery. It taught me what sort of things I must do if I design *Volpone*. I can only alter the colours and backclothes, all the rest has to be permanent.

Lunch with Theodore Burton Black. His room is in a dark court. It is delightfully decadent—beautifully carved furniture, Persian carpets, silks on the wall. There are long brass candle-sticks, carved boxes, weird colours and rows of interesting books.

When I came in, Burton Black stood with his back to the fire. His hair looked lankier and his face whiter than ever. He wore a bright blue silk shirt and collar, a vivid emerald tie, a white sash round dark trousers, white socks and black slippers. Over the shirt was a short kimono of black and pale yellow. He smoked a cigarette through a holder about two foot long, so thin that I wondered how smoke could get down it.

I was very amused and sat down to a decadent hour or two. Burton introduced me to a dull boy who was tiresomely childish. We waited for Hunt to come to lunch, then decided to wait no longer. I enjoyed lots of oysters and concluded that my host was like an oyster. The boy with the childish manner behaved stupidly about the oysters: he hadn't had one for six years and would rather like one now, but no more. Then we ate cutlets, ending with angels-on-horseback as Hunt arrived at the gallop. He had had a note from someone saying, 'Don't come today, come tomorrow.' But the note hadn't been sent by B. Black.

Conversation now became most edifying. We talked about art and looked at books on Cézanne and Picasso. Hunt held forth about the theatre. He is going on the stage, and spoke of play construction. He said it was his whole principle in life that rules should be observed. He then broke the rules, becoming annoyed with Burton Black for dogmatising, for being so affected and wearing a kimono. He said Black looked like a tinned hermaphrodite. I howled with laughter, thoroughly enjoying myself.

We left together. Hunt commented that Burton Black could be an extremely nice person if only he were periodically severely kicked. I did not think, however, that kicking would do much to improve B.B.'s designs for *Oedipus Rex*, over which he sits up until five o'clock in the morning.

Undated

Mama and I walked down past the University Arms Hotel. We looked at antique shops, and Mama saw a little old gate-legged table which she said I ought to buy if cheap. Then I said good-bye.

I felt rather brutal when I realised I didn't mind going back to my rooms alone. What a change! I can remember the time when I cried in bed at night because my governess told me that in Heaven peoples' shapes were different. I didn't want my mother to assume another shape.

How I have grown up. How sad to be so much less affectionate and dependent.

Undated

All the intellectuals in Cambridge turned up at the ADC for the Greek play. I saw Adrian Bishop, who looks like a decadent Roman Emperor or a Spanish Oscar Wilde, Stewart Perowne, Dadie Rylands, miraculously blond, Denman, Hazlitt, Sebastian Sprott. Hunt was selling programmes. Lytton Strachey and Irene Vanbrugh had come up specially from London.

The first act seemed patchy. The scenery was cheap, ugly and messy; the lighting couldn't have been worse. Arundell made an absurd apparition as Oedipus, and his acting was monotonous. Everyone laughed when Herbage as Jocasta insinuated himself on to the stage. His salmon-pink gauze dress was a travesty; his bosoms had been padded as large as balloons. Only Clinton-Baddeley survived the disaster.

During the interval, the audience rushed to the club room to shout and smoke. Lytton Strachey peered at everyone through thick glasses, looking like an owl in daylight. He is immensely tall, and could be even twice his height if he were not bent as a sloppy asparagus. His huge hands fall to his sides, completely limp. His sugar-loaf beard is square and reddish, but the hair on his head is thick and dark, worn long in the fashion of an arty undergraduate. Topsy Lucas,[1] Eton-cropped and draped in a Spanish shawl, held a reception in one corner. Irene Vanbrugh, I noticed, did not leave her seat. Apart from her scarlet and gold turban, there was nothing stagy about her. Without make-up, her complexion reminded me of crumbled dog biscuits.

We had something of an improvement in the second act. Arundell did splendidly; and the intensity of the tragedy sustained even poor Herbage, though his final exit was superbly ridiculous.

The play got terrific applause at the end. When we came out, the streets were filled with Rollses.

---

[1] Wife of F. L. Lucas, Fellow of King's College and Literary Critic.

Part II

The Vacation and Family Holidays
1923 and 1924

December 10th, 3 Hyde Park Street

Lunch was rather startling. My father kept asking me awful questions about Cambridge—questions that were impossible to answer. He asked questions like this: How many St John's people are there in the rugger fifteen? How many John's people in the cricket eleven? I don't know any of these things. I don't even know the names of the athletes; except for Tolley who plays golf. To crown it all, my father asked what the St John's colours were. I was covered with confusion, while Nancy and Baba giggled.

It is awful nowadays that I don't bother to get myself interested in anything, except art, society and the theatre. I must try and pull myself together or I shall become most frightfully dull.

When this upsetting lunch came to a close I read a book on Leonardo in the drawing room while Nancy and Baba tinkled the piano. I become sick of their everlasting piano playing.

27

December 16th

I decided, all of a sudden, to ring up and get a ticket for the last matinée of *Dear Brutus*. The theatre had nothing left; Webster's, fortunately, had one dress-circle seat.

Happy at the thought of seeing the play again, I hared off to do a lot of shopping. I went to the Times Book Club, renewed my membership, took out Mrs Asquith's second volume and Elizabeth's new book of short stories, *Balloons*. I tried to get Kitten on the Keys at His Master's Voice in Oxford Street, but they were out to lunch. Other errands, and I came home hung with parcels.

Lunch, of course, was late: Papa hadn't come in. I gobbled some cold meat and bussed it to Wyndham's, so fearful of being late that I arrived too early. I waited in the vestibule and saw the crowd dribble in. It was a dowdy intellectual crowd. Fifty little girls swarmed through the vestibule, all very excited.

I watched the performance attentively from beginning to end, enjoying it even more than my four previous times.

I was struck with the wit and beauty of things I hadn't noticed before. I realised how splendidly the play was acted. Ronald Squire is excellent, Gerald du Maurier incredible. The Dream Child scene was more exquisite than ever. In fact, it all impressed me as too tragically beautiful; also fresh, spontaneous, polished, intricate. I waited for Moyna Macgill's 'Never, forever, forever, never'; and Gerald du Maurier's 'It's so frightfully unfunny'. I drank in the greens and the dim colouring; the wood, the greys, Faith Celli's silky hair and green clothes and green voice. I loved the birds and the tune that Coady dances to; Lob's roses, Lob's room with the soft yellow light inside; and the moonlight on the standard rose trees outside.

In the interval I went to the box office and bought the *Dear Brutus* poster by Shepperson. It was one of my happiest afternoons, and I knew how wise I'd been to go alone. What if someone else hadn't shared my enthusiasm?

The reception after the play kept the curtain going up and down about eight times. I moved round to the side of the dress circle for a close look at the stage, wanting to remember the little room I was seeing for the last time. I etched the details in my mind: the shiny round table, the low flower bowl, the *Tatlers*, Lob's fireplace, the oak beams.

I walked into Leicester Square with tears on my cheeks.

28

December 28th

The golf links were covered with hoar frost, but it was exhilarating to play on crusty ground. Reggie[1] and I will never be champions, yet once or twice I hit the ball an enormous distance! Towards the end of the morning the frost began to melt. Soon the green was soggy, making me wish I hadn't dressed so unsuitably. But golf isn't romantic when played in plus fours.

After tea I went to get my negatives from Selfridge's, but was disappointed because they seemed underdeveloped. I then went to Kodak's and bought a portrait attachment, some gaslight paper, developers and fixers.

The whole evening was spent excitedly printing by gaslight in my room. It was the first time I'd ever done this, and Reggie and I were all agog. The results looked awful. But I have wonderful plans, and am going to do marvellous things in photography soon!

December 29th

Tonight Reggie and I did some printing by gaslight again. Nancy and Baba came up to look at the magic. The sock wrapped round one of the electric lights started to scorch, making a stink in the room. Our efforts were more successful, and we took the basin downstairs to show the others.

We had dinner: smelts. Smelts are almost my favourite fish, and we talked tonight, thank God. Afterwards we played bridge. It was a mistake not to play for money as everyone overbid.

ST CYPRIAN'S

February 19th 1923

St Valentine's Day. I wonder why I thought about St Cyprian's today? All sorts of things about my first boarding-school came to mind.

When preparing for this school, my mother was horrified at the length of the prescribed list: 12 pairs of socks; 6 pairs of pyjamas; school cap; blazers; 3 pairs of football shorts; 1 serviette ring and 1 Bible. Reggie and I were each given a 'play box' in which to put our favourite personal possessions. This box had

---

[1] My younger brother.

B*

29

black metal corners and large initials on the lid. (I hated my C.W.H.B.: cricketers are always known by impersonal initials. I want only to be Cecil Beaton.)

In a specially reserved Pullman Reggie and I went off to Eastbourne together with a group of other boys. We were seated on the far side of the platform window. As the coach started to glide I had a glimpse of my family waving goodbye. I realised we were in for something serious. Mother looked anxious in spite of her smile. Would we mind the wrench from home? She didn't worry about Reggie. She knew *I* was the one to have qualms about. Something in her well-dressed appearance or sweetness touched me so much that to be parted from her now seemed the most awful thing. I bit my lip. But before the coach window moved out of sight, my face crumbled, I broke into a torrent of sobs.

During those first days at Eastbourne, I blubbed at the most unsuitable times of day and night. I would suddenly be overcome by waves of homesickness and burst into tears in the middle of a sentence. When we marched in crocodile file over the downs towards Beachey Head, the tears almost froze on my face in the winter wind. I got into the habit of waking early, so that I could go to the lavatory and weep alone.

By degrees, I accepted my fate. It was only after a 'suitable interval' that Mrs Vaughan-Wilkes,[1] with her rosy cheeks and ape-like grin, said she had a surprise for us in her private sitting room. We found our parents there. I couldn't see or speak for tears.

St Cyprian's was probably better than most schools during the war (it certainly is one of the most snobbish). But the food was bad. Reggie and I developed papillomas on the soles of our feet. Dr Whaite said they were caused by undernourishment. We had to have them burnt away with acids during the holidays by Mr Cooper, a chiropodist with a mahogany *toupet*.

It was always cold at St Cyprian's. Whenever possible, I clung to tepid radiators in the corridors. Here I developed the chilblains from which I still suffer agonies. It didn't help matters much when we had to jump into an icy swimming bath every morning.

The gymnasium was mediaeval torture to me. In spite of my weak arms, I found myself obliged to climb the rope. Half way

[1] The wife of the headmaster.

to the ceiling strength would give way, and I hung in terror by weakening hands.

There were agreeable moments. In summer I enjoyed being allowed to pick gooseberries. I also had a square-yard patch of garden in which to grow mustard and cress, phlox and poppies from seed packets.

Most of all I enjoyed the theatricals. At the end of term we performed a curtain raiser by W. W. Jacobs, with Cyril Connolly in mob cap and curls playing the barkeeper's daughter. There followed a potted *Pinafore*. In the *Mikado*, I sang plaintively, waving a fan I had painted with periwinkles. As Nanki-Poo, I got two plums: 'A Wandering Minstrel I' and another singer's 'Willow-Tit-Willow'.

My greatest success, however, came at a concert given for the wounded soldiers in a nearby camp. Faced with a sea of blue flannel uniforms and scarlet ties, I sang 'If You Were the Only Girl in the World' and 'Chalk Farm to Camberwell Green'. I remember the evening ending abruptly as we were all bidden to pray. I knelt on the platform while the camp cat wove its way between the wooden chairs and on past my nose.

Of all the boys at St Cyprian's, Cyril, or 'Tim' Connolly was certainly the strangest, most fascinating character to me. He seemed so grown-up. Even his face was dotted with adult moles; and his long fingers ended with filbert nails. We admired one another, though I got a bit of a shock when I discovered how much he knew about life. A few of us vaguely realised that someone's parents were rich or titled, or had a large motor-car. But Cyril knew which of the masters had a financial interest in St Cyprian's, and which were only there on sufferance. He said it helped you to know how to behave towards them.

What made me tremble was that Cyril's greed seemed stronger than his sense of self-preservation. When it came to food, he did the most dangerous things. If he'd been caught, he would have been 'out of favour' with Mrs Vaughan-Wilkes. Flip, as we called her, had more influence than all the masters put together; if you crossed her path, life was not worth living. Cyril's taste in literature being far above everyone else's, his standing with Flip kept him 'in favour'. Yet after breakfast, during Flip's alarming scripture lesson to the assembled school, Cyril seemed unable to resist continual nibblings at the bread and honey. While we still sat at our places in the dining room, Flip, from one end of the central table, would instruct various boys to recite the collect for the day. Her beady eyes darted throughout the hall, quick to discover anyone not paying attention. Cyril, barely two yards from her, surreptitiously extended a filbert-nailed hand towards the big bowl of rough honey in front of him. Dip went the sop into the stickiness. Then it was brought by slow motion across the table, over his green sweater front and up to his mouth. By the end of the meal, it seemed as if a hundred snails had been travelling forwards and backwards between Cyril and the honey bowl. Astonishingly, I never remember Flip catching him in the act.

As for me, I regarded Flip with terrified awe. Generally I remained her angel, for I knew how to suck up to her and curry favour. I pretended to read books that might impress her with my good literary taste. I even mowed the school lawn, and painted Christmas cards for her. In fact, I became such a positive favourite that she often took me down into the town of Eastbourne on her domestic shopping visits, and gave me a mid-morning coconut cake.

Once or twice, however, I fell from grace. There was a particularly cold winter's afternoon when Flip went up to London for the day. Boldly, I refused to change into icy football clothes and run round the frozen sports ground. Instead, wearing an overcoat and scarf to keep warm in the equally cold indoors, I hid myself from view. Bored, I wandered from corridor to corridor, migrating towards the improvised theatre built over the swimming pool for our forthcoming production of *Pinafore*. As luck would have it, Mr Vaughan-Wilkes was showing some prospective parents round the school. He spotted me looking out of a window at the wintry scene. By slow, appalling degrees he tracked me down. Oh horror, the party entered the theatre! I crept to the back of the stage. They followed closer. There was nothing to do but squeeze under the platform. Footsteps echoed overhead. My place of refuge in the darkness was discovered by a large torchlight playing on my doubled-up form. The victim was dragged out from under the stage, covered with shavings and sawdust and doubly shamed in view of the prospective parents. Weakly, I said I'd been helping the carpenter. This immediate disgrace proved bad enough, but when Flip returned from London I came to realise the full horror of what I had done.

Another dangerous moment came when I was caught by the matron of St Cyprian's, doing a pantomime 'principal boy' stunt outside the dormitories each side of a long passage. Rows of heads peeped from every cubicle or above the partitions, as I goose-stepped up and down. My pyjama trousers were rolled up to my middle; I wore a corps cap and tunic and held a little riding crop. Suddenly a great scurry: *cave*! I whisked off the buttoned-up tunic in a second, jumping into bed just as the matron came into my cubicle. She laughed, and being a good sport, didn't tell Flip.

THE BEN JONSON PLAY

March 18th

I went to a performance of *Volpone* given by the Phoenix Society. Mr Ensor[1] had been successful in arranging seats for me. I gave fifteen shillings as a contribution to the Society and waited for Boy to arrive.

Wonderful people were there, all very artistic. Bernard Shaw stood talking to the Fagans. Mary Grey[2] stuck her face almost into his, pouted her lips and puffed out her cheeks. I thought Shaw looked very pale, scraggy and watery-eyed and old; but then, I suppose he *is* old. Lopokova came in, smiled and bowed at me. She wore the same huge moccasins and almost transparent dress I had seen her in at Cambridge. How small she is, how unaffected without any powder. David Cecil arrived in a taxi, together with a frightfully affected person from Oxford.

I waited outside a long time. I felt sorry for a little old woman. She peered into every taxi, but her friend still hadn't arrived a quarter of an hour after the show began. Neither had mine: Boy, it turned out, went to the wrong theatre!

March 25th

The alarm clock woke me successfully at 7.30. I lay in bed, wondering whether after all I would get up and go to church.

I would; I did. It took me ten minutes to dress, one minute to unbolt the front door and three more to reach the church at the

---

[1] Aubrey C. Ensor, a former schoolmaster at Heath Mount.
[2] Mrs Fagan.

SARAH
AS JOAN

Delacroix gypsy. And they say that at one time she became so thin you could only see the ghost of a skeleton emerge from the hansom cab when it arrived at the theatre. In later life she was heavy but made a none the less grandiose appearance, muffled up in lace, chinchilla and violets, with a huge sable extinguisher on her head. Her voice must have been golden, but I missed my only opportunity when, one-legged, she last appeared in London. . . .

The Divine Sarah

end of Southwick Place. Few people were there. I didn't like the church at all, but felt pleased to have been to Communion.

I came home fresh and full of energy, then read the papers while waiting for people to come down to breakfast.

Poor Sarah Bernhardt is dying! It seems like some final part to be played with those grandiloquent, yearning gestures (after all, hadn't she always wanted to die on the stage?).

How I loved her red frizz, her white face, hen's beak and kohl-rimmed eyes. She was beautiful when young, like a

The following vignettes are included, for all their detailed banality, to show something of our family life.

Perhaps they stress too much the misunderstandings, irritations, and clashes of temperament which are so often part of a large household with its conflicts of age and interest: For, in fact, we were a united, happy family, always wanting to share our delights and joys, particularly those of the country—pleasures which only city dwellers know. But it was during those periods of enforced enjoyment of the family holidays that the strain sometimes brought about scenes that were tragi-comic.

In defence of my own smugly critical attitudes and fantasy-snobbishness little can be said. The fact that as the eldest of the children I had had glimpses of the grandeur of adult life, cannot excuse my callow condemnation of the very people of whom I am most deeply fond.

IN THE COUNTRY WITH MODOM

April 9th, Turner's Hill

Aunt Jessie's Danish friends, the Petersens, sometimes lend her their weekend cottage at Turner's Hill. As I was recovering from my sixth bad cold this winter, she suggested a few days in the country. The Petersens would send us down in their motor.

The idea of 'the country' has always excited me. I put on my coat and waited impatiently. Modom buzzed about, making an inventory of the supplies we were taking with us—candles, tea, coffee, sugar and peppercorns.

Of course, the motor was ten minutes late; and it took another ten minutes to get the luggage on board. I asked the chauffeur if Turner's Hill was in Sussex or Surrey. 'Sussex,' he replied. Nancy and Baba rushed into the house, screaming, 'Sussex, Sussex.'

It was a bitterly cold morning. We sat comfortable and airless in the Petersens' huge car. I looked at the squalid scene while Modom held a pencil and jotted down the names of passing places. 'Oh look,' she exclaimed with unwithered enthusiasm, 'this is Purley, Balham Hill, Tooting. And here's Wandsworth Common.'

I felt vaguely sick at the very mention of absurd suburbs which had always been a joke before. I couldn't imagine why we didn't go past Wigan!

35

It was snowing outside, the first snow of winter in spring. I shut my ears to Modom's enthusiasm and read the last act of *Advertising April*.

It stopped snowing. The countryside became green, dotted with pink and white blossoms. I was now very curious to see what sort of place we would arrive at. Modom kept saying, 'Oh, it's all very nice.' But then, she considers such weird things are nice. I asked a lot of questions. 'Is the cottage pretty? Is it old? Is it grey stone? Is the countryside hilly or wooded?'

'No, no, no,' Modom replied, making me suspect the worst. Then we arrived; and my suspicions seemed confirmed. Before us stood a new, red-brick cottage.

A white-haired woman opened the door. Her name is Mrs Eagles. She has known the Petersens for many years, and quickly informed us that a kinder man than Mr Petersen didn't exist. 'He is the kindest, goodest man God ever created in the whole world!'

Inside, the cottage proved pleasant in spite of its newness. A great log fire burned in the open fireplace. Pots of primroses stood on the window sill. There were red walls, quiet oak furniture and bowls of wild flowers. I thought the pictures un-suitable, but they would have to stay. Books included volumes on Velazquez, Franz Hals, Millais (I now quite like Ophelia), Rossetti and Holman Hunt.

Aunt Jessie went into the kitchen and started to talk sob stuff with Mrs Eagles about *Madam Butterfly*. 'It's so beautiful, so sad. She is waiting for him, you know. It's his child. And then she kills herself.'

Mrs Eagles repeated the last word of each sentence and added, 'Oh yes, I've read about it in the papers.'

Again they talked of Mr Petersen, the world's paragon. Aunt Jessie agreed, 'He's the kindest man. I adore him.' She laughed and warned, 'But you mustn't tell Mrs Petersen that!'

Screams of laughter from Mrs Eagles. It made me so on edge I pinched myself. I tried to get absorbed in the Pre-Raphaelites and not listen, but the two women chattered and laughed loudly.

Mrs Eagles bragged, 'Yes, I'm fifty-three, and I can still carry two slop basins down the stairs.'

Modom said how happy she was now that she had no servants or money.

Picking primroses: C.B. and Baba at Turners Hill

The Christmas dinner

My Father and Mother

'Yes,' Mrs Eagles replied, 'What I say is, "Waste not, want not".'

'Absolutely. Oh, absolutely.' Then Modom brooded: 'What shall we have for dinner tonight? I'm trying to get thin, you know. I only want one good meal a day. It's healthy.'

'Oh yes, absolutely,' Mrs Eagles agreed. 'I have only had one meal a day for fifty-three years and I can still carry two slop pails,' etc.

'Some steak, some onions,' Modom suggested. 'I've been abroad a lot, you know. My husband was the Bolivian Minister. He died.'

'Oh, yes, my husband was a taxi driver,' Mrs Eagles took up the refrain. 'He left me with five children, and Mr Petersen sent me a pound. My daughter is a between-maid.'

'Oh? My sister Etty is so sweet and kind and considerate. She keeps five maids, but none of them are good to her. Oh, Mrs Eagles, you must see her. I hope she's coming down here for a day. Her between-maid won't get up in the morning,' etc.

At last Modom issued forth from the kitchen. We went out for a walk. I couldn't admire the village, with new cottages so infernally hideous and suburban. I became a little tempery when we walked along a tarmac road. It's all very well, but one can do that in London.

It started to snow again, then stopped. In spite of the wet, we trudged on to Lord Cowdray's estate and were rewarded. Birds twittered in the avenues of huge grey trees. We sat on an up-turned trunk by a gurgling stream. All seemed calm and quiet, except for the birds' song. Modom discovered a beautifully made nest, as smooth as the inside of a coconut, which held two greeny-blue eggs with brown specks on them.

Then we came to a primrose field, with thousands of little faces looking up at the sky. Trying to get near the biggest clumps of yellow primroses I jumped into a bog. My red tie got splashed.

Whinings in the distance: Aunt Jessie couldn't jump over a little stream scarcely a yard wide.

'Don't be absurd,' I laughed.

Timidly, Modom lifted her black skirt to reveal pink knickers. Now for the jump across the stream. It was quite easy to do, but —splosh! 'Oh, oh, oh, I've gone over my ankles! I'll catch my death of cold.'

37

At six o'clock we came home footsore. Modom loved it all, even the tarmac road. We had tea and I ate a lot, then lay back in a huge chair. I thought of the green groves, quiet woods, grey moss, fawn-coloured birds and the trees silent and beautiful. I felt happy.

Modom made a wonderful supper from her Bolivian recipes—*Empanadas*—little pies filled with meat and raisins—then *picante* chicken. It was spicy, peppery and good. I gobbled while Modom talked in a whisper. She always does at mealtimes, as though the act of eating were something forbidden. Methodical, diligent, dainty and precious, she watched my plate. 'Let me give you another pinch of *Aji*.'[1]

'No, thank you.'

'Oh, but yes, only a nip,' and she heaped my plate with mounds of everything.

After supper I lighted twelve candles, ignoring the oil lamp. I lay back and read about Rossetti. Who would have known him to be so voluptuous and horrid, taking chloral in later days? Poor man, he turned out to be a brilliant disappointment.

Early bedtime. One had to be quick in undressing: it was cold away from the enormous fire in the room downstairs.

April 12th

Overslept and came down in my dressing gown to eat an egg which had only just been laid. The sky was dark grey with clouds. There were no letters. I deliberated for a long time as to whether or not to go to the post office and telephone home. Perhaps if the family thought of coming down, then they had better be warned of the wet weather.

It took only a minute to get through to London. Murphy answered the telephone. Though I asked thousands of questions, she still didn't know who was speaking. 'No, Mrs Beaton has gone away for the day with Miss Nancy and Barbara and Mr Reggie.' They had started at 9.30!

I ran to tell the good news to Modom, who sat in the kitchen exchanging 'absolutelys' with Mrs Eagles.

A flurry of excitement ensued. Auntie worked very hard, polished tables and chairs and the window sill, hurried upstairs,

---

[1] South American dried and powdered fruits, pronounced *A-hee*.

put on her grey and black suit, made up her face as if for the stage and ran off to buy a leg of lamb. Mrs Eagles flurried for rhubarb and vegetables from the next garden. I was left to Rossetti's chloric.

After a bit, Modom came back with a gargantuan joint.

All of a sudden the sun came out. The sky cleared and it became hot. Brrr, brr, brrr, brrr, the little Calthorpe chugged slowly up the hill. Inside were Mummy, who drove, and Nancy, Baba and Reggie—all of them squashed up without hats.

Everyone screamed and rushed about. I seized things out of the car; two films, hair lotion, letters, chocolates, Roquefort cheese and baskets. Nancy and Baba jumped with hysterical excitement inspired by my letters of the past two days.

Indoors, the 'absolutelys' rose to a crescendo. 'Isn't it lovely! Isn't it sweet, delightful! Now this is my idea of a country cottage. Oh, isn't the fireplace cosy? What adorable windows,' etc.

Nancy jigged up and down. 'I wish we could stay the night, Mummie, can't we sleep here?' With Baba in her wake, she sped upstairs to the bedrooms, then she sped down again.

Modom's voice soared and swooped: 'Beautiful eggs, just out of the nest and only one-and-sixpence a dozen!'

While the sun still shone, we hurriedly decided to go into the woods. Reggie drove: Nancy, Baba and I sat on different parts of the car and whizzed along with the wind blowing through our hair. An old woman, looking rather like Great-Aunt Clare, lay sleeping on some logs. Her hands were behind her head, her hat on her stomach. Our laughter was so shrill that we woke her up.

We got out at the Red Lane. Baba thought she was being so clever in 'going down the Red Lane'. Arm in arm, the four of us trooped across Lord Cowdray's preserves. We hurried through the wet grass, climbed banks and hedges with boundless energy, and invaded the wispy woods. Nancy and Baba shrieked with ecstasy at the sight of pheasants and partridges, small rabbits and a squirrel. They danced around trees, gathered the primroses, scooped up the star moss and listened to the crackle of leaves and twigs. We bolted home with baskets full.

After the joint (undercooked!), we braved the afternoon rain. Everyone put on thick shoes and overcoats and went out. We walked over sopping fields and climbed gates. Nancy looked so pretty, her hair getting curlier and her cheeks pinker every minute. Baba was being chirpy about her botanical diary. We came to the boggy wood and fought for gowans—Nancy and Baba eager, Reggie so dashing.

We picked quantities of the yellow blobs. Nancy chirped from the middle of a bog. 'Mummie's bought a new hat.'

'Oh, what's it like?'

And Baba in a throaty voice, 'It's a little cloche,' etc., etc.

On our way back over the wet fields, we saw newborn lambs, and I inspected the thrushes' nest with the two bright eggs inside it.

It began to rain. Back in front of the fire, shoes and socks were hung up to dry while the women separated the primroses, gowans and wild violets, busily tying them into separate bunches with cord. Nancy *did* so want to stay the night, but no: time to put on the socks and pile high the motor-car with foliage, flowers and eggs. Then space must be found for the occupants. At last the Calthorpe drove off. And it seemed so quiet, dull and lonely.

Darling Modom *will* go on talking in whispers at meals, and if only she wouldn't refer to lunch as 'dinner' and dinner as 'supper'. Yet she has even *me* doing it. Why won't she allow me to help myself? She even tries to give me salt and 'that's bad luck!' 'There, there,' she says, all full of breath. 'There!' as with eyebrows raised to heaven and lips pursed into a cupid's bow, she takes spoon and fork in her fat little shiny white hands.

Modom has other peculiar habits. She often leaves off in the middle of a sentence and goes on with some other half sentence. It is tiresomely abstract. 'So you're blue, yellow, green and red,' five minutes later, I discover she's talking about my Fair Isle jumper.

She affects a foreign accent. She pronounces 'potato' or 'tomato' like a Spaniard; she talks about 'a negge' or 'a nahpple'. Instead of swearing she exclaims 'Och ta tai.'

Yet Aunt Jessie is wonderful, I love her. She has a heart of the purest gold. Her courage and gallantry is heroic. What other woman, so essentially feminine, could survive without any trace of bitterness such a reverse of good fortune? Once she was 'Her Excellency' with the entrée at Court. She was flirtatious and admired. Rich yet happy! Her dinner parties were listed in *The Times*. Then, suddenly, her husband's fortune in the rubber plantations of Bolivia was lost, and she became a destitute widow. Hardly any of her colleagues in the Diplomatic Corps bother about her now, though she still has staunch friends who appreciate her for her extraordinary generosity of spirit and gaiety.

For me, as a child, she was not only the most resplendent human being, but she gave me my first unforgettable taste of adult luxury. To see her today is less comic than tragic as she simpers out of the room with all the airs and graces of yesterday but with the fag end of a cigarette yellowing her upper lip, and a vegetable dish poised in either hand.

I judge Modom so harshly because I am an insufferable snob. Besides, she has interrupted me twenty times while I write this. 'I can't think what you scribble so much about in the evenings.' I reply arrogantly that it is my 'work'. It isn't, and hating myself for my swinishness I go unhappily to bed.

August 30th, Instow, Cornwall

At loose ends, with nothing to do on a cold morning, I took out Daddy's large box camera and decoyed Matilda, the grotesque servant at the hotel, into the garden. If her photograph comes out it will rival 'the Ugly Duchess'. I could hardly hold the camera still for laughing at her wig (like cotton wool dipped in Bovril) and huge hourglass figure encased in black.

Reggie and some man had been messing about with the man's car while Matilda postured. Baba said the man had exclaimed about me, 'What a terrible looking person,' and asked Reggie who I was. Why didn't I get my hair cut, etc.

Reggie (foolishly, as I at first thought) replied he didn't know me. But on thinking it over, I'm glad he denied acquaintance. The man would have told everybody about his *faux pas*: 'And do you know who he was? Why, his own brother.'

I pretended I didn't mind a bit, but I do mind—a lot.

Somewhat dejectedly, I went for a walk beyond the cricket ground, wandering slowly up the hill to the church. On the way I stood gazing for ages at an old stable of the most unique shape. The light dappled through the trees threw moving shadows on the Devonshire cream cracked walls.

I felt an urge to do something about the stable—perhaps photograph it, but then the plum painted doors and windows would be lost. I rushed home for my paints and was lucky that Reggie brought me back again to this spot in the car.

But rain came down periodically, and the shadows disappeared. The sketch was an utter failure, which made me profoundly desolate.

September 3rd, London

Tokyo and Yokohama have been wiped out by an earthquake. There is no proper news yet, but over 200,000 people are estimated killed. The papers were just one mass of this earthquake and the return of Pavlova. I read all about it after breakfast, then lotioned my hair with that evil-smelling muck.

September 5th

My father came back from the office with the news that he is going to America on the *Berengaria* on Saturday. What exultation at dinner! We all talked American—like rich Americans because we don't like to think there are any poor Americans.

September 8th

Reggie and I helped down with Father's luggage: apparently it was still too early for the servants to appear. At Waterloo it was almost as good as being in New York to see all these sumptuous millionaires and their families going back after their holiday in London. Most of the women wore orchids and some were taking home a perfect dog. The men immaculate and nonchalantly self-possessed. Daddy, hanging out of the window looked so human and appealing with his kind blue eyes full of fondness for us, his comparatively meagre family of well-wishers.

At last the train went off, full of sumptuousness. One American girl remained on the platform. She was very pretty and small. As she waved, she slowly wriggled her body all the way down; it struck me as being terrifically sexual!

EASTER AT BOURNEMOUTH

April 12th 1924

Packing was finished. Upstairs I got distinctly annoyed at having to lug so much of it downstairs when six maids sat doing nothing. Tennis rackets, books and ignominious paper parcels littered the hall.

I had discovered that last night's photographs which I had squeegeed on to plate glass wouldn't come off, and at the last minute had to be put in the bath again. I tried to dry them in front of a gas stove, as I wanted to take the batch with me to Bournemouth. In my haste I almost burned to death, while Papa and Reggie hollered for me. I grabbed the photographs and *The Forsythe Saga*, gave final instructions to Nurse[1] about taking care of the love birds and plummeted into the car.

After all the panic, it took so long to start up I needn't have burnt my fingers after all. Papa, as though he were the butler, was carrying out the last of a thousand humiliating packages, including two bottles of whisky. Why on earth hadn't he packed them? Papa has no pride at all. I felt certain that all H.P. Street was peeping from the windows. More parcels got crammed on top of me, Then an additional trunk had to be put on the carrier at the back. Reggie tied it on with a ball of string; Papa shouted No-No-No, the string wouldn't hold, and found some dirty rope. I thought we would never get away. And to top it all, Mrs Philip Guedella came by.

[1] My sisters' nurse, Alice Collard, sometimes known as 'Ninnie'.

Reggie drove. I had fits at the back of the car because Papa kept shouting, 'Steady! Steady!' This sent Reggie into defiant skids. We had ten close shaves: Reggie can't resist passing cars at inopportune moments, especially on narrow roads with another vehicle coming towards us like a bat out of hell.

At London Hall Hydro on the outskirts of Bournemouth, the hall porter greeted us in a very dirty uniform. The most suburban people sat about in the meagre lounge, reading cheap novels and drinking tea out of enormous white cups. Everyone stared hard. I felt ashamed of the two bottles of whisky.

Daddy excitedly ordered tea, wanting to do everything in the first five minutes. Of course, the tea took forever to arrive, which sent him into the most terrible passion. He cursed, swore and puffed. Reggie and I sat trembling in silence, wishing to goodness he would keep calm and quiet. Daddy shouted, 'Waiter, waiter,' adding his rarely used, 'For God's sake, hurry up!' Daddy always has a row with the waiter if he can.

We went for a walk. I tried not to be miserable, but my stomach churned with anger. The road into Bournemouth might well have been the road to hell.

'Aaaaaaccch!' My father took in a huge amount of air and let it out again. 'This will make your whiskers curl,' he promised, then read out the bathetic names of every cheap little house, hotel and boarding house. Papa observed about a horrifying residence surrounded by a hedge of repugnant shrubs. 'That doesn't look a bad sort of place.' I nearly went mad.

How I abominate English seaside towns! When I'm on my own I shall never subject myself to such squalor. As I walked along in misery, I kept thinking how romantic it would be to go to Italy. My whole soul cried out for something exotic. Why, in Bournemouth it wasn't even warm.

Papa reminisced about the hard times he'd had here at school. We looked into cheerless shops, we stared at even more cheerless seaside people. The smell of Daddy's filthy pipe insulted my nose.

We had to change for dinner: it was *de rigueur*! The other guests, their faces like logs, sat erect and wretched. Afterwards, we withdrew to a lounge. I read a bit of Saki while Daddy and Reggie, bored, stared vacantly into space.

There was an entertainer woman, the worst thing I've ever heard of. Fancy having a stranger introducing people to one another! She rang a bell and shouted instructions to the whole room to mingle for a family whist drive. With each ring, a would-be comic in the audience shouted, 'Muffins, Muffins, I loike muffins, but I prefer crumpets. Ha! Ha!' We sat in our corner criticising, then went to bed early as the clocks were being put forward for summer time.

Even from my bed I could hear that entertainer ringing bells.

April 14th

We discovered that Mrs Patrick Campbell is on a tour of *The Second Mrs Tanqueray*, playing at the Pier Theatre tonight. Daddy generously got tickets. I perked up, as it would be a great chance to see our living legend and compare her performance with Gladys Cooper's.

I've read the old play a lot. It's still a good vehicle—a bit artificial, but well constructed and full of theatrical situations.

Later:

Pinero would have winced. His *chef-d'oeuvre* got mutilated tonight; especially by Aubrey Tanqueray, who was stiff, prosy and absurd.

Mrs Pat looked physically unbelievable—like a huge, falling blancmange. It's tragic that at this stage of her life she should be appearing in the same role that 'made' her in the heyday of her beauty. Poor old thing, she did seem a repulsive sight, twice as large as any man on the stage.

Still, one could see more than remnants of the great actress. She has a wonderful voice, and employs certain splendid little tricks. She laughs, 'Ho, ho, ho, ho,' deep and unusual—this device brought into play each time she gets upset. She gives out a long, breathy sigh, 'Ooorrrr, I'm so happy!' And she has an effective sniff.

On the whole, I thought her performance less convincing than Gladys Cooper's and certainly much quieter. Or did it merely seem that way to me because Gladys looked so marvellous? Mrs Pat, by contrast, might have been a terrible old landlady, all insolent ways and untidy black hair about to fall down. Gladys's cockney, flashy *bravura* added to the character; not to mention Molyneux's encrusted gold and chinchilla dresses. Poor

45

old Mrs Pat, she must make do with pea-soup hand-me-downs and washed out old Spanish shawls. She was continually meddling with fringes and pulling at bodices to keep her dresses from falling off her shoulders.

Mrs Pat was horribly to the front each time she sauntered on-stage, even when she ought to have faded into the background. Instead of quietly playing the piano, she strummed so loud no one could hear a word being spoken by the other actors. Twice she was late for her cue, and once kept the audience waiting for what seemed like three minutes. I've heard many stories about her beastliness to other actors and her jealousy. But she knows she is a monster, is the first to laugh at herself.

The way she took her call struck me as highly amusing. She waddled to the footlights, leaned forward, held up her skirt with one hand and bowed with a grotesque sneer on her face.

Daddy sat bored throughout. I must admit, I was a little embarrassed myself by the last act. I didn't think Mrs Pat at all good in it, but perhaps the play tails off badly.

We came home to the Hydro, thankful to have missed the hotel dance. I drew myself naked from the glass. It's good practice; and with a shilling in the gas meter, I felt warm enough.

April 15th
'What car was that that passed, a Rover?'
'No, a Ruston.'
'Are they good cars?'
'Fairly.'
'Steady! Steady!'
This stimulating conversation passed the time as we jolted and jogged to Poole. Daddy and Reggie wanted to see an old man in the hope of selling him some timber.

I sat in the car, shifting on the hard seat and reading bits of *Apollo*, though it is much too exhausting a catalogue to read for long on end.

On our return, we played tennis. Daddy was longing to have a four, but Reggie and I rudely declined, determined not to know any of the undesirable residents in our hotel. Daddy played single to our double, winning every one of the five sets, though we had some energetic rallies. And I did serve well!

After dinner, while the professional entertainer was doing her worst, I found, fortunately, a more delightful source of amusement by quizzing an old woman who arrived here yesterday. I thought her pert and perfect, an inspired little bird in smart London clothes. She is spiky and wrinkled, with a Botticelli forehead and thin, Renaissance eyebrows. She's almost bald but, clever little darling, doesn't wear a wig, simply parting her thin, moth-eaten hair very slickly. She sat in the lounge with a frown on her face. She, too, tried not to listen to the entertainer but I could tell what she was thinking from her expressions of semi-amusement, astonishment and disgust.

I sat watching my new-found friend long after the others had gone to bed. I wanted to pluck up courage and talk to her, but instead drew her very badly on the end-page of Saki.

VISIT TO SANDRINGHAM

July 30th

It was a cloudy day. But we decided to make an excursion to Sandringham and visit the royal gardens while they are open to the public. The entire family squashed into the car; laughing and twitting, alive and witty.

When at last we arrived, we discovered with delight that it was the day of the flower show, the first I had ever visited. Huge tents had been set up, bands were playing. It was a festive opportunity to see the gardens at their best. We sat under trees and pretended to be 'royal guests'. But the pretence couldn't have been more ridiculous with thousands of country yokels swarming about, eating food from boxes and bags.

Then, unexpectedly, Queen Alexandra arrived. For me, she had always been a fantastic figure from an unbelievable past grandeur. In her day, court ladies spent the entire morning being laced into corsets, patiently submitting to florid adornment with jewelled pins, brooches, Prince of Wales feathers and fenders of diamonds. Gone now were her stately banquets, presentations, balls and palmy splendours. She would be eighty years old on her next birthday, but she was still a queen. One caught jerky glimpses of her in newsreels—arriving by motor instead of by carriage, nodding to the multitude. In these motion-pictures she still appeared trussed and trimmed, though black sequins had replaced the *aurora borealis* display of early years. A tight cake of formal curls seemed clamped upon her head. It was rumoured that she never appeared in public without being tremendously made up, 'enamelled', as Modom used to say. In my mind's eye I had created a mask of white and pale magenta, propped upon pearl dog collars beneath which the *décolletage* was festooned with trinkets and charms.

All the country folk hurried forward to the ugly red brick of Sandringham House as the Queen came out, followed by several aged crones. And of course she wasn't at all as I had imagined—not a bit enamelled or grotesque. She seemed merely a charming old lady with a very beautiful, pale face, a sweet smile and expressionless eyes. I had never seen anyone so frail. Her body was like a Knossos figure, neat and waisted. Her head, with a black sequin toque perched atop a high coiffure, seemed like an egg stuck on a hatpin; for her neck was so slender I wondered how it could support a human head.

She tottered slowly towards us. My mother curtsied. We heard her talking in a guttural jerky voice to a weeping baby. Then she went into a tent to see the exhibits. The crowd waited patiently and silently for her to come out and drive away—a spindly little hag in spider's-web black.

We thought of her as we walked further round the estate. We wondered what she would eat, and conjured up a picture of her messing about the ugly house and being taken to bed at six-thirty. Mummie kept our fancy on a practical level with, 'Oh, well, you see the Queen wouldn't . . .' As though Mummie were in the know! We teased her about it, but Mama insisted firmly as though she had been specially invited, 'I remember last time I was here . . .'

The royal gardens, in spite of an impressive orderliness and formality, showed no imagination. It was only near the house, in contrast to the red brick, that the mass of ramblers and yellow privet hedges acquired a stolid Victorian charm.

As we passed close to the house on our way out, we looked up at the bedroom windows. A huge standard lampshade was visible, all yellow silk with layers of silk frills. In fact, driven by curiosity, I even peered through one of the ground floor windows. I caught a glimpse of the old Queen pottering about the sitting room. Stopping at a crowded table she picked up a silver-framed photograph of the Duke and Duchess of York, taken by Bertram Park in soft focus.

August 7th, Melrose, Morris Street, Sheringham

Seaside life brings out the worst in me. If only Boy were here to talk interestingly to! But Boy, quite rightly, would loathe it bottled up here with my family. Meanwhile, I mess about, reading Chesterton on Browning and not absorbing anything very much, playing tennis badly, drinking gallons of barley water and bathing in a slate grey sea. This morning Modom got knocked over by two successive waves, panicked and rushed out of the sea. We laughed; the crowds on the beach laughed. But Mama shouted and waved for the rest of us to come out. How ridiculous: if anyone gets a mouthful of water, you'd think they had drowned. Yesterday, Nurse bumped her leg on that breakwater. She, too, got into a panic, calling to Nancy, 'Come to me, come to me!' As she was being led to the beach she got knocked over twice by waves and of course we never heard the end about how easily accidents can happen, how she might have been drowned and a mournful procession home, etc., etc. A lot of rot, but it terrifies the family.

August 10th

Morning spent on the beach sitting on hard stones, thinking of nothing and trying not to look at the people around me.

Daddy and Reggie arrived after lunch, short of temper, hot and dirty.

We heard a lot about the cricket tour. Reggie told me later Daddy hadn't allowed him to do this, that or the other. It seems Daddy went to bed at nine o'clock every evening, whereupon Reggie slipped away to gad and dance at all the seaside hotels. It sounded rather cheap to me, but Reggie enjoyed himself.

Dinner became an awful strain, with Daddy saying such terrible things they made me gasp. To Reggie: 'Your hair is getting a terrific length. Why don't you go to the barber and ask him to cut as much as he will for fourpence?'

During the evening walk, Reggie and Baba became over-enthusiastic about a new Astaire step they had just invented. They danced it down the street when, bang!—they fell.

49

A terrible commotion ensued. Baba's face was black all over, with three huge graze marks. Reggie turned white as Daddy turned red. I thought it a nasty accident, but why not leave it at that? No, Daddy persisted in working himself into a rage, crying, 'What a silly fool you are, Reggie! You utter idiot! I nearly

Baba

shouted for you to stop your tomfoolery, but I knew you would take no notice. I always said one day there would be an accident and now you've done it. If you fool about again, I can tell you you'll get it.' This threat was repeated over and over again, while everyone looked at poor Baba's face. She didn't cry; nor did it hurt, nor was it bleeding.

We came back and watched the victim being cleaned up in the bathroom. Nancy very naughtily and irrelevantly remarked that Baba looked as if she'd been up a chimney. Mummie continued where Daddy left off, 'It's a wonder this, it's a wonder that. She might have had her nose broken. She might have this, she might have that.'

Baba said, 'Never mind,' kissed Reggie and went to bed, after which things settled down slightly. That is, until Nurse came down in a tantrum and complained in front of everyone about Reggie's conduct. She insisted that she was very *ashamed*, then went on to say she'd seen Nancy and me bobbing about outside the house, and no doubt the neighbours thought we had a tile

missing! I exploded at the old hag's audacity. I shouted to her to mind her own business and get out!

Next morning Baba looked terrible, her eye swollen and yellow, also a horrid place on her face. As soon as breakfast was over, Nurse went out and bought a bandage. Baba's head got tied up, making her look a marvellous nut. We joked and ragged her a good deal.

August 12th

I loaf around doing absolutely nothing but complain. It's a relief to exhaust myself playing tennis, and at this I'm becoming quite energetic and can give Reggie a run for his money.

This afternoon I drove the car. My parents shouted at me the whole time. I went round a difficult corner with a shrieking chorus from the back seat, 'Another car wants to pass you!' Several minutes later, a lot of vehicles got stuck on a steep and bendy hill. I stopped, then daren't start again for fear we would roll backwards and hit the joy-riders behind. The pater changed places with me while Lord Cholmondely rolled down the hill in a black automobile done up in that yellow basketwork which used to be smart years ago. He looked at us as if we were mad. Later we looked in at the Cromer tennis tournament as N. and B. were entering for some of the sports competitions. They had started off the afternoon badly but Baba was determined to win the running race for under twelves. Reggie ragged her mercilessly, but for one thing she has guts. We were very amused to see her run. She was so determined! Eyebrows knitted, chest puffed out, and fists clenched! She got the prize, and N. and B. also won a second in another race and that meant chocolates.

August 13th

Rather a sad day, as Modom left. She seemed flustered and happy, kept saying how satisfied she was now that she'd had a holiday which would keep her well for the winter.

Lunch without Modom proved an ordeal. I dread Papa's vulgar heartiness at meals—clicking his tongue, eating cheese off a knife, and everlastingly wanting Nancy to kiss him or hold his tongue. The smell of his pipe makes me want to vomit, but then I don't know what's the matter with me. I'm so disgruntled and bad tempered, nobody seems to do right by me. When my mother remarks upon how pretty Sheringham is, I jump down her throat. To me it's ugly beyond measure. Only when one has walked for miles into the netherlands does the scenery become free of apartment houses and lodgings.

August 15th

We started off to Norwich directly after breakfast—a dull day and a dull run.

Mama and I went to the cathedral. Papa waited outside. Norman architecture is so bare and subtle in colour. I should like to have a room at Cambridge built exactly like some of those hidden apses and chapels. It would be a long, massive room, all whitewashed stone with enormous arches and one or two theatrical but simple pieces of dull gold furniture. A huge fire could burn at one end of the room; a gold dining table at the other end might have a cloth of gold on it, with gold plate and red

The family on the sands: my Father, Nancy, my Mother, C.B., Baba, Reggie

C.B. at Sandwich

gladioli in tall vases. I'd have people come to lunch, just to terrify and impress them.

This reverie was followed by shopping. My mother is too impatient to wait for anyone, and as a result we spent a lot of time trying to find her. The Norwich shops didn't inspire me to buy anything (I had no money in any case). Papa hovered in front of cheap clothes shops, looking at cheap hats. I went into Faith Brothers with him and did my best to influence him. But he bought a 4/9 hat that couldn't have been more offensive, then left the shop all hunched up with the absurd little thing on his head. He smiled, thinking how *clever* he'd been to buy a hat for 4/9.

IN MEMORY OF BOBBIE HORTON

August 23rd

As I was printing some snapshots in the sun, Mrs Middleton came round with *The Times*. She showed me the obituary column: 'Robert Schofield Horton, youngest son of Mr and Mrs Horton of Bolton House, near Rugby; at Fishbourne, Isle of Wight, of pneumonia, aged 21.'

Bobbie Horton! He is the first dead person I ever knew well. I kept thinking about him all evening long. . . .

We first knew one another at St Cyprian's. Bobbie was huge, delicate and red-headed. People laughed at him when he went down to his bath in the morning, wearing a grand Jaeger dressing gown and carrying a mammoth sponge.

At Harrow we shared a room during our first term. I tormented him with all sorts of mean tricks. I used to spill a jug of water on Bobbie and his bed when he wasn't looking. Or I would rush up behind him as he sat on a chair, tip it over and yell with joy when he landed on the ground with a nasty click. Most malicious of all, I waited till he knelt down to pray, rubbing his feet together in the typical way he had. Then I would give him such a hit!

Bobbie was a gentle soul. Though bigger than I, he could rarely be provoked to hit back. Once, however, he jammed his huge sponge into my mouth and I bit it in two! I shall never forget his beady little eyes at that moment: all astonishment. After lights out on that particular night, I went on at him for ages; insisting that it was brutal of a great lout like him to bully

c

a little thing like me. Bobbie, though in the right, took my cheek and then asked if I would come to breakfast tomorrow with him and his mother at the King's Head.

Bobbie wanted our Harrow room to be pink; I wanted blue. To convince him I said, 'Your red hair clashes with any pink.' (I got my way the following term, when I had a room to myself and turned it into a blue nightmare. Even the window boxes were painted blue. My housemaster became furious, lecturing the whole house. 'What are we coming to?' he asked. His answer, 'blue ruin', became a house joke for weeks afterwards.)

Bobbie Horton is dead. He was the most unphysical, pi person that ever existed. He was the essence of everything nice and clean, of everything a well-brought up boy should be. His red hair was cut short and slightly greased. His pink and pale complexion was immaculate; his eyelashes and brows were interestingly pale; his slightly parrot-like nose indicated good breeding.

He dressed in quiet but sumptuous clothes, wore silk shirts and silk pyjamas.

I envied Bobbie many things: his prowess at tennis, his handwriting, so large and distinctive. Also, the Hortons were rich. Bobbie had fine quality luggage and ivory-backed hairbrushes with his monogram on them. He had Ovaltine, malted milk and chocolate or digestive biscuits which he generously shared with me. He had a picture of his mama taken by Rita Martin; it was framed in expensive leather and stood on his roll-top desk.

Bobbie was a lesson in perseverance. Though quite ignorant when he started at Harrow in the bottom form, he learned and remembered much. By the time he left, he'd caught me up. He became proficient at history.

It took a long time for Bobbie's quiet virtues to be known and liked at Cambridge. There must have been many times when he felt lonely in that large, dark room of his. If I wanted something to do and couldn't stand my own company any longer, I went to see Bobbie. In his own flustered and anxious way he played the considerate host, always so polite and careful to do everything right for his guest.

Thinking of Bobbie's death tonight, I realise how terrified I'd been of death when I first went up to Cambridge. I remember thinking that I was going to die before I got there, because certain omens made me feel queasy inside. It had been the 3rd of the month—my lucky day. Yet written beneath the calendar for the day was a quotation from Joubert: 'This life is cradle of the life to come.' Strange that I should have noticed that: ordinarily I never look at calendars.

Why should Bobbie have died and not I or someone else? Poor Bobbie was absolutely sinless. I don't believe he ever said or did anything bad—not because he was ignorant, but because he was incapable of doing so. Certainly his behaviour towards me could not have been kinder, and I don't think he really liked me all that much. I hadn't much in common with him; I made a bad tennis partner and talked viciously about people.

I wonder if Bobbie went to see me act in *Henry IV*? He always promised he would see me next time, but said he was so busy working he couldn't spend an evening at the theatre.

The way I harp upon it, one would think I had lost my best friend. The truth is, Bobbie wasn't an intimate friend. If I feel intimately touched, it is because of our common past, of the many adventures we'd been through together.

He bored me, but he was charming.

August 16th

Spent the afternoon in the woods, feeling edgy and tense. I found a fallen tree that was rather comfortable, then lay on it face downwards. The sun shone hotly. I propped myself up on my elbows and read about basilicas for a while. Then I decided to lie in the bracken, where I smelled the damp leaves, the cool moss and earth. It gave me a peculiar sense of being alone, aware of my body. I don't know why, but I took my clothes off. It made me feel closer to things around me—the birds, a fluttering white moth, the stiff saplings. After a while, the sun sank behind a branch. I shivered and put on my clothes again.

I walked home, arriving late for dinner.

MEMORIES OF ARLEY

September 9th, 3 Hyde Park Street

I came back to find Modom making fudge. I ate a piece, had a bath and dinner. Afterwards, Reggie and I danced with Tecia and

Nancy. The pater had to go to a committee meeting. The mater went to bed, as she felt ill.

Exhausted from dancing, we lay back smoking cigarettes and reminiscing about Arley, where Reggie and I had been to stay with Aunt Cada and Tecia[1] when we were perhaps ten years old.

I couldn't remember as much as Reggie, but Arley remains in memory a lovely little village (now completely changed and trippery). Our holiday there seemed unlike anything we had known before. This was the real, pure country we never ordinarily saw. My parents, always more conventional than the bohemian Chattocks, felt bound to wear a 'collar and tie', so to speak. Most of our childhood was spent in suburbia; for summer we inevitably went to detestable seaside resorts, with asphalt paths and those oily shrubs that harbour horrible insects, and the slate-grey North Sea never far away.

Arley is a village in the heart of Worcestershire, with Arley Castle and (at that time) only a few dove-coloured stone cottages. The Chattocks used to take the curate's house for weekends and holidays, until the 1914 war created a housing shortage that put an end to the arrangement.

The curate's house, very small, had an outdoor earth closet that seemed surprisingly pleasant. In the next door cottage lived the keeper and his wife, who would lend a hand whenever we called over the wall to her: 'Mrs Co-oles!' They kept a tame magpie that we used to tease.

Our garden was sweet-smelling, with a stile that led into the park and a quiet, mysterious wood from which rabbits emerged and sat twitching their noses in the twilight. Here, too, I had my first alarming glimpse of ferrets, with their pink eyes and sharp teeth.

Opposite the house, a low stone wall surrounded an apple orchard, where the twisted trunks of fallen lichen trees gyrated on the ground. In this orchard I painted my first 'masterpiece', a picture of Tecia sitting on the wall and making a daisy chain, with the orchard behind her in full blossom.

Arley was altogether an inspiring place for me to work. I had been given the box-room above the porch, where I could mess about to my heart's content. I made a toy theatre out of three sides of a hat box and ambitiously put on my own miniature

[1] Aunt Cada's daughter, Letecia Chattock, now Mrs Fearnley-Whittingstall.

production of the musical comedy, *Oh! Oh! Delphine!* First I cut photographs of the chorus ladies out of the *Play Pictorial*, painting their faces in full stage make-up. Then the evening dresses were washed with pastel colours and dotted with gold and silver liquid paint that had such a strong acid smell it remains in my nostrils to this day. I faithfully reproduced the rose and wistaria scenery, then turned an electric torch on to the tableau.

ISOBEL ELSOM.

Characters were pushed on stage by means of tin clips attached to long handles. It remained only to make them perform, which I did by acting all the parts and singing the score myself.

Here, in remote Arley, my theatrical dreams flourished. And a prize addition to my gallery of stars was provided when Aunt Cada went away for a day, coming back with the week's *Tatler* that contained a large photograph of my goddess, Isobel Elsom. She stood in profile, her long swan neck and prize-fighters chin straining towards a cluster of hydrangeas.

Reggie had more sporting interests. Often he played Red Indians with Tecia and Tess.[1] Sometimes I joined him for clock golf. And one day, in a more high-spirited mood, I very nearly killed him. I was swinging him in the hammock, higher and higher and higher. Crack! He fell out on to the top of his head. I shall always remember the sound. Apart from a terrific head-ache, Reggie was not hurt. But the incident terrified me; years

---

[1] Tecia's younger sister.

afterwards, I would wake up in the night and relive it with horror.

Reggie, Tecia and I dredged up all these and other souvenirs tonight. Do you remember the way down to the village? Do you remember the Ferry across the Severn river? What about the fair at Bewdley? Oh, and the wild bamboos in the water garden of Arley Castle! And the peacocks on the old stone walls! Can you picture the Forest of Wyre? No, but I remember being aware for the first time of the shrimp redness of japonica. I remember the frogs in the well, the painted lady butterflies resting on a fallen tree trunk and flapping their wings lazily. Who could forget the evening peace of the garden, with Aunt Cada and cousin Ella smoking cigarettes, and only the hooting of an owl to disturb the serenity?

'Mrs Co-oles, Mrs Co-oles,' we used to shout. But I don't remember what she looked like.

It was a perfect holiday. Reggie said, 'The happiest time I've ever had.'

THE ASTAIRES

August 30th

There was a large crowd of people outside the theatre, and a pinned-up notice: 'House full'. It was the last night of the Astaires in *Stop Flirting*.

I've seldom enjoyed myself so much. The music is bright and full of life; the whole show, modern and clever, goes with such a smack. A flashy orchestra played ragtime that made me almost sick with delight, while the chorus buzzed about mad with life.

I laughed terrifically at Jack Melford, who last time I saw him had given me double nausea. Helen Gilliland had nice shoes.

As for the Astaires, they are so indescribably loose limbed they can only be compared to animals. In fact, you could bend them into any shape without hurting them. Their dancing is ultimate, original and effective. The quick and witty steps could only be the invention of people who really observe and enjoy being alive. Some of the routines, so true and grotesque, are almost epigrammatic. There is one delightful bit where both dance together, doing not quite the same steps and stabbing out at both sides with their feet to create a precise and strong effect.

Adele is thin, energetic and such a little snip.

Fred makes the word 'marvellous' sound clean and manly. After him, I'd like to go home and cut off my hair; I'd like to change my whole self.

At the end of the evening Adele tried to make a speech, but broke down and gave a half cry and half giggle. Fred insisted, 'Don't be silly! We've got a bit more to say.' Old charwomen shouted from the gallery, 'Come back soon!' Fred answered them all. Adele piped in her high little voice, 'Don't forget us!' and everyone wanted to cry.

Christmas Eve

Nurse was away for the day, so Nancy and Baba had dinner with us. I kept ragging Baba and told her to go to bed. She chirped, 'I thought you said dinner was only bearable when the brats came down!'

Dinner conversation certainly has been less awful lately, but tonight it seemed unfortunate. Mummie said she felt ill. Daddy suggested, 'Let's go and live on a golf course and lead the simple life!'

A little silence and Mummie replied, 'Well, we *do* lead the simple life here,' meaning we go out very little. Later she asked, 'Are you going to the office tonight in the car or by train?'

Reggie parroted, 'Are you going to the office again tonight?'

Daddy burst out, 'Yes! To complete the living of a simple life!' He was furious. He puffed and bit at his cigar and trembled. 'I work my hardest at the office all day. I don't mind that. But to be told we lead the simple life. It's really too bad!'

Explanations followed. I felt very depressed. We left our parents in the dining-room. Later Mummie volunteered, 'I'll come to the office with you.'

My father, contrite, said, 'Oh, no, no, no, of course not, no, no!'

Reggie said *he'd* go. 'No, no, you needn't come.'

I offered to bring my diary and write. 'No, no.'

Well, Reggie went. Mother sat in a chair and talked. 'We can't afford this house. We'll have to sell it and live in some cheaper place. Business has been bad. Ever since that brute of a Fox left, things have been getting slacker and slacker. Now you know

Daddy has lost the American business. That brute Bowers has taken it away and given it to a man in Manchester. It'll make an awful difference: half of our income gone. No wonder your father's worried and edgy tonight. There's a cargo of stuff from Finland which may mean a dead loss of six thousand pounds. That's why he's gone to the office, to see if any telegrams have come in.'

My spirits sank. I love this house, and I enjoy being a little extravagant. It'll be a disaster if I'm not rich. I almost despise a man that isn't rich. Anyhow, I'm sure I shall be. I felt very disheartened about Life with a capital L. If we *do* lose our money, I'll not know how to look at people: Basil Bleck, for instance. I'll have to put up with friends like Leonard Tregoning; he wouldn't mind our being penniless. I'll have to make do with such friends, but I like my rich ones more: they're so polished and clever.

My mother sat on in the chair, looking lined and wretched. Then she took up a pile of presents to put on Nancy's and Baba's beds.

Papa and Reggie came back fairly cheerful. I dare not ask about the six thousand pound cargo.

A FAMILY CHRISTMAS

Christmas Day

I woke with a start. Very dark it was. Reggie called me to get up to go to church. Ugh-r-r-r! It was so cold. I lay in bed a bit longer.

Baba's clear, throaty voice floated up from downstairs, excited and busy. Then she came into my room to give me my present, the one she had said 'looks expensive'. It turned out to be a handkerchief; some sort of *crêpe de Chine*, black and yellow and red. Baba is clever with her presents.

Mummie and Reggie had already gone off to church. I ran all the way, with difficulty as the roads were icy. What a cold morning! The church was crowded, but by luck I saw Mummie and Reggie and sat next to them.

The congregation looked the most dowdy imaginable—so dowdy they were almost exotic. Church was decorated with narcissi and poinsettias.

Mother nearly fell on the way home, but Reggie and I caught her without slipping on the ice ourselves. Breakfast, while Nancy and Baba sat about opening all their presents: a stumpy umbrella from Mama, a box of paints from Modom, fountain pens and books. Baba got twenty presents, Nancy just as many. Papa was pleased with the cigars. Nurse came in and crossly gave us agreeable things: me, a pot of pink dwarf tulips.

The family went out in the park, then came back. Nancy was in despair at having lost one of her new silk handkerchiefs. Reggie had given it to her, and she'd got such a good collection.

We had a small lunch of smoked salmon, Stilton cheese, mince pies with burning brandy. The brandy was so old it took ten minutes to light. Then we played little card games: Pitt, which I gave Baba for her present. It was a noisy game.

I sat in the drawing-room and read *Antic Hay*. It's open and frank and cleanly dirty.

Papa was bored and wanted exercise. He started off on a walk to see the Willes.[1] One would think the Crosdales[2] and the Willes were the only people we knew!

Modom arrived soon after tea. There were hoots and screams for her. 'Thank you a thousand times for the lovely present! Oh. Auntie, you are a naughty girl!' People screeched and kissed. Then it was the Beaton family's turn to give presents. Modom uttered a different scream for each parcel she opened. 'Just what I wanted!' Scream, scream. She was very pleased with the mincing machine.

Nancy came down in a new party dress, so pale and ordinary that one wouldn't look twice. I ragged and teased her until she became desperate. 'Nightgown,' I said. 'Disgusting, coming to Christmas dinner in a nightie.'

Uncle Wilfred arrived, blinking shifty walrus eyes above drooping walrus moustache. He's very, very nervous. Papa says it's all put on, which I think is the funniest thought imaginable, He's certainly a character with his double chaff, exaggerated nodding of the head and his far too far-fetched jokes. He gave

[1] Mr and Mrs William Willes, an aged, bewigged couple who somehow or other had become fast friends and always appeared at family festivities. This year, however, they had become too infirm to make the expedition from Willesden where, suitably, they now lived.

[2] Mr and Mrs Gordon Crosdale, another inexplicable addition to the extremely limited family circle.

some silver purses to Nancy and Baba, but of course nothing to Reggie and me. I'd been fuming, before he came, and thinking of *demanding* a present.

Dinner was served, but no Bee.[1] We waited a little, waited a bit more and then started. We had soup and were on the fish course, drinking the health of the Willes when Bee arrived, her huge black eyes blazing with delight and surprise. She looked charming; the table looked charming with that Georgian silver basket, scarlet carnations and four scarlet candles.

The champagne was fizzy, the turkey huge. Papa kept talking about old man Willes and how we missed him. Nancy and I fought for salted almonds. I ate a lot of olives.

Uncle Wilfred rambled on about the latest plays he'd seen. He hardly ever enjoys the theatre nowadays, but used to have a great passion for Gilbert and Sullivan: he went to see *Iolanthe* over a hundred times, and lost count with his favourite, *The Mikado*. He's the most eccentric man I know—and such a miser. He might have been a great success at anything, but just lives alone, never sees a soul and never wants to. He doesn't read or write. I suppose he spends his life blinking at the wall to save a sixpence.

My father now became sentimental. It was twenty-one years ago today that he proposed to my mother. Papa asked Mama if she were willing to spend another twenty-one years with him. Mummie said 'Yes,' very happily and sweetly. She would go on living with him for another twenty-one years, never realising that they had nothing in common.

The Christmas pudding was brought in to great conviviality. Everyone got half sovereigns; I, the bachelor's button, Mummie a ring and Bee a thimble. We pulled crackers; wore caps; ate Karlsbad plums and dates and fruit and were very merry.

Papa talked mostly cricket and O. Henry to Uncle Wilfred when the ladies departed. I fidgeted a lot, but pricked up my ears as Papa started to discuss his friend, Lady Smith-Pebble, who has just been fined for shoplifting.

At last we went upstairs. I brought out my designs and photographs for the Cambridge play to show to Bee. She was interested. Bee is now painting lamp shades at a furious rate and stepping out besides. Last night she went to four dances—the Embassy, Ciro's,

[1] Beatrice Alberdi, a Bolivian friend of Aunt Jessie.

the Savoy and Rector's! She is lucky the way she gets taken about and given presents. Her mother gave her a gold watch.

We danced and became rowdy. We played oranges and lemons; all of us against Uncle Wilfred and Bee, who were left sprawling on the floor while everyone else stood round screaming. We threw paper streamers at Modom till she was wound in them. We danced an energetic Sir Roger. Papa kept missing old man Willes.

In bed I read a lot of *Antic Hay*. It gets much better after the first hundred pages. I especially like the part where the two people go to bed, stroke one another all over and fall asleep.

Part III

Bayswater and the City

1925 and 1926

My last two years of Cambridge life are recorded with nauseous detail in nearly twenty scribbled notebooks; these hysterical volumes emphasise the determination with which I escaped being 'educated' and avoided partaking in the orthodox activities of college life.

Never a mention of the lectures on architecture, history, or literature, which I should have attended. Instead, there are lengthy accounts of visits to London to see picture exhibitions or plays, or more local jaunts motoring round the countryside, visiting churches and antique shops or going to Newmarket races.

The journals record the highly aesthetic lunches in his Renaissance rooms, with Steven Runciman, who wore heavy rings, carried a parakeet on his fingers, and had his hair cut in an Italianate fringe. But, although the sprinkled names of Rylands, Shepherd, and Ord, remind me that I was acquainted with other intellectuals in King's and Trinity, it is evident that the undergraduate's easy and spontaneous ways of companionship, of 'dropping-in', were beyond me. Still deeply insecure within myself, I took refuge behind a façade of formality, and but for the companionship of Boy Le Bas would have been extremely lonely. Boy, however, had his other interests to occupy much of his time, so I became absorbed in the productions of the Amateur Dramatic Clubs. No triviality connected with my multifarious participation in these plays is considered unworthy of the written word: every grievance, rivalry and typical stage intrigue is committed to paper to my ever-lasting shame: I have spared the reader.

When my university span had passed—in as untypical a fashion as any undergraduate's could—I was again faced with the problem of my future. I now found myself more than ever without convictions, in fact the obstacles I placed in my own path were becoming insuperable. Back in London I could only await possibilities with a vague hope-fulness.

The picture that follows is of a miserable creature full of self pity, jealousy and envy. My frustrations and pretentiousness must have made me as exasperating an element in the free-and-easy atmosphere of my family, as they were hateful to me.

January 14th 1925, 3 Hyde Park Street

My birthday. I feel very funny when I realise that I am now twenty-one. That's more than half one's nice life. It will be dreadful when I'm over thirty. My whole excuse so far has been my youth!

September 7th

Daddy didn't seem to mind my coming down from Cambridge without a degree, but he's getting in rather a state since then. Yet I can't think what to do! I only know that I want to do *something*. At the moment, I'm just spending, or thinking of extravagant ways to spend more.

September 22nd

I'm utterly stagnant except for a few paltry engagements. Tuesday I went out on the tramp for a studio. Round by St James's Square there was a small house that would be ideal—but certainly beyond the price-pale.

I'm desperate about the necessity for work. I don't just want to take photographs, which would be a petty waste of time. But where in hell will I get the money to start an establishment where I turn out theatrical designs, paint and take photographs—all at the same time?

Meanwhile, I can't be seen sitting about, in case the Pater comes into the room and starts yelling again, 'Why can't he do some work?' Mama is so harassed and upset about Reggie's appalling headaches that she has no energy left to cope with me. Boy prods me to work, but I can't seem to get started on anything.

September, undated

I had a second look at that house in St James's. It's pretty pokey, but that wouldn't matter if I once got inside and had my notepaper stamped. I ought to inquire about the lease.

The Pater hasn't said anything more for the moment, but I get in a panic as things slide on. I'd really like to go away, but one needs a lot of money for that. At Cambridge, one *was* away. In fact, now that I look back on those days they seem positively halcyon. One merely spent and tried vaguely to pay the bills.

October 15th

The whole week has slipped by, and nothing done. I had hoped to have out a whole series of designs to show to Nigel Playfair.[1]

Good Lord, I resent wasting time like this. Where will it all end? I feel so annoyed, going to theatres and picture places and seeing others shine. I want to shine myself! I'd like to act, but what terrible parts one would get if one got a part at all! So I go on, feeling discontented and grudging everyone's triumph.

November 10th

The axe has fallen! Today my father said, quite agreeably, though I could see he'd been planning his speech beforehand, that he would like me to get a better idea of business by going to his office and keeping accounts. I replied that I would. But gosh, how I'll loathe it!

That puts an end to my hanging about doing no definite

[1] Actor-manager of the Lyric Theatre, Hammersmith.

work. As it happens, I've been pretty busy lately with designs and photographs. But Papa thinks of these things as a hobby.

I lied to Boy and said I had *decided* to go into my father's business. He was shocked. When his parents heard the news they gloated. 'Ah ha! So he's had to knuckle under and throw to the winds all his fanciful ideas,' etc.

Realising that I had only a little freedom left, I put a sprint on and did a tremendous amount of work. I got fagged out mounting enlargements, a long, laborious task during which I became covered with foul-smelling secotine.

MY FIRST DAY IN THE CITY

November 20th

The City, oh God! I got up early and was ready to go at 9.30, but Daddy said I'd better wait for him.

Last night at dinner, Reggie and N. and B. and I talked about how we'd been brought up in such awe of the 'office'. N. and B. decided it was really a complete farce, a mere excuse for taking up Daddy's time. They made it seem funny, but I didn't see anything funny this morning.

I walked to the tube station with my father and a thousand other men, all smoking pipes, all carrying morning papers under their arms. I didn't buy a paper. I glared and glowered at the people in the train, intent on their papers and themselves. They never looked about them.

Daddy lectured me with earnest impatience: 'The first rule in business is . . . to put it another way . . . the simple plan is . . .' These expressions echoed over and over again in the midst of a long harangue I didn't understand at all. I replied dutifully, 'Yes,' or 'No.' I was more or less resigned to my fate, except for one thing: I would never wear a bowler hat.

We arrived at the office. A series of nondescript men slid into my Father's room with letters, their expressions as dreary as their collars.

I had rather a headache. The radiator-heat atmosphere of the building didn't help any. I hadn't had time to visit the lavatory after breakfast, which made my depression total.

Then, abruptly, I heard Reggie[1] talking professionally and

---

[1] Reggie had gone straight into our father's office from Eastbourne College.

67

competently on the telephone. How important! I began to think the place wasn't such a farce after all.

Mr Tarr came in. Mr Tarr had a white face, red hair, drooping moustache and a pale, silky voice. He looked like a Velazquez portrait. But what a freak of nature—so methodical, punctilious, neat and tidy as a silly old virgin.

I had to read one or two typewritten letters, but I couldn't understand them any more than Daddy's pompous explanations. He created an aura of great hurry, kept tapping his fingers and became impatient with the poor clerks. I was made to do a lot of figures in a book. Each figure (feeguire as Daddy calls it) had to be put in exactly the right spot or else sharply rubbed out with an indiarubber. Daddy keeps one in a drawer of his desk, wrapped up in a piece of paper. Each time the rubber is used, the paper gets unfolded, then folded up again.

At one moment, the pater rang up that cheery Hampstead cricketer, Geo. Hickson. I am to do a caricature of him for a cricket club menu; which means I'll have to sit and look at his Ally Sloper face and draw him making ludicrous expressions— eyebrows up, mouth stretched like a slot and cheeks all wrinkled.

By lunch time I had copied out a lot of feeguires. Reggie took me to the place where he generally goes. I'd imagined worse, but it was two o'clock and the crowd of young men at Birch's, as the place is called, had thinned out. We went downstairs, crossed a sawdust floor, stood at a counter and ate: ham in roll sandwiches, beef sandwiches, rock cakes, chocolate biscuits. We drank punch.

Afterwards, we went to the Jamaica place for coffee. This I did think revolting. The coffee couldn't have been worse, the bowler hats stiffened my determination not to wear one. I had the impression of a lot of dirty beetles fighting for existence.

Back at the office, I decided that the whole building smelled like an underground lavatory. I wrote some more feeguires in the book and was faced with the task of doing additions. I have always been bad at arithmetic, finding it an agony to add anything up. Now I must needs do the best I could. My head went round and round. Exhaustion overtook me. I struggled for hours.

What a squalid place! The tall chairs were falling to bits; the oilcloth had holes worn through to the floor. Dust and dirt were everywhere, creating a musty smell. And here I was, hacking away at this damned arithmetic. The purple ink had dwindled in the well; with the pen nib so thin, my entries looked completely meaningless and without character.

At last we went home, with a million other bowler-hatted business men now carrying the evening paper. Queen Alexandra was dying—'sinking' as the placards had it. Since we were all going to the theatre tonight, the pater and Reggie began to worry in case the Queen should die and the theatres close.

I felt sick of hearing about the Queen. All I knew was that I was tired and bad tempered. My headache persisted, I felt cold and wanted to get home so that I could have a bath, rest and think about something decent.

At length I *did* get home, in such a state of rage and despair that I wept as soon as I was alone. I slammed everything on to the floor, clenched my teeth, swore more filthily and freely than I'd ever done before.

I felt in a happier state of mind after I'd been to the lavatory and had a shave. I trailed down late for dinner, but didn't care a damn. The lazy, silly females had done nothing all day and the house looked ugly, without even any flowers. Mummie appeared thoroughly dowdy.

N. and B.'s Angela Duveen came to dinner. What a delightfully precocious midget, all of twelve and speaking as though she were thirty.

Daddy (as bad as Uncle Wilfred) suggested that Reggie and I go by bus or tube to the theatre. I damn well wouldn't, and we went comfortably in a taxi. It was my second time seeing *Mercenary Mary*, but I enjoyed it, thanks to champagne at dinner.

I'd forgotten the whole day to wish Daddy many happy returns on his birthday. I hadn't any money for a present, either.

My first day in the City: I pray that there won't be many more!

November 24th

Up at the last minute; on with the clothes that lay crumpled by the bed. My shirt was dirty, but what did it matter in the City? Nothing mattered. I looked a wreck with my suit unpressed, with filthy collar and cuffs. Down again in the tube, directly after breakfast. No time to finish the photographs I wanted; no time even to fill the orders on hand—and there are quite a few of them.

The same office, the same petty work, the same routine. I wrote out receipts, filled up the ledger, wrestled with averages and sums until my head was splitting and my hands clammy.

In the luncheon interval, Reggie and I were out over an hour. We ate at Simpson's, a chop house. We had a great lump of meat, beautifully cooked. The men there looked dreary, everything seemed dreary. Worse, I felt more resigned than yesterday. If it went on much longer, I'd gradually lose interest in everything I ever hoped to accomplish.

As an end to a perfect day (of horror) Reggie took me to the woodwool factory. We went in the bus to the most God-forsaken place: Bethnal Green! The factory was noisy, repellent, etc. Reggie put on a businesslike air with doddering old Baldwin, the factory head.

On the way home I tried not to read the papers. But there was nothing else to do in the train.

November 30th

Today I didn't mind the office boy's face. I felt rather sorry for him.

Mr Twist is the only one I don't feel sorry for. He oozes malevolence with his huge chest and stomach, his vulgarity, his nastiness. In his indolence he reminds me of a fat woman with a rich cough.

Lunch at the Stock Exchange Lyons, where we tried in vain to get rid of a foreign coin that had been given us as a shilling.

December 3rd

The pater stayed very late at the office and came home in a foul mood. He turned Reggie out of the room, then ticked me off about the books. He said I couldn't do work that a child of twelve could do. What with mistakes, scratchings out and blanks, I'd put the files in a chaotic state. In future, he would be afraid to let me handle them. Why, I couldn't do the simplest addition of feeguires. The business would soon be bankrupt if I continued. He even went so far as to say he didn't want me at the office again, but at the same time wouldn't tolerate my doing nothing.

I felt untouched by his fury. It just seemed far away. Inevitably, of course, I knew my work had to be checked; and I felt certain I'd made a few slips. But in all ignorance, I couldn't have guessed it mattered so much. Apparently, when something has been written down wrong, one must take a ruler and put a ruled line through the mistake, not just draw a line through it by hand.

I had a very hot bath, so hot that I almost fainted in it. I lay back with my eyes shut and hoped I would lose consciousness. As a matter of fact, I wouldn't have minded drowning. I felt numb, uninterested in anything. I had no ambition, was surrounded by difficulty and thoroughly depressed. Generally, the thought of death terrifies me. I want to live and do what I am going to do next week or the week after. But this evening I could have faced it with equanimity—not because I was unhappy, not for any particular reason, except that there seemed nothing immediate to live for.

December 6th (Sunday)

At lunch, 'Where's Cecil?' At 3.30, 'Where's Cecil?' At tea, 'Where's Cecil?' All through the evening my father's anxiety continued. It wasn't because he wanted the pleasure of my company. No, he worried for fear I wouldn't get the cricket caricatures done.

When at last I did come home (and it's *my* business where I've been) I found the family playing bridge. I drank some whisky and soda to get less irritable, then started the damned caricatures. They were quickly done; I thought the one of Hickson quite good. I took them to Daddy, who promptly expressed his delight. He leant on the piano, chuckling over them. Having been grumpy all day, he was satisfied now. He asked me if, as a reward for the caricatures, I'd like to come to the cricket dinner. I had carefully to say that I didn't think I would enjoy it, but thank you all the same.

December 7th

At breakfast this morning I asked, 'Are you expecting me at the office today?'

The question baffled my father. He didn't know. He had had to engage a Dutchman (evidently of an unexcitable nature) to scratch out my mistakes and clear up the books.

71

I said, 'I have enough orders for photographs to keep me busy a whole week.' This was true.

'All right,' and he clicked his tongue.

I rushed Mrs Joicey[1] through by ten o'clock, packing her up neatly. Then I took the pictures to the Berkeley, walking there and back in the snow. It gave me a thoroughly thankful feeling to have got them off my chest. I also felt glad I hadn't given her poor prints. It is important to do a print over again when the first results aren't good enough.

THE MOVE FROM 3 HYDE PARK STREET

February 23rd 1926

Farewell to number three Hyde Park Street. Tomorrow a van comes to cart all the rubbish in this house to the sale room. We'll not be able to get half our things into the new place.

I spent hours sorting out papers in my room and tidying my desk. Gosh, what a lot of utter muck! The love letters, the soliloquies I wrote at Harrow. It all seems housemaid sentiment now, but how deeply I felt things at the time.

Then there were all my old theatre programmes to go through. With what fervour I collected them! It seemed a major disaster if one was left in Rumpelmeyer's after the matinée. I'd have to go back to the theatre and haggle with a commissionaire. These mementos were clipped away in a *Schauenburg schellhäfter*, a filing contraption father got from Germany.

The programmes are faintly interesting still, but only to stir memories. What raptures I went into about musical comedies: the 'fakeness' of the scenery, with netting in the trees, and painted artificialities. Lily Elsie and Gertie Millar were my heroines. And I used to pray that there would be a full page of rabbity Florence Smithson in the *Sketch*. There never was.

Oh, those embarrassing letters! Long ramblings from Beresford-Jones about art; descriptions of studio parties and 'wonderful talks'. Courageously, I threw them all away at last. I've been meaning to do so for years. It would be a scandal if I fell ill and someone discovered them.

Then there were all the painstaking water-colours I did at

[1] The mother of my friend Magda, a Hungarian lady of wealth and flamboyance, whom I had photographed professionally.

Harrow. In those days I sketched anything. It didn't matter what. I wanted to make things look as they looked. But now I see a sad lack of tone, a conventional realism I thought was art! Alas, a great many people *still* think so. My parents observe wistfully that I could draw in *those* days.

In the afternoon I went through my magazine clippings. How I worshipped the actresses in their ridiculous clothes. What enthusiasm I had. Nowadays, nothing makes me so genuinely ardent as I was then. Of course, it seems self-indulgent in retrospect. I must try never to be self-indulgent again.

February 24th

In the midst of this wretched house-moving, I haven't for a moment forgotten my plight. I still have no work, am sick about what work I shall do and when.

Meanwhile, my father slaves away and naturally feels disgusted with my idleness. Pig that I am, I almost wish he would force me to take action. But I'm no bloody good in that office. The Dutchman is still undoing my damage.

This afternoon we all went round to the new house in Sussex Gardens, Paddington. It's much smaller and less elegant but we'll have to make the best of it. The blue door has dried badly.

Papa took us for a run in the country, but as usual we never got farther than the Uxbridge road. And he must shout 'Get out' at people when they dare to cross the street.

February 25th

The move! Yesterday the men packed up our glass and small stuff. Today, in good earnest, things were carted out and plonked on the pavement before being put in the van. It offended my eyes to see servants' bedroom furniture cluttering the pavements—wash stands, china chamber pots.

At the new house, Nurse muddled about bossing everybody. She's such an old tartar.

February 26th, 61 Sussex Gardens

Where are we to put all the furniture? The drawing-room is stacked so high I had difficulty getting a ladder placed in order to

73

pick out the mouldings with gold paint. What a labour, and how precise one must be! During all this dead man's work, the turpentine fumes gave me a big headache.

Our last meal at H.P., with just the dining table left! I wandered about, making a goodbye tour. The empty rooms looked dirty and forlorn. They'll want doing up now. Still, it's been a good house; living up to it was something of a triumph.

April 7th

I have looked through my Cochran designs and can't understand why C. B. didn't use any of them. I've rung Miss Scrimshaw many times, but get no satisfactory reply.

The Pater is furious: Why hadn't I got a definite contract, etc.? I admit it must be exasperating for him to observe my unbusinesslike ways. Yet Cochran definitely told me it wouldn't be 'a waste of my time'.

April 8th

I had an idea for a stage curtain decoration: a family of Marie-Laurencin fauns leaping about, pale pink with dark, liquid eyes. I started to draw contentedly.

Mum came up to my room and said, 'Oh, dear, I do wish Cochran would accept your things. Your father is threatening to put you in Schmiegelow's[1] office!'

I refused to contemplate such a fate and went back to my pink fauns.

---

[1] A Danish business man and friend of my father.

Part IV

Holborn

1926

April 10th 1926 (Saturday)
At breakfast, Daddy brusquely asked if I had found a job yet.
I said, 'I'm afraid not.' I started to explain that I might possibly
get a job with Nigel Playfair at the Lyric, Hammersmith.

Daddy interrupted rudely, 'Well, if you haven't, I have. Mr
Schmiegelow will take you in his office. You start on Monday
morning at half past nine and get one pound a week. I'll leave you
to work your way up from the bottom.'

I went crimson. Of all the humiliations! If I had to go into an
office, I could have asked Mr LeBas to let me into his—his really
is a good one. But Schmiegelow, that young Danish friend of the
Kiaers! Schmiegelow, who plays tennis with Daddy!

But how could I argue? After all, I'd done nothing for a year.
For that matter, I'd done precious little at Cambridge.

If only Cochran had accepted my designs!

An office! I would only be as incompetent as I was at my
father's. I suppose he thinks he's being sensible, firm and strong.

75

He read an article by Arnold Bennett in the Sunday paper, all about 'fathers' sons', about how the Swiss hotel proprietor sends his son to the neighbourhood hotel to work his way up. That's what my father thinks he's doing.

Yet he won't let me start from the bottom in my own line. He doesn't realise I've made more than a pound a week, just dabbling with photography in my spare time. The trouble is, when I get a cheque for seven pounds I immediately blow it, half on some extravagance and the other half on paying debts.

After all I've dreamed and hoped for, to be chained to an idiot's task in a meagre office!

My grievance festered all day. I felt thoroughly venomous. I would be as unpleasant as possible to Schmiegelow. If I could get any other work at all, I would immediately plank down a pound note and quit. I would *not* be damned in an office. I would *not* give up the opportunity of doing work that interested me.

April 11th

With Schmiegelow's office staring me in the face tomorrow, I tried to do a bit of journalism for the *Daily Express* or some such paper. I spent the morning sitting in a large arm chair desperately trying to finish a snobby article about 'Society'.

I'd get a spasm, write masses, then gradually alter it all until there was nothing left.

I am no good at writing. I often try doggedly to write an article or a short story. But it's too bloody difficult.

Soon the family returned from Birmingham, my mother with a cold and sore throat. My father handed me a slip with the address of Schmiegelow's office on it. I argued a bit, making him feel uncomfortable.

I am sitting in bed now, wondering whether I really will have this hell foisted on me? Perhaps I can manage to create a last minute argument at the breakfast table and get myself free.

GETTING TO KNOW MR SCHMIEGELOW

April 12th

At breakfast I said nothing, just munched and felt an empty, throbbing feeling in my stomach. Mummie stayed in bed with her cold. At breakfast Daddy asked if I needed any money for lunches this week, as Schmiegelow wouldn't be giving me anything until Friday. Oh, no! I'd rather starve.

I left directly after a second piece of toast and marmalade. At any rate, the address was a Bloomsbury one and not in the City.

I enjoyed the bus ride. It was a sparkling morning, the air fresh with spring. I felt superior for not having a morning paper to read. In fact, I had the odd impression of being tremendously alone and independent. It came over me all of a sudden, something akin to what one felt when going back to Harrow or Cambridge, after the holidays. One was conscious, for the first day, of oneself; of oneself doing this or that, or walking alone in the street.

But then the hard reality struck me again. Far from being independent, I was in a trap. Indeed, out of spite I had put on my oldest suit—the brown one all covered in gold paint spots.

I wandered about Bloomsbury trying to find Southampton Row. Funnily enough, I discovered that Schmiegelow's office was in the same building occupied by a photographer whose work I often looked at in my days of leisure. Those days seemed a long way away.

I found the room and entered on my guard. Mr Schmiegelow wasn't in. But a little man with an intimate and kind manner said, 'Oh, yes, you're Mr Beaton, the son of Mr Beaton who owns the woodwool works. You've come to help Mr Schmiegelow, haven't you? Well, he can't be long and won't you sit down.'

I sat sordidly on a chair, my coat collar muffled up above my ears. I boiled with spleen. My father thought I'd done nothing all this time. I had, admittedly, been lazy. But how difficult to work in the family atmosphere, with one's mater always busy wasting time. And anyway, I'd done a lot in spasms. I daresay I've made fifty pounds with my photographs during the past year! Moreover, hadn't I slaved on a rickety ladder gilding the house into a state of respectability? Just look at the suit I was wearing! And what about all the work I did for Cochran? I wasn't to be blamed if he didn't look at half the things I showed him. My designs are definitely good. I feel confident about several being really original.

The door burst open and in flew young Schmiegelow, bright and cheery and taking long strides. He wore tortoise-shell glasses;

77

he seemed nice looking. To my relief I found him Danish and foreign, instead of middle-class.

I took my coat off, feeling it mightn't be as bad as I had imagined. An old virgin huddled in and took off her hat and coat, too. I was introduced to Miss Robertson, who hurried about giving me papers and telling me in a firm but motherly way what to do. She sat me at a typewriter and I started to work that, very slow and somewhat careless about mistakes.

It seemed a less awful place than my father's office. There's only one small room, but it's well-proportioned and light, painted various unobjectionable shades of green.

A busy morning: copying first one thing on the typewriter and then another. I was told to do one or two easy sums.

At lunch time, Schmiegelow said he'd like me to go out with him. We went to the Holborn Restaurant, a place which, in my days of leisurely shopping, I had looked at with curiosity and wondered if anyone ever went inside. They did: I found hundreds of business men having a mediocre lunch. We had some particularly nasty steak and kidney pudding and talked hard.

S. understood that I didn't like this sort of thing, that I was an artist and not a business man. We got fundamental, exchanging energetic views about how hard life was; about how, when one was at Cambridge or in polite society, one never realised the unpleasant fact that life was really governed by cash. Gentlemen didn't talk about it, but pounds and shillings determined everything. When it came to business, friendship meant nothing if one could get a bit of money by doing someone else down. We took, as an example of a typical dishonest-honest business man, Mr ——, that little Danish bounder who does anyone down if he can. He doesn't care a damn for art except in relation to pounds, shillings and pence: 'This must be good because it cost me five hundred pounds!'

Schmiegelow seemed to understand what I felt about business men. He has apparently been going through a disturbing period since he left the Danish Legation. He realised with a bump that cash was everything, and without much money has been finding things difficult.

He considered my problem, saying that what I wanted was a manager, just as Carpentier had Descamps. 'It would pliss your faghter if you could earn money with your artte.' (It would

78

please me, too, but doing my own work would be the greatest pleasure.) S. then promised to see if he couldn't find me some work congenial to my talents. In the meantime, there were a few things I could help him with in the office.

It was a long and interesting wrangle. By the time we returned to the office I had thrown off my sullen state of despondency. I tapped the typewriter like a woodpecker. Schmiegelow became vivacious at tea, adopting a funny and airy attitude to the things we'd been serious about at lunch.

I went home pleased. This morning, I had pictured myself returning in fury and despair. By contrast I now felt full of beans, and immediately started gilding a fireplace.

April 13th
Arrived at the office fairly early. S. didn't turn up until late.

Miss Robertson is a nice old bird, feminine and giggly. Though fond of routine and practical, she loses her head in an emergency. She speaks in a high, cooing-dove voice with a pretty accent, pronouncing her u's in a pointed way. I wondered if she could be Danish, then found out she was Scottish. I got to like her more and more as the day passed. She is matey and pally, if unstimulating.

I didn't know where to eat in my luncheon interval. I abominate those big teashops and would sooner go hungry. I went to the British Museum, requisitioned some books on costume and waited so long for them that I had to leave just as they arrived.

I came back to the office, felt rather hungry and decided I must have some coffee. The café downstairs is evidently run by prostitutes. I sat in fear of catching syphilis from the coffee cup.

The p.m. was spent copying out invoices. I pecked away, feeling my hopelessness and incompetence returning. By six o'clock I squirmed with irritability. I came home in a cracking temper, insulting everybody. I hated myself for it.

April 14th (Wednesday)
This morning I arrived laden with books to read and letters to answer. I am determined to be energetic every moment that I have to be here, unlike the other people in this office, who slack away doing nothing. There's hardly any business accomplished.

79

Miss Robertson yawns, gossips about her Scottish relations, her flat or her idea of a perfect holiday. She makes cups of tea and looks out of the window. The room gets squirted with eucalyptus by the little girl who serves as secretary for Mr Skinner. Mr Skinner is the nice man who greeted me on Monday.

I suddenly realise how different these people's world is from mine: no snobbery.

Time drips on. The tea interval is greatly looked forward to. Schmiegelow plays the comedian, ragging old Miss Robertson. She answers back in her fluty Scotch accent, yelling with laughter.

After tea I'm restless to bolt as soon as possible. The others seem content to stay on till the bitter end, even though they know there is no work for them to do nor any possibility of there being any. I suppose they have nothing to get away to.

April 15th

I felt it was a bit too late in the day to ask what E. & O.E. meant, but managed to do a lot of credit notes.

During the luncheon interval I again went to the British Museum. I tried to pretend I wasn't hungry, but finally bought some bars of milk chocolate. In the B.M. I had difficulty about a reader's ticket. Anyhow, I did get a squint at the mediaeval costume books.

In spite of my resolution against idleness, I spend a lot of time gassing away with Miss Robertson. She is forever brewing tea. She stands and pours it out into cups, while the teapot leaks and drips into the fireplace. She ogles Mr Skinner: 'Two spots more?' Mr Skinner cannot resist, replies embarrassedly, 'I don't mind if I do.' Miss Robertson is delighted. 'That's right,' and she throws the dregs of the first tea right on to the fire. Sp-r-r-r! There is a terrible spitting noise, almost a pop, followed by a burst of grey smoke.

INSPIRATION FROM HELEN MACGREGOR

I rang up Miss Helen MacGregor, the photographer, and arranged to meet her at six o'clock this evening. I was looking forward to seeing the studio and the good work she and Maurice Beck are doing.

Helen MacGregor is rather like an apple that has been kept for a long time in a loft. She might be one's fairy godmother—benevolent, with a benign twinkle in her eye.

As we talked 'sharp' (shop), I looked round the studio at a large screen which was papered with silver foil, the lacquer chest, and other oriental props I'd seen photographed by her in *Vogue*. Then Miss MacG. put on a spotlight and showed some examples of her work: the things she really liked. I gazed in amazement. Every picture struck me as being the work of an alive person, with a gifted imagination.

H. MacG. seems to have taken pictures all over the world. She favours Chinese things—owing, I suppose, to the fact that Maurice Beck lived twenty-five years in China.

I looked at the photographs; I listened to her talk. Her flow of bright ideas made me glow. We talked of photographers, pictures and paintings. I felt attuned to her attitudes. I confessed to being a lost soul, striving to fight my way against the difficult difficulties of youth.

It was already late, but we talked on and on. I wondered where this funny little frump, so plain yet so alive, would have her dinner.

I nearly missed mine. But what did it matter? I had greatly enjoyed being with a creative person. She'd inspired me with all sorts of notions for getting amusing textures by varnishing cheap brocades and canvas or taking photos of people reflected in piano tops. In fact, my head is buzzing with ideas which I must find time to realise.

April 16th

I mapped down little diagrams on the blocks at the office of photographs I'm going to take: heads of Nancy and Baba upside down or crown to crown like a *Janus bifrons*; double reflections; and other compositions, all very modern, inspired by the Mac-Gregor.

By persevering I have learnt lots of typing etiquette. One must not use the ' & ' mark for 'and'; one must place things on the paper in a certain way. Mindful of these things, I copied out a lot of statements.

Miss Robertson has been telling me more about herself. She

loves crossword puzzles. She would like a nice little car so that she could go off on her own and play golf. She was in a munitions factory during the war, and has worked ever since, though there is no essential need for her to do so. I suppose this routine must be a drug enabling her to go on and get through life. She has a flat of her own and is tremendously proud of it. Displayed in one room are masses of unexploded bombs from the last war. I laughed when informed of this, though neither she nor Mr Skinner thought it a bit funny that an old Scotch bird's room should be decorated with bombs.

In the lunch interval, I felt rather conscious of myself, with nothing to eat and being intellectual in the B.M. reading-room. But lunch is merely a matter of habit; one which, as soon as I drop it, will allow me to edify myself instead of wasting time *and* money in some bleak eating house. Of course, I could do as Miss Robertson does: she goes out and buys food, then eats it in the office.

Perhaps my eternal readiness for tea is because I can't eat lunch! But it's a welcome break for everyone. We sit around while Miss Robertson spreads a dirty paper tablecloth on a desk. We chat and gossip, we drink her tannic acid. I derive a certain amusement from watching Schmiegelow rag poor Mr Skinner. Today they both ragged *me*, talking in the most mercenary way of how, if they were able to paint, they could make 'cash'! Mr Skinner, I'm sure, is conscious of every farthing he spends. He's hard-working and businesslike, but without any imagination. He must be all of fifty and, I suppose, as poor as a church mouse.

MY SISTERS AS MODELS

April 18th (Sunday)

I was feverish in my bedroom doing designs—things I'd thought about in spite of the office humdrum. Bright sunshine flooded through the window. I could almost hear the buds popping open on the delicate trees.

Reggie, Nancy and Baba burst in on me, 'Spring is here!' Away we went in the open car, greedy for air and sun. We would pick large branches of fresh green. What could be nicer than foliage in a London house? Father didn't want to come along, which was just as well: he makes everything humdrum. He says,

'Very nice,' when you ask him if these primroses aren't splendid. But he doesn't even mean *that*.

Reggie drove. It would have been an anxiety for me to find the way. During the past week, after office hours, I've been going out with Reggie to drive in Regent's Park. But though I feel more confident at the wheel now, the sense of impotence is still there.

At last we reached a country lane and climbed into an orchard which was a fairy haze of blossom. We broke off huge swags of flowering apple, then gathered spidery, green shoots out of hedges.

We streaked back home, the car laden with springtime plunder, What a satisfactory feeling to think one has got something for nothing! I jammed the branches in an accumulator tank and lugged it into the green and gold drawing-room.

At lunch, N. and B. were most unwilling when I expressed my intention of photographing them this afternoon. I asserted rudely that I hadn't taken any pictures of them in three months, and they ought to be damned willing as I would very likely get the results into some papers. I got my way. Baba irritated me by keeping a perpetual eye on the clock. I had definite compositions with the love birds in mind. We got all gadgets, electric light, camera background, etc., ready in the conservatory. But Reggie had impertinently taken it upon himself to feed my birds directly after lunch, and as they were no longer hungry they wouldn't come on to Nancy's hand.

Hastily, I improvised other shots. I took one of Baba in front of the blossom. She looked romantically disdainful in her silver Italian dress. Nancy, by contrast, seemed plain as sago pudding this afternoon. Both girls were exasperated and very grudging. Undaunted, I worked with eager determination, experimenting with the startling highlights given off by the mackintosh background.

We were having a tea interval in the pink room when, to my great surprise, Boy arrived. He has remembered, at long last, to bring the shell flowers under the dome. I am glad he has let me buy them from him.

Boy couldn't stay long. Hurriedly, I showed him my new designs to see if he liked them, which he said he did.

Afterwards more photos. N. and B. were outraged, Baba so annoyed that she nearly wept. I coaxed and cajoled, yet wouldn't bribe them. I used to pay them 6d. per picture, but that is expensive and photography already costs me much too much as it is. I got a waxwork effect with Boy's glass dome placed over Baba's head. She knelt down with the back of the dome on her shoulders and the front resting on the edge of the table. At first her breath clouded the glass, but I told her not to breathe for a while. She nearly asphyxiated.

April 20th

With business slack and S. off to a wedding, there was hardly anything to do.

In the lunch interval I hared off to Selfridge's to get the negatives of Sunday's photographs. Would they be as good as I had hoped?

They were; they were very good, especially N. and B. having two heads each from reflections in the piano lid. The glass dome was also a success, and the mackintosh material may well become my favourite exotic background. The only drawback is that the negatives are so thick. They'll take an eternity to enlarge.

Being near home, I decided to have lunch for a change. Lunch

My sister Baba under the dome

My sisters Baba and Nancy reflected in the piano lid

was late; everyone seemed on edge. The house is under-staffed, and with Mama still ill in bed the servants complain about 'extra work'.

Aunt Jessie was there. She provoked me by saying in front of Loins[1] that Nurse is an old fidgeting fusser. All the servants repeat to one another anything nasty which they hear people saying about them. Not long ago, I had a row with Nurse because she showed Loins something she happened to find. The 'something' was a design of mine, and on the back I had written a list of Loins' faults in the hope that my mother would have an opportunity to tell him about them one day. I never intended anything so crude as for him to be shown the list. How he must have quivered! Anyhow, he seldom makes the same mistakes now. There were about twenty faults put down, things like: 'Do not omit to say Sir or Madam or Miss as the case may be; ask politely if people would care for a little more; claret to be decanterred; cheese and butter not to be plonked down on the table as in a boarding house, etc.'

Modom became very annoyed about my telling her to 'Shh,' and told my mother I was getting bad tempered of late. I suppose I am. It's living among such uncongenial people. I can't abide this haphazard way they live: they let things slide, they never 'do' or think.

After a rushed curry I bussed back to the Kingsway office, where I spent the afternoon knifing and scraping my negatives. It was a hot day and a sticky job. My eyes ached, but I had to re-touch for enlarging tonight.

Immediately on arrival home, I brought out all the gadgets and basins of acid. It was still too light to start before dinner, as I cannot make my room dark enough with the curtains drawn.

Enlarging is messy and nauseating. But the job had to be done. Gradually I worked up enthusiasm. The results were so good that I went on and on and on until about two o'clock in the morning. Then my mother came from her bedroom to tell me to shut up, I was waking the whole house with the running water.

I felt cockahoop with the results. Till now, my pictures have been ordinary attempts to make people look as beautiful as possible. But these are fantastic and amusing. They strike me as being an achievement—something personal.

[1] The butler.

April 22nd

Instead of lunch, I went into the National Gallery. Of course it was a 6d. day: it always is when I go there. But it was worth my money to watch the odd old hags that make what they think are copies of the pictures. I sat in front of El Greco for ten minutes. I like Bronzino's Venus, Psyche and Cupid more than ever. I hurried through the Gainsborough and Reynolds room.

Back at the office, I looked out of the window until the ostentatious building opposite got on my nerves. There is a lump of stone on its summit: a Victorian goddess with Victorian children. On top of the goddess' head is a lightning conductor!

April 23rd

I was given a clean one pound for my week's wages! And I'm happy to get that!

April 24th (Saturday)

Half-day at the office; I wished I needn't have come.

Schmiegelow keeps telling me I'll have a great deal to do when he drafts out a circular about some ebonite. But Miss Robertson and Mr Skinner insist the letter will never be drafted, as it has already been put off from day to day for nearly a year.

Back home I worked for five hours on some stage designs I had got an inspiration about, but my shoulder blades ached so much I felt I must go out: so I rang up Billie Williams[1] and asked him to come and dine at the Eiffel Tower. I like that place because the food, though expensive, is terrific. Also, the people who go there are smart, arty, and the set I must get in with. I knew that I was going to spend a lot of money, but it would be worth it and I would damned well enjoy it.

Billie came to the house first, as I wanted him to see my new work. I hungered for praise, and certainly couldn't hope for it from my father. He would probably have said, 'What's this? Which way up? Who is it?' Billie liked my Macgregoresque photographs. 'I can tell they're by you.'

Reggie drove us down to the Eiffel Tower. The whole of London swarmed with people up to see the football final. The

---

[1] Now known as the writer and critic Robert Herring.

hooligans were already half drunk, and one man spat at the car as we drove by.

The Tower was fairly empty. I felt slightly apprehensive, as the waiters are apt to be rude to people who are not *habitués*. We settled down at a good table, smoking Russian cigarette after Russian cigarette. I enjoyed the unflashy surroundings—dark Victorian ferns in polished brass containers, and a high-spirited canary in a cage hung from the ceiling by a wire spring.

The people were dull to begin with: very few celebrities, except for Augustus John, who sat very seriously wine-bibbing.

I jawed Billie about the importance of being given a chance to get on and do what one wanted to do. But one had to be strong-willed to overcome difficulties. What I didn't say was that I thought Billie most admirably placed now. He seems to have won his way into J. C. Squire's heart, and will soon be his right-hand man. Squire has already got Billie's book, *Discussions on Travel*, accepted by a publisher. I feel terribly envious.

We drank a lot of brandy. I became slightly tipsy, but the bill sobered me up.

April 25th (Sunday)

My father wanders in boredom about the house. I am perpetually hiding from him.

I sneaked off to Wyndham's[1] and found a small tea party made up of old people. Lady W. was vivacious. She wore a little coatee of gold cloth, so effectively theatrical it looked as if liquid metal had been poured over her arms and back. A Mr Somerville performed on the piano and addressed everybody in an involved way. Wyndham took me by the arm and whispered for me to remain till the others had gone.

We sat in front of the fire. She said, 'Now I'm going to talk to you like a mother.' Take it from her, this office work would do me no harm whatsoever. I'd get an inkling into business, which would be an enormous help. We spoke about my designs. I complained of Cochran treating me rather off-handedly. Wyndham said she'd like very much to help me and get me introduced to some theatre people.

I listened gratefully. I thought, 'If only I had *her* courage.'

[1] Lady Wyndham (Mary Moore, the actress), widow of Sir Charles Wyndham.

Poor W. has been stricken with a kind of elephantiasis disease, as a result of which her face and hands have become tragically swollen. Even her tongue is enlarged, making it difficult for her to articulate. This, for someone who was so exquisite on the stage, must be doubly hard. But she rises above her physical disabilities, enjoys seeing people and gives a tea dance every Sunday. Who could not love her? She has such a big heart.

Admirable is Wyndham's attempt to keep up with the times. To be modern, she explained, was her aim. New things came as a bit of a shock to begin with, but she soon got accustomed to like them. I commented on her gold coat. She said she would also have liked to wear black satin trousers caught in at the heels, but people would have said she was too old. W. showed great interest when I told her I had taken it upon myself to decorate our new house. She intends to have hers done out next year, as she realises how old-fashioned the place is. I said, 'Yes, old-fashioned. But I like it because it's personal.' This was not mere politeness: there is, of course, a lot of rubbish, but it's unique, interesting and funny. Historic souvenirs of Sir Charles's stage triumphs mingle with affectionately signed photographs of celebrities. Here and there, too, are some fine bits of glass and china. Yet, determined to be modern, Wyndham insisted upon seeing our coloured ceilings and bottomless beds. She is coming along on Friday.

April 26th

I took an enormous, cumbersome portfolio with all my drawings in it to the office. Billie had arranged to get me a look-in with Squire. I was nervous at the prospect and felt sick all morning. Miss Robertson helped to work me up, so that I was in a state of panic by noon when I left to go to the *Mercury*.

After a little difficulty I found the place. I was shown up to the holy of holies where Squire sat trying hard to be natural and hearty. He looked like an old bird's nest, but had the eyes of a mole. He enthused over my pictures, kept using the same adjectives. Billie helped the situation with his free and easy manner, blurting out useful suggestions. I had nothing suitable for reproduction in the *London Mercury*, but Squire said he'd try to get me a start with book jackets or illustrations. Altogether, he was charming, though nothing definite was fixed upon.

After the interview, Billie took me to a chop house in the Strand for lunch.

April 27th

I am getting much better on the typewriter, and don't have to strain so much to avoid mistakes. Schmiegelow was beginning to get annoyed with me for wasting his office paper. It seemed to me that he made a ridiculous fuss about the placing of things correctly in a business letter, but now that I have learnt to do as I am told, it is all rather dull. Before, I had great fun placing things artistically. I created beautiful effects by underlining words with spots, by making long and short dashes and using pretty asterisks, ***
'& & &' signs, ÆÆ and ooOoo, etc.

But this evening, as luck would have it, I had to copy out a long letter on the typewriter just as I was about to leave, and because I wanted to do it quickly, I made mistake after mistake. The first time the letter was read through and checked, I'd left out two lines. The thing had to be done perfectly for some bloody judge. I got desperate. I went on and on, throwing sheet after sheet into the waste-paper basket until after seven o'clock.

No wonder I was exasperated with Loins for giving me no wine at dinner.

AT THE EIFFEL TOWER

April 28th

The Chenil Gallery was crowded for the Sitwell recital: not a seat to be had. Allanah[1] and I stood, along with masses of other thrilled and expectant people. Half the audience seemed nicely arty and the other half merely revoltingly arty.

The poems started. Accompanied by modern music, they were spoken through a megaphone that had been shoved through a hole in a painted representation of a face.

I liked Walton's music. I liked the poems, too, but felt restless and couldn't properly settle down to understanding them. Also, the effect got spoilt by distractions—arty people moving about, arty people in the outer room talking too loud. In the end, the

---

[1] Allanah Harper, a wealthy young lady with newly acquired artistic tastes.

programme seemed much too long and monotonous. But the reception couldn't have been more friendly and enthusiastic. The Sitwells gave repeated encores.

Afterwards we all went on to the Eiffel Tower, or at least the mob of rather arty people that Allanah moves about with did. Everyone behaved hilariously in the car. Allanah drove so casually that we nearly had two bad accidents. Zita,[1] Baby[2] and a Rosemary Somebody left us before we ever reached the Tower, but the party was still quite large.

The Tower crowd had decided to be social tonight. They shouted, calling to acquaintances by their Christian names. At our table sat: Allanah, Inez Holden, vivacious and alert, though she annoys me; Curtis Moffat, who affects to be pompously middle-aged, Dick Wyndham, whom I like now. Dick is crude and unfinicky. At first this seems bad manners or conceit; but he's good-hearted, generous and rich. He ordered some magnums of champagne.

There was a lot of trafficking between tables. A little old man sat with us, name unknown but intelligent and without a wrinkle on his fat, baby face. Michael Sevier got plastered, looking a sight with his dead-white face and sparkling eyes. He kept saying indecent things. Allanah had two alternate responses: she showed shock, or else she giggled weakly. It surprised me to see Lord and Lady Milford-Haven at the *Tower* but I hear they often come for a good guzzle and drink of wine.

Tallulah[3] arrived late, went to every table and was quick-witted at each. She has developed her personality to such an extent that she always seems natural, but it is only acting.

Augustus John became somewhat playful, making sporadic grabs at some silly little idiots dressed up as Sapphists. There was a whole group of these young women, all with their hair cut off, tailored suits, collars and cuffs, watch chains and gardenia buttonholes. They tried to talk and move like ventriloquist's dolls.

We stayed on until very late. Stulik, the fat old proprietor, waddled about sleepily begging people to go. The little canary dozed in a corner of its cage.

---

[1] Miss Zita Jungman.
[2] Miss Theresa Jungman.
[3] Miss Tallulah Bankhead.

May 3rd

Lugged my portfolio to the office again, as J. C. Squire kindly gave my name to Longman's for an interview this afternoon. I hate going about with the portfolio: I feel everybody is sniggering at the poor struggling artist.

The people at Longman's were warm and jolly. I don't think Mr Robert Longman understands anything about painting, but he'd heard from Squire that I was good. Squire had evidently been funny to him about me, said I'd been in an office for six weeks and didn't yet know what was sold! At any rate, it was decided that I should do the dust jacket for Billie Williams's book *The President's Hat* and get four guineas. I didn't think four guineas much. Robert Longman said they paid from three to five guineas for these things. If I were well known, I'd have been paid five; but I suppose if Squire hadn't said, 'Here's a young man that is going to be good one day,' they'd have paid only three guineas. All in all, I was pleased.

My next move would be to take the portfolio to Nigel Playfair, who is doing such interesting things at the Lyric Theatre.

When I got home hungry and depleted, everyone was talking about the strike. Tomorrow there would be no trains, no buses, no newspapers. I didn't relish walking to Hammersmith, so I asked Reggie late in the evening if he'd like to motor me there now, before the strike. He wouldn't and I understood and didn't get annoyed. But Papa flew into a towering rage, shouting at me, 'You want everyone to wait on you hand and foot! You never think of the expense for petrol and the run of the car. Why didn't you think of it earlier?' Etc.

I flared back at him, beside myself with bitterness. 'The car has been running up to the Hampstead Cricket Club twice or three times a day lately. Reggie takes it whenever he likes, and never has the cost of petrol been taken into consideration. Is it any further to Hammersmith than Hampstead?' Daddy became livid at being answered back. Effectively, too, I told him that if I'd suggested going to that morbid middle-class club in Hampstead there would have been no outburst. 'Get out,' Daddy shouted.

I got out. I sat in my bedroom feeling venomous, loathing my father. Here I was, at the damned office all day long. Unless I got some definite work in my line I'd never be free.

I reached a pitch of hatred and frustration when Mama came up and said, 'Why did you want to take your designs to Hammersmith?' I broke down completely, blubbing as I hadn't done for years.

Mummie sat looking worn and unhappy. She tried to make me feel a little forgiving, to respect my father or, at any rate, to try and put up with him. I, meanwhile, overtired from working late on my drawings and skipping lunch, continued to weep hot, fat tears. I could hardly breathe.

After Mum left, I blew my nose. I lay on a wet pillow and didn't go to sleep for a long time.

May 4th

My mother did her best to create an amicable atmosphere at breakfast, but I never spoke a word to Daddy. The General Strike meant no underground or buses; unless one had a car, one must walk to the City. I felt like an independent parlour-maid, and wouldn't have stepped inside my father's car if I'd been asked. I wasn't asked.

I set off to walk to work, enjoying my dejection while everyone else seemed to be enjoying the strike. People felt important for being a part of the general crisis. Apart from the many pedestrians, a stream of unfamiliar traffic moved slowly through the streets. Lorries were piled high with giggling typists; old carts were chock-a-block full of women dangling legs and loving it all. 'Such a lark,' they seemed to be saying, 'so new, so amusing, so bohemian.'

I walked in a straight line from Bayswater Road along Oxford Street to Holborn. I was the earliest bird. Soon the others dribbled in, all with stories to tell. That little wretch of a Miss Wildman, who still ought to be at school, had hiked it from Clapham. She was one of the heroines of the day. But then we found the greatest heroine in the tea shop below: she had walked for four and a half hours!

Mr Skinner prodded me to get off a letter to publishers, asking if I might pay them a visit to show my designs for dust covers. I drafted out a letter—original, unbusinesslike and impertinent. Mr Skinner's alternative struck me as cringing and drab. I think that must be why people like him don't get on. At length we decided on a compromise, which I typed out many times and sent off.

May 6th

I walked back from the office this evening and was pleased to find an array of letters from publishers willing to see me. Also Miss Todd of *Vogue* had written to say she is favourably impressed by my photographs and will let me know how many they will be publishing!

This was a beginning. I pictured myself inundated with orders for dust jackets, photographs, stage designs and paintings. Then I remembered that I am always being disappointed.

I went up the ladder—the one in the dining room. I am still gilding the moulding round the ceiling. What a messy job: my arm ached above my head, the treacly paint trickled down the brush on to my hand, my fingers stuck together and the smell gave me a headache.

May 8th (Saturday)

The mater was still in bed, but she had her heart set (at least *I* had) on being well enough to get up and present a scroll to the Queen at the Gentlewomen's Club Meeting. Mum did go, looking very nice indeed, pale and smart. As her name began with a letter early on in the alphabet, she found herself first to make the presentation to the Queen, who looked 'extremely handsome'. Her Majesty had a pristine pink and white complexion and rigidly waved white hair. She wore an ankle-length skirt and shoes with toes 'turned towards heaven' as N. and B. would say. She dragged her inevitable umbrella into the drawing room.

I went on with the gilding (I've only been at it three months). Loins came in to gossip. He told me about the days when he was butler to the Newtons in Regent's Park. The Newtons had been neighbours of Gladys Cooper, who sued them for letting the bath water run into her house. She got sixty pounds damages, but six weeks later Gladys Cooper's bath water ran into the Newtons' house, and they got their money back!

Gilding took the entire day. I felt once removed from myself by night time. The strike got on everyone's nerves. Loins became terrified when, from the height of the ladder, I threw a cigarette end into the fireplace. There were sparks. He jumped and gave a terrific, 'Oo-er!' Later he said he thought a striker had thrown a bomb through the curtained window.

During the night a lorry broke down outside the house. The driver tried to start the engine again, which banged and misfired. All the servants hurried in fright to hide in one another's rooms. They thought a revolution had started! They'd heard wild stories about how the strikers were so desperate to win, doing this, that and the other to buses, old women and volunteers. All of which was, of course, poppycock.

May 25th

When I went to see Squire, I was nervous and awkward, dropping my umbrella and hat, convinced that everyone was secretly laughing at me. But nowadays I feel superior and definite. I march smartly in to see people without blushing or being clumsy.

Today being exceptionally slack at the office, I was able to visit quite a number of publishers. This morning to Fisher Unwin, where I got treated like the meanest commercial traveller.

I then went to Heinemann, and after keeping me waiting for twenty minutes the man who looked at my designs dismissed them as 'rather rough'!

I went home and got down to enlarging photographs. Paul Cohen-Portheim has been writing me frantic letters from Germany because I haven't yet sent the pictures for his arty magazines.

Baba helped me for some time, but the prints were so bad that I went on alone until the early hours of the morning.

May 27th

I don't seem to have got anywhere since leaving Cambridge. The truth is, I don't know what I want to do or be, and one can't be successful until one knows what one wants to do. If I felt convinced about acting I could go 'all out' for the theatre, possibly even have a success. But then it occurs to me that Lady Curzon would think it rather low of me to go on the stage; she would immediately drop me. In reality, however, I don't even *know* Lady Curzon! So my snobbery is wasted and useless. As a matter of fact, I am surrounded by the awful sort of people who go to charity balls. For them, it doesn't matter a hoot whether I go on the stage or not.

Here I am, terribly swanky and snobby but utterly penniless, unable to afford all the things I would like to do. I loathe my existence at the office; the drabness of the underground and Holborn saps my vitality. I'm in an awful groove and don't know how to get out of it. I know it is silly and wrong, but I believe I enjoy wallowing in my dejection.

June 1st

My God—June the first! And I'm still looking at the goddess with the lightning conductor on her head. That really does cut home!

None of my visits to publishers have come to anything, so I've cheapened myself for nothing. At Cambridge I used to have such a high opinion of myself. But now I see what a snob I am, even in my most sincere moments I harbour absurd and petty notions about fame. It all leads to nothing, only everlasting disappointment. Perhaps I am after wrong and impossible things— that is very likely true. Yet I want these things, I should like these unreal things to happen.

I haven't seen Boy or any stimulating people. How can I, when it costs money and I am in debt? I try occasionally to earn a guinea or two from photographs in papers, but the fee barely pays for materials.

June the first—what a catastrophe! I ought to be enjoying my summer, instead of sitting in Holborn collecting moss. I'm twenty-two years old. That's almost twenty-three. After twenty-five, I'll be old.

I have almost lost confidence in my endurance. Yet I know that I'm talented in many ways. And I've got a tremendous personality. Something *must* happen!

June 8th

To Selfridge's for the negatives of Mama resplendent in court dress. They were thin and not very sharp. It exasperates me when my photographs turn out badly—such a waste of time and money. I spend hours arranging things, dressing up sitters, dragging out all the lights. To have disastrous results is heart-breaking.

The negatives retouched and the evening was spent enlarging them with Baba's help. But we couldn't get the right exposure. Every attempt turned out so pale that a fortune in expensive paper was ruined.

June 11th

Schmiegelow sent me on an errand to Peter Lind, Ltd. I was to find out about some lost cement bags. I hadn't even the money for a bus fare, so hoofed all the way.

When I arrived at an enormous building, I produced my little card: 'John P. Carr and Co, represented by C. Beaton.' This is the sort of identification travellers bring out with a flourish, but at the critical moment I fumbled and dropped it. The gentleman who received me, a Mr Hill, fixed me through his pince-nez while I grovelled under his desk.

'*You* are John P. Carr?'

'No, I'm C. Beaton.'

'I see. What is the nature of your business?'

'Cement bags.'

'You make them?'

'No, I believe we're looking for some.'

'*Here?*'

'Well—uh—I—uh—don't really know. I'm so incompetent.'

'If that's the case, I don't know what you're doing here.'

The cement bags were not found.

June 12th

I am always in a panic for fear that Schmiegelow, by some mischance, will arrive at the office before me. But though I arrive late, sometimes very late, he arrives still later. What is the point of arriving early, anyway? There is hardly anything to do. Schmiegelow asks, 'Would you go and pick up some theatre tickets for me? Take this note to the Danish legation.' Etc.

When I got home this evening, I found another, 'the editor regrets...' So now my article on the Charleston has been returned by *all* the papers. At any rate, if I couldn't sell the Charleston I would learn how to do it. Cousin Tecia was returning to Birmingham, and N. and B. and I made her try to teach us before she left. We hung on to backs of chairs, jumping about like cats on hot bricks. Tecia made it look easy; she is brilliantly expert with her firm steps and unwobbly ankles. Yet jig, kick and laugh as we might, we couldn't seem to get the knack.

CAMBRIDGE REVISITED

June 13th and 14th
I went to Cambridge for a night, just to visit old friends. Topsy Lucas was delighted to see me on Sunday afternoon. I told her I'd come up for Richard Sykes'[1] party. She said, 'I am amazed to hear that you even know the hunting set.' She said they sounded nice, but added, 'Will you be a success with them?'

Lytton Strachey was staying with Topsy. He soon appeared in the doorway, cutting a marvellous figure, tall and anaemic. His beautiful hands are pale yellow, long and thin but useful. His voice is ridiculous—high-pitched, nervous, affected. He speaks quietly, each syllable most distinctly pronounced and rather dragged.

Topsy boasted of my affiliation with the hunting people. Lytton showed interest. His eyes twinkled as he commented that he would like to be liked by the cultured, hearty hunting men more than by anyone else.

Topsy uttered a horsey scream, 'Oh, nohohh!'

Lytton, in his genteel dairy-maid voice, 'Yes, yes I would. We've all been wanting to get in with that set for years.'

Dinner was over. The candles guttered in Richard's room. Jack Gold and I, Richard and Ambrose Congreve lay about in a haze of port and brandy. Soon Jack became quite tipsy and started to reminisce (he enjoys doing that). He sang Lee White songs out of 1914 revues: 'I shall see you tonight, dear, in my bee-eautiful dreamland'; 'Goodbye, Madam Fashion,' etc. Then we both sang Ethel Levey songs and remembered how unique she had been.

We were talking about Gaby Deslys and the King of Portugal when Richard Sykes observed, 'You're too young to know about such things.' I replied proudly, 'I have always considered myself

---

[1] Sir Richard Sykes.

of the Gaby Deslys period.' Jack roared, 'You go back farther than I do.' We soon realised that to the young, Richard and Ambrose, we were being 'old bores!' We had never before considered ourselves anything but young and modern; it seemed funny to pretend that one's 'period' had passed.

Jack and Richard said, 'We're going on a motor tour to visit the châteaux of the Loire at the end of July. Won't you come with us?' I said, 'I'd love to go. Ask me again when you're sober.'

Ambrose Congreve sat quiet as a tomb. Richard started to play the piano. We did a Charleston to the newest ragtimes. Jack leaped into the air like some cat doing a death dance. We then sang more revue songs, imitating the whole company doing the finale.

Ambrose was still bored when Charles Cavendish, Robert Adeane and John Ramsden barged in from a dinner party at Newmarket. Kicks and yells ensued. Robert pounced on Charlie and tore open his boiled shirt. In the mêlée of legs and arms, someone knocked the sofa over. Someone else got hurt: 'Oh, you are a bloody fool.'

I laughed. Jack, rather sober now, sat eating an apple.

At last the evening broke up. There was some difficulty as to where I should be sleeping. I suggested the sofa, but John Ramsden had first claim on that. Robert, Jack and I then staggered off to the Blue Room Hotel and knocked up the night porter. No room was available. That meant I'd have to go to Simon Whitbread's dirty sheets (he'd gone away for a day or so).

It was now three o'clock. I didn't relish climbing the ten-foot railings of Trinity in pitch blackness. Besides, I had my heavy leather bag—the new one Reggie gave me for my birthday. Robert Adeane helped with the luggage. Jack clambered over the nails and spikes without much difficulty. But when it came my turn, my trousers caught. I hung on for grim death, miles up in the air. At last I got free. Robert hoisted me the portmanteau; I lowered it to Jack, who let it down with a bang. I jumped into black space and we scuttled away, thinking the night porters would surely have heard.

It was blind man's buff groping in the darkness of Trinity. I went first, but forgot a descent of six steps and came a cropper. Jack immediately hared off like a rabbit. Porters scurried about, flashing torches through the darkness. Dazed and stupid, I staggered in the vague direction of Jack's room. The stair^s creaked. What a nightmare to be caught doing this sort of thing: in the ordinary course of events, one could be sent down.

With a terrific sigh of relief, I found myself in Jack's room, but he hadn't arrived yet. I then went to Simon's room and found Simon in bed! He had returned a day earlier, so I would sleep on Jack's sofa after all.

I returned to Jack's room, wondering where he was (he still had my bag). I undressed, then waited. Had he been caught by a porter? Perhaps he'd crashed into a pillar and was lying hurt somewhere. I thought I'd better search for him. I felt my way along Neville's Court, half naked. At length Jack was heard creeping along. All was well, he had simply gone back for the leather bag. No damage, thank goodness, and the porters hadn't spotted him. 'If they had, I'd have bribed them,' he said grandly.

Jack decided to be gallant and unusually selfless, insisting on my having his bed while he took the sofa. Exhausted, I immediately fell unconscious, though my dreams were troubled at the thought of having to get up so early tomorrow and return to the hell of Holborn.

June, undated

I'd been wondering lately if I couldn't get a job talking on the radio. I wrote to the BBC offering my services, and received a summons to be tried.

In fear and trembling, all bunged up with a bad cold, I found my way to the broadcasting place. This really was an adventure! I hadn't told anyone except N. and B.

I was interviewed by a tall, rough man named Sieveking. He said, 'Read!' Suffering from acute embarrassment, I started to drawl a bit of a short story I'd written. But I had hardly got going before he shouted, 'Stop!' I couldn't think what disaster had occurred. 'No, I'm afraid it's no use. Your voice just isn't any good!'

'Couldn't you hear me?'

Yes, Sieveking said he could hear me very well, but mine was a voice that didn't 'take'.

I asked, 'Does a cold make any difference?' 'It would.' 'Well, I have a bad cold.'

99

At last Sieveking confessed, 'It's no good pretending. With most people I beat about the bush and make false excuses. But if you won't be grossly insulted, I'll tell you just what's wrong.' 'Yes, I'd be interested.' 'Well, when you're broadcasting you're talking to the masses—the lower middle-class masses. These people don't like being talked down to or patronised.'

What he was trying to say was that I had an over-cultured, up-stage sort of voice! This was a bitter shock to me. I'd always thought I spoke in a less affected way than my friends. No, Sieveking stood firm, I didn't speak English as it should be spoken. I talked with an Oxford accent.

'Surely not! I went to Cambridge.'

Sieveking then gave me an imitation of my voice. It sounded so exaggeratedly high-class as to make me almost sick! Why, I talked just like the silly ass in musical comedy—the nut with spats, large buttonhole and eyeglass! I felt annoyed, but flattered that the man had told me the truth. I said I could easily get rid of my faults if I practised, and would come again when my cold was better. I'd try to talk to the masses in a straightforward way.

I came home and ate worms. Hell and damn!

June 18th

Spent the morning at the office retouching the prints of Billie Williams. Mr Skinner and Miss Robertson became excited. 'Why, you *shouldn't* be here wasting time! You should be making "big cash"! Oh, it's a sin for your father to send you here!'

We then debated how much I should charge for the photographs. I thought they had roughly cost me about seven shillings and that I couldn't charge Billie more than three pounds. But when I worked out a more exact estimate in terms of light, time, materials, etc., I found the work cost me nearly twenty-five shillings. I was amazed. As a matter of fact, I think I could make 'cash', if only I had the money to start in a fairly respectable way. But with one pound a week, I can only joke about my wages.

Peggy[1] rang me at the office, suggesting lunch at the Eiffel Tower. I had to say, 'Bring lots of money, as I haven't any at all.'

[1] Peggy Broadbent, a cousin of Jack Gold, now Lady Hudson.

My brother Reggie photographed by me in the attempted
manner of Bertram Park

An experimental picture of my sister Baba

Mrs Mosscockle in the kennels at Clewer Park, Windsor

Venice: C.B., Mrs Alison Settle and Mrs Violet Whish
half hidden by her daughter

Magda Joicey joined us. We drank too many cocktails, I laughed about my plight. A dish of kidneys arrived, all mucked up in a rich sauce. I do like the Tower: it is such a gourmand's paradise.

Afterwards, I bought Peggy and Magda some caramel rock from that cheap Canadian candy shop.

MRS SALISBURY'S PREDICTIONS

July, undated

Directly after Miss Robertson had thrown the tea dregs into the fire, I said, 'I wonder if you could not spare my valuable services for the rest of the day?'

They did. I had made an appointment with Mrs Salisbury, the clairvoyant. I found her in her house off the Fulham Road.

To my surprise, Mrs S. was neither weird nor eccentric looking. She eschews pretence, wears no headband of scarlet silk, and does not hang her room with pseudo-Egyptian drapery or rubbish from the Chinese Emporium in Oxford Street. As a matter of fact, both she and her environment seemed much more impressive for being completely natural. Yet she communicated a subtle personality behind the frail, nervy exterior.

I began to snicker when, straight off, she started by looking at my hand. But soon the laugh subsided in amazement. This woman knew nothing about me; she must indeed be clairvoyant. 'You are very sensitive. You have a great deal of confidence in yourself but lack the American push. You're artistic, fastidious, delicate. And I think you possess much more resistance than people imagine.'

I said this was all true.

'Ah,' Mrs Salisbury went on, 'You've a great eye for colour and diplomacy.'

Diplomacy? I didn't understand that at all!

Undaunted, Mrs Salisbury took up the crystal and cards. 'There is dramatic instinct here. I see you going abroad on two separate journeys in the immediate future. At the moment, of course, you're restless and undecided. But someone will make a suggestion to you. You'll take it up enthusiastically, you'll work hard until you are a success. I see you decorating a house, and you'll definitely do designs for the stage—mostly in America.

Yes, you'll be in the public eye, so to speak. You'll realise your ambitions.'

I listened willingly. It bucked me up to such an extent, hearing these incredible things.

Mrs Salisbury assessed me: 'You're the mercurial type, and will always look younger than your age.'

I nodded. In spite of recent haggardness, I don't nearly look twenty-two.

'You'll have a lot to do with royalty.'

This sounded so grand as to be utterly unbelievable. It sobered me up. Indeed, I began to wonder whether anything she said could possibly be true? Where would I get the money to go abroad? I'm poor, my father is poor, and no one is going to leave me a halfpenny.

Still, I felt soothed to hear Mrs S. talk solely about me all this time, promising an interesting and happy life instead of the drab, unsatisfied existence I'd been leading. It seemed an edifying way to have spent a guinea.

ETRETAT

Beginning of August

I am writing this (strange as it may seem) in the Casino at Etretat. What a miracle, to have got out of my groove for even a week!

As I sit on the terrace, surrounded by the gabble of hard-faced, smart Frenchwomen, Holborn seems far away. I can hardly remember the cooing of Miss Robertson's Scottish accent. It has been replaced by nasal grunts and trilling r's, though I must admit I don't understand a word these people say. As for talking back, I can only manage: 'C'est formidable.' and 'C'est épouvant-able!' Mostly I keep my mouth shut, scrutinising the various women. They screw up their noses when they laugh; they bare their teeth viciously and roll their tongues.

It all happened quite suddenly. I came here to stay with Peggy and her mother, Mrs Dillon,[1] who has rented a villa called *La*

---

[1] Mrs Arthur Dillon (now Hilda, Viscountess Dillon), with whom I stayed in her sulphur-coloured stone house near Banbury. In spite of not being an enlightened race-goer, accomplished horseman or expert bridge-player, I enjoyed my forays into the Hunt Ball world. Moreover, Peggy, her daughter, was an enthusiast of Mr Cyril W. Beau-mont's ballet bookshop in the Charing Cross Road, and an ardent admirer of the novels of Rose Macaulay and E. M. Forster.

Bicoque for the holidays. I felt rather a dog leaving for the 'abroad' on my own. Peggy met me at the station café, helped me through Customs (*Monsieur n'a rien a déclarer*) and whizzed us through the countryside in her powerful open car. The labourers all shouted as we went past. But then, everyone shouts in France. On the way we noticed a great number of fights: people swearing at one another with demented fury. The next minute they seem to forget everything.

I reacted like a child. It surprised me to find that the hedges and grass were just the same in France as in England. Even the common fly looked no different. I did notice, however, that there were none of the enormous trees one is accustomed to at home. No large spreading oaks or chestnuts, but a lot of tall, spidery specimens.

Etretat has thus far been great fun. Everyone seems to have a lover and a high-powered sports car. People lie about taking sun baths in their bathing costumes. I'd always longed to do this, but it is seldom warm enough in England. Now that I had the chance I felt worried at first by the disgusting array of spots round my back and on my arms. Generally I'm spotless. It is disturbing to see spots: they seem to me a complete 'giveaway' of a person's secret immorality.

Our leisure has been busy. We swim; we go to the Casino for cocktails, dancing and gambling. There's been a lot of tennis; rather alarming, as the standard of the French is high. But I compete and haven't made a fool of myself yet.

Réné Lacoste, the champion, is here. When I first saw him he struck me as repulsive. Now I think him comical, with his long nose, fat lips and black eyes. I'd like to make a picture of him looking miserable, with his chin down.

Today I felt stagnant and not a bit confident. I had a mood on such as I've not suffered for ages. I felt numb and was dumb. Peggy's mother remarked, 'You've become little Pierre Sergine!'

Peggy laughed, 'Cecil's always analysing his feelings.'

Jack Gold (who joined us yesterday) retorted, 'If you were like him, wouldn't you?'

I couldn't rally to this backchat, though ordinarily Peggy stimulates me to make funny remarks. The truth, I suppose, is that I was still suffering from last evening's upset at the Casino. . . .

Every night we've been doing the Charleston. Peggy's a wild partner—always game for anything. With her dimples and my long legs, I thought we made a winning pair. But gradually I realised that a good many young men took objection to me. I always seem to stir up a certain enmity: in this case, they blamed me for kicking out too much! I caught a rude remark from one of the outsiders, which worried me enough to put me off the Casino for good.

Generally, those who take exception don't know me, which makes it all the more exasperating. Perhaps I give the impression of being effeminate and affected. Whatever the reason, that rude remark made me completely miserable. It's an awful shock to one's self-esteem to be the recipient of a cruel jibe, just as one is getting on well at a party. What if one's dance partner heard it? Very likely she didn't. After all, I'm unusually quick at over-hearing what people say. But still . . .

Etretat

Friday, the 13th (naturally!)

The return home was an awful let-down! It was living death to be by oneself in a shut-up house. Everything looked ugly, including Nurse who was acting as caretaker. Nurse said, 'Oh, I didn't expect you back so soon.' She didn't seem best pleased.

I wished that I had stayed on at Etretat. I could have ditched old Mrs Mosscockle and her ridiculous invitation for this weekend.

There were a lot of letters, all disappointing. 'The Editor regrets,' also unwelcome bills and an annoying note from Boy. I had written beseeching him, if *worse came to worst* and I couldn't get it from any other source, to lend me the money to go to Venice. Boy's casual pencilled note made me furious. 'Sorry, can't lend you the money as I haven't got it.'

I sat down and wrote back a whopping lie, saying that I was now on very good terms with my father and everything would be all right. Then I spent the rest of the morning sorting out suitable photographs for magazines, as I am desperate to get some published. It took an unconscionable time, and there were lots of other things that wanted doing. I put out drawings too, deciding that I would brazenly go down to certain offices and hand in the portfolio myself.

I set out after lunch, traipsing all the way to the *Sketch*. I waited in a lobby where several spotty young boys cracked dirty jokes to a slut of a girl. The portfolio was taken from me, then returned five minutes later. 'They thank you very much, but they are awfully sorry they are full up.'

Off I went. No more luck at a couple of other places left me defeated. I ought to have gone to see old Miss Robertson and Schmiegelow, but I hadn't the energy. Instead, I returned home and did up parcels of photographs and drawings which I would send off to the *Tatler* and other papers.

MRS MOSSCOCKLE'S HOUSE PARTY

August 14th

My father was surprised to see me this morning. He didn't even know I was home, as I'd gone to bed early last night and he'd come in late. 'No idea you'd be back so soon. Had a good time? Let me think, it was Etretat you went to, wasn't it?' And that was all he asked.

After breakfast, Daddy said, 'I'm off to Sandwich for the weekend.'

I said, 'Oh, I'd like to join the family there for a few days, after Mrs Mosscockle's.'

'Right.' But all the time I knew my father was wondering

when, and if, I intended to return to Schmiegelow's office.

I wondered what it would be like at Mrs Mosscockle's. I hardly know the woman, have only seen her casually at parties. She is always laughed at; I laugh at her improbable married name and her whimsical maiden one—she was born Rita Sparrow. She married a man old enough to be her father, lived modestly with him in some meagre square in Kensington. When old Mosscockle died, his will revealed that he'd been a millionaire. The great wealth was left entirely to Rita *née* Sparrow, who promptly took a suite at the Berkeley while deciding where to live and how to spend the money. She plumped for Hertford Street, Clewer Park, Windsor and dogs.

Today, Rita Mosscockle must be pushing eighty. She looks like a macabre travesty of Queen Alexandra. In fact, some Eton boys actually think Rita is a reincarnation of the Rose Queen and, to her great delight, they take off their hats when she drives through Windsor in her carriage.

As I took the train to Windsor and taxied to Clewer Park, I wondered why I had accepted a weekend invitation which might result in deadly boredom. It was my penchant for the grotesque that made Mrs M. fascinating to me. But to stay in her house seemed rather a risk!

From the gates, the long, impressive drive led to what I had more or less guessed—an enormous early Victorian house of startling red brick.

An antique butler answered the bell. Huge and fat as a bulging baby in his grimy clothes, he might have been Mr Pickwick. I was shown into the presence chamber, where my hostess sat bolt upright in a vast drawing-room, all white and gold, with crimson brocade hangings and a thousand knick-knacks.

Mrs Mosscockle's cheeks were daubed with pillar-box gashes. Perched atop her marmalade wig was a funny little white hat, like a *timbale* selectly trimmed with lace, tiny rosebuds and for-get-me-nots. Crowning this confection, a moth-eaten aigrette quivered. Her dress was cream shantung, sentimentally sprinkled with pearls, diamonds and turquoises. Champagne-coloured tulle had been wrapped round a drain-pipe neck. Sad dog's eyes peered out resignedly from circles of sooty *maquillage*. Poor little hag, what an effigy!

We sat round having delicate afternoon tea in delicate cups and saucers. I stuffed myself with plain Victorian cakes and scones, while Mrs Mosscockle gibbered away like a mechanical marmoset. Her face, during this stream of formal conversational remarks, remained immobile so as not to crack or wrinkle. She never moved her upper lip.

A Mr Pelion-Smith had arrived five minutes before me. As he was about forty-five years old, Mrs Mosscockle directed her chatter more towards him. The man somehow reminded me of a nasty bit of raw meat.

Mrs Mosscockle

Mrs Mosscockle said, 'I'm sorry the car couldn't meet you at the station. But Princess Marie Louise, who is staying here, wanted to pay some calls and she had to have it.'

A rather ordinary but cultured young secretary came in; Miss Wilberforce looked pale and aquiline; she spoke in a metallic voice that indicated she was well-bred but poor. Mrs M. prompted her to show us the garden. We trailed outdoors to admire the well-kept lawns, specimen trees and monkey puzzles. The herbaceous borders were a blaze of antirrhinums, gladioli and geraniums.

Miss Wilberforce effectively hid whatever she thought or felt behind an expression as completely dead as her voice. But I liked her none the less, and felt that I should be able to get at her.

I studied Mr Pelion-Smith more carefully. He wore a blue suit, genteel and badly cut. His new black shoes had dull leather, rounded toes and carefully tied laces. His head had been shaved almost like a convict's. He smoked gaspers one after another, putting his hands in his pockets and talking with the cigarette wobbling away on the edge of his lips. He talked in a breathless, sing-song way. 'Yes' was 'yais' with a sort of bend in the middle, as though he were a nursemaid talking encouragingly to a child.

Soon Miss Wilberforce spilled the beans: the Princess staying here was not our good royal Marie Louise, but a Bourbon Princess Marie Louise, Duchess of Seville. The Duchess appeared, a sallow little dumpling in black stockinette with jet beads around her neck. She spoke with a clipped accent.

Another visitor arrived, a worldly, white-haired man named Mr Algernon Bowing-Levey.

Mrs Mosscockle discussed pedigree with me. Mr Bowing-Levey, now, was of a very good family; Mr Pelion-Smith, too, came of the Smith-Clarendon clan. And, of course, Miss Wilberforce had good antecedents: Mrs Mosscockle herself was connected with that family. No doubt I could trace a respectable lineage, too.

On a more complete tour of inspection, we now visited the glass houses, saw the pheasant in a cage, then went to the kennels. Here were an astonishing number of Japanese dogs—some silky white, others black, all long-haired, panting, goggle-eyed and looking very decorative. Eight yappers occupied one room, while six more barked away in another. The kennel maid looked like a fat old pet herself. In still another small room we came upon ten additional black and white dogs!

Mrs Mosscockle adores her darlings, and intimately knows all twenty-four of them. Coming of good families, they have taken many kennel prizes!

We left the kennels and walked across the lawns. Eleven white blobs of silk rushed panting and waggling round our diminutive hag hostess. Pansy-faced and bizarre in her antiquated clothes, she staggered gingerly on delicate feet.

Our destination was the dogs' cemetery in a corner of the garden. With tears in her eyes, Mrs Mosscockle said, 'This is a sad spot for me. I come here to throw flowers on their graves.'

We gazed down at a score of miniature mounds with Lilliputian headstones. The inscriptions on the tombstones (I came later with a pencil and copied them down) commemorated gone-but-not-forgotten household friends. 'In fondest memory of Champion General Kuroki of Mayfair. The beloved and faithful little friend of Mrs Mosscockle. Died November 6th 1913'. 'In loving memory of dear Fushimi and dear Yum-Yum, passed away 1916. Much beloved by Mrs Mosscockle.' 'Darling little Tartar, fondly loved by Mrs

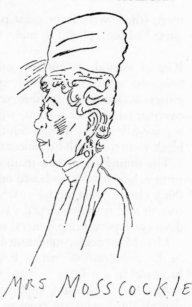

MRS MOSSCOCKLE

Mosscockle, June 21st 1909. Also in memory of dear old Ruby, my friend for over twelve years. Died December 1st 1911.' Other Mikado names included Mimosa, Mizu, Yoko, Shu-Shu and, oddly enough, Dot.

Pictures of the dogs, both dead and alive, had been made by 'lady artists'. Coloured photographs of them were framed about the house, and two particularly small corpses had been stuffed and placed in glass cases in the drawing-room!

We retired to change for dinner. I looked forward to act two of the play. I chuckled away to myself in the clean, white bed-

room (there were forty guest rooms, I learned), where a pot of asters had been placed to make me feel 'quite at home'.

Rise of second act curtain: our hostess is discovered wearing turquoise satin embroidered with moonstones. Diamond stars glitter in her coconut-fibre wig. The Duchess has chosen an overmantel of black sequins, while Miss Wilberforce plays safe in a *jeune-fille* frock. Pelion-Smith does *not* play safe: he wears a black waistcoat with his tailcoat.

The dining-room is a mausoleum lined with red silk and—surprise!—over the sideboard one fine Nicholas Poussin. A white shiny cloth covers the table, while scarlet gladioli tower in silver tureens and trumpet-shaped vases, blocking the view of *vis-à-vis* diners and preventing general conversation.

Mrs Mosscockle, undaunted by the *épergne,* contrives to 'make conversation', while Pelion-Smith interpolates unctuous bromides in a voice so rich one feels bilious.

Mrs M.: 'I hide in a cupboard during thunderstorms. I hope that all those who are cruel to animals will be punished in the after-life,' etc.

'Yais.'

Brightly, I mention that lobsters can be heard screaming in the pot while being boiled up.

Mrs M., her rickety little frame shaking and shuddering with horror, gasps, 'Fancy, a poor squealing fish!'

After dinner, we have barely settled in the drawing-room when our hostess (fearful of things not going with a swing) drags us off to a billiard room that smells as though it had never been lived in or utilised before.

A rusty old gramophone is put on. Miss Wilberforce and I snigger slightly at the excruciating sounds. Bowing-Levey shows no feelings at all. Pelion-Smith piles Pelion on Ossa, raving emptily about Albani as she wails away like a stray dog. Why, even old Mrs Mosscockle believes there is something wrong with her favourite soprano tonight.

The wireless proves no greater success: it cannot be heard. After a scrap of billiards, Pelion-Smith suggests dancing. To a foggy, grinding record of *The Blue Danube*, he and our hostess waltz on six square feet of uncarpeted floor. P.-S. looks like a Soho waiter in his baggy tailcoat, the pants sloppily sagging at his knees. He holds his preserved partner at arm's length.

The Duchess whispers to Bowing-Levey to turn off the stove, as the heat is asphyxiating. A few minutes later she complains of a headache and retires. The second act has reached its climax. The ladies curtsey, the men bow.

P.-S. holds up the curtain. 'Might I have a nupple before I go to bed? I always have a nupple before going to bed.' This request occasions a lot of bother, but the butler eventually brings a nupple up.

Third act breakfast tomorrow at ten o'clock. And everyone must be assembled on time!

August 15th (Sunday)
The *pièce de résistance* of the weekend was provided this afternoon when Mrs Mosscockle expensively hired a launch to take us up river for a trip. *Empress of China* had room enough for two hundred and fifty people, and we were seven. It went smoothly, elegantly, but oh so slowly. We glided along, a living Tissot, as everyone exclaimed at the view. 'Oh, isn't that picturesque? Look at those willow trees, and all those Dorothy Perkins!' Every other house on the river had white-painted balconies and a wealth of scarlet geraniums. Windsor Castle, in the distance, looked as it does in Victorian water-colour sketches. Mrs Moss-cockle sat in a wicker chair, revelling in it all. 'Capital, capital!'

At dinner, the scarlet gladioli had been changed for salvia. Last night's pickings had been poor, but now Mrs M. provided caviar and champagne. She herself eats like a butterfly, but Pelion-Smith guzzled greedily. Between mouthfuls he said, 'That's a lovely diamond bracelet you're wearing, Mrs M.'

She replied, 'Yes. In memory of my husband. A snake, you see. Eternity.'

We then went on to discuss literature and art for an eternity. 'Thackeray,' P.-S. managed between mouthfuls, 'Oh, I like Thackeray. He's got bite. *Vanity Fair* is strong meat.'

Miss Wilberforce introduced the subject of modern poetry. She thought Kipling very bold. 'I don't like him myself, but he has a great public.'

'What do you think of the Sitwells?' I ventured. But nobody had heard of the Sitwells.

Pelion-Smith regarded me with suspicion. 'In my humble opinion, the modern tendency in art is the cult of the ugly.'

Mrs Mossockle shuddered, 'The cult of the ugly! How horrible!'

Typical of the cult was Sargent. 'How cruel and merciless his portraits are,' said Bourbon Princess Marie Louise, Duchess of Seville.

'Portraits should be idealised,' Mrs M. agreed. And the matter was left there.

After dinner our hostess was induced to play the piano and sing. A travesty to end travesties, she sat playing mostly wrong notes as she squawked out *Il Bacio*. *The Rosary* and *A Little Brown Bird Singing*. I bit my lower lip savagely in order to maintain the proper reverence. She wheezed; she wobbled on the treble notes, inevitably three tones flat. Even as a funny skit it would have seemed overdone. Pelion-on-Ossa seemed too embarrassed to gush. It remained for Bowing-Levey cleverly to intersperse the necessary encouragements. After a particularly screeched 'To kiss the cross, sweetheart, to kiss the cross,' however, he could only remark, 'That must have been a very tiring and difficult one to sing.'

SANDWICH: PRELUDE TO ADVENTURE

August 17th

It was midnight when the train arrived at Sandwich. Mama and Aunt Jessie met me on the platform, both looking wild and unkempt in old clothes, but elated by the excitements of their holiday; the pageant at Walmer Castle, antique shops in the back streets of Deal and the Prince of Wales on the golf-course. All the news they gave me as we walked in Stygian darkness to the cottage which is about a mile outside Sandwich.

Next morning Nancy and Baba greeted me early, alert and bright. I was pleased to get a fresh impression of them. They are both very pretty indeed, with pale faces and hair that has got bleached from the sun. Baba has the more classical features but is going through a gawky, ungraceful period. Nancy, by contrast, knows what to do with herself and can be most decorative.

N. and B. showed me about the cottage, small and primitive, but they've been happy with it. The garden's not bad, and there's a kitchen garden, orchard and some hens.

We bathed at Deal: the water grey and filled with jellyfish.

Lunch seemed more like a picnic. We ate grilled ham and breakfast foods. I had a gargantuan appetite.

Afterwards, Mum and Modom busied themselves with domestic work. Modom concentrated on catching fleas off the dog. It appears that the cottage had been infested with fleas. No sooner had the family arrived than all were bitten. Mummie wrote a 'strong' letter to the owner of the house, who became outraged and wrote back: 'How dare you? I have a horror of fleas.' Meanwhile I lay on the lawn: How pleasant to be lazy and do nothing but watch the clouds or the cabbage butterflies hovering around, or the various little insects in the grass. I read some letters of Chekhov.

From then on, the incidents of the holiday have no sequence. . . . Days went by while I sat in a wicker chair in the garden, reading. For the first time, I read all the Jane Austen novels, and made drawings of the heroines. I discovered Samuel Butler's *The Way of All Flesh*. What could be more piercing than: 'He found a theory on which to justify himself and went to sleep?'

I also came across Ronald Firbank. A little story called *Caprice* is the best; the others are too inconsequential to be funny for very long. Robert Byron's excellent *The Tower* made me appreciate Byzantine art for the first time. It was a shock to discover that Robert, a person I had always considered a dilettante-white-mouse, should be so erudite.

Other works: Margot Asquith's trashy novel, and Rebecca West's essays. In fact, I read more than ever before. But how slow I am: Nancy and Baba can read twice as fast.

Every evening we went for a walk through the cornfields: It was enormously nice. Before dinner, we sat on the window sills outside the house and read, while a late sun shone warm. Sometimes we would sit enthralled, listening to the group of villagers. Against the hedge which divided our lawn from the walk by the ramparts are public seats. On these, old ladies gossip to one another to pass the time of day.

'I believe in children eating their crusts.'

'There's been such a horrid smell down there.'

'Aaah, you mean the drains! The sewer! We had to shut all our windows during that very hot weather. We couldn't stand it.'

By gaslight, I made quick pen and ink sketches of Baba. The results encouraged me, and I filled many pages. The gas hurt my eyes; in addition to which, it smelt and killed the cut flowers.

Gradually we gave up and did nothing after dark, just walked outside and went to bed absurdly early. Not tired enough to sleep through the night, I'd wake and read by candlelight while moths spluttered and popped in the flame. In the orchard outside, I could hear the thud of apples falling.

Baba

Ninnie had come out of retirement for a holiday, but insisted upon becoming maid-of-all-work. She sang to herself all day; and as her sense of tune is non-existent, the noise we heard was like an old hen clucking in the yard.

The Chattocks came to stay, which pleased Nancy and Baba especially. I was left alone to read and write and draw. When the Pater came down for weekends (most unsuitably clad in city clothes), the little Mill House almost burst its walls. Ninnie's songs turned to a dirge. Daddy's mood was a bit sullen. He's no more interested in Mummy's or N. and B.'s enthusiasms, than he is in mine. And if the truth be told, we are not interested in *his* enthusiasms either. Behind all our frivolity lies the unhappy awareness of this incompatibility. No one thinks about it if the abyss can be avoided, but the abyss is nevertheless there.

'Best summer for many years,' said the postman as the sun continued to shine on our holiday. We over-ate ourselves with village chocolates, marshmallows and ice cornets from Mr Medlicott. I started smoking again and bought cigarettes. I bought papers and magazines at the station: the society ones on Wednesday morning, the *New Statesman* and *Saturday Review* on Saturday. I bought Indian ink and inspiring notebooks from the stationer's. Each time I did this I passed through the churchyard with its old and new graves and wizened villagers tending them. We played tennis a lot. My laziness was such that I could never bother to put the racket back in its press after the set.

One evening while we were eating a cold supper in the kitchen, I talked airily of my plans about going to the Lido on Sunday. 'Two journalists, Mrs Whish and Mrs Settle, are off to Venice to write about Baroness d'Erlanger's costume ball. They suggested I tag along with them.' What I didn't say to the family was that I am desperate to go, though I don't know how I'll manage it. The alternative—returning to Schmiegelow's office— was not very cheerful. Suddenly the telephone rang. It was Daddy relaying a telegram for me from Peggy: 'Very sorry impossible. Writing.'

August 19th

Damn! Damn! Damn! *Now* how was I to get to the Lido? The fortune teller had said two journeys abroad, and one of them wasn't even going to materialise!

Mum asked what the message meant. I told her I had written to borrow money from Peggy. Mum turned white. 'Have you gone mad? It's the most disgraceful thing for a young man to borrow off a young girl. What a caddish thing to do! You're abusing her kind hospitality. No one will ever lend you money for pleasure. You must never do such a thing again.'

I suddenly felt abashed and squeamish. I hadn't thought of it in that light at all. Being perfectly honest, I would have paid the money back as soon as possible. It wasn't as though I were stealing. Anyway, I wrote to Peggy immediately, saying how sorry I was and that I suddenly realised I shouldn't have done such a thing, but out of desperation, etc. . . .

I felt stranded. All my high-falutin' talk had been worthless and silly. I couldn't go, not even if I sold all my leather bound books so carefully collected from old David's bookstall at Cambridge.

I went to bed, sick with the thought of not seeing Venice this year. I wouldn't be meeting my saviour after all.

August 20th

Nancy and Baba wondered if they couldn't get their money out of the bank and lend it to me. I said no, that wouldn't do. I asked Mum what she thought. 'The only thing to do is write to your father and explain the matter. See what he says.'

Could I? I hadn't really thought of that, but it was my last hope. I sat down and wrote: 'Will you lend me twenty pounds to go to Venice?' Then I listed all my reasons, and even boldly stated it was a waste of my time to remain in Holborn when I could earn more than a pound a week standing on my head.

Baba had the note 'express lettered' to London. If I rang my father this evening, I'd have his decision.

I spent the rest of the day being sick with nervousness. Whenever the telephone bell went I had pangs of agony. False alarm: the wrong number. Mummy began to worry with me.

The telephone rang again. This time it was my father. 'If you intend just to go for pleasure, I'm afraid I must refuse.'

'But it isn't for pleasure. I really think I might be able to get something out of it.' 'Well, you see, I can't go on forever with these great expenses. You've been a year doing nothing. I can't really afford . . . don't think I'm being unreasonable . . .' Then, after, a long pause, 'If you *do* think there is a chance of something coming of it, I'll let you have the money.'

I exploded with gratitude. Daddy became gruff. 'You see, as usual you leave everything till the last minute. If you'd known this all along we ought to have discussed matters thoroughly. And your passport: that'll have to be seen to.'

The rest of the evening was panic. I'd leave here first thing in the morning; I started to pack and looked up the earliest train to London. Then it was discovered that none of us had any money,

Stephen Tennant's House Party at Wilsford

Rex Whistler, The Sacheverell Sitwells, Eleanor Wylie, Rosamund Lehmann, The Hon. Edward Sackville-West, Borden Harriman, Zita Jungman

My Mother and Aunt Jessie

and I couldn't buy a ticket without ten shillings! I had sevenpence, Nancy and Baba about sixpence between them, Mummie a few odd shillings and Modom a religious medallion of doubtful value. We looked in every drawer of the cottage, in every purse. We scraped together seven-and-six, which wasn't enough. Then Mum found a pound note. It shamed me to take these scrapings, but I couldn't turn back now.

There was no alarm clock in the house. I wondered how I'd wake up in time to catch the early train. Baba said, 'I can make myself wake up any time I want to. I'll wake you at six-thirty.'

August 21st

Baba's pale yellow face appeared in the doorway—triumphant, beaming and sprightly. 'Exactly six-thirty! I woke up on the stroke.'

All flea bitten and miserable, I got up and dressed hurriedly. The clocks seemed to show different times. Baba had gone back to sleep, taking her watch with her. I thought there was time to spare but Mum agitated me on, saying how awful it would be to miss the train. I bolted off to the station. It seemed longer than a mile, and I began to grow panicky. I had to catch that train, otherwise I wouldn't arrive in London in time to get my pass-port. I ran the last lap in agony. My clothes stuck to me; my hands were grimy and aching from the effort of lugging the heavy bag. Ready to give up the ghost, I reached the platform just as a train was going out. Then I suddenly saw a clock: I was half an hour early!

During the journey I thought: how selfish I am, how nice the family is being to me. But how wonderful to be going to Venice! It only remained to face my father this evening, an ordeal which might prove embarrassing. I'd felt master of the situation on the telephone, but it would be difficult to look him straight in the eye. . . .

It wasn't difficult. When Pop arrived home he seemed calm and quiet, hardly mentioning my trip. I just thanked him very much. And, almost by tacit agreement, we never alluded to Schmiegelow or the office. We had dinner. As there were no servants, I helped with the food. I drank a lot of whisky and soda, felt quite drunk and talked freely and easily.

E

In my room I started to put out the photographs and designs I was taking to Italy to show to my 'saviour', whoever he or she might be!

August 22nd

I was ready to go. I called a taxi. I kissed Daddy goodbye, not having kissed him in months, almost years. Then, with my pink flannel scarf round my neck and neat luggage stowed away, I set off for the Lido.

Part V

Venice

1926

August 24th

Venice! I stand at the window of the Pensione Casa Petrarca. There is no view, but effective shadows fall on the white stone walls outside. What a blinding sun! What a glut of sun! I never realised before, but in England the sun comes in precious small spasms. Here, it shines all day.

I feel alive and alert. I enjoy my *café complet*. The only thing I can say to the maid is *Caffé completo* and *Grazia*. The coffee, heavy with chicory, leaves a nice taste on the roof of one's mouth. And I like the Italian bread, dry and indigestible.

I walk down all the odd, dirty, bright vistas. Everything is picturesque—a word which, until now, I've always considered taboo. I take turnings and wind my way through twisting little alleys, overcrowded with people and glittering with shops.

Suddenly I stumble on the Piazza San Marco. What a shock! All seems incandescent. St Mark's is a shimmering cluster of oriental beehives. The Doges' Palace stands luminous and flushed, like a flame through porcelain. Thousands of pigeons are so much confetti; the glaring whiteness of stone filigree carving completes a theatrical unreality. I want to stand and gaze forever, but my companions have arranged to catch the boat to the Lido.

We arrive at the Excelsior. What a hideous Moorish hotel! Its vulgarity and bad style make me think of a Hippodrome revue

Venice

—meretricious but rather fun. In the marble lounge, women sit about wearing the most expensive pyjamas (with designs of dragons and birds of prey hand-painted in brilliant, sickening colours) and no shoes. The men, too, saunter about in fancy pyjamas. It is all quite absurd, fantastic and smart.

On the sumptuous stone terrace people drink aperitifs in the shade of large umbrellas. A flight of alabaster steps flanked by oleanders leads down to rows of bathing *cabanas*, all gaudily striped. In the sand, people lie practically naked as the sun burns them an even deeper red-brown. The yellow sands are almost too hot to walk on.

Impatient to be a part of it all, I strip into my bathing costume— the scarlet and white one I wore at Etretat. Here on the Lido, no man wears a top to his costume: just small trousers, the smaller the better. I must buy a pair immediately.

The Adriatic is pale and tideless. Strange, to swim about in a leisurely manner for as long as one likes and still be thoroughly warm. I paddle along to the place where there are rings for swimmers to pull themselves from the water. Accidentally, I kick someone. It is Nancy and Baba's Angela Duveen! We are both surprised to see one another, though without her tortoise-shell glasses she doesn't recognise me for a moment.

Venice is the place! How provincial of people to mess about at that petty Etretat.

August 25th

Mrs Whish and Mrs Settle, in need of copy to send home, arranged to visit the d'Erlangers and hear their plans for the pageant. I was allowed to follow in their wake. We set off blindly, taking the *vaporetto* or whatever it is called. We got lost, then found a guide who intricately steered us to the *palazzo* of the Baroness's daughter, Princess Faucigny-Lucinge.

When we arrived at an unprepossessing back entrance, there was a lot of shouting to a man leaning out of a window. He proved extremely polite, ushered us through a courtyard of vine leaves, white stone walls and old, terrifically artistic looking well-heads. We went up to the *grande sala*, an enormous room with mottled marble floor and red brocade wall hangings. The furniture was sumptuous and Italian; there were Greek scrolls of gilt and tall gold lanterns. The room ran the whole length of the *palazzo*, and must have been a hundred and fifty feet in length.

The two journalists were asked to go into the Princess's bed-room. I wished I'd seen her: from her photographs she appears a mixture of Persian miniature and organ-grinder's monkey. But I had to remain behind, busying myself with browsing through the books on the table, seeing what sort of cigarettes were being smoked, what gramophone records played. The records were flippant ragtimes. The books seemed very good style, mostly belonging to Lady Wimborne, who had written her name across the fly-leaves.

In the large adjoining room, green brocade hung in folds on the wall, and the ceiling beams had been painted green and gold. There were high-backed throne chairs, needleworked sofas, large glass tubs of lilies with shiny leaves and white tuberoses. A few modern touches had been introduced: the lamps, in round bottles filled with water, were covered with fashionable, pleated parchment shades.

Presently the journalists reappeared. They'd got all the pageant news about who was going to appear as Water, Seaweed, or the Moon. For further details they must ask the Princess's mother.

We went off to a neighbouring *palazzo* and found the Baroness d'Erlanger with her companion in the garden. The Baroness had scarlet hair and wore a magenta satin dressing gown. She was busy gilding some pumpkins on a huge stone garden ornament. With all these last-minute preparations for the pageant, she didn't seem to know quite what she was saying. All that the journalists could glean from her staccato mumblings was that the Crown Prince of Italy had promised to come to the Ball, and that Diana Cooper had been in a few minutes before to take away all the remaining costumes. I thought the Baroness rather curt with Mesdames Whish and Settle, but they didn't seem to mind much.

After a bit, I left the journalists to file their stories. I felt eager to explore more of the sights of Venice. I peeped into dark churches where my eyes, still dazzled by sunlight, took considerable time to make out the Tiepolo fresco or Carpaccio frieze. I wandered along small canal-ways and over stone bridges, abruptly discovering some lofty piazza decorated with an equestrian statue or fountain. I found myself in a main artery again, and was swept along in the crowd, past sellers of beads, filigree silver and spun glass to the statue of Goldoni and the Merchants' Rialto. This was really worth living for!

When the light began to fade I made my way to the Piazza San Marco and had an ice at Florian's. The ice was good, about six different flavours in compartments. I ate *brioches* and smoked, enjoying the warm, still evening, and the light that changed from minute to minute.

Lady Diana Cooper appeared, wearing an enormous apricot-coloured garden hat. Surely, she must be the most beautiful English woman alive today. I stared in awe. Her face was a perfect oval, her skin white marble. Her lips were japonica red, her hair flaxen, her eyes blue love-in-the-mist.

With Lady Diana were: Lord Berners, who looks more like a figure in a tailor's shop window than a composer; Mr St John

Hutchinson, huge, jocular and Regency in his arty clothes; and Maurice Baring, who I believe writes novels.

Whish and Settle returned from the Lido to announce that the beach had been buzzing with the sensational news of Rudolph Valentino's death. Rumour has it that several flappers shot themselves dead on hearing the news, while thousands of others flocked to see the corpse. Rudy is the first big film favourite to die.

August 26th

This evening we got into a gondola and went to hear the *grande serenata*. Half Venice was out of doors. Crowds lined the Grand Canal, faces stuck from every window. Driven by an unromantic steamboat, a huge barge came into view. On it was a bower-like pavilion strung with electric bulbs and sheltering a full complement of orchestra and singers. Hundreds of gondolas (filled like ours with English trippers) plied about the launch. The gondoliers were loving the performance; and as it was a festive occasion, they overcharged outrageously for their boats.

I got tired of it all. The gondola dropped me at the nearest striped landing pole, and I started to plough my way back to the Casa Petrarca. The *festa* mob outside seemed almost impregnable. I couldn't push my way through to the door, and waited in the hope that the diva on the floating palace wouldn't scream all night.

How the Venetians loved her! If any child in arms was unmusical enough to squeak during her song, hundreds of irate women and men would 'Shhh' for all they were worth. Other singers then throbbed out their chests, pouring forth pent-up, soul-swelling melodies in a sentimental, unrestrained wallow. Thousands stood breathlessly thrilled, until a prolonged shriek brought immense clapping.

It was already one o'clock. I had overdone my sunbath and now stood so red and raw that at the slightest jostle I winced in pain.

At last the illuminated dome moved far enough down the canal for me to get to bed.

In my room I gingerly unpeeled each piece of clothing in torment. I couldn't bear to put even my fingertips on my body. I laughed with pain as I crawled under my mosquito netting.

Outside, the operatic merrymaking continued. Periodic flares were let off, flooding the room with livid daylight. The Italians seem never to go to bed before two or three, and tonight they'd very likely not go at all. Just outside, I could hear peals of laughter, raucous shouts, and then such animated excitement one might have thought a murder had been discovered. It was probably only two men saying what a nice day it had been.

BARONESS D'ERLANGER'S COSTUME BALL

August 27th

The journalists wanted to watch the dress rehearsal for the pageant. An ungainly party, we trooped into the Princess's *palazzo*. Poor Mrs Whish looked her worst, hot and sticky in dusty black. There were screams when she appeared, and Mrs Robin d'Erlanger let fly at her in the most surprising manner. It seemed that Mrs Whish was responsible for Mrs d'Erlanger's costume being lost. Mrs Whish looked thunderstruck. Messengers were sent off in every direction. We sat soddenly apart, ignored while the scarlet-haired Baroness plopped about on flat feet. By degrees, self-conscious young Frenchmen and Italians put in an appearance, dressed as Tritons in bright blue and green sequins. A press photographer waited about, eyeing me and my Kodak with suspicion.

Mrs Whish regained her journalistic ardour as soon as the lost costume was found. She gushed at a social lion who had no forehead or chin but impressively protruding teeth. He seemed brainless and quite forty-five! Mrs Whish said, 'Do let me introduce you to Mr Beaton. He wants to photograph you!'

The lion showed more of what was already showing. 'Oh well, I'm afraid . . .'

I thought, 'So should I be, if I'd got a face like yours!'

Lady Wimborne appeared, wearing a crinoline of wheat sheaves embroidered in gold. She wagged her hips, pranced about, 'talking common', and shouted to the Duc de Verdura, 'Allo, dearie.' Mrs Evelyn Fitzgerald glided in, wearing a poison-green sequinned crinoline. But the best was Princess Baba Lucinge, who really looked the part of 'Water' in a flowing armour made of hundreds of strips of tin and a *casquette* of florin-sized sequins.

The photographer took the most ordinary group photographs.

It seemed to me a wonderful opportunity, but I didn't dare barge in and ask if I might take pictures also. I felt completely ignored, along with Whish and Settle. Everyone else was offered a cocktail except us.

Suddenly I plucked up courage and asked Faucigny-Lucinge if she'd let me take some snapshots of her. I explained that I was rather an amateur and didn't wish to vie with the professional, so might I take them in another room? No, there was nowhere else; if they were to be taken at all, it must be here. I wished I'd said, 'Well, don't let's bother then.' I felt acutely embarrassed as I somehow clicked three photographs under the professional press photographer's nose. My amateur tripod kept slipping on the marble floor, while Princess Lucinge giggled with her foreign men friends and posed awkwardly. She seemed surprised when I asked her to move this way or that. I feared the photographs would be the dullest imaginable, yet wanted to capture that perfect head with its high nobbly cheekbones and huge domed crown. Some profile views would do it, if only her hat were not hiding so much. I asked her to remove the *casquette*. No, that wasn't suitable: the hat was an intricate part of the costume. I faded away, fuming to myself.

The Ball took place in the gilded La Fenice Theatre.

Mrs Settle was having difficulty with her borrowed fancy dress skirt and train. Mrs Whish, wearing her inevitable black, looked like a Holbein creation. I felt self-conscious as a mediaeval page in stencilled tunic and tights.

Since the Crown Prince was expected, there could be no dancing before he arrived. A blatant band blared, while people wandered about aimlessly, growing tired of looking at one another. Some began to yawn.

At long last the Crown Prince took his place in the most royal royal box. He bowed formally from the hips and the pageant unfolded. The d'Erlanger 'elements' hobbled in, trashy as a *Folies Bergères* revue (but, of course, none of the group could do right for me!). Towards the end came Lady Cunard in a highly unsuitable Spinelly outfit of pink ostrich feathers and top hat to match. She looked surprised. Lady Diana Cooper was to have been part of a group of Porcelain Figures. But her prepared costume, a white mackintosh dress with mask, had to be

E*

abandoned: Italian etiquette forbids wearing a mask in front of royalty. Home she went, returning in a crinoline and Turkish turban. She looked furiously beautiful now, sitting in her box energetically picking her nose. Lady Abdy and old Princess San Faustino were a study in dramatic contrast. Lady A., like a huge lioness with her mane of oatmeal-coloured hair, wore a black-and-white velvet dress. The bread-stick Princess looked a religious curio in her abbess's habit and wimple. It gave me a shock, however, to hear this distinguished widow speaking with the most twangy American accent.

The Prince continued sitting erect in his glut-of-gilt surroundings. He never danced. The brass band trumpeted away. Few people knew there was a room upstairs for supper, and the general rush was for a railway-station buffet, where a crowd fought to buy glasses of beer and sandwiches. With the whole evening so disorganised, it came as no surprise when most of the guests started leaving soon after midnight. A lot of money had been made, but no one had enjoyed the proceedings.

We trailed home through moonlit Venice. Mrs Settle lagged behind, still having trouble with her train. Whish saw the humour of it all and howled with laughter: fancy her articles telling millions of readers that tonight's dazzling pageant would make Venetian history!

'Wait! I can't keep my shoes on,' moaned poor Mrs Settle from the far side of a ghostly *piazza*.

AN ENCOUNTER WITH DIAGHILEV

August 31st

I went to the Lido, bathed and felt restless. How could I justify my visit to Venice in my father's eyes? So far, I'd not met my saviour.

As this was my last day but one here, I persecuted Miss Gibson, another journalist who had promised to introduce me to Diaghilev. If only I could get a look-in with him! At last Miss Gibson said she had an appointment to interview the great man in the Piazza San Marco at six o'clock. I could join her there.

I rushed to get back to the *pensione* and collect my portfolio of drawings and photographs. From San Marco I took what I thought would be a short cut, but lost the way and was soon hurrying through a hopeless maze of back alleys and streets. Knowing no Italian, I hadn't much courage to ask the way to the Casa Petrarca. In desperation, I retraced my way back to San Marco, then started off again the long way round. By the time I found the *pensione*, seized my portfolio and ran back to the Piazza to meet Miss Gibson and Diaghilev, I was in a sweat.

After an anxious time, Miss Gibson appeared. We waited and waited, but Diaghilev never arrived. I seethed with disappointment and dejection. How dare I go home to England and confess having spent all that money if nothing came of it?

Seven o'clock and still no Diaghilev. Miss Gibson became paler and paler, more unhealthy looking. We kept thinking we saw him in the distance, but when the person approached it was somebody else. Miss Gibson couldn't understand it at all. He'd seemed so eager to see her, had even volunteered to bring some photographs of the ballet if she cared to publish them.

At last Miss Gibson gave up. He wouldn't come now. She went off to send a note from the Danieli, but I sat and continued to wait, just on the off chance.

Oh God, there he was with Lifar![1] I catapulted forward and spoke in English. 'Miss Gibson was to have introduced us but she's gone and may not be back and mayn't I show you my portfolio?'

Diaghilev stared at me in surprise. In spite of his colossal stature and dignified mien he reminded me of a pale and fat baby. He was impeccably dressed in white flannel trousers and blue, double-breasted coat with a tuberose in his buttonhole. He wore a formal Panama hat with an Edwardian flourish to the brim. Lifar was identically garbed, but somehow in spite of the natty armour, continued to look like a street urchin.

They sat down at my table. D. held himself very erect, speaking meekly in pidgin English. I couldn't think what animal he reminded me of—perhaps a mole or a very nice monkey.

I fumbled with the knotted strings of my portfolio. Diaghilev pompously, yet carefully, studied the sketches I brought forth, making no remarks but nodding like a mandarin and showing definite interest. Lifar, too, seemed more than polite. Some of the designs I tried to pass by, as I didn't think them good enough to exhibit. But Diaghilev wouldn't have that. He looked carefully

[1] Serge Lifar, the dancer.

at everything. I asked his advice on one or two designs, and with astonishing sensitivity he quickly indicated what was lacking or where each had failed. Some he said 'nice' to, others 'original'.

I gushed; I stammered and overdid the politeness. I spilled an avalanche of sketches and photographs I had never intended to show from the portfolio.

Diaghilev bent down with difficulty, taking up in his ringed fingers my picture of a double-reflected N. and B. 'You take photographs, too? I like this. It is very curious.' He smiled and went through other photographs.

The waiter appeared. No, the gentlemen wouldn't have anything as they must be going. Bows and exchange of compliments. I thanked D. for seeing my things. He thanked *me* profusely, while I still wondered what animal he looked like. Then they walked away. And that was that!

Miss Gibson returned and found me in a daze. She turned pale grey when I said, 'Diaghilev's been here and you've missed him.'

'Golly!' Miss Gibson was American.

I said, 'Don't worry. He promised to meet you here tomorrow at the same time. Perhaps you can find out what he thought of my work.'

I then carted my portfolio back to the Casa Petrarca, feeling rather dejected. Mrs Whish greeted me tactlessly, 'Well, I'm afraid your holiday hasn't been quite successful.'

It was all over; and in spite of disappointments it had been beautiful. Oh, but if only I were returning home with a job: if only I'd made some money! I felt squeamish: no success, and I'd taken twenty pounds from Daddy. Including Etretat, my holidays this year had cost fifty pounds.

I took a gondola to the railway station—such a beautiful station, unlike most. The gondolier tried to rob me. The fare from the Casa Petrarca to the station should have been twelve lire. I gave him twenty-five as I felt particularly kind to Venice. But he pretended that was not enough: he wanted fifty! I felt alarmed, weakly gave another ten to his delight, and boarded the overflowing train to return to—what?

Part VI

Charmouth

1926

Since my return, the subject of Schmiegelow's office has never
been mentioned. It would only be weakness if I went back there.
Schmiegelow doesn't want me, anyway: I'm no use to him, and
so it's a complete waste of both our time. In any case, I felt
determined not to go to his office today, even if I had to begin
again tomorrow.

Besides, there was a lot for me to do: many photographs to
cope with, including all the Venice pictures to pack and post to
magazines. As always, I'm enthusiastic about submitting the
work, though it will probably come back with the polite,
'Go away, you're not wanted.'

Also, I had Hazel Owet's photographs to do. Two pictures
of her will pay more than a week's work at Schmiegelow's.

I remained quiet as a grave in my bedroom until my father
had gone off to his office. Then I rang up Schmiegelow and
said I'd come tomorrow to do some typing if he liked. There

129

was nothing to do anyway. Miss Robertson was on holiday. But if I came in tomorrow morning for a talk, he would like that. I agreed.

On with the photos. A packet of Venice negatives arrived. I went out and bought more printing paper to enlarge them. When the results were dry, they went off to the papers.

With a charcoal pencil I retouched Miss Owet. I gave her more eyelashes, cut irregular lumps off the dress, made her look prettier and more uninteresting. Silly people don't want to look interesting.

Jack Gold rang up, eager to hear all about the Lido. We arranged to meet for lunch. He was intrigued and amused when I told him about Mrs Whish. He wanted to hear all about this journalist from Barnes, whose work took her to wherever the *haut monde* congregated.

I said, 'She's a very good sleuth, and has worked on *The Times* under a man who is fascinated by all the perversions.'

'*All* of them?' Jack raised his eyebrows.

'Yes. She's an expert on the sins of society. And I must say I admire her for being philosophical when she gets such offhand treatment from the high and mighty.'

'They snub Whish?'

'She just laughs. She told me, "I give the most beautiful of those women seven years." Besides, she sees herself as others see her. She has no taste and she knows it. She gushes at flamboyant trash in shop windows. At teatime, when most people like a *brioche* or shortbread, she eats one of those unbelievable cakes all smarmed with apricots and puffed cream, and layers of jam and coconut.'

Jack said, 'You must write a play about Mrs Whish on the Lido.'

'But I couldn't hope to write a well-constructed piece. It might have a certain grotesque vitality, but to tell a story for two and a half hours on end——'

Jack talked very large. 'Well, you hear of these successful first plays. I don't see why you shouldn't have a hit. I could help you with the bones of the story, if you like.'

The suggestion was stimulating. Jack and I had been successful enough at Harrow, collaborating on a satire of Elinor Glyn's *Three Weeks*. We decided now to spend *one* week reading plays,

then go off to some quiet place and write. We would use a
pseudonym, calling ourselves Ada Meadows.

On our way to buy books on play construction at the Times
Book Shop, we passed Cathleen Nesbitt. She was looking her
most severe and staid, gaunt about the face and dressed in an un-
spectacular fashion. I told Jack whom we had just passed. He
said, 'Oh, I wish I had known. I would have taken off my hat!'

'Why? Do you know her?'

'No,' he said, and smiled. I was amazed. 'You old dog.'
Really, it is fantastic how formally Jack behaves—like an old
Regency club bore. He is younger than I am, and certainly too
young to be doffing his hat to actresses in the street, whether he
knows them or not.

When I left Jack, it was with the feeling that Venice had
perhaps justified itself after all. If it had not given me a job, it
had given me the character of Mrs Whish. I knew her pat. It
might be funny to see her going through the hoops, against the
bright setting of Venice, always wearing the same old black dress
and black picture hat.

Other main characters would be: a stiff upper-lipped duchess,
impoverished but unwilling to lower her gunsights; and a pushing
American hostess, a 'shooting star' closely based on Mrs Corrigan.

I went home and quickly filled many pages of a notebook. All
we needed now was a plot, which quite possibly might evolve.

Meanwhile, there were still a lot of photographs to be printed.
I darkened the bedroom, but Ada Meadows kept intruding on my
work. Every now and again I leapt into the air as things to put
in the play occurred to me. So many parts of the jigsaw were
falling into place. I felt that, at last, to be on the verge of giving
birth; doing something myself, not just watching others perform. I didn't mind a bit facing my father now that I had a plan.

I went on enlarging and came down to dinner in dirty, acid-
eaten rags. Before Pop could say anything about Schmiegelow
or ask if I had been there today, I announced, 'My next mad
scheme is to write a play!' That more or less took his breath away.

'Jack and I plan to go to Cornwall, find some quiet village and
write for ten days.'

'Where are you finding the money to go? Who will pay?'

I answered that I would. Hazel Owet was sending a cheque for
her flattering photographs; and Jack had volunteered to settle a

three pound ten debt for pictures I had taken of him a long time ago wearing a pink hunting coat.

'Well good luck to you!'

In bed I started to read Ibsen and Galsworthy plays for hints on construction. I found that more often than not I was just led along by the story, unable to realise the craftsmanship. I was encouraged by studying *The Queen in the Parlour* but discouraged by *Our Betters*.

I studied until dawn. My elbow got stiff. A decorative circus bed may be fine to look at, but it's most uncomfortable for reading in. With nothing to lie up against at the pillow end, one has to lean on an elbow.

I twitched with restlessness and longed to start work.

MR SCHMIEGELOW'S SECRET

September 7th

A hurry to be at Schmiegelow's office by ten. When I came out of the underground, Holborn Circus looked just the same. That haunting man with scarlet eyes and face half-eaten away was still smoking a dry pipe and selling shoelaces. In Southampton Row, our building hadn't changed by a scratch. Clara, the buxom, fresh-faced lift girl, took me up to the fifth floor. How sad to think that the inevitable had been going on in the same way ever since I'd left! Hundreds of letters had been received and posted, and perhaps just enough profit had been made to justify the office staff remaining on and on, in the same groove. Yet perhaps that's what they like—being in a groove.

Schmiegelow was alone in the office, slowly tapping at a typewriter. We sat and talked. I asked him to smooth matters over with my father, to explain that I was marking time when I might be doing much better on my own. In any case, I could get a job somewhere else and earn more than a pound a week.

He agreed in his clipped, baby Danish accent. 'Yess, it tiss a vaiste. But you see, you faghter iss a businesse man and wornts you to have your feeghte on the ground.'

I told Schmiegelow that I *had* my feet on the ground and was now toddling off to write a play. This interested and impressed him. I said, 'Do tell my father that I'm not at all a slack sort of person. I really have great ambitions, and even when I'm doing

132

nothing definite at home, I'm busy with photographs or painting.'

Schmiegelow promised to clear the air. I felt relieved. As I was leaving he said, 'Don't joordge your faghter too harshly. He just wants you to be dissciplined. He knows you'll never be a businesse man. In fact, I'll tell you a secret but don't effer repeat it.'

'What secret?'

'Your faghter hass been paying me the one pound a week that I pay you.'

I was flabbergasted.

September 8th

I read *Mrs Cheyney*, or at least most of it, in the Times Book Club. It seems cleverer than it did when I saw it. But at that time, my level of a good play was so much higher than it is now that I am starting to write myself! I still don't admire all those old-fashioned epigrams, though: they're very Oscar Wilde, remote and unreal.

At lunch I read Granville-Barker's *Madras House*.

TWO CHARACTERS IN SEARCH OF A PLOT

September 13th

Jack and I took tickets to Lyme Regis. We had decided that Cornwall was too far, too expensive a journey. I had about one pound for my stay away, but with what Jack owed me I thought it would do.

The train started. We shouted ideas at one another, more suitable for short stories than a three-act play. It seemed difficult to get hold of a strong enough plot to carry three acts without being mechanical. We decided against murder, mistaken identity and above all robbery. How tiresome to have to invent 'Who was the last person to put the pearls in the box? Who placed the box on the *écritoire*?' We didn't want any unpleasantness, no sex; yet the play had to give people the impression that they'd been amused and had their money's worth.

At Axminster we still had no plot but decided to get off there. I carried a small attaché case and no change of clothes except for some socks. It would be simple and crude. We took a taxi through perfect scenery. It was just beginning to get dark as we arrived at the top of a steep hill to find the village of Charmouth. Here was where Harriette Wilson had come from, and here we would stay.

We inquired at two pubs but neither could offer anything except a double bed; and though we were collaborators, I thought that was going too far. We said we preferred lodgings anyway, not an hotel. Most of the villagers came out to consult with the taxi driver. 'Try so and so; no, they've got people in.'

The driver, who looked like Massine, took us to six lodgings before we found one grey haired woman with eyes sparkling like stars in the glow of the candle she held. 'Yars, yars,' she could do us for two and half guineas a week but couldn't manage dinner tonight. 'Mrs Childs I am. Mrs Childs of Charmouth.'

We asked what her address was. 'Oh, this is Waterloo House, but Childs of Charmouth gets me from all over the world.'

September 14th

I was wakened by Mrs Childs of Charmouth shouting at me outside the door. She had brought my breakfast and the hot water. Too modest to bring them in herself, she slowly opened the door and slid the tray and can along the floor like a toy engine. I roared with laughter. Mrs C. of C. must have thought me quite mad.

Jack was pompously unhurried, having breakfast in bed and reading the papers. An hour went by before he decided to have his bath. I, meanwhile, ached to get started. I didn't give a damn about the London papers.

The morning was spent in fruitless discussion. Each time we got hold of a notion, some booby trap would suddenly send us flying into space. We went round and round in circles. Jack was all for murdering poor Whish at the end of the first act but I would have none of it. Perhaps the stiff upper-lipped duchess might put Mrs Corrigan's pearls in the *écritoire*. Or Whish might have known Corrigan when.

At last we sat silent, dried up. Jack said cheerfully, 'You must have your bath now. It's getting on for lunchtime.'

September 15th

Even if we haven't yet got a plot, we do think we know how to introduce the characters. Without knowing what would happen later, it seemed best to plunge into Act One. The wet, cold day prevented our going out, and so we did quite a bit of work. My mind buzzed with significant things that must be said by Whish, Corrigan and Stiff Lip. We were pleased and excited actually to be writing dialogue.

We still, alas, have no definite link to bind our characters together. In fact, I begin to wonder if we haven't been counting our chickens before they were hatched. In our mind's eye we read raving reviews of the play, made a fortune and envisioned the audience crying, 'Author, author, we want Ada Meadows!' We saw ourselves pulled onstage while Lady Curzon of Kedleston applauded from her box. But will all this ever become a reality?

After tea, Jack suggested that we part company until dinner—a welcome break from having seen one another continually for three days. Jack took his map and set out for a long walk. I went my own way for aimless miles over wet fields. I found myself hedged in, but with ridiculous determination pushed my head through thick hedges, getting my hair caught in twigs and my old trousers torn by thorns. I walked up and up, then sat on a gate at the top of a small mountain. I got out pencil and paper, but my mind was blank.

September 16th

This morning we sat in Mrs Childs of Charmouth's clean sitting-room, looking out at the drizzle. At last Jack said, 'Let's give up this bloody trio and start on something else.'

'Oh Jack, how can you? They're my own flesh and blood. I'm fond of them!'

It was a deadlock. If we stayed together much longer we'd start to bicker. More separate exercise: I set off for a long walk in the rain. I sloshed through a field of clover and felt that a four-leafer might bring us luck. I found one within the first few seconds of looking. But one of the leaves was a bit malformed. I felt determined to find a proper one for luck. The rain made all the clover look silver, though my touch turned it to green. I went on looking until my back ached; I thought I was a damned fool not to be content with the poor example I'd got already. I didn't find another.

This evening we more or less came to the conclusion that Charmouth is not the place to find a plot. We may part company for a few weeks, to think about things. If either gets an inspiration, we'll join forces again and continue.

September 18th

Jack has gone. Perhaps I'll hack away at the play more successfully by myself. I wonder if his three pounds ten will see me through? Or will I grow restless by myself and become too introspective?

After he left this morning, I tidied up the minute sitting-room. He had left *Country Life* hanging about, also his map and some rotten fruit.

Mrs Childs asked, 'How long will you be staying?'

'I'm afraid I can't tell you, Mrs. C.'

I sat down cheerfully and began to scan our notes for the play. Suddenly I realised our efforts were crude and amateurish—utter rot, rot.

Mrs C. of C.'s sitting-room faces the road, and her house is on top of this huge hill. As a result, one can hear in the distance every single car that comes buzzing up the hill. The buzz grows louder and louder as gears are changed. By the time the car arrives at the summit, the noise is infernal. I hadn't noticed this distraction so much while Jack was here, but now I seem to be aware of nothing else.

Working alone is more satisfactory than collaborating. Whenever I go stale, I type out what has already been written. Mrs Childs' daughter comes in to lay a meal or clean the remains of one away. Mrs Child occasionally says, 'You've been hard at it today, Mr Beaton.' So I have; I had no idea what concentrated work a play requires. I went up the lane for a breath of air before lunch, but otherwise slogged non-stop 'til midnight.

September 19th

The morning was spent weeding out the titbits of what Jack and I have concocted and trying to zigzag them into place. After lunch I typed until my back ached.

I went out. Charmouth, with its grey stone and large, dark trees, looked peaceful in the bright sunlight. I walked down to the shore, then wandered for miles along the beach. The sky was as vivid a blue as one sees in Italy. The sands were yellow and hot.

Completely alone, with no one likely to be in sight for miles, I stripped naked and lay on my towel reading Congreve. Swarms of sandflies hopped about my back and legs. I went into the sea, thinking they would leave me alone if I were wet and salty. The water was cold and bracing, but when I came out the insects still buzzed about. Determined, I looked at my notes for the play, then decided I couldn't do much unless I settled down to a table and became really wrapped up in it.

I dressed and walked further, deciding to scale the cliffs and explore the wild country. But it wasn't so easy to find a place where I could climb up. After a long while, I came to a small stream that ran down the cliffs into the sea. Here there were many pampas grasses, and by clutching them I managed to reach the top of the downs.

I gasped with delight. It was all primitively wild, with not a sign of a cottage in sight. Rabbits scuttled, birds flew up from thickets, God was in His heaven and all was right with the world. I walked along the downs, or rather waded through bracken as tall as myself. I came to an enormous greystone farm, with beautiful barns.

I was tapping away energetically when Mrs Childs came in and said, 'Not finished the whole play yet?' She looked amazed when I told her I'd only just scratched the surface of Act I.

September 20th

Mrs Childs obviously thought I'd gone potty when she heard me reading my absurd play aloud. But in spite of her attempted interruptions, my dry throat and hoarse voice, I was determined to time, by my watch, the length of the first act. It was much too long, and of course there would be laughs. (I hoped.) Cutting could be done later. But what was going to happen in Act II?

Morning's end and I still had no idea! The wastepaper basket was overflowing. I felt entitled to give my brain a rest, so would spend the afternoon blackberrying along those downs I discovered yesterday.

I set off with an enormous basket. It would be a gesture to send the blackberries to Mrs Whish!

Though the blackberries were enormous, I kept thinking that the ones out of reach were bigger. Before ransacking the place in front of me, I would plunder the next grey bush. With their long, barbed branches, they reminded me of the details in a Leonardo drawing. I picked until my hands looked dipped in ink.

Worn out from pinching the black carbuncles off their sockets, I started back along the top of the cliffs. A fantastic idea came to me. Supposing a young man were to wake up and find himself here, in this wilderness? He stumbles across a sign post, 'Trespassers will be shot', and then to his panic hears distant dogs barking. The sounds come nearer; he sees farmers marching towards him with guns.

'Bang! A young man shot out of nowhere, rushing along in white flannels. His face was serene and shining. He, too, had been overcome by the remoteness of the place. He got as much of a start on seeing me as I had on seeing him. He said, 'Tricky path, isn't it?'

'Yes, very.'

And he bounded off like a spring lamb.

My hands were scratched with thorns, my only pair of trousers torn from brambles and barbed wire. I staggered past the grey-stone farm and continued for a long distance, looking for a way from the cliffs down to the seashore. I tripped up over roots, but each time managed to regain my balance before falling and dropping the blackberries.

At last I reached a cleft where one could scramble down without too much difficulty. Then I came a real cropper, tumbling squash on an eiderdown of blackberries. Hundreds spilled from the upturned basket and trickled down the cliff.

My hand was cut. Blood mingled with blackberry juice. It was useless to try to collect the fallen treasure: it would be too crushed and dirty to eat. Damn! To have an accident within four yards of safe, sandy ground. Why hadn't I fallen at the beginning of the day?

The way home seemed interminable now. I trailed along the shore, dripping blood. My feet sank in the sand. At Waterloo House, Mrs Childs of Charmouth produced iodine and a strip of clean linen. 'There's no harm done. We must give you a good tea.' And she did! Jam tarts which I heaped with Devonshire cream.

This evening I looked over the typescript. I can think of nothing more to add to it. There's no point in staying on here if I can't work. Why not admit defeat? I'll go home tomorrow with one act under my arm. And if my father wonders why we didn't finish this opus, well, after all, Barrie wasn't able to continue with *Shall We Join the Ladies*!

Part VII

London: New Directions
1926, 1927 and 1928

Perhaps word had got around that my charges for home-made photographs were modest; certainly it became apparent that the new friends, whom I photographed, had friends also interested in being perpetuated by my Kodak, for the front door bell now never ceased to ring. Although this brought complaint from Loins that he was run off his legs, it meant for me a steady trickle of 'cash'.

It was Allanah Harper, more than anyone else, who showed me a London life less conventional than the one at home, and gave me my first glimpses of the 'illuminati'.

I had first noticed Allanah—bored and cowlike, dressed in an apricot tube at a ball, at the Hyde Park Hotel. But Allanah had broken away from the débutante world, and, much to her mother's disapproval, discarded her ostrich feather fan and silver kid-shoes in favour of a highwayman's cape and buckles. She now made a niche for herself in the half-worlds of Chelsea and Bloomsbury, and gave me the key to that fascinating other-life for which I had always been searching.

My appetite was uncurbed for closer acquaintance with those glorious people whose works were published by the Hogarth Press, who painted in mud colours or lived in Gordon Square in rooms decorated by Duncan Grant. I longed to be included among those fortunates who eat at the Eiffel Tower or at Boulestin before going on to a Private View of Marie Laurencin or Gaudier Brzeska at the Leicester Galleries. I hankered to be one of the 'first-nighters' of the Phoenix Society or at the expressionist German film 'Dr Caligari'. Surprisingly, I succeeded in making friends with some of these splendid creatures: Raymond Mortimer included me at a luncheon in his dining-room with walls covered with varnished foreign newspapers. Talk was not of Mr Baldwin and unemployment but of 'Les Six', D. H. Lawrence, Lydia Lopokova's marriage to Maynard Keynes, and Lady Ottoline's contretemps with Siegfried Sassoon. The blood seemed to quicken through my veins and I sensed a marvellous freedom of the spirit. The glow on my horizon was not fashionably muddy but rose-dawned.

October 18th 1926, 61 Sussex Gardens

I worked on a book jacket most of the morning. Whenever I felt stale and yawny I went upstairs and danced energetic Charlestons to the gramophone, wishing I were on the stage. In the evening, Allanah Harper rang me up to go with her to a dance. I arrived before Allanah—so embarrassing—to find an incongruous, anonymous crowd who had got together for no apparent reason. A fair-haired woman, who had seen me on the Lido, took compassion on me. She introduced me to the host, an equivocal, furtive little man of sinister complexion.

It was an inexplicable assortment of people—one or two fat débutantes in taffeta, with fat dowagers whose dresses smelled of camphor. One woman, whom I discovered was named the Countess Lovatelli, seemed to be disguised as a tree. She stood smiling enigmatically wrapped in green and gold brocade with a wreath of smilax on her green turban. I made futile conversation with a Lady Parker and her dull-as-ditchwater daughter. I wished Allanah would come. The fair-haired lady who had seen me at the Lido smiled every time I looked up.

At last Allanah! But with her was a nameless man with pale canary hair parted in the centre, looking like a plump Victorian housemaid. I took a violent dislike to him. He struck me as being a pig and an unpleasant personality to boot. His buttery lips and cheese-smelling nostrils reminded me of a dairy shop.

Allanah—a nice, dimpled baby—was the favourite of the evening. Everyone rushed up to her. I could hardly get a word in edgeways. Lady Dean Paul monopolised her, a magpie spectre, with her hair half white and half black. Eventually Allanah looked surreptitiously around her, murmured something about this being a bore and shouldn't we go to the Gargoyle.

Then we spotted Teddie Gerrard, the retired revue star. I hadn't seen her for donkey's years, but used to think her the last gasp in the days when she innovated backless dresses and huskily croaked, 'We're so glad to see you're back, dear lady!' (That was in my favourite Palace revue, *Bric-à-brac*.) She looked like a panther, then; hard and cruel eyes turned up at the corners. She was the essence of sex appeal.

Tonight, Teddie Gerrard seemed more remarkable than ever before. Her skin was burnt a cigar-leaf brown and was as firm as an arab boy's. She wore a dress of black satin with white-bead embroidery, also short, white kid gloves and diamond bracelets. Tight round her neck were the largest false pearls I have ever seen. Her hair was bound up in black satin. Her eyes still seemed as slitty and chinky as a Mongolian's.

I stood agape, watching her from the top of some stairs. She was quite drunk, quite unaffected by the years—a perpetual tomboy. She hooted with foghorn laughter. She sat on someone's knee, tried to be a vampire and toppled over backwards on to the floor, hurting her elbow.

Dancing began. I jigged with good old Allanah, pure and sane. Then I found myself partner to Teddie Gerrard, who whirled me round the room singing at the top of her voice and shocking the last of the dowagers off to their beds. I felt a little wild and un-respectable, dancing with this drunken houri! But our abandon inspired Lady Dean Paul's daughter Brenda to rival us with an energetic and hilarious Charleston.

Teddie Gerrard doubled up and tried to do likewise, but couldn't. She yelled in her hoarse voice, 'I only do that sort of thing when I'm paid for it!' She then became more and more tight, rushed round the room waving her arms and (without being paid) sang songs of days gone by. She took delight in teasing Allanah, dashed up saying, 'You're a great, fat lump! Lump, a great lump! Great, fat lump!' Once or twice, beside herself, she shouted out such obscene retorts as 'balls!' Then, through the alcoholic veil, she realised she had over-stepped the bounds. Her eyes would pop and she'd cover her open mouth with a gloved hand.

She then assumed dignity as she surveyed the scene through *lorgnettes*. This prompted her to clutch my face and say, 'Oh, you're beautiful, beautiful! Look at your eyes! you've got no lids! Neither have I. That makes the space between your lashes and brows so marvellous! Augustus John says it is the most important part of a face. You've got no eyelids and neither have I. Oh, I adore beauty!' She clutched my face again, turning it to see me in profile while Allanah and the 'dairymaid' giggled. Teddie Gerrard decided to start a club for people without eyelids and made me a charter member: 'I'm giving a little party here tomorrow. You must come!'

Her exit was spectacular. Too drunk to walk, she pretended that her little toe hurt, then lurched up the stairs. Her cloak was given to her. She pulled it over her back as though it were a bath towel. There followed a deafening crash and Miss Teddie Gerrard had vanished.

Attention now shifted to Lady Dean Paul, who played her own compositions at the piano. 'I'm drunk,' La Poldowska, or whatever she calls herself professionally, candidly remarked to her audience. Yet in spite of this confession Lady D. P. remembered everything she had ever written—*Femme Laide*. The Caledonian Market Suite, Midnight Blues, and one vulgar but effective number called Those Cud-Cud-Cuddle Blues.

We danced, we played Nuts in May, we did Viennese waltzes and lancers and a Children's Dancing Class. Everyone 'talked common'—the smart thing to do at the moment: 'That's a bit of all right; I don't mind if I do; oo-er!' How tiresome it becomes. I looked at Allanah and appreciated her nice baby air among all these fly-blown revellers.

I came home in a taxi, sharing it with the 'dairymaid'. I suspected he was a sponger and, sure enough, he borrowed ten shillings from me.

October 19th

I got ready for Teddie Gerrard's party, shaving carefully in case she should clutch at my face again.

143

Off again in a taxi to Yeoman's Row. (How is it that one goes twice to the same place, by the same route, and yet the fare on the meter is different?) I met Allanah on the doorstep. Together, we faced the music.

Teddie was all dressed up to the nines again. She wore an embroidered silver dress and a tiara. She looked thoroughly sheepish as she met my eye.

Two old men, who had been drunk last night, arrived and started to get drunk again tonight. The 'dairymaid' sidled in. Irene Dean Paul tottered about, looking like a Marie Laurencin poodle in a checked, tailor-made suit with a pink blouse. She said, 'I'm a disgrace. I'm not dressed, I'm not clean, and my head wants re-dipping!' There were now about two inches of white hair showing at the roots.

With Teddie Gerrard tonight was her young lover. I'd met him on the Lido, but he didn't utter then or now. He always looks completely miserable. I suppose it is his pose, or else he's blasé. At sixteen he was reputed to be the most precocious youth ever, driving racing cars and having affairs with all the most famous beauties in continental casinos. Now he gives the impression of an unhappy puppy, bored and insolent. Teddie Gerrard is mad about him.

At dinner I sat next to Allanah. Teddie Gerrard, despairing of her silent lover, chipped in on our conversation about Gertrude Stein.

After dinner Lady Dean Paul played as usual. It was impossible to believe we weren't in hell, repeating last night's festivities all over again: the same people, the same dark room and the same dingy things in it.

Then we danced. Once Teddie's silent lover forgot himself so far as to do a Charleston and stand on his head. But he soon went back to a sofa with a wrinkle on his forehead, there to be pawed by the old vampire. I didn't feel best pleased with Teddie Gerrard tonight, partly because it wasn't *my* face she was clutching!

Butter lips shared my taxi home. This time he borrowed a pound.

November 22nd
Baby Jungman started to taunt Eleanor while she was being

photographed. 'That's right. Put on the well-known Lady Eleanor Smith, wistful expression.'

Later, when I was trying to photograph the two heads together Eleanor mocked Baby in return. But instead of employing her usual hyperbole, 'I would have you know you'll be the cynosure of all eyes!' Eleanor made grunting noises like a pig, and jabbed Baby viciously in the ribs with a wicked elbow. They then both became two peevish children fighting: 'Oh, Baby, turn your ugly face away, you annoy me.'

'Shan't.'

'Shall.'

'Shan't.'

'Shall.'

'Oh, dry up.'

'Your face makes me sick.'

'So does yours!'

This made the photographer's instructions somewhat of an irrelevant interruption.

November 23rd

I went to Selfridge's and was bitterly disappointed at the negatives of Eleanor.

With all that badinage, she moved just as most of the pictures were snapped. Also, I took any number of them out of focus! In my excitement at having 'got' Lord Birkenhead's daughter, I lost my head and misjudged the distance.

Life is hard for a climber!

November 27th

Cyril Connolly paid me a visit, though I've hardly seen him since our days of friendship at St Cyprian's.

Odd that a person so devastatingly intellectual should give the impression of so little aesthetic sense. He falters when talking of pictures.

Cyril is devilishly amusing. He can be very scathing about other people, but I think he likes me! We talked about the paintings in body colour on brown paper I used to do at St Cyprian's, also our intrigues against Flip. We discussed book covers. Cyril asked me to do a wrapper for the psychological travel book he is completing.

I showed him photographs. They obviously didn't interest him very much.

CYRIL
CONNOLLY
RESTING.

BABA AS HELPMATE

December 4th

I made preparations for a whopping batch of enlargements. I mixed acids in four different wash basins, spread an old mackintosh on the carpet and wrapped the usual scarlet flannel shirt around my bedside light bulb. What an amateur darkroom! But it works—sometimes.

Baba and I set to printing cheerfully after dinner. We distracted ourselves from the labour by talking ghastly French or imitating poor Auntie Jessie. Modom is an invitation to mimicry, yet one never exhausts her idiosyncrasies. She speaks in a sing-song, mysterious voice, employing slang expressions. She has the excitable yet humble *naïveté* of a child. The slightest thing amazes her: the women in the bus are 'so well dressed!' She screams with pleasure at receiving a post card or just looking out the window. She enjoys working people up, like a tot telling a fairy story. She relishes mentioning awful things.

Shortly after ten o'clock, Baba begins to yawn audibly. I take this as a hint that she wants to go to bed. She goes, but I continue by myself. Sometimes I am unable to stop. I get cold and stiff; my joints crack. Then the batch of photographs is taken to the bathroom, where they are left swirling up and down and round in a basin of running water. I clear up the mess in my bedroom. I am as careful as possible not to drop acid on the green carpet.

The floor boards creak horribly, which I fear will waken my father, whose snores can be heard from below. Later, the running water is stopped, the prints are put on an upturned screen, I open wide the window and sink into bed.

December 5th

The whole day spent mounting and retouching last night's enlargements. My back ached with leaning over so much. Photographs sap all my energy; but once I've started I go on in a state of coma, doing the dull spade work without thinking.

After dinner Baba and I again set to work enlarging, doing a number of prints on shiny paper—these for the press. The enlarger light was switched on for the exposure. One, two, three. Sometimes the negative was so opaque that we had to count up till forty. The light switched off, we then slipped the paper into the acid. Our technique has certainly improved. We used to get such poor results, as I am not a bit scientific and never keep a record of time exposures. In fact, I am ashamed of being so inept at the technical side of the game.

At last Baba dropped a yawning hint. I hate to see her go, but even ten o'clock is late for a gangling schoolgirl. Yet I won't feel guilty: I pay her fivepence an hour.

I went on by myself; and later, in an experimental mood, decided to make dada-like designs by placing various objects on sensitised paper. It was my first attempt at this sort of thing. I experimented with shapes and textures, using glass animals, vases, bits of flowers and scattered birdseed.

Excited by the results, I crept downstairs to the drawing-room and conservatory to collect suitable loot for further endeavours. If anyone had encountered me on the stairs, they would surely have thought me a burglar laden with bits of chandelier, wire netting, a dishcloth, pieces of cotton, matches, vases, brooches and spiky coral necklaces.

I created any number of designs. Each effort encouraged another. It was fascinating to produce such contrasting tones and subtle textures, much finer than the results from any lens photograph.

At five o'clock I went to bed. My brain buzzed with new ways to employ this method.

December 6th

I took photographs of a spoilt rich woman who had been sent to me by Billie Williams. I was alarmed to discover she had a glass eye that somehow always looked in the opposite direction to her good one. Yet I tried to find the kindest angles.

When the pictures were heavily retouched and mounted, I telephoned to her. The message came back: please to go round and show them at once. I went, feeling a little uneasy. I waited with the package in a florid drawing-room. Then the lady clacked in in bedroom slippers, a gasper wobbling on the end of her lips.

'Let's see.' With her one eagle eye she pierced the proofs. 'Ow, I like *that*! Ow, *that's* a good one! Ow, they're lovely!'

I felt overwhelmingly relieved. I came away a quarter of an hour later with a cheque for seven pounds ten in my pocket! A good day's work done already, and it was still only eleven-thirty.

EDITH SITWELL

December 7th

Allanah was to bring Edith Sitwell to lunch. Afterwards, I'd take photographs.

Edith arrived, a tall, graceful scarecrow with the white hands of a mediaeval saint. At first I felt she was 'making conversation', but soon she relaxed completely. She told stories with measured flourish and effect. A great actress, she can keep a room in fits of laughter.

I had expected Edith Sitwell to be ethereal and beyond worldly concepts. But to my surprise, she embarked upon a pungent assessment of people and events. She fired comic broadsides at Drinkwater and Squire, also shaking a little pepper on Ethel M. Dell, Hannen Swaffer and Tallulah Bankhead. Gradually, I found her formidable aspect less striking than her sympathetic girlishness. In spite of her cadaverous appearance, her complexion is as fresh as a convolvulus, and she has a disarming girlish manner of not being able to contain her laughter.

Lunch was a success. Edith ate heartily of a piping hot fish *soufflé* which was a triumph, except that it had bones in it. Manley[1] offered red or white wine at the same time, and to make matters worse had placed the bottles on a mingy little tray he had picked

[1] Our butler, Loins's successor.

Dame Edith Sitwell, surrounded by Tchelitchew drawings in her
Manresa Road flat

Osbert, Edith and Sacheverell Sitwell

up from heaven-knows-where. Edith, when approached, entolled in her bell-clear voice, 'White, please.' During dessert she recited a bit of Gertrude Stein's 'Portrait of Tom Eliot': 'Silk and wool, silken wool, woollen silk.' How precisely and richly she spoke. She could make any rubbish sound like poetry.

Edith Sitwell

I could hardly contain my impatience and delight as we went up to my sisters' bedroom for the afternoon's photography. She posed instinctively. No matter how many positions I had already taken, I felt loth to call a halt. Surely this was an unique opportunity. I must perpetuate the image in front of me, of a young faun-like creature sitting against my leaping-fawn design, looking surprisingly Victorian in her crudely-cut Pre-Raphaelite dress, with her matador's jet hat, and necklace, her long mediaeval fingers covered with enormous rings. When the hat was discarded, she became a Brontë heroine, and her pale silken hair fell in rats' tail wisps about her face, while the big teapot handle bun made the nape of her neck appear even more impossibly slender.

As the afternoon wore on, I suggested more exotic poses. I even persuaded her to asphyxiate under the glass dome. She became quite hysterical kneeling on the floor, her knees and

F

joints popping and cracking. A Chinese torture she called it, but loved it all the same.

I, meanwhile, had my own agonies. The camera kept going wrong, the film got stuck and couldn't be wound further. I excused myself, crossed the landing to my room, pulled down the blind and unrolled the film.

At last Edith left to 'finish a poem' she was in the middle of. I caught an approving twinkle in her eye as she left. It meant that we were going to be friends. I remembered a letter Kyrle had written to me in answer to a *cri de coeur* of mine. I had begged for his advice. 'What on earth can I become in life?' He had replied: 'I wouldn't bother too much about *being* anything in particular, just become a friend of the Sitwells, and wait and see what happens.'

After today's photographic session my eyes ached from looking into the unshielded photographic bulbs. I could see wiggling scarlet and green worms everywhere. Hastily I changed for dinner, as Billie Williams was taking me to the ballet.

What a rush life has become!

A RUSH OF ORDERS

December 9th

The telephone bell rings all day long. It seems that the young girls I've lately come in contact with have nothing better to do than to call me: 'Take me out; take my photograph again and let me bring Tanis, Meraud, Honey and Rosamond . . .'

I'm generally in a compliant mood. If there is any complaint, it's simply that I spend too much time on the drudge work connected with photography. Lately, however, I've been giving Selfridge's photographic department nearly all the developing. This morning I traipsed there for the fifty millionth time to get the results of Edith Sitwell. The camera had leaked: light got in and spoiled a number of negatives. It would!

Soon after lunch, Inez brought Honey, Rosamond, etc., to be photographed. After almost every pose the camera got stuck; I had to go into my darkened bedroom and tug at the film.

Inez, very businesslike, suggests that I give her a commission on each girl she brings to be photographed. It sounds all right to me.

The girls sat round in various stages of *décolleté*, as I like to take bare shoulders. With everyone in her slip, the room looked like a dormitory. (When I was photographing the Du Maurier sisters, outspoken Daphne said it looked like a brothel.) Inez chatted and smoked cigarettes, sometimes holding the lights above the girls' heads for me.

We had a riotous afternoon. Inez's friends kept saying they hadn't enjoyed themselves so much for ten years; in fact, not since the last time they'd been photographed. Meanwhile, I tried to keep my head and bring into play all the stunts and tricks I've developed.

December 18th

There were endless photographs to be done. A glut of Tanis Guinness turned out beautifully. I love her fat face, her enormous eyes with tulip-petal lids.

I sat for hours under a light, retouching prints with pencil and paint. Then I steamed them over a kettle in the cook's den downstairs; mounted them with secotine and put the cards to press under the leg of some heavy furniture. Then more hours enlarging: I persisted in making endless prints of the same picture until I got one worthy of being sold.

I stopped at ten o'clock, as I was invited to Madge Garland's bottle party. Mum knew I was going out, but we had to keep it from Dad. Last night Reggie had been stupid enough to stay on at a nightclub until five o'clock. Dad is generally a sound sleeper, but by some misfortune he woke up and heard Reggie returning surreptitiously. There was a terrific row. I had difficulty getting away unnoticed. Mum kept *cave* for me. I couldn't stop laughing at the sight of her in her nightgown, face soused in grease and terrified eyes beckoning me to come on or go back. She allowed me to take a bottle of champagne to the party, as it's Christmas.

December 20th

The Christmas rush is on. Everyone wants last-minute photographs taken for presents. I am up to my navel in work. This morning was such a pandemonium I hadn't a jiffy to shave or dress smartly. I grovelled on the floor in a dirty old sweater and flannel trousers, mounting and retouching masses of prints. The pink work room got strewn with rubbish. My mother came to the door, looked and sighed woefully, 'This room will never be the same again.'

Anyway, I did a good day's work and sent off several large packages, including the glass-eyed woman's order.

January 14th 1927

Today is my twenty-second birthday. Yet the last few years have meant so little to me, compared with my early life. How impressed one was, how cut with emotions as a child! Now I feel that life has slowed down to half pace. I'm rather thick-skinned, and things don't seem quite as important or vital as they once were. Life has become more or less routine.

Twenty-two, damn it! Hell take it! Or no! I do believe it is twenty-three! Yes, I was born in 1904. Good Lord, I'm twenty-three!

In my suit of plus fours, I felt like a new person. I then went hunting for a place to use as a photographic studio. Now that my photographs have become well-known, I can make a great deal of money if I start in a business way.

I went to estate agents. I'd like a mews in Mayfair, an amusing place where I could not only click away but also paint and read and telephone my friends. I want to do the place up to look like my own, with cages full of chirping birds.

WEEKEND AT WILSFORD

The weekend party described below was the first of many others to be spent at Wilsford. This Elizabethan-esque manor-house in the Wylye valley, was created by the mystical Lady Glenconner, at this time married to Lord Grey of Falloden. Living with her was her youngest son, Stephen Tennant, a golden-haired young man who resembled the youthful Shelley. I had first met this remarkably poetic-looking apparition while he rode the papiermâché horses on the roundabouts at the Olympia circus. He was surrounded, as usual, by an adoring group of Guinness girls. He wore a black leather coat with a large Elizabethan collar of chinchilla. As he blew kisses to left and right, he created an unforgettable sight.

Ever since Stephen had published, at a very early age, a book of his poems, The Vein in the Marble, *illustrated with his own Beardsleyesque drawings, he was brought up, by his mother, to be a genius. Although he lead a semi-invalid life, which no doubt encouraged him to evade the more unpleasant aspects of reality, his health had recently improved; in fact he created an impression of galvanised vitality.*

Stephen could give a verbal fireworks display that was brilliantly funny. His ability to make people laugh was brought out, not in repartee, but in declamations on a definite subject, or in descriptions of past experience. Sitting around his silver bed, such critics as Rebecca West, Elinor Wylie and Arthur Waley, would be sent into paroxysms of amusement while Stephen regaled them with fantasies about restocking his reptillery or ordering all the exotic specialities from the bottled fruits department at Fortnum & Masons.

It is always difficult to re-create the humour of the past: so much depends on the timing and the nuances of the performer's personality. And, jokes that strike us as original at one period, soon show signs of becoming dated.

Since I never wrote down any of Stephen's flights of inspiration, I cannot vouch for their successfully bridging the gap of years. I can only state that, at the time, they were inimitable.

WILSFORD

January 15th

I was met at Salisbury station and motored through the dusk to Wilsford Manor. It turned out to be a greystone manor house, with parrots, lizards, Morris chintzes, and flagstones. The long, panelled drawing-room created a comfortable and informal air with its enormous soft chairs, bowls of fat hyacinths, sweet smelling freesias and an untidy litter of books.

Lady Grey, plump finger tips in the air, beamed her greetings, eyes bright and small. Stephen wore plus-four trousers and a lizard-skin belt. Zita and Baby Jungman both looked countrified in wool and tweeds. Dolly Wilde,[1] raven hair shingled, and oyster face plastered with powder, wore vitriolic purple and reclined like a decadent Roman empress.

We sat on the floor in front of a great log fire, at which an

[1] Miss Dorothy Wilde, niece of Oscar Wilde.

153

extravagantly exotic scented elixir was burnt in a long handled spoon. I felt awed by Lady Grey, gracious and queenly as a fairy godmother. But soon she left the young people to themselves.

Stephen talked like a rocket going off. Dolly, never expecting that she might have inherited her uncle's wit, continually managed to say clever, funny things as if by a fluke. Her eyes widened with astonishment at each *bon mot*, and she exploded as heartily as anyone in the ensuing laughter. Baba Brougham[1] hunched her shoulders, chuckled in spite of a cold and encouraged cleverness with, 'Oh, that's good! Oh, my! That's very witty!' Baby tossed a strand of flaxen hair out of her eyes and chuckled contagiously; Zita looking like Trilby with her page's cap of hair, had a gentle quiet voice like honey, or milk that is slightly off. I love them both.

Steven Runciman added a note of erudition. He told historical anecdotes, including a grotesque account of Louis XIV's heart. It seems that, many years after the Sun King's death, his heart was transported to England with much ceremony and reverence. While being exhibited on a salver at some reception, it was mistaken for a little cake and eaten by a short-sighted clergyman!

At dinner, I warmed to Lady Grey when she regaled us with nonsense. She told about the woman who wanted to have diamonds put in her teeth so that she could even say. 'Good morning' brilliantly.

Afterwards we played a game of 'Analogies'; also various word games, including one called 'Interesting Questions', I was very bad at that, being so ill-educated. But, by dint of being funny instead of knowledgeable, I managed to come out fairly well. Steven Runciman wrote about me: 'My Mother: Lady Colefax. My Father: Cardinal Mazarin. My Teacher: Leonardo da Vinci. My governess: a piece of porcelain. My skeleton in the cupboard: a kind heart. What would I save from the fire: myself.'

I considered this weekend the beginning of a new life. At last I found myself among people with kindred interests. Moreover these people seemed to like me, whereas at home I feel misunderstood, somewhat of an idiot and a nuisance. Undressing in front of the fire that glowed welcome to me in this strange Honeysuckle Bedroom, I was happy and thankful after so many months of having fought desperately. If I hadn't made a move from

[1] The Hon. Eleanor Brougham.

the Holborn office I should still be at odds with the world—miserable, unsuccessful and undeveloped.

MY PARENTS' SILVER WEDDING

March 7th, 1928

Today was Mummie's and Daddy's silver wedding day. At first there had been vague plans for a party. Several weeks ago, Mum suggested 'having some people in' and even employing a pianist; but since she inevitably avoids making any move or decision, nothing had been done about it and no one had been invited. It was just as well: this house is too small for a party. Besides, whom would we have asked?

We all foregathered for such festivity as had been hastily planned this evening. Aunt Jessie, wearing an old evening dress under a day overcoat, was in high spirits and determined, whatever happened, to enjoy or at least make the best of the event. I hadn't seen Mum earlier in the day, and tried to be nice. But I couldn't congratulate her, couldn't tender wishes or whatever one does on a silver wedding day. I was deeply shy and uncomfortable, wishing the whole thing had never come about. It seemed merely sad that my parents should have been married so long.

Worse, I felt miserable and beastly for judging my parents' life as being drab and dull. What a fatuous fool I am, living in a largely self-invented world of wit, brains and money. How dare I judge my parents' humble efforts? I detest myself for it, yet their world is not for me. Their aura warps and rots me until I am without any spirit.

Anyway, I was a part of tonight's family party and must enjoy it just as Aunt Jessie seemed to be doing. After dinner, there would be the inevitable theatre. Whenever any of us has a birthday or anniversary, dress circle seats are taken at a theatre where the play is sure to have been running for some considerable time. Tonight we would see Gerald du Maurier in a piece that had received bad notices. But the choice was made in desperation: Daddy vetoed everything else. He'd read through the list, hated George Grossmith so that cut out *Lady Mary*, couldn't bear Noel Coward so *The Second Man* had to be forsaken, and so on.

I sat watching Daddy mix three crude, orange-coloured cocktails. Mama and Modom held the results high in their fingers, then sipped. Poppa, who had already changed, kept pulling out his heavy, old-fashioned gold watch and chain. I subsided on a sofa, listening to Modom's jovial reminiscences of the wedding day. It is extraordinary how unintimate we are with our parents. They never talk about things past. I've no idea what sort of people my mother's parents were, what their house in Cumberland was like, where my parents met or any such sentimentally interesting items. Yet here was Modom spurting out all sorts of amusing gossip. 'Oh, Etty, do you remember how it rained? Do you remember the thunder? Do you remember how that boy lost Ernest's hat? Ernest said, "Now be careful, don't lose it." "No sir," and then, of course, when it was wanted it wasn't to be found. Oh, the thunder! I shall never forget the peals of thunder when you were cutting the cake. The carriage horses were terrified! Had it stopped raining by the time you got off?'

'Got off? A very suitable expression,' said Papa. This rather typical joke of his struck me as being chillingly unfunny, but Modom threw back her head and screamed with golden-hearted laughter. Daddy looked at his gold watch again.

Dinner was rather more elaborate than usual, with extra ornaments on the table; salmon, roast chicken, champagne and toasts.

'Well, here's luck for health, wealth and happiness during the *next* twenty-five years,' Aunt Jessie raised her glass.

'Best wishes,' was all I could gulp. Then my father nearly killed me, as he held his glass in front of his mouth, nodded sheepishly to my mother and said, 'Well, I'll take on the job for another twenty-five years.'

Reggie exploded with laughter, his face red and shining. 'I think that's jolly funny: take on the job for another twenty-five years!'

Sitting next to me, Baba remained very quiet. She is sensitive, and I daresay it was all as painful to her as it was to me. But we didn't discuss it afterwards.

No one at the table would ever think about this scene again.

After dinner the gold watch came out again. 'Oh, Ernest, there's plenty of time. It doesn't take a minute to put our things on.'

'Well, you always say that, but in point of fact it does take time.

I was only suggesting that you should start to put your things on.'

Aunt Jessie and I went in a taxi, as there was not enough room in the car. Modom talked hard all the way. I tried to concentrate: what was she saying? Something about walking so far this afternoon in order to save some bus fare! Yet Auntie, on this anniversary, had filled our drawing-room with lilies. I thought, 'Here I am, having spent the day jumping into taxis, and I didn't even buy my parents a bunch of violets.'

The six of us sat in a line in the fourth row of the dress circle. Daddy wore his spectacles and hunched his shoulders. Mummie had on a home-made dress and an old moleskin cape that offended my eyes. The light in which she sat made her hair appear tangerine, though I noticed it was pale at the parting. Baba looked white and anaemic; Reggie was just an ordinary young man. Auntie burbled next to me, her hair dyed rotten, then crimped and curled and kept in place with many slides.

I was suddenly overwhelmed. My heart cracked in two for love of them, and with shame at my snobbish uneasiness over their appearance and the ordinary commendable goodness of their lives.

The play was bad as it was said to be, but I saw it only through a veil of my private unhappiness.

THE PHILOSOPHY OF BOY LEBAS

April 1st

Tremendous omission: I forgot to write about such an important thing as going to see Boy in his flat.

It was an impressive visit, and I came away filled with admiration. Not so long ago Boy was moping about, looking ill and refusing to speak much. Then he left his family; since that time he is living every moment of his life, thinks hard and works hard. Even his leisure hours are spent reading good books, not smart rot.

It is positively inspiring to see what a strong person Boy has become. I've more confidence in him than ever before. He has even become sufficiently detached to look upon my half-baked social world with tolerance.

Boy's apartment, on the top of a fat Georgian house in Golden

F*

Square, is typical of his new life—completely utilitarian, with no ornaments or silly art effects. The whole place has been white-washed out; the furniture could scarcely be simpler. On huge book shelves he keeps only the books he will read, having sold that half of his collection which he knew he would never begin.

As a result of his mind training, Boy doesn't waste a single minute of the day feeling half dead or taking things for granted. Every experience is vital. His only motive is a determination to perfect himself. He has long since got beyond wanting fame or any of the nonsense *I* want.

Boy says, 'One cannot escape from oneself. One *is* oneself at every moment. One must keep oneself as true and right as possible. It isn't good enough to know that one is doing wrong and then continue to do it all the same.'

He didn't show me any of his paintings; but I have a feeling Boy will achieve greatness because he thinks the right way, which is what matters. In fact, I got so carried away when he started to analyse *my* position that I nearly decided then and there to give up the petty, self-indulgent life I lead.

I suddenly saw myself as lazy and sloppy compared with Boy; my life is such a finicky frivol. Boy explained that I had got into this state by taking nothing seriously at Cambridge. As under-graduates, we were cynical, smart, amusing, publishing our failings and faults and laughing about them. We were too busy with foolishness to realise how sterile our existences were. How perverse and disgusting!

I really *lived* in Boy's room. I felt freshly inspired with vigour. The evening was so much better than anything I'd done for ages. How stupidly and consciously affected my designs are. I *am* I, too, and I am capable of being better. I should become like Montaigne and renounce the world at a certain age, giving up all vain thoughts of fame. Fame is only the desire to win recognition from a mob I fundamentally despise.

We had a simple dinner. Boy cooked the new potatoes. His eyes sparkled like a baby's when he opened a tin of expensive coffee. It was expensive, it was good, and he thoroughly ap-preciated that to the full. Out of custom, I should doubtless have opened the tin without any feeling whatsoever.

I didn't leave until an unearthly hour of the morning, but went away with my brain working at full speed. I read Montaigne in bed, and it was almost dawn by the time I fell asleep.

How I envy Boy! I hope I shall see him always. I shall go to him whenever I want freshening up. I shall go to him for Holy Communion.

As a result of Boy's influence, I have since felt alive; not merely soddenly comfortable, unquestioning, unnoticing. Before, I would very likely have eaten a Turkish Delight without fully appreciating the enjoyment. But suddenly I realise that at this very moment I am eating T.D. Is it good? Oh, yes. So good! Mm, mm! I am happy to be squelching this delicious, succulent jelly in my mouth.

EASTER OUTINGS

Good Friday, April 2nd

Reggie was up early. In a great state of excitement, he put on his new grey flannel trousers and went off to Brighton with Raymond[1] for the Easter holidays. They are staying at Harry Preston's hotel, being charged thirty shillings a day. God, what a holiday! I should loathe it: Brighton! And expensive, too!

Mum and Daddy quarrelled, as they couldn't decide where to go for Easter (and Mummie needs a change very badly indeed). Each blamed the other for not having come to some definite conclusion beforehand.

In any case, we went for a picnic in the car. I decided to be thoroughly lazy and good-natured, but to enjoy myself none the less. At all times, I must control my mind and not sit like dead mutton. Thanks to Boy, I will henceforth live as fully as I can.

It was a little difficult to do this in a cramped car. Everyone, including Becky[2], came along for the ride. Also, how can one keep alert and alive with unstimulating people?

The weather was unexpectedly brilliant; the trees were just budding and nature, at any rate, seemed alive. We motored to Turner's Hill, intending to have our lunch trespassing on Lord Cowdray's estate. But since our last visit, the preserves have become more formal and inaccessible. So we drove about the neighbourhood, looking for a suitable picnic ground. At last an

[1] Raymond Crump, a school friend and cricket enthusiast.
[2] The family dog, named after the character in my father's favourite book.

ideal place was found. Down through a field we went, into a valley of wiry saplings. Here it was prettily carpeted with delicate but fat primroses, wild violets and a few early bluebells.

The bluebell wood started a chain of thoughts in my mind. It was just the sort of place I used to sketch at Harrow, when the art class went out on half-holidays with W. Egerton Hine, our art master.

Poor little white-haired Eggie (Boy tells me he is dead). He dearly loved sketching in a bluebell wood. He wasn't much of an aesthete; but he had great technique, and under his guidance we became enthusiastic disciples. Here's another landscape! And another! The whole countryside—cottage gardens, moors, churchyards, farmyards and even manure heaps—all was grist to his effortless output or our glib imitations. Using a lot of raw sienna, burnt umber and a touch of prussian blue, we covered the Wattman Nott with fake W. Egerton Hines masterpieces.

Eggie and his assistant Mr Vallance took us on many enjoyable expeditions. By Metropolitan railway we went to neighbouring stations (Ruislip or Pinner) where, apart from art, there was the joy of a cream tea at a farmhouse and surreptitious cigarette smoking in a church tower.

Once each winter we were herded along to the National Gallery in London, where Eggie made no bones about resenting the inclusion of the El Grecos. In summer he would take us to the Royal Academy. But first we'd lunch at Frascati's, where Eggie and Mr Vallance always haggled over their portions of food. 'Now, Mr Vallance, if you will give me that potato, I will give you a bit of my spaghetti.' 'Mr Hine, if you would give me a bit of your meat, I will give you one of these sausages!'

How Boy and I laughed! In fact, most of the pupils ragged the poor man terribly. A legend even sprang up, to the effect that poor Eggie had never in his whole life been to the lavatory.

April 3rd

Papa was determined to motor down to Brighton and see Reggie for a minute, as it was his twenty-first birthday. Momma suggested Reggie wouldn't relish seeing us: he was there for a holiday. But nothing would stop my father, so off we trooped in the car.

I looked forward to seeing Brighton again. I wanted to go to the antique shops in the Lanes. And it would be amusing, at last, to get a glimpse inside the Royal York Hotel with its celebrities room. My only worry was that Father would plan our afternoon: he dislikes the Oriental Pavilion and insists on being on the sea front to get the air.

Poor Reggie was trapped. When we got there, Papa had nothing whatsoever to say to him: and, in fact, perhaps through exhaustion at having driven so far, he was in a bad temper. By the end of a dreadful meal at the Royal York, he had worked himself up into a towering rage. Reggie sat at a different table with Raymond. My mother said she thought it the most extraordinary thing that we should motor to Brighton to see Reggie on his twenty-first birthday, and then not have lunch with him and buy a bottle of champagne.

Part VIII

The First Rung

1928

From now on, the diary entries become more sporadic. I felt somewhat guilty at the sight of my journal lying apart like a discarded lover: but life had become too busy for regrets.

Exciting new friends appeared like mushrooms—some brilliant in promise, others already eminent. They became willing sitters for extremely unconventional photographs, and contributed towards an exhibition which a hospitable gallery in Bond Street had offered to promote. Also to be on show were my somewhat amateur stage designs, and some impertinent caricatures, so the exhibition should not be lacking in variety.

The invitations to the Private View were duly addressed and stamped, when Ninnie (called back to give an occasional hand), on her way to post them, slipped and fell in the gutter. Little sympathy was extended to the hurt knee, but anxiety felt that the envelopes should not arrive splashed with mud.

In spite of their grimy summons and a pea soup fog, the crowds arrived in such unexpected numbers, which combined with the density

162

of the atmosphere, almost shut off the exhibits. I knew that success was in my palm when Lady Colefax, a hostess of discrimination, not only spent the morning with her blackcurrant eyes darting from catalogue to people, but returned to do battle in the afternoon's mêlée.

Newspaper journalists pounced ravenously on the more startling aspects of this show, and my name became known, even to the extent that that old walrus, Uncle Wilfred, reported to my family in bewilderment, that it had been used as a joke by a red-nosed comedian in an Edgware Road variety theatre.

Among my new friends the Sitwells were not only helpful in giving my professional career every stimulus, but they comforted me with their allegiance; by finding me good company, they gave me a certain and necessary confidence in myself. In spite of her somewhat forbidding appearance, Edith proved to be the most understanding of human beings. In her Bayswater flat, she was girlishly flustered and surprisingly maladroit. One's heart went out to her as she clumsily knocked over the big brown teapot on her way to answer the door bell to admit Mr Yeats. She would hoot with deep laughter and apologise, 'That's me all over.'

One was never daunted by the intellectual discussions on poetry that followed, although I have no ear for poetry and was quite incapable of playing a part in these debates. Edith, however, was convinced that her problems were the same as everyone else's, and, for my delectation and opinion, would later send me her new poems, written out by the ream in her loping handwriting.

As for the Sitwell brothers, both of them had established a mode of aesthetic existence that completely satisfied my own taste. No detail of their way of life was ugly or humdrum. They managed to give a patina of glamour to a visit to an oculist, a bootshop, or a concert. Each catalogue they received from a wine merchant or a bookseller in their hands became a rare volume. With their aristocratic looks, dignified manner, and air of lofty disdain, they seemed to me above criticism.

A whole new world of sensibility was opened to me while sitting in candlelight around the marble dining table in Osbert's house in Chelsea. Here, it seemed, witty observations, and an appreciation of dolphin furniture, were more important than poor forgotten Mr Skinner's 'big cash'.

I learnt a great deal about the art of living while staying with Sacheverell and his newly-married Georgia in their home in Northampton. Here Sachie held forth, in the deepest coke-crackle voice on *such diverse subjects as the castrati, Offenbach, Norma wreaths, Ingres, or Ronald Firbank. He would produce his rare books on plants and birds, and while listening to a vast collection of gramophone records, he would wear an expression of resigned helplessness or wistful exaspera-tion as he smoked large Turkish cigarettes in boyish, unformed hands.*

More new friends, some of them to become important ingredients in my life, were coralled when a sequel to Lady Grey's Wilsford festivities was staged in the South of France.

A villa was leased by his mother in which Stephen could be cherished by dozens of Guinnesses and other exquisite young girls while conval-escing in the winter sun.

Here, too, for companionship and visual contrast, was old Mrs Belloc Lowndes, a French pastry cook's version of Queen Victoria, digging her podgy fingers deep into the resilient cushions of her dough-coloured face, and rolling her r-r-r's in greedy relish of the succulent meals.

Another face unknown to me among my fellow guests belonged to a rather swarthy and formidable middle-aged woman wearing a tall purple pixie hat. She seemed to eye me with definite disapproval. Lady Grey, always so intently busy communing with birds and the stars, was vague about mundane matters; only fitfully did she think of intro-ducing her friends to one another. When I asked Lady Grey who this critical lady was, the answer in no way gave promise of less forbearance.

'Miss Olivier comes of an old Huguenot family, and is a figure in the archaeological and ecclesiastical life of Wiltshire.' Later I discovered that this was true; but the description was far from resembling the dashing, dazzling person who so soon was to become a lifelong friend. After we had confessed our mutual shyness and struck a chord of mutual sympathy, I began to rely upon Edith Olivier for advice on every conceivable variety of subjects. Until her death many years ahead she wielded over me a wise and efficacious influence.

Edith Olivier had spent most of her life, until his recent death, in quietly looking after her exacting father in the Wilton Rectory. Sud-denly the country robin emerged as a bird of paradise. Her small Gothic dairy-house in the park at Wilton became brimful with such varied characters as Ronald Storrs, Leonard Woolley the explorer, Siegfried Sassoon the poet, and, most cherished of all, Stephen's Slade school friend, Rex Whistler, the promising young painter whose murals at the Tate were not yet completed. Edith started a prolific career as an author; the first of her numerous novels was now about to appear, and her interests became boundless.

The painter Louis Eilshemius in New York

My first New York apartment: Leonide Massine, Oriel Ross, Beverley
Nichols, Miss van Rensaellaer, C.B., Carl Erickson

The bathing pool at William
Randolph Hearst's ranch

C.B. and Anita Loos

William Randolph Hearst

Jigsaw puzzle at St Donat's Castle: Marion Davies, Constance Talmadge, Hedda Hopper, Mrs Samuel Goldwyn

C.B. on the *Edmund Goulding* set in Hollywood

Rex was also staying at the villa, and although he remained always in the background of any gathering, and at first gave an impression of exaggerated retirement, I felt as proud as when a child completely accepts and returns one's friendship, when Rex revealed to me his great gift for intimacy, and decided to come forth from his shell to wield his irresistibly potent brand of charm.

Rex's poetical appearance—the profile like an ivory cameo, and pale unseeing eyes—was, I soon discovered, in contrast to his rugged health and independence of character. In spite of his vagueness and inability to cope with worldy affairs, he could be extremely caustic and was by no means removed from the down-to-earth reality of high life. Rex was always a refreshing companion: each time one met, his frankness and honesty of purpose seemed to grow in effect. Everyone reacted with delighted surprise whenever he entered a room.

At Cap Ferrat, at the suitably named La Primavera, the days went by as we laughed and talked in the sun. The evenings were spent playing guessing and writing games, or somebody would read aloud 'Papillée', Marcus Cheke's fantasy about Paris under the Directoire, or selected pieces from Shelley, Conrad, and Emily Dickinson. The formal parterres blazed with purple spring flowers, green terraces led to gnarled pine trees, grey limestone rocks, and dashing, lashing sapphire sea; existence seemed to consist of day to day delights.

August 1928

August in London can be very pleasant. I enjoyed getting on with my work. I hoped to have some pictures in the Salon of Photography, and also to finish the photographs to be used in the new Arnold Bennett play.

This morning, Viola Tree, vague but confident, said I could come with her to the dress rehearsal of Bennett's play. Viola was typically late, and I had to wait a bit at the stage door. Lady du Maurier, russet-cheeked and flashing of smile, saw me, was horror-struck and flew into a fluster: 'The last person we want to see. He's so hypercritical. If the secret of the play gets out, all is lost.' (The secret was that the play had been written as an up-to-date version of Faust.)

Gerald du Maurier didn't give a damn about the secret, but worried about his make-up. He called to his wife across the footlights in his dry pumice stone voice, and asked if it looked all right. 'Oh, no, Gerald, too pink and white. And the eyes are too dark.'

Gerald waggled all over, then grunted stertorously, 'Well, I'll take some of this muck off my eyes.'

Grace Wilson, the nondescript leading lady, then asked if her make-up was satisfactory. No one bothered to answer. But there followed a long discussion about the length of her skirt. Muriel du Maurier complained that it was too short, showing her knees. Arnold Bennett said he moved in the highest circles; and, 'Believe me, they are worn short.'

Muriel chimed, 'Oh, well, perhaps they are in Paris.'

To my surprise and delight, I found that Osbert and Sachie were in London. Osbert asked me to dine with him and Rex Whistler at Boulestin's, the prettiest restaurant in London, with its deep yellow varnished walls, cloudy mirrors and Dufy designed silks. We sat on *banquettes* and in the most leisurely and epicurean manner, enjoyed Osbert's talk, the cheese sauces and red wines. Osbert has very early in life acquired the grand manner without pomposity. He tells a story with interruptions of 'Huh Huh' as he himself enjoys the humour and looks quickly from one face to another for approval. He is generous in his appreciation of others' attempts at wit, snorting with painful grunts of suppressed laughter during an imitation of some new friend or rival.

When leaving, Osbert fell up the stairs and said, somewhat surprisingly, 'That means good luck.' It seemed so out of character.

Rex and I hadn't seen one another for months, so that there was so much to discuss that we could not now call a halt to the evening. In fact, when Osbert was bundled into a taxi-cab an impetus was given to the outpourings on many subjects in which our host could not have shared. Yattering so volubly that we were oblivious of the direction in which we were going, we walked until I got a hole in my sock. Then we sat on spiked railings, and unaware of the chiming of clocks, gossiped about friends: Stephen's relapse of health, his strange relationship with his mother, his recent friendship with Siegfried Sassoon, a paradoxical combination of characters, the one so flamboyant and the other so retiring.

We talked of Edith Olivier, with whom Rex had just been

staying. Edith, at the best of times, likes to lie on a chaise-longue with her head lower than her legs, while she reads or converses in her sibilant, jerky tones. This time, Edith, having cracked her knee-cap, lay prostrate on her terrace while she read the proofs of her new novel, *As Far as Jane's Grandmother's*.

We discussed Osbert's vicissitudes with his father, who, with his ivory complexion and ginger beard, looks like a Victorian Tintoretto. It seems that, much to Osbert's exasperation, the father's extravagance is now manifesting itself in the removal of an ornamental lake from one side of the Renishaw park to the other.

Rex has a *bonté* towards mankind. Curious about all aspects of his world, he finds the complicated behaviour of some of his friends completely baffling, but his interest in gossip is never malicious. Rex, so romantic with his luminous face, Roman nose, and large crown to his head, exudes warm-heartedness and sympathy, but he is a strangely remote person. I doubt if many people even impinge on his inner feelings. He seems to accept me as a new bosomer, but I wonder if, apart from his deeply reciprocated devotion to Edith, he has really loved anyone.

It was half past two when I left Rex. I felt chilly. I had to wake up Daddy and bathe his eye, as he had poked it badly when looking for a tennis ball. He had visited the oculist several times, but was still in agony.

IN AN AEROPLANE

September, undated

Englebrecht, a Dutchman whom I saw a lot of at Cambridge, has for several years been asking me to see Holland under his guidance. I agreed at last; but as I could only spare a weekend, decided to save time and take an aeroplane. There has been a daily air service to Holland for the past five years and more. It would be 'modern' and commendable of me to go this way; also daring and adventurous.

On the other hand, what if there were an accident and I did not return? I have never wanted to die less than I do at the moment.

I made the decision and bought my ticket. This morning I woke early, shaved in cold water, dressed in a hurry, rushed down before breakfast was ready and waited about with queasy stomach. I wrote important letters in case of my demise until the coffee was ready. My father tramped in, a mass of leather from riding in the Park. He greeted the news of my departure with surprise. 'By aeroplane, really! Hm! Hm!'

I motored to the Victoria Hotel, whence the bus takes one to the Croydon aerodrome. I arrived early and waited in the hotel lobby, feeling unreal. The sensation was very likely helped on by my having taken Mothersill to prevent air sickness.

The aerodrome proved large, clean and new-looking. Distant aeroplanes could be heard starting their engines. My fellow passengers were mostly Dutch, stolid and ugly. The men had short hair and bad complexions. One woman, typically Dutch, looked like a fat pig with silky skin and red hair worn in a soft, old-fashioned way. Atop her head a beaver hat was perched high; and her clothes were unbelievably dowdy.

Everyone was excited. The Dutchmen laughed. We marched towards our aeroplane—no turning back now. I chose a good seat and stuffed cotton wool in my ears. The engines started, buzzing and roaring and racing to a deafening whirr. I laughed aloud. Two blocks of wood were pulled from under the wheels of the plane and off we went. I bent my head forward, touching the window to see everything there was to see. It was like being in a large limousine as we raced round an enormous field on two rubber wheels with the engine going all-out. The rubber wheels whirled round madly, like runaway motor wheels. Then I knew we were ascending: in an instant the grass field had sunk away from us, became smaller and smaller.

Our rubber tyres still revolved jerkily, but with less force and rapidity. Slowly they slackened and stopped. No longer did we depend on them: we flew of our own accord.

The most incredible things were happening outside the window. Everything seemed so unreal as to drive fear out. We scarcely moved, yet below passed a slow procession of absurd scenes: bird's-eye views of churches, town halls, villas, main roads and by-roads peopled with infinitesimal specks. It was impossible to realise that that doll's town below could be the world one lived in. Minute toy houses, complete with Lilliputian back yards, marked out tennis courts, ponds, a patch of grass worn away where a horse was tied. These things surely belonged to an elf.

Washing, hung on a line, looked like the smallest fragments of broken china; sheep might have been fairy lice; and country lanes were mice's tails across green velvet.

Certainly it was impossible that real people should inhabit those tiny boxes; that people should be born, live and die in such confined smallness, eating, sleeping, visiting the lavatory and having love affairs down there. Such a pretty microcosm could not contain any unpleasantnesses. Each cart-horse and labourer looked so finely wrought and elegant; nothing was clumsily hewn; coarseness and squalor had disappeared, leaving a pattern of exquisite delicacy.

I couldn't believe we were high in the air. Flying gave no sense of proportion at all. Sitting in a quietly purring limousine, my body seemed just the same as ever—the skin round my finger nails dry and jagged, my overcoat covered with the usual bits of fluff, yet the world outside had been transformed.

Now, according to the map, we were over Kent. Motionless blue smoke hung over a wood: it was a little cloud. And now for the sea—a thrill, this! It was a motionless blue carpet, occasionally flecked with white feathers of waves. Below us a small moth glided across the water smoothly and steadily. This was the shadow of our own aeroplane, cast by a bright sun. The sea changed colour every minute—from blue to pale green, then dark again. Hovering white specks proved to be seagulls. Light-houses were no more than golf tees painted scarlet.

In a minute, it seemed, the moth had crossed the Channel and traversed the coast of Belgium. Occasionally our limousine encountered an air pocket, swooped up and down and gave one the sensation of being on the Giant Racer. The red-haired Dutch lady laughed and lay full length on the floor.

The scenes below now comprised small square 'samples' of tailors' materials pieced together to make a patchwork quilt for a midget's bed. Tweed, corduroy and poplin were combined in different tones of browns and fawns—and occasionally a sere yellow.

Lor'! The patchwork flew up at us—nearer, nearer, nearer! The aeroplane turned sideways. The big rubber tyres were no longer motionless in mid-air, but whirled madly round and round again. Suddenly they were carrying the aeroplane with them, revolving slower until they stopped. We had arrived.

Fellow passengers laughed at one another, pulled orange-waxy cotton wool out of their ears and lumbered out. There stood Englebrecht waiting for me—my *cicerone* in a foreign land. And with him was a nice, dowdy lady, who must be his mother.

LONDON

This was to be the great party time: scarcely a night without some impromptu gathering. Quite often fancy dress taxed one's resourcefulness but added to the fun.

Loelia Ponsonby, Zita, Baby, and others of the Guinness contingent, organised 'stunt' parties; paper chases, find-the-hidden-clues-races, bogus impressionist exhibitions, and bizarre entertainments based on the fashion of the latest Diaghilev ballets.

Loelia, of the raven's wing shingle and magnolia complexion, had a quiet retiring manner, yet was a great 'animatrice'. Greedy for more intelligent forms of amusement than those surrounding the Court circles in which she lived with her parents at St James's Palace, she, for many years before her marriage to the Duke of Westminster, enjoyed devising ingenious ways of eking out her income while living at a spanking pace. She was the first to give parties at which the guests were bidden to make a contribution, not only by giving impersonations or doing a particular 'turn', but also providing something high in the gastronomic scale such as oysters, a croûte of foie gras, or a bottle of champagne. Under Loelia's baton, the Bright Young Things were not only bright but talented. The name, however, when taken up by the gossips, soon acquired a stigma. A 'bottle party' became synonymous with drunkenness and squalor, and no longer had any connection with its charter members long before a not very 'bright' middle-aged woman shot someone under a piano.

Meanwhile Mrs Beatrice Guinness had ordered breakfast foods and the Embassy Band for the King of Greece and Charlie Chaplin, while Mrs Brigit Guinness was planning an ambitious costume ball complete with a ballet on a raft. For me life had suddenly appeared easy. Friends seemed all important, and of them I now had my share. Yet, without my fathoming the reason I realised, on occasion, that I generated hostility among certain strata of people who did not know me. Perhaps my manner was innately effeminate. But surely not flamboyantly so? Nevertheless, this hostility boiled over every now and again, part-icularly one late-summer's evening, when the self-assurance I had been

building was dashed in cold water at a ball given among the glories of
the Vandyke portraits, Kent gilt furniture, and ruby velvet of the
Double Cube room at Wilton.

A DUCKING AND OTHER MEMORIES

The festivities were to celebrate the coming-of-age of Lord
Herbert. Edith Olivier had asked me to stay in her house in the
Park for the event. After dinner our party walked along the river
and over the illuminated Palladian bridge, across the smooth
lawns to the house. In the gloaming the Inigo Jones façade looked
its most noble with the long range of tall lighted windows.

It was a grand occasion, and I was over-awed. I remember Mr
Rudyard Kipling with his plebean moustache: his flat chest was
pasted with medals. And a more handsome couple could seldom
have been seen than Lord and Lady Anglesey! she looking so
cool and wistful, with white face and black hair, and carrying the
weight of the world and a tall spiked tiara on her poetical head.

I walked on the lawns in a dream.

How beautiful the night scene was! How calm and visionary!
But my reveries were short-lived. Suddenly they became a
nightmare.

Out of the darkness a group of tail-coated young men surrounded me and, without a word of explanation, highjacked me
across the lawns at enormous pace towards the river. I remember
my head was raised in a Guido Reni agony which seemed to be
unending. In the panic that assailed me, the emotions of humili-
ation and shame were stronger than those of fear. The black night
whirled past me, batlike, as the phantasmagoria journey continued,
until abruptly, with a vicious thrust from all my attackers, I was
catapulted into the darkness. With a tremendous splash and
plopping of stones, I found myself standing hip deep in the
Nadder. Too stunned to know what to do, in my startled misery,
I merely stood silent. This had the effect of a clever ruse: my
enemies now became somewhat apprehensive lest their treatment
of me should have ended in my complete disappearance. The
group above me on the river bank murmured, 'Do you think
the bugger's drowned?' I continued to stand motionless in the
water. Someone—I think it was Roger Chetlock—shouted, 'Are
you all right?' I did not answer. More murmurs. But perhaps I

feared further retribution, if some would-be rescuer were to plunge after a supposedly drowning man and find him no worse off than wet to the white waistcoat. 'Where are you? Are you alive?' Eventually, in a rather dead voice, I replied, 'Yes, the bugger's alive,' and I trudged up the stones and mud into the comparative light of the lawns. My attackers had vanished.

The night was still comparatively young. I was determined not to leave the ball. While the water ran down my legs and oozed out of my shoes, I remained by a window of the Double Cube room making conversation to an eminent Field Marshal ... Later I danced with some of Edith's young nieces. They did not seem to notice my damp trousers, or that the squelching soles of my feet dragged without their accustomed smoothness across the parquet.

Walking home, as dawn lightened the skies, down past the river that I had come to know so intimately, I joined airily with the others in a post mortem on the party. 'Yes, it was a glorious ball. The best I've ever been to.' About one thing I was determined: the incident would never be mentioned by me. So far as I was concerned, it had never taken place. Although Edith's servant must have been surprised to find my soused clothes next morning, she did not draw my attention to them, nor did Edith ever allude to my shame; and her tact increased my love.

A week or so later in London, Roger Chetlock, accompanied by a self-consciously giggling Katie Maitland, came up to me in the interval of some theatre and taunted me: 'I haven't seen you since Wilton. You remember Wilton? That place of the Pembrokes in Wiltshire? On the Nadder, I believe. I think you were there for the ball, weren't you?' Katie Maitland waggled her kiss curls in a delirium of amusement.

Years later, there was some sort of wry compensation, when, out of the blue I received a letter from Roger Chetlock, saying that he'd heard I was a collector of Victoriana, that if I was interested he had a number of paper weights for disposal. I let him off scot-free.

It was, however, quite surprising to me that some of my attackers eventually became close friends.

Perhaps this experience confirmed a lesson I had been taught the very first day I had been to school: that however terrified one may be, one must never show one's quaking fears. If it is possible to put up an authoritative front or assume an aggressive attitude in turn, then the bully himself will be the first to collapse.

I was not a particularly puny boy, but I was an excellent bait for bullies, for I failed to conceal an inner fear that marked me out as a prospective victim. On the very first morning that Reggie and I set off to the day-school, Heath Mount, Hampstead, I tried not to disclose to my younger brother my dread of the Dickensian cruelty we were probably about to face. But, as we walked along Hampstead Heath with our emerald green caps and satchels, my stomach was queasy at the prospect of having my knuckles slashed with a sharp ruler by some sadistic master, or my backside swiped until it bled. It was with relief, on that cold autumn morning, that I heard the whistle blow for the eleven o'clock break. Half the morning, at any rate, had passed without disaster. The masters I now knew were not sadistic. Now the entire school was let out to rampage over the asphalt playground. The older boys formed their own posses of interest, others were playing the hearty games continued from last term. All the new boys seemed rather lost and did not know where to go; but none looked more ill at ease than myself. Suddenly, out of nowhere, the bullies arrived. They had recognised their quarry in me. Growling like wire-haired terriers, they were large and solid, with hairy stockings and rough tweeds. Their leader was a boy half the size of the others, wearing Barrie-esque green tweed knickerbockers. Recognising from a distance that I was the most obvious lamb for the slaughter, the leader, having darted silently towards me at great speed, halted a few inches in front of me with a menacing wild stare, while the bigger boys circled me and growled louder. He then stood on his toes and slowly thrust his face with a diabolical stare, closer and closer to mine, ever closer until the eyes converged into one enormous Cyclops nightmare. It was a clever inauguration to the terrors that followed, and my introduction to Evelyn Waugh.

But the 'breaking-down' process, the preliminary to the bullying proper, had not yet been completed. After the Cyclops eye had several times been retracted only to be brought back again in its symbolic horror, Waugh then stood baring his teeth at me. By the time the physical onslaught began, fright had mercifully made me only half conscious. That the tortures were devilish in their invention I can be fairly certain, since they were conducted under such expert leadership. Exactly what torments were endured I have forgotten; however, twenty years later, during the war, when I found myself in China in some military mess, a huge grey-haired major, middle-aged and respectable, came up and said, 'Well, Beaton, I haven't seen you since the days at Heath Mount when Evelyn Waugh and I were beaten for bending your arms back to front.'

Part IX

America

1929 and 1931

I was still living with my parents, and continued to take photographs in the drawing-room. Sometimes photographic lights and strangely improvised décors had not been cleared away before guests arrived to lunch or tea with my mother. The surprised visitor would see a room through which a tornado might have passed, leaving scorched tinsel, mountains of crumpled American-cloth, spilt water and empty vases on the floor, and various W. Heath Robinson arrangements of dead gypsophila hanging from billiard cues balanced on wooden towel racks.

The conditions for work were hardly ideal, yet the results were successful enough for me to be able to summon almost anyone to look pleasant and watch the birdie. Only Queen Mary and Virginia Woolf were reluctant to do my bidding.

Why, at this busy and exciting time, when new vistas were opening for me every week, did I want to discover a whole new world by visiting America? Since childhood it seemed to me that my father was always in the process of leaving for, or returning from, business-trips to the

*United States. He was reticent about his experiences in this land which
seemed to be all dollars and honey, but his shiny sepia snapshots of life
in the South showed glimpses of Pensacola and Mobile that looked
inviting. Jolly, prosperous families laughed on verandahs, or in garden
hammocks, surrounded by darkie servants and palm trees.*

*He would also bring back the theatre programmes with their illus-
trations of Laurette Taylor of the surprised crescent eyebrows, of Hazel
Dawn, the 'Pink Lady', or Leslie Henson in* Tonight's the Night.
*These invested my father for me with a little extra stardust and first
whetted my appetite for Broadway.*

*More recently the glowing reports of New York from Beverley
Nichols conveyed the impression that any visitor would be welcomed with
the same fanfare as the author of* Twenty Five *and these doubtless
influenced me to look for the pot of gold on the other side of the Atlantic.
But whereas on two continents Beverley Nichols was a full-scale
celebrity, I had achieved only a small notoriety in England. This would
not have preceded me across the waters. It was perhaps rather foolhardy,
armed with a No. 3A pocket folding Kodak and a crate of water
colours, to set sail towards a land where only half a dozen souls knew
of my existence.*

November 3rd 1929

It was still grey outside when Papa called me with some joke
about, 'Get ready for the Skylark.' I felt cold, empty and quivery
as I dressed and packed the last necessities—also some odd bits of
tinsel and cotton for possible future backgrounds.

The luggage was strapped on the car. Across the road a tweeny
sleepily shook a rug; a policeman trundled by, a few carts moved
slowly, cats and dogs appeared. Gradually little clerks in black
were hurrying Citywards, and a few buses had started. By degrees
the light became less fogged. When we passed the rear of Buckingham Palace, there was a throng of scurrying bowler hats. By
Westminster Bridge the crowds were thicker. The day's hubbub
had begun.

It was a gloomy wait on the station platform. The family
looked white and drawn. I could hardly bear their words of warn-
ing: 'Don't be too polite; don't let them get the better of you!
If you feel ill on board, send for the doctor.' The atmosphere
was potent with suppressed emotion. Goodbyes, kisses, last hand

waves. My mother, wearing a fur coat, her face worried but smiling, became smaller and smaller and smaller.

I sank back into my seat. I was off on a journey of adventure, to conquer a new world. It was to be a pleasure trip in a luxury liner; yet I felt as if I were going to my doom. In the little towns outside the window, the inhabitants were already busy with the day's work. A painter in a white jacket stood atop a step ladder and painted a sign over a shop window: 'Alice Grey—Milliner—Robes'. I hoped that Alice Grey would thrive.

The boat turned out to be a hotel full of dementedly rushing visitors. Its wide, imitation-marble staircase was thronged with an incessant stream of ant-like comers and goers. The gilded, super-ornate gates of the lift clanged every second.

In contrast to all this *va* and *vient*, I had nothing to do. Where to go? One couldn't walk aimlessly. It had taken only a short while to unpack in my cabin, but what next? I explored the pseudo-Adam drawing-room, the grill room, the baronial hall of a smoking-room. Fake eighteenth-century pictures were let into the moulded panelling of various reading-rooms, and there were fake fireplaces as well. The dining-room, Louis Seize in style, had carnations at every table—at least fifty thousand tough little carnations sprouted from metal vases. The decks were be-decked with potted palms and growing chrysanthemums.

November, undated, At Sea

I wander about the ship feeling and looking unlike myself. Stripped of personality, I am just another anonymous passenger. I prowl the decks, lie in armchairs in stuffy rooms, and wonder why I hadn't realised what a long journey I was in for. Cigarettes taste differently, perhaps because of the sea dampness. I stifle in the fuggy reception rooms, in the airless corridor leading to my cabin.

For distraction I watch my fellow passengers. There are the rampageous exercise lovers, who, with the resignation of lions in a cage, prowl the decks and suck in the ozone, snorting or marking time, bending their knees like stage policemen and going through a whole parade drill all by themselves. Others, as the first shyness wears off, nod or smile at one another. They exchange cards, play toy races, putt, ping-pong and crawl about on all fours looking for lost balls. They bet upon the slightest provocation, paying small fortunes in drinks.

A few, like myself, are odd men out. I wonder about one woman in particular, who is never without a plate of green grapes on her lap. And there is a sleeping beauty lying full length on a sofa in the Palladian lounge, with her shoes off for comfort.

I reach a zenith of boredom. I am tired of over-eating, of gazing at real flowers that look artificial, of listening to the hopeless band tooting in the lounge.

NEW YORK

November

Little white cubes shone in the sun, tug boats began the slow business of herding a giant up river to its Manhattan pier.

There were crowds waiting to welcome everyone but me. Fellow passengers pushed excitedly.

'Excuse me for doing you out of your place, but I'm crazy to see my mother!'

'Ah, that's my wife!'

The taxi drive was a trail of shocks. New York's tall buildings were lost somewhere overhead. It became dark enroute to the hotel, and the scene turned to a frozen fireworks display. From my eighteenth floor bedroom window the view appeared even more dramatic: the Hudson shining in the distance below, stars shining, brightly-lit buildings contrasted against shadowy edifices in the foreground, and rose-coloured church steeples.

November 15th

Yesterday I went to tea with Miss Elizabeth Marbury, to whom Osbert gave me a letter of introduction. I had been told much about this great figure in American theatrical life, but meeting her proved surprising nonetheless. A maid ushered me into the little house on the East River. Immediately I felt the Chelsea-ish charm of jumbled books, photographs and pictures.

Miss Marbury sat by the window in a chair heaped with cushions. She looked like a dear, enormously fat Victorian landlady. She wore her hair scraped high as any old farmer's wife, and was in a black satin dress that Queen Victoria herself might have worn. Surrounded by rolls of fat is the face of a parrot; her arms are as thick as one's own body, and her bolster-like legs have been strapped to iron supports to bear such colossal weight.

Bessie Marbury, as she is known, has a personality as grandiose as her figure. I felt at once that I'd made a new friend as strong as a wall. She explained about New York life, about the buildings and the plays. She told me of many ways in which she could help me.

Soon, to my regret, a stream of visitors appeared—friends who came in ceaseless numbers to pay court to her on her throne. There were an old actress and a young actor; one Italian and one English author, both of great renown; and her house guest, Elsie de Wolfe, who recently became Lady Mendl.

Bessie Marbury regaled the company, saying, 'Oh, Arctic explorers are such bores. They are so earnest, have no sense of humour and consider their vice a service to the country. They tell one such long and boring stories. I will show you how long and boring their stories are.' And she did.

The others roared with laughter, but I became conscious of my grimacing and theatrical pretence at listening appreciatively. I would rather have been alone with Marbury, listening to the whole story of Oscar Wilde and his trial (she was a close friend of Wilde's at the time). I wanted, too, to hear about Bernhardt and Lillie Langtry and Mrs Vernon Castle.

At last I did have an opportunity to talk quietly and alone with this huge old Buddha. But the *tête-à-tête* consisted of her giving me some sound, motherly advice. She told me I shouldn't be out with such a bad cold as I had today; I must go home and take a strong cathartic. I didn't know what a cathartic was. She laughingly suggested I write to Osbert to say that Miss Marbury had become my grandmother, and advised me to go home and take a cathartic.

I wrote to Elizabeth Marbury this morning, thanking her so much for her friendliness. I said I had taken her advice last night, had come home and gone to bed with a very strong Catholic.

December 2nd

I saw the most sadistic incident in the street. A crippled woman, with one badly malformed foot, hobbled along leaning on a

stick. Some urchins stood by, their eyes glued to the foot encased in its shining black boot. One of the little monsters inquired,
'Shoe shine?'

The cripple shook her head and politely said, 'No, thank you.'

ASSIGNMENTS FROM VOGUE

December 7th

Friday is a bad day for me. It marks the end of the week, and the
hotel bill arrives. This week my bill seemed much higher than
before. There are very few cheques left in my letter of credit book.
It is terrifying and depressing. I have begun to loathe the Ambassador Hotel. 1805 is a nice room, but even if the numbers *do*
add up to my lucky number fourteen, it has been a jolly expensive fourteen.

Suddenly the telephone went: Mrs Chase bid me go round to
Vogue and see her at once. The photographs I had taken for them
of Natica, Condé Nast's daughter, were admired. I felt relieved,
as I have been here already a month, and it's time I started to
work in real earnest.

I met Mrs Chase's second-in-command, Mrs Snow, who is the
American editor. This meeting was very satisfactory. Mrs Snow,
looking like a fox terrier, seemed pleased with me, and we arranged that I should do various jobs for her. Around her sat Miss
Case[1] and Miss Voght, taking down notes of what I was to do. My
assignments included an article on New York's night life, for
which I would be taken to various joints and have an opportunity
to meet Erickson, as he is to do the illustrations. I would also
write another article on theatres, to be illustrated with my
drawings. *Vogue* would supply tickets for all the plays I hadn't
seen. I wish this had been arranged before, so that I could have
saved my fast depleting dollars!

Mrs Snow has the most satisfactorily ordered life. She is never
flustered by the vast amount of work to be done at the office,
yet has time to devote to her husband and children, a house in
New York and another in the country, while still she manages
to travel in Europe. It seemed typical of her to plan three different
evening-entertainments for me—one to be passed in a lounge
suit, another in black tie, and the third in tails! She said, 'Well,

[1] Miss Margaret Case, who became a staunch, steadfast friend.

Walking on the downs above Ashcombe: Rex Whistler, Edith
Olivier, Peter Watson, Christabel Aberconway

Tchelitchew painting Peter Watson

that night you'll go to the movies after dining at the Caviar. You can try Casanova later. And this will be a good night to go to Harlem.' The itinerary was as carefully balanced as if a gourmet should say, 'Well, after the juicy steak, a little *soufflé* should be washed down with a glass of Chateau Yquem.'

LONG ISLAND

December 8th

I was asked down to Long Island to spend the day with the Harrison Williamses, whom I had never met. The prospect was terrifying. I waited in the lobby of my hotel to be picked up by an unknown quantity with a motor car.

Mr Arthur Fowler proved a harsh, glum schoolboy of sixty. Further acquaintance revealed that he is a shrewd business man, yet 'passionately' interested in portraiture. This struck me as being odd. He looks the least aesthetic person, and I imagine his painting is ghastly.

Snow was falling. It was a raw, ugly day. The drive through uninteresting country seemed interminable. Mr Fowler and I had so little in common that at any moment we were likely to dry up. But we eked out conversation to the bitter end, talking about American versus English humour and the people I would meet today. I was informed that our prospective host had two hundred million dollars.

The car turned through tall gates and made a semi-circle along the gravel drive, stopping before a sumptuous country house. I noticed odd, crate-like structures of canvas and wood littered all over the garden. It seemed as if a circus were pulling up stakes. But on inquiry I found that box trees (a sign of antiquity on Long Island) were put under these tents for winter protection, making the garden an eyesore for four months of the year.

The house was new and neo-Georgian, filled with English Hepplewhite and Sheraton. Among the paintings were a fine Bronzino and two Tiepolos.

Our host and hostess greeted us. Mrs Williams is fascinatingly beautiful, like a rock-crystal goddess with aquamarine eyes. She moved with pristine and smiling ease among dozens of guests. Harrison Williams has a wrinkled parchment face, a blunt mouth and tired Chinese eyes that have seen everything. His low, deep

G

voice crackles like coke. Although I had little chance to get to know what sort of a man this great mogul was he seemed extremely sympathetic and was obviously somewhat aloof and only tolerably amused by his guests. I must admit that, for the most part, they rather put me off, especially Charlie Hayden, an old bachelor parrot who gambles on the stock market and enjoys social success. He's almost startlingly quick, getting in his remarks with more facility than anyone. Charlie held forth about how he knew 'everybody', including someone who was 'very much of a lady, not a bit Jewish-Christian faith, you know.' He related stories about how he holed in one and had to give five dollars to the caddie and five hundred dollars to the club to build a new green. Or he went to the bicycle tournament and paid five hundred bucks for a sprint. He took a party here; he made a million dollars there.

Knowing nothing about stocks and bonds, I thought I should go mad listening to market quotations about what shares went up or were going down. Most of these people seemed to treat a hundred thousand dollars as a mere bagatelle. The loss of a million was another matter: 'Oh I've known people commit suicide when that has happened.' This depressed me very much indeed: I, who have about twenty pounds left out of the two hundred I brought to the States with me!

After lunch came tennis in the new glass-domed enclosure which is artificially lit so that people can play all night if necessary. Also enclosed here were a huge swimming pool and gymnasium. I feared the standard of tennis would be far higher than mine; as indeed it turned out to be. I watched in awe and silence while the Parrot slammed volleys and yapped, 'Atta-boy!'

More people arrived for dinner—all celebrities of Long Island, all indefinite in appearance and definite in thoughts. They emanated self-assurance, and I felt alarmed by everyone except one fat old Mrs Tiffany, a terrific personality whom everyone calls Nannie. She was amusing and shrewd; she had a wry sense of humour. She talked like a lady in a play, offering her formula for getting thin: for three days now, she had had nothing but hot and cold water and the juice of one orange.

On my left at the dinner table was a Mrs Henry Russell. Earlier in the day she had taken no notice of me, but now seemed flattered that I should ask so many questions about the people present. She was a mine of information. That hard woman there had recently married a prince and was keeping him penniless. The overtired lady, with bloodless lips and incessantly blinking eyes, had a debutante daughter who needed closer chaperoning than she had received.

After dinner there was more talk of bull and bear markets, also bridge. Mrs Williams, Nannie Tiffany and myself begged off. We made conversation. I warmed to a sense of *entente* with our hostess: she was so unlike the others. She radiated serenity and sympathy; she seemed utterly selfless. Without her, I would have felt at a loss, hobnobbing with the weightiest names of Wall Street. As a matter of fact, what good did it do when one had nothing in common with them?

I sank into a car and was driven back through miles of Long Island bleakness to New York. I hoped I would see Mrs Williams again, as I felt we should become friends. If only she weren't so rich, so sought after, it might be easier.

In my hotel room, the windows were all shut, the steam heat terrific, my puny vase of cheap flowers was quite dead. I found urgent notes and telephone messages from Elisabeth Marbury asking me to meet Amelia Earhart.

Undated

Today is the 14th, my lucky number. Then the weekly bill gets swished under the door—not so lucky! Well, let's see the horror. Oh, good! Less than it has ever been: ninety-three dollars isn't really much. This afternoon a sitter comes to be photographed for sixty pounds, which will pay for two weeks' bill straightaway.

I am very pleased with life. I cannot believe that I ever felt depressed here, with nothing to do.

Undated

Quite a glut of sitters—and impressive ones too. At this afternoon's session I was amazed at my own patter: Don't budge an inch, I beg you. That's fine. I do thank you for keeping so still. Now lower your chin—lower, much lower. You see, with this little camera I'm like a dog looking up at you. Still a little lower. Don't worry about the double chins. I'll knife them later. Pretend you're looking down a well. Good; perfect.

Dear old Mr Frank Crowninshield appeared and, to my great delight, raved about my photographs. He liked some of the paintings, too. I felt that praise from the editor of *Vanity Fair* augured well. Gosh, it was good to hear him enthuse so extravagantly: myself, Steichen and de Meyer the *only* photographers: 'But it's so amazing that you can do things like this with a toy camera.' And he stayed three times as long as he had intended.

With enticing offers of work and invitations from my new friends it was not surprising that I crossed the Atlantic again the following autumn. I discovered that, quite naturally, all picture galleries in New York were long ago booked for the winter season, and no one could exhibit my efforts. When Elsie de Wolfe offered me the boiseried showrooms of her interior decorating establishment, I accepted with gratitude; though perhaps I might have wished for a gallery of more serious standing.

A goodly number of pictures, however, were sold at prices much steeper than they were in London. When the New York exhibition closed, I took the remaining pictures to Palm Beach where the prices were marked even higher than on Fifth Avenue. Here I reaped a great harvest: a sketch of a bluebell wood, done in the Harrow sketching class under the eagle supervision of Mr Eggie Hine, was sold to Mr Ralph Beaver Strassberger for a thousand dollars; this was gratifying.

But more exciting still: a delightful and witty group centring around Addison Mitzner[1] became my first real American friends. They went into peals of laughter when I tried to make a joke or relate an anecdote. They seemed to find me sympathetic. Yet in spite of their encouragement, so full of tiresome misgivings, so shy, and lacking in self-confidence was I, that when Addison first asked me to stay around for dinner and spend the evening with Anita Loos, Marjorie Oelrichs[2] and others, I lied that I had something else to do. Although more than anything I wanted to be accepted by these vital people, I could not bring myself to believe that they really accepted me as one of them. This diffidence on my part, possibly inexplicable to others, made it difficult for people to like me, and was particularly baffling to Americans. When Marjorie telephoned to me immediately on her return to New

[1] The giant-sized architect who had peppered Florida with his grandiose Spanish taste.

[2] Marjorie Oelrichs had shocked the more conventional members of New York's well-bred families by showing an unconventional taste in friends, and a rebellious spirit that manifested itself when she was among the first to give her illustrious name to a testimonial for Lucky Strike cigarettes.

York—in fact before calling any of her other friends—she proved conclusively that I was not just a holiday acquaintance, and gave me the most gratifying surprise of my first American winter. Altogether, with her subtle ways and acute sense of humour, Marjorie became one of my most admired human beings. More than any other woman I had met before, she was responsible for giving me a modicum od self-confidence and the satisfaction of having gained some worldly experience. Her death, giving birth to her son, left me with a sadness I shall never forget.

With a group of new friends to cheer my departure and a bulky contract to work for Condé Nast, I sailed home pleased with the fact that I had made even the slightest ripple in the life of New York.

CRITICISM FROM NOËL COWARD

April 5th, At Sea

The last week in America was stuffed to the gills with work and play. I feel exhilaratedly independent now—surrounded by people I like and who like me, whose tastes and ways are strengthening the struts of my world. I have even had one or two diversions with young women where I would never have expected such success possible. At any rate, I live at a much higher speed than I've ever known before.

When the hour of parting came, intimates wept and waved me off on this boat. Others sent tragic telegrams. Horns tooted; the boat sailed.

I don't think I slept for more than a few hours during the last week in New York. I've started a very bad cold now. My throat feels relaxed and sore, the boat rocks up and down. After two days of semi-coma in an airless inside cabin, I staggered from my bed this morning, dressed in plus fours and managed to walk to my chair on deck without being ill. There I met Noël Coward and Mrs Venetia Montagu, whom I had always imagined to be charming and interesting people.

At once they attacked me. 'Why do you write such malicious articles? Why do you say such nasty things about Mr Coward?'

I staggered, my knees quaked. 'You must please not attack me now. I am feeling ill.'

'You must expect to be attacked if you write such horrible things.'

They told me my writings were impertinent, malicious, mean,

full of untruths and utterly superficial. They exaggerated, of course. But there was much truth in what they had to say that I could not deny it. The blows came raining down upon me.

Mrs Montagu is the sort of woman I admire: tall *raffinée*, gaunt and grey-haired with a hawklike profile. There are few good books she hasn't read and remembered, never forgetting the name of a character or the gist of a situation. At crossword puzzles and writing games she is quicker than anybody else.

As for Noël Coward, the truth is that I've wanted to meet him for many years. I admire everything about his work: his homesick, sadly melodious tunes, his revues, his witty plays, his astringent acting.

Why, then, have I hated him? Perhaps for the very reason that I've not known him before and wanted to. I hated him personally, out of pique. I was envious of his success, of a triumphant career that seemed so much like the career I might have wished for myself.

Since my friends in New York had told me how *unmalicious* I was, I could now hardly believe my ears. Mrs Montagu lashed out at me, determined to give me a lesson for several reasons: (a) because she disliked me and (b) because I obviously needed putting in my place. Coward showed more aplomb, investigating me out of a detached curiosity. Yet both came to the same conclusion: I was flobby, flabby and affected.

I moaned tragically, 'But believe me, I'm a wad of guts and gristle.'

They died of laughter. They mimicked me: 'Oh, it's too, too luvleigh!' My arms were said to fly in the air. This I thought was going too far! I denied it. My walk was said to be undulating, my clothes too conspicuously exaggerated.

I fell speechless with inferiority. I had wanted enormously to be liked by Noël Coward, and now he thought nothing of me. I thought nothing of myself. My gloom was total.

It will be so unsatisfactory to break an acquaintance like this, without convincing them both that I'm not as low as they think me. There may never again be a further chance of making explanations, excuses or amends.

I arranged to do a drawing of Noël Coward and went to his cabin:

'We've been absolutely beastly to you,' he admitted. 'But you've shown spirit and let's hope you've learnt a lesson. It is important not to let the public have a loophole to lampoon you.' That, he explained, was why he studied his own 'façade'. Now take his voice: it was definite, harsh, rugged. He moved firmly and solidly, dressed quietly.

'I see.'

'You should appraise yourself,' he went on. 'Your sleeves are too tight, your voice is too high and too precise. You mustn't do it. It closes so many doors. It limits you unnecessarily, and young men with half your intelligence will laugh at you.' He shook his head, wrinkled his forehead and added disarmingly, 'It's hard, I know. One would like to indulge one's own taste. I myself dearly love a good match, yet I know it is overdoing it to wear tie, socks and handkerchief of the same colour. I take ruthless stock of myself in the mirror before going out. A polo jumper or unfortunate tie exposes one to danger.' He cocked an eye at me in mockery.

We dine together every night! I still wear my plus fours on deck, but my two critics seem less severe. In fact, Mrs Montagu paid me the extreme compliment this evening of saying she no longer disliked me. She has promised to call me up in London after our arrival tomorrow!

HOLLYWOOD WITH ANITA LOOS

December 1930

I travelled from New York with Anita Loos and her husband, John Emerson, to spend Christmas in Hollywood. Anita, at the age of sixteen, wrote the scenario for Mary Pickford's film *The New York Hat*. Ever since, she'd been one of Hollywood's most popular citizens. So I was assured of seeing the film metropolis under good auspices.

On board the train were exclusively film folk. The talk centred almost entirely on the 'recent advent of talking pictures.' Some-one bet that Garbo would be no good in talkies; her downfall was certain to be as rapid as her rise. John Gilbert's reedy voice had caused him to be eased out of his contract. Clara Bow, it seemed, was suffering from appendicitis.

For three days we ate enormous tenderloin steaks in the confines of a metallic dining car. In Chicago, a frenzied porter wheeled a barrow most painfully into the back of my legs. At Las Vegas, John Emerson bought a bow and arrow from an Indian. And at San Bernadino we alighted from the train.

A car and chauffeur had been sent by Mr Joseph Schenck. The limousine had been given to Mr Schenck as a birthday present from Al Jolson. Five years previously, it had won first prize for its body in an exhibition of modern art in Paris. It was decorated with inlaid woodwork, engraved glass and tortoise-shell. The seats and carpet were woven with a design of paradise birds whisking among futuristic globules.

It was a relief to be out of the train, whizzing along in comfort. The daylight faded. The sky turned to copper. In the distance, mountains were purple; a warm and velvety evening air was heavy with the smell of orange blossoms. I sniffed happily, but felt a stab of longing for some sort of love affair, so that the palm trees and warm evening could be appreciated even more.

We were keyed up to observe everything. A huge electric sign read, 'Ye Olde Gas Shoppe'. There were many such 'shoppes', with Merrie England propaganda abundant. On we sped, past wooden bungalows, imitation Spanish haciendas, and weird constructions where the traveller stops for ice cream. These were decorated to look like gigantic ice grinders, or puppy dogs or dolls with hats and yellow curls.

Every little bakery had been built like a windmill, theatrically illuminated. Gardens were inhabited by pottery elves and gnomes with long beards and red caps. We passed the Hansel and Gretel kindergarten school for girls and boys. Perhaps it was these children who had been allowed to run amok with their whimsy, creating a dotty never-never land.

The chauffeur explained that Hollywood Boulevard was being officially renamed 'Santa Claus Lane' for the holidays. Its sidewalks were lined with huge Christmas trees, all tarted up by vari-coloured lamps.

John Emerson mopped his brow. 'Phew, the heat!' We all felt breathless in the sultry, subtropical humidity.

All at once there was excitement. Coming towards us a lorry, equipped with spitting blue lights, towed in its wake a giant sleigh on wheels. Merry Christmas! In the 'one-lorry open sleigh' a group of Eskimo, wearing white fur, sat placidly enduring an artificial snowstorm. The lorry men whipped themselves into an arctic hysteria, shovelling mounds of white confetti through a wind machine that spewed clouds of white over Nanook and Nanette. This was Hollywood! If anyone doubted it, a rival lorry driven by outraged puritans proclaimed: 'The Lord Jesus came to save sinners, not to worship Santa Claus in Hollywood!'

We arrived at our hotel. The Roosevelt turned out to be a mock Moorish conceit with patio, fountain, and shawl-draped balconies. Its lobby was crowded by desperate blondes in black satin, osprey and furs. Though the climate varies little the year round, Hollywood ladies insist on wearing the same season's clothes that are being worn in the East. Little matter if the December sun is broiling.

A swarm of songwriters greeted Anita and John, overwhelming them with an avalanche of invitations in which I was generously included.

Apollos and Venuses are everywhere. It is as if the whole race of gods had come to California. Walking along the sidewalks with Anita, I see classic oval faces that might have sat to Praxiteles. The girls are all bleached and painted with sunburn enamel. They are the would-be stars who come to Hollywood from every part of America, lured by hopes of becoming a Mary or Doug, a Joan Crawford, Gloria Swanson, Richard Barthelmess or Gary Cooper, whose autographed pictures are part of nearly every shop window display. Few of the hopefuls ever 'make it'; some are realistic enough to admit their failure, in time to leave before their savings have been exhausted. The diehards hang on, buoyed by empty prospects and promises, eking out a piecemeal existence by working at 'drive-in' quick-lunch counters or as shoe shiners.

Some of the women, accepting their failure to dazzle on the silver screen, mate and make babies which they are convinced will become a gold mine like Jackie Coogan. They encourage them to be tarts out here from the age of five. Younger still: by the time a brat is three or four, it has been mercilessly trained in the art of sophistication and artificiality. Cheeks are painted, noses powdered, hair permanently waved. The girls are dressed in

G*

189

tight-fitting little frocks, so short as to barely cover their rumps In doorways, elevators and lobbies, mothers and aunts can be seen titivating their prodigies. They moisten fingers and smooth plucked crescent brows; they encourage the lashes backwards.

One little horror of six took our breath away. She was coming out of a draper's shop with her mother. Her sausage curls were peroxided canary yellow to match mother's tresses. Her eyes were large and blue, her cheeks had been painted like blushing roses. A frilly pink bonnet surmounted the head, while the tiny body had been squeezed into a skin-tight, sleeveless frock. To complete the picture, a *corsage* of blue and white flowers was pinned to her little chest, and coral bead bracelets dangled from each dimpled wrist. We stared so hard that both the tot and her mother became self-conscious.

Whimsicality soars to new heights. Beauty shops advertise 'face exchange' or 'face aesthetics'. In the household stores, hand-painted velveteen cushions are decorated with lake-side scenes of bewigged love-making, or stuck with bas-relief roses of acid-tinted putty. One cushion was affixed with a small statue possibly made of chewing gum; another depicted two psuedo-classical nude figures clasping one another on a draped 'couch'. Both these art works were exhibited as being 'suitable for milady's salon'.

Weary from window-shopping, we sit down on a sidewalk seat that advertises a dentist, a doctor or a funeral parlour.

Wilson Mizner[1] joined our entourage. Anita told me some of the events of his career, which has been even more varied than the rival fortunes of his large and remarkable family of brothers and sisters. Certainly, he is one of the most unique characters one could meet. He has got into all kinds of scrape, run every sort of racket and been connected with a dozen inconceivable organisa-tions. He has twice been a multi-millionaire; he had a play run-ning on Broadway for years. He has drunk and doped enough to kill ten people, is tough as the toughest hobo, yet kind-hearted as the good Samaritan. He claims to be an inventor (among his innovations is the 'rubber pocket' to help waiters steal soup!). Wilson should write his life-story, but he is much too lazy to do anything except hang around the Brown Derby and gossip to passers by, or regale us with bizarre anecdotes of this strange city.

[1] Brother of Palm Beach's Addison.

Of burly build and six foot six in height, he makes a striking
contrast to Anita, who looks like a ventriloquist's doll with her
famous fringed hair and clothes bought from the juvenile department.

Anita and I went into a cheap tie shop to buy a joke Christmas
present for Fred Astaire. There were long cravats in orange,
green and purple, the iridescent colours swirling together; there
were bow ties with wired flaps, like enormous butterflies. We
had to pretend to buy these things in all seriousness, but it was
hard to keep a straight face. Anita's voice became more quavery
and childlike: 'Oh, that's *very* nice,' holding out a spotted
atrocity or a hand-painted creation of a sunset behind palms. I
selected a cascade of nude ladies sprawling in positions of abandon.
Fred won't appreciate the joke very well, but it gave me a kick
to think of him opening the package. Fred, who looks like an
unborn colt with bleary, cowlike eyes and fat lower lip. . . .

Anita and I walked up to see a young 'starlet' who had vaguely
asked us to tea. The house proved much further away than we'd
imagined. We were pretty blown when at last we arrived. Anita
was quite interested to see the girl, as she hadn't set eyes upon her
since the mother worked hard to make a New York débutante
out of unlikely material. Now the mother seemed resigned:
'If my daughter prefers California and wants to dine with Mary
and Doug instead of with more suitable friends here on Long
Island, it's her own affair.'

We entered and found a group of young people sitting about
on the floor. 'Welcome strangers,' one said. 'Cutie Pie is in the
kitchen.'

An hysterical scream sounded, followed by ear-splitting yells.
'Cutie Pie' appeared, looking like a flagstaff in a red velvet jacket
and red and white check trousers. Her hair had been tied up in a
piece of tinsel ribbon. She was unwashed and sweaty.

We were introduced to the rest of the company. One young
man made a dead set at Anita, sat almost on top of her and held
her hand. He was so drunk he looked embalmed. As a matter of
fact, they were all pretty sour-breathed, rolling about on the
floor while Cutie Pie screamed and screwed up her face like a
monkey. Soon her nose was on a level with her eyes. A young

swain on all fours chased her round the room. Prussic acid and vitriol were dispensed from a bottle labelled 'Kentucky sourmash whiskey.'

Slang expressions that puzzled me flew about the room. Then someone came in with a large brown paper parcel. 'Dandy! Eats! Oh, whoopee!' Young men tripped over the dog or empty-drink trays, as they hurried into the garden to wee-wee. Some returned in a torment of prickles, having fallen into the cacti.

The house looked informal. The flowers on the mantelpiece had long since died, the 'snack' table had been ravaged by this horde of locusts. 'Won't you stay and have a bite? Bill's going to cook us some goodies.' A sharp clapping of hands and more yahoos from the cockeyed young men followed the announce-ment of Bill's imminent prowess.

Anita and I apologised to Bill, said goodbye to Cutie Pie and sneaked off. Once out of earshot, Anita summed up her im-pressions. 'I love the idea of Cutie Pie's mother having visions of Pickfair for her daughter. I'll bet if an electrician smacked our débutante on the rump and said, "What're you doin' tonight, baby?" she'd be thrilled. Anyway, she's enjoying herself; she's at least broken the silver cord.'

Inside the Paramount film studio, the stars' dressing-rooms are built with façades of various styles of architecture. Thus, when occasion demands, they can be used as backgrounds for films about England, Holland, Germany or Russia.

I soon discovered that most buildings had no interiors, were merely shells of Civil War plantations and Istanbul nights.

In an enormous cafeteria, actors, producers, cutters, photo-graphers, caption-writers and scene-writers had congregated for their salad-and-coffee lunches. An old monk in mediaeval habit was scrutinising the menus through pince-nez. A dowager duchess, in ball dress and tiara, sat eating spaghetti by herself. There were Hugo-esque beggars, Dickensian executioners, creole beauties in crinolines and hospital nurses from 1914.

I was introduced to a series of people whose names I knew from the movie magazines I'd been reading. 'Meet Mr Lubitsch.' A cigar twisted from one side of his mouth to the other, while I remembered his *The Marriage Circle*, the first good film I ever saw. 'Meet Mr Richard Arlen.' A nice, clean-looking young man

wrinkled his forehead and smiled. 'This is George Bancroft.'
The twinkling tadpole eyes didn't seem a bit thuggish off the
screen.

Then, suddenly, a rather horrible surprise—of all people I
encountered Elsie Janis! A great revue star in London during the
1914 war, she was one of my hottest boyhood's enthusiasms. She
sang in a fogged voice, 'Give me the moonlight, give me the
girl, and leave the rest to me.' Also she did impersonations I
thought were the final proof of her brilliance, and I did imitations
of her impersonations. What chic she had—this enigmatic dun-
coloured frog-faced revue actress with a curl in the middle of her
forehead. She loved Basil Hallam, her jeune premier, who was
sent white feathers, then joined the Balloons, and was killed when
his parachute failed. Now Elsie is writing scenarios, *soi disant*,
looks spinsterish and school mistressy, and although she fights
gallantly and keeps going, her pithy wit is blunted and she exudes
everything that is *démodé*.

A Mr Al Kaufman now took me to see the man who made
Wings. He was busy producing his next picture, which featured
Gary Cooper. A shot was in progress. Over and over again, Gary
Cooper had to address Fay Wray as 'Miss Calhoun'.

Cooper is warm and friendly with everyone. The electrician
offered him a cigar. 'Are they all right?' 'They should be: the
three of them cost twenty-five cents.' Gary lit up, and the cigar
did not explode.

This ingenuous cowboy's success has sky-rocketed. He started
in the business only three years ago, and now it saps him entirely.
He pines to get away but can't. He can't even spend his money.
He longs for the sun to stop shining, but it never does. 'Terrible
weather this, for the day before Christmas.' The sun was broiling
hot.

On the next set, a 1914 wartime party was in slow progress.
The men strutted about in khaki; the women we had already seen
in the cafeteria, wearing aigrets and beaded tunic dresses. Blinding
arc lights sputtered, scorching in their heat. An endless supply of
assistants, electricians, dressers and small-part players cluttered
the set. After interminable preparations, the camera moved down
a vista with the hero and heroine. Then a yell: 'Cut from here.'
Everyone sighed with relief that the scene was 'in the can' after
twenty-five retakes. The heroine shouted 'Whoopee,' and did a

shimmy shake. The hero warbled joyously, the director clasped his little son.

On another stage, William Powell was being extremely serious in a typical detective drama. Immaculately dressed, he sat at a desk and frowned. His cool white hands were crossed. He spoke in a rich, unctuous voice, due perhaps to the relish with which he enjoys his great success.

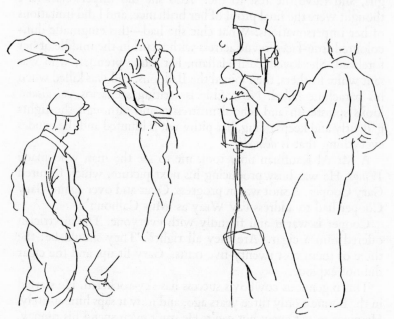

Film engineers

While various technical gadgets were adjusted before a new take, Powell talked shop to bystanders. 'Why is it that Barrymore is so lousy nowadays? I haven't seen *General Crack*, but I hear he surpasses himself in over-acting. I suppose he's up to his old tricks.' An imitation of the old tricks convulses electricians and propmen with sycophantic laughter.

Encouraged, Powell went on to discuss the interpretations of another famous actor. 'He's acting in an eighteenth-century play, isn't he? I suppose that means he does the snuff business.' There followed an imitation of snuff-taking.

An electrician, lying in the gantry above, roared with laughter and shouted, 'The pansy!'

'Okay,' the director bellowed. And they proceeded with the next scene.

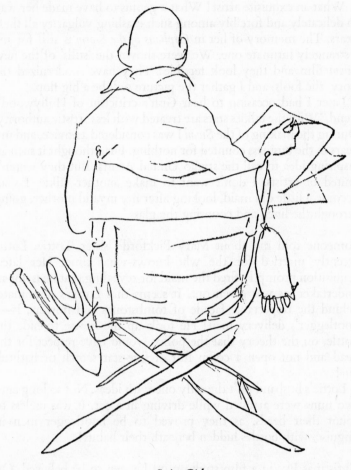

Script Girl

Anita took me to United Artists about photographing Lilian Gish.[1] But the film had been finished, and the publicity man doubted if Gish would ever make another 'talkie'. So by witness-

---

[1] Lilian Gish is still giving distinctive performances to plays and films.

ing peradventure, that defiant little spinster, wrapped in a squashed strawberry-coloured shawl and walking with such martial tread back to her dressing-room, I had been present at Gish's exit from the screen world!

What an exquisite artist! What a genius to have made her way so delicately and forcibly among such crashing vulgarity all these years. The memory of her in *Orphans of the Storm* is still for me a strangely intimate one. We were shown the 'stills' of the new *Swan* film and they look terrible! They have modernized the story, the fools, and I gather the picture will be a big flop.

Later I had occasion to hear Gish's criticism of Hollywood's trend. 'With the talkies stars are treated with less artistic authority. During the making of the *Swan* I was considered a novice, and my years in the business counted for nothing. I had thought it such an inspiring idea to call the studio United Artists. But they weren't united or artists. I don't want to make another talkie. I shall become a little old maid, looking after my invalid mother, going through the linen and counting the glass.'

Someone told me about Mary Pickford's sister, Lottie. Lottie recently married for the who-knows-what time. Her latest acquisition promptly fired the maid for revealing that he is not an undertaker, as was given out. It seems that Lottie's new mate, behind the respectable façade of tombstones and flowers, is—a bootlegger's delivery man! He took up the hearse to hide the bottle, on the theory that the police would have respect for the dead and not open a coffin full of five-star scotch or bathtub gin!

Lottie's husband isn't the only one with ideas. Not so long ago, two nuns were arrested while driving in a car. It was useless to count their beads, as they proved to be bootlegger men in disguise, with bottles hidden beneath their habits!

Christmas Eve in a film studio must be seen to be believed. On Wellman's new film, we were given a demonstration of the director-genius at work. He did weird gymnastic exercises; he mouthed, gesticulated, swayed and switched coloured lights on and off. Finally he screamed, 'All right! Stop! God, this scene is a bastard!' The 'bastard' entailed much moving of cameras and sound apparatus while a pretty German spy was busy doping the

hero home on leave, so that her accomplice could get hold of the
secret papers.

It was very nearly the end of the day's work. Yuletide exaltation became exaggerated. Wild-eyed stenographers were
whisked under doorways to be kissed beneath sprigs of mistletoe.
One young man, a total stranger to me, rushed up and asked,
'How are you going to spend your Christmas?' When I said I
didn't really know, he almost shed a tear for the poor limey bum.
A stenographer rushed into the room, picked up the telephone and
barked, 'Hello, you silly sucker. Merry Christmas to you!' Then
she hung up.

The whistle blew. The studio became a scene of pandemonium
as its inhabitants, laden beneath mountains of fancily wrapped
packages, rushed forth like school children let out for their
holidays.

We went to a Christmas party given by a newly married couple
of stars who live on the top of a hill. The bride is considered to be
a woman of temperament. The bridegroom has a reputation for
drinking to excess and becoming violent. There have been
rumours that the marriage is already somewhat turbulent.

Tonight, we found her handing out a plethora of smiles, displaying too many white teeth. He, too obviously on his best
behaviour, wasn't touching a drop himself, yet poured drinks
for everyone else. He talked brightly and politely; he showed
us the twinkling lights of Los Angeles from the balcony.
He offered a brief tour of the loggia, the sun parlour, the
swimming pool and the expensive indoor tennis court. Such
extreme civility from a man generally known to be *farouche* was
ominous.

Somehow, the party missed being a success. The stars present
behaved like self-conscious stars as they received and opened
hundreds of presents. One movie queen lay on the floor and
played with a toy tank, letting it crawl over her stomach. Lilyan
Tashman continued to act the vamp off-screen, displaying an
exquisite figure by taunting a fox terrier with her black lace
handkerchief. She raised the handkerchief quickly out of the
animal's reach each time it leapt into the air. This pantomime
continued for several minutes. The dog jumped higher and
higher, barked louder and louder with a wild glint in its eyes.

Screams ensued. 'Well, there goes thirty dollars worth of lace!'
The exhibition had been worth it.

Next morning we heard that the newly married couple had
ended the night in a first-rate brawl. The husband rolled downhill
while his wife clung fast, scratching and biting him in their
communal descent.

AIMÉE SEMPLE MACPHERSON

Anita and I decided to join the flock and hear Sister Aimée
Semple MacPherson preach in her Angelus Temple. We arrived
punctually, but the enormous, vaulted building was already
crowded with some three thousand people. More were fighting
for admission.

The temple would have done Santa Claus proud. Mass decorations of tinsel fringes, silver cardboard stars, frosted paper leaves
and poinsettias were displayed against crimson flannel curtains.
The holy tone of the proceedings was set by a representation of
the domed buildings of Bethlehem framing the proscenium arch
of the stage. Round the auditorium were imitation stained glass
windows depicting tableaux of brothel angels.

A hush. The curtains drew apart to reveal a cinema screen on
which were projected the typewritten words of hymns. The
congregation sang solemnly. Mrs MacPherson stood unob-
trusively to one side of the stage, screaming at the top of her
voice, jumping up and down, wildly wielding her arms or beating
time on a tambourine.

Aimée Semple even *looked* like a force of nature. Her horse face
sported snorting nostrils and flashing teeth. To compensate for a
sallow skin, she wore a bright gold wig of hair in elaborate coils
and curls. She was dressed as an angel in floating white tea gown
with butterfly sleeves and flowing cape. A huge silver cross was
stamped upon her bosom, while on her shoulder sat a corsage of
mauve orchids and lilies-of-the-valley.

The audience appeared to be a conglomeration of all the odd
faithfuls that gravitate to Los Angeles. There were doubtful old
men, ambiguous widows in pince-nez, anaemic, spotty youths,
sad morons, grey-haired ladies with vapid, benevolent faces, and
an alarming number of sinister crackpots.

Faces broke into life as soon as Mrs MacPherson began her

performance. Warmly she shouted, 'Who's here for the first time tonight? Put your hands up!' The novitiates smilingly raised their hands. 'And who's been here more than twice before?' Enthusiastic hands shot up.

Aimee Semple Macpherson

First-comers had promptly to be made to feel important. 'I want all of you here for the first time to come up on this stage. I want to hear your name. I want to hear it loud so I can shout it to the rest of the audience.' Wild applause at that. Commands to shake hands with your neighbour and say, 'God bless you' filled empty lives for a brief moment.

Aimée created a dynamic effect, with never a let up. Attention was being paid to the downtrodden. A feeling of pride swept through the assembled mass as every cipher realised he or she could become the centre of the stage while Aimée shook hands. Their moment had come. Old men perhaps got some sort of sexy kick out of it.

199

Aimée now tapped her toes and clapped hands to the rhythm of religious jazz played through a Wurlitzer. Her voice, somewhat corn-crakey, had a great whine and a husky crack in it. She eulogised her wonderful audience through the megaphone. She directed traffic to the stage as sheep crowded through the gates of salvation. She shouted out the name of the state from which each person had come, while the rest applauded.

Anita and I joined the procession to get a good look at Sister Aimée. By the time Aimée shook hands with us she was exhausted and mechanical. A contorted smile froze on her face. First the left hand went out to a passer-by with 'God bless you.' Then the right hand pumped away, 'God bless you.' She hurried through the queue like someone with a train to catch. When she bared her fangs at Anita she took another look, sensing an alien spirit. I tried to muster a pasteboard smile in return for the corpse-like grimace.

Introductions over, Sister Aimée now seemed to be distracted by the radio machine in front of her: the evening's performance was being broadcast. She paid more attention to her unseen audience than the disciples on tap.

'Now, all those who have found Jesus with me—put up your hands!' A few fingers were tentatively raised. Whereupon she yelled wholeheartedly, '*That's* splendid! *Oh*, that's fine! Why, it makes me so glad to see you all holding up your hands in this beautiful building with its dome one thousand feet high.'

She shouted invitations for us to buy her publications. The *Evangelist Times* had an inspiring picture of her at the piano, composing words and music for the wonderful Christmas oratorio that had been performed for the first time and had taken two hours to be sung. Buy also Aimée's magazines, *The Bridal Call*, and buy her *Life Story* for three dollars, and let's have a Christmas collection now, and let's make it a paper collection— no silver, only dollars!

The collection renewed her vigour. Aimée preached a Christmas sermon about the nicest present she had received. It was a huge box done up with ribbons. When she untied the strings, she found her mother inside. 'What could be nicer than having your mother sent back to you for a Christmas present?' (Anita whispered explanation to me: Aimée and her mother had been deadly enemies of late, and the mother sued Aimée for misuse of funds collected at the Temple.)

Aimée babbled on in an endless tirade. Each time she said 'Jee-sus,' it sounded like a swear word. She told about her children, and how she liked to be their equal—more of a sister than a mother. When they swam, she tried to outswim them. When they dived, she tried to dive higher. When they rode, she rode faster and farther. Now she was about to impart a secret! Her children didn't call her 'mother', they called her 'baby'. If a lot of important people came to luncheon, Aimée's daughter leaned right across the table and said, 'Baby darling, will you pass the salt?'

This intimate anecdote had a purpose: 'Baby' introduced her son, who would now preach the second sermon of the evening. He was about sixteen years old, and terribly shy. Sister Aimée stood in the background, trying to hide her tears. She laughed with maternal pride at his jokes; she fluttered like a proud old hen. The boy confessed that he had only found 'Jee-sus' three weeks ago tomorrow, and therefore he couldn't preach well because he hadn't prayed enough. But he was going to pray hard for the Lord to make him a good preacher. The audience responded with chuckles, rounds of applause, and tumultuous cheers at the end of the sermon. Aimée rushed to kiss her son in a spontaneous outburst of affection. For the rest of the entertainment he sat with bowed head, meekly holding his Bible.

Now for the *clou* of the evening: baptismal rites. 'What a wonderful thing,' said Sister Aimée, 'to be baptised!' Just sprinkling with water didn't mean a thing! No, one had to be *buried* with Jee-sus, submerged, and then one would rise from the water a new person, sins all washed away!

Crimson curtains parted to reveal a canvas representing a blazing flower garden. A tiled tank of water, with steps leading down into it from each side, had been placed in the centre of the stage. Coloured arcs went on to floodlight the proceedings. Sister Aimée screamed, 'Get ready to watch the baptisms!'

Aimée, having donned a long-sleeved shift, walked down into the tank. The water came up to her waist. One of her male disciples, wearing collar, bow tie and similar shift, joined her in the bath. Together in their shifts, they received each convert to the amazing ritual. A fat and plain young girl walked into the tank. Aimée and her assistant took the poor sinner by the arms. 'This is Natica Cramp. She found Jee-sus three days ago. In the

name of the Father, the Son and the Holy Ghost.' Down went
the fat girl under the water. Aimée held aloft the girl's right arm,
though her head was still submerged. At last the redeemed one
struggled to the surface. Spluttering and trembling, she staggered
out of the tank.

'Next, please!' The procession was so outrageous that Anita
and I had to hold our breath and pinch one another to keep from
laughing. A grey-haired old hag tottered into the holy pool and
was given the most appalling ducking. Brothers and sisters were
dunked together. One white-haired grandmother croaked into
the microphone, 'I'm now going to be buried with Jee-sus.'
Aimée shouted, 'Isn't that beautiful?' The grandmother very
nearly got her wish. Old men followed. They, too, were submerged longer than a pearl diver.

Then came the spell-binding finale. A cripple was brought into
the glowing arc lights on an invalid chair. Aimée squalled, 'Isn't
she brave? Give the courageous little girl a big hand!' Everyone
cheered and chair and girl got dunked. The cripple's hair, a
moment ago so fluffy and curled, was now lank. Aimée apologised that tonight there were only forty baptisms. Next Thursday,
which would be New Year's Day, she expected a hundred and fifty
people to hold their breath. This was just what Anita and I had
been doing during most of the evening's performance.

A HOLLYWOOD WEDDING

We had to be on time for Bessie Love's wedding. I felt spruce
in my evening tails, with a gardenia in the buttonhole. It was the
first time I'd worn the thing since we arrived in Hollywood.

A large and excited crowd waited outside the church. Inside,
the aisle had been decorated with gilded baskets of pink gladioli
tied by yards of pink tulle. A woman in surplice and cap sang
semi-religious love songs while the congregation assembled.
'Kiss me again,' she pleaded. The organ throbbed and made fluty
noises. The congregation consisted almost entirely of cinema folk,
including a number of cutters, photographers and electricians.

The stars, as befitting them, arrived late. Lilyan Tashman,
with an escort of eight or nine vaguely *louche* young men,
looked ever so ladylike in a chinchilla cape. Her scrambled-egg
curls were done in a Greek fashion. Anita obligingly whispered

the names of those I might not know or recognise. Mae Murray, with painted pout and daffodil-yellow hair, was a miracle of agelessness in spite of being a grandmother. She looked a fat, dimpled cherub in a Kate Greenaway dress of silver lace. She chirped away to her sweating, long-haired husband, Prince Mdivani. Other celebrities came in waves. 'Hedda Hopper,' Anita hissed in my ear. 'Cecil B. DeMille and family. Jetta Goudal.'

Not to be outdone, I whispered back, 'William Powell, one hundred percent peach-fed. And a very self-conscious Ronald Colman.'

'There's Louella Parsons,' Anita countered. 'She's the most important columnist in Hollywood. That's Laura La Plante. This is Pauline Stark.'

Excited screams could be heard from the crowd outside, heralding the arrival of the bride. The organist was having the time of his life, pulling out all stops. The air vibrated with thunderous fanfare.

One by one, at intervals of six yards, the bridesmaids moved up the aisle with jerky, funereal pace. And what bridesmaids! Divorcees and mothers alternated with famous stars, all wearing large hats and flower-trimmed crinolines. Rather naively, I still believed that most bridesmaids were virgins. But perhaps they realised they couldn't find enough; so the retinue had been culled from the bride's friends, both married women and divorcees. Norma Shearer crept towards the altar, looking chiselled from alabaster. Her unseeing eyes stared out of a flawlessly complexioned face. Bebe Daniels, once a Mack Sennett bathing beauty and now a big star, walked behind Blanche Sweet, the maid of honour.

Here comes the rock-pippet bride! Bessie Love entered on the arm of her very proud and over-dressed father. She wore a shroud of white tulle and looked like a terrified bird. Bessie radiated love.

The ceremony was short and sweet, performed by an affected minister. The bridal couple walked down the aisle towards an hysterical crowd outside.

Scuffles ensued. By the time most of the guests had reached the church door, complete chaos had broken loose. The police were outnumbered, the pavement littered with the shattered glass of photographic bulbs. Two old painted twins, dressed identically and looking like demon schoolmistresses gone wrong, assaulted Ronald Colman. 'Oh, please sign this, Mr Colman!' Mr Colman obliged. 'Oh, Mr Colman, we want to tell you what a great personal success you are in *Hong Kong*. We loved *Bulldog Drummond*, and our hearty congratulations on your performance in *Condemned*.'

The wedding reception was held at the Ambassador Hotel. Anita tugged me in Mae Murray's direction. She had read in a newspaper that 'while in Hollywood Mae Murray was going to make a film and lecture on Universal Peace.' 'Auntie Mae,' Anita asked, 'what do you have to say about Universal Peace?'

Auntie Mae considered for a moment. 'Oh well, I became interested in Universal Peace by reading the old Persian philosophers. This stupid picture-making isn't everything, you know.' She cooed and screwed up her face, leaning a little blonde head on Prince Mdivani's shoulder. She then stood stiff as a ramrod, head back so far and chins in so tight that I was tempted to poke her and see if she toppled backwards like a ninepin. Yet, for all the mannerisms, Auntie Mae seemed the most *naturally* affected person I had ever watched.

The bride's mother joined the Universal Peace group for a moment, tapping Anita on the shoulder. 'You know,' she said confidentially, 'the groom is just as lovely as he looks!'

AT W. R. HEARST'S

January 2nd 1931

Anita, John and I were invited to stay at W. R. Hearst's ranch for New Year's Eve.

We were to take Hearst's special train, leaving Los Angeles at eight o'clock in the evening. The train would arrive at its destination around two in the morning; but we could sleep as long as we wanted to, and, when everyone was awake there'd be a communal drive out to the ranch.

The party assembled at the station. Everyone was in high spirits. Tough blondes, hams and nonentities mingled with directors and magnates. Eileen Percy, the gay spark of the crowd, wisecracked, laughed hilariously, swished round on one heel and boxed anyone within reach.

W. R. had taken a train from New York. His car was now slowly linked to the private train that would transport our raucous mob. An official hurried along, carrying a huge bouquet. Flashlight photographers sought out Marion Davies. They love her because she is unlike any other star. Not a bit stagey, she doesn't clasp a bouquet and smile with shut eyes and raised brows for the cameras. She is genuinely surprised by the bouquet: 'Oh, but how nice.'

The party surged on to the train. Time to be off, but Anita and Alice Head were being flashlit and the train must wait. 'Once more, please. A close-up this time.'

We were all ravenously hungry and made a dash for the dining car. Hearst, Marion and Ambassador Moore were edging their way along the corridors. Marion dined quietly with Hearst, and only occasionally dashed across to whisper to her girl friends about how she had lost a bracelet or had her hair dyed a different colour.

I ate in the company of two blondes: Eileen Percy, gayer now than ever, and Julianne Johnston, a nice film actress with no particular personality. With us was Colleen Moore. I had seen pictures of Colleen looking pretty and cute. Now she was here in the flesh. I marvelled. It is one of the tricks of fate that Colleen Moore photographs so well. She looks utterly different in the flesh and I couldn't keep my eyes off her.

Colleen Moore said not a word during dinner. Afterwards we joined Anita and John. I had a spurt of vitality and was in good form while describing a brawl at Zoe Akins' party, when someone knocked a goldfish bowl on to Gloria Swanson's chinchilla coat. The blondes and even Colleen Moore screamed hilariously, spurring me on to fresh sallies.

Later in the evening, John took a redhead in tow and brought her to Anita's compartment for laughs. I have never heard such laughs. Miss Stork (we found out her name) was quick and witty, and so dirty that we yelled in an agony of laughter.

At last Anita and John, their ribs aching, decided to go to bed. I was to share a compartment with a natty little counter-skipper named Eddie Kane. The compartment reeked with fumes of alcohol. Eddie and an old-girl actress were rather tight, talking over-emphatically to one another. At last she tottered off. The beds were made up, and in the space of a few square inches we undressed. We spun a coin; I won, and slept on the lower bed. 'Good night, old man,' Eddie said. I replied, with as much energy and spirit as I could muster, 'Good night, old man.'

A tap on the door. The porter's voice saying, 'It's after nine o'clock and Mr Hearst is up,' was a command for us all to get ready. The king had arisen; now his minions must rise.

The awful Eddie Kane made early morning noises. He dressed and departed, looking both pathetic and smart.

I joined Anita and John. After a slight delay, we started off in a motor for the ranch. There were about ten cars in all; and the party dribbled up to the ranch in twos and threes.

The air was sharp and crisp, with a tang in it. We admired glorious scenery, we gaped at enormous green hillsides that made remembered mountains seem like mole hills.

At length the car shot through a gate, and we were on the grounds of the estate. A sign warned: 'Danger! This road dangerous to pedestrians on account of wild animals.' Soon we passed herds of buffalo, striped zebra, deer and antelope, exotic birds that looked like white ostriches.

Abruptly, in the distance, at the top of a tree-spotted mountain, we caught sight of a vast, sparkling white castle in Spain. It was right out of a fairy story. 'Gosh,' I said. The car moved closer and closer to the vision. Through the cypress trees we could distinguish statues. And then we had arrived.

. The sun poured down with theatrical brilliance on tons of white marble and white stone. There seemed to be a thousand marble statues, pedestals, urns. The flowers were unreal in their ordered profusion. Hearst stood smiling at the top of one of the many flights of garden steps.

As we stepped out of the motor the housekeeper, a white-haired, dark-eyed woman, came forward and shook hands. Then we were shown to our quarters, with footmen conducting us.

My room seemed gigantic. There was a carved gilt ceiling; great, hewn Jacobean beds with gold brocade covers; old, tinselled velvets hanging on the walls. The view from the window revealed a panorama of pale green mountains, blue, misty hills and a silver sea in the distance.

I walked outdoors. The castle consisted of a main building and five outbuildings. The main portion loomed like Wells Cathedral, with an assembly room and a dining-room both the size of a great church. The outbuildings were almost as impressive.

John and Anita's accommodation were even better than mine. Brocade lined the walls of their sitting-room from floor to ceiling It would have bankrupted you to buy one square foot of the material for a cushion. The Italian furniture was of museum quality. The ceiling, like the one in my room, had been carved with full-sized gilt angels. And the bed, an affair of oak tooled to resemble drapery, had the most elaborately embroidered coverlet upon it.

We went outdoors and toured the formal terraces, then wandered in the vast garden. Some of the statues, I noted with surprise, were not up to scratch, even cheapjack. Perhaps it was by intent; we'd been so overpowered by Donatellos and Della Robbias that it made the place come alive to see a nypmh with bobbed hair eating an apple, or three very obviously Victorian graces playing together.

Inside the cathedral-like assembly-room the party now gathered, all bemoaning the non-arrival of their bags. Some stood in awe at the grandeur of their surroundings. Those who didn't, the tough blondes and nonentities, had been here before. Blasé, they made efforts to explain what certain pieces were, where they came from and their date. This aesthetic assessment ended in shrieks of ribaldry. In fact, Eileen Percy was already making whoopee, rushing about with a sword she had picked up for an impromptu bacchanale.

The lunch table looked like a scene in some epic film about the lives of the Caesars. A never-ending length of table was literally covered with food—bottles of pickled fruits of all descriptions, chutneys, olives, onions, squares of every kind of cheese, bowls of fresh fruit. Purple glass goblets, vivid hanging banners and urns of poinsettias completed a Lucullan sight. The food turned out to be as good as it looked. I gobbled away, while the blondes became increasingly hilarious as they planned a cockeyed New Year's Eve.

Trunks arrived. I retired to shave and put on entirely new clothes. In doing so, I lingered too long. Feeling spick and span, I came down from my Jacobean magnificence to join the party but could find no one. Every guest had disappeared.

I wandered about, rather unadventurously trying to explore.

Occasionally, a secretary hurried through the marble garden. I got out my camera and spent an hour or so trying unsuccessfully to photograph myself with a timing gadget. It kept going off prematurely, clicking the shutter before I could even get into position. Still no one. I wrote a long Hollywood letter home, skimmed through newspapers, ate chocolates and nuts, smoked cigarettes.

At last I found some of the party drinking in the kitchen. The blondes were in riding breeches and bright-coloured sweaters. They had had a glorious ride. Secretly, I wished I'd been with them, though years had elapsed since I last rode a horse. It also turned out that I'd missed joining the throng when they went to watch the animals being fed in W.R.'s private zoo.

The sun now set; the lights in the garden were put on, illuminating the swimming pool. I went indoors and found Marion Davies arranging the placement for dinner. She was wearing Wedgewood blue, which accented her white, freckled skin, her drooping aquamarine eyes and shining, pearly teeth.

Marion Davies is pretty as a Greuze, and what a character! She is kind, humble, shrewd, blindly generous and madly inconsequential. When I photographed her a few weeks ago in New York, we wanted a bare shoulder which the small neck to her dress would not allow. In spite of its being a new dress, worn for the first time, she seized a pair of scissors and ripped it down.

Marion is never alone, always surrounded by a gang of twenty or thirty hangers-on. In New York, her party kept arriving at the theatre so late they once trooped in ten minutes before the final curtain. When she went to Europe last year, she took a retinue of twenty-six people who could buy anything they liked and charge it up to her. The scent bills alone came to thousands of dollars. But then, Marion must spend more money than anyone else in the world. . . .

'Marion is most attentive to all sorts of people,' Anita later remarked. 'I've often gone into a shop where she knows the salesgirl, and the salesgirl says, "I had a post card from Miss Davies this morning".'

Marion's nephew, Charlie Lederer, was in grand form at dinner, celebrating his eighteenth birthday. His codfish face made him look older than his years. He behaved like a roué, with a silly goat laugh and a very dry tongue. Brought up in an atmosphere of sophistication, he knew all and seemed unshockable. During the meal, Charlie sat mixing a concoction of cheeses, sauces, butter, onions and paprika, all the while displaying his astonishing gift for making jokes. In reply to a toast, he got up and made an outrageously funny birthday speech, about how inadequate he was to live up to these surroundings, how annoyed Hearst was with him each time he put his foot through a Goya. It was great impertinence, as everyone sat scared stiff of Hearst.

A very ordered party went out onto the terrace to see Marion's latest picture. The cold air sobered us up. Or perhaps it was the dull film. I wondered why Marion should spend her time making such bad movies. The production of this one seemed particularly poor. I went to sleep once or twice, but a blonde Miss Lloyd nudged me incessantly.

Indoors, the mob crowded the assembly-room and waited for midnight. We drank champagne, tried to be hilarious, exchanged kisses all round. But the party was so large that many of the guests remained strangers one to the other. Bells ringing, sirens going off and a whining moan in the distance announced that the New Year was in. Eileen Percy put a cushion on her head, then turned somersaults in front of the colossal chimney grate. Colleen Moore drank silently. Marion had sudden spurts of energy, did a Charleston, shook her hands frenziedly, then hurried out of the room to consult with Hearst. Gradually, all hopes of an orgy disappeared. We dwindled to bed.

I had no sooner put out the light than Charlie Lederer came in. He had opened his bedroom window and a wasp's nest dropped in. If he couldn't find an unoccupied bedroom, could he come here and sleep in the other bed? But there were corridors of empty rooms and he did not return.

New Year's Day. The sun poured through the windows. The mountains sparkled. I was early for breakfast. Colleen felt like death, but wandered out with me to look at the zoo. We found every kind of animal in wired cages—lions, tigers, giraffes, bears and a gorilla. We sent telegrams from the telegraph office in the garden.

Snapshots had to be taken of everyone. I clicked Eileen Percy in riding clothes astride a white marble unicorn.

By lunch time, Charlie Lederer had dressed himself as a film cowboy. He made me laugh so much that I almost choked of hiccups. Again he concocted his mess of cheeses.

In the early afternoon there was a lull of half-hearted wise-cracking. With Eileen Percy laid low by a headache, the party lost its spirit. Then Anita and I decided we would ride. It was a brave moment, as I hadn't been in the saddle since St Cyprian's School. Riding clothes were soon lent me; I fancied myself enormously. With cold feet and an uncertain sinking in my stomach, I went towards the mounting block. The cowboy told me about the reins, and once on I felt all right.

We jogged over even ground. Clop-clop over stones; crack; twigs and dry branches snapped. We descended through woods, down the mountain for miles. Jog-jog; my innards were being well shaken up. But I felt jubilant and decided to ride a lot in future. I liked the smell, the click of the hoofs, the crunch and the creaking of the leather saddle, the balmy air.

Miss Lloyd, a film rider in scarlet, rode first, Anita and I and the cowboy followed. My legs were beginning to quiver with the strain. At last we came out onto an open space and cantered, then galloped. Though pretty shaken and wobbly, I did quite well for myself.

The sun set. The sky became blue-violet, the white palace at the top of the mountain seemed literally a castle in Spain. Deer and antelope bounded past with incredible grace. The scarlet blonde shouted 'Whoopee!' It was what I felt, only I wouldn't have described it that way.

Then came the accident. To keep wild animals away from the main grounds, fences have been erected on W.R.'s property. This entails the opening and shutting of many gates when horse-back riders go afield. One kind of gate we opened by tugging at a long rope which, attached to a lever, pulled the whole gate to one side. But we had to pull hard. My horse clearly didn't enjoy going too near the gate, and became nervous. I got the gate open; but in order to shut it, the rope had to be pulled again. The animal had no inclination to turn back to the rope: he was all for galloping off home. Still, the gate must be shut. Anita and the cowboy had already disappeared. The scarlet blonde cantered off, leaving me to perform this task. I managed to get the horse near enough to the gate. But no sooner had I pulled the rope than the creature bolted. I clung to the saddle with one hand. Stupidly, I also held on to the rope with an ungloved hand, and not quite strongly enough. My bare hand streaked down the length of the rope in a painful second. The skin on my fingers was seared almost to the bone!

Agony ensued. My hand smarted and throbbed until I howled with torment. I galloped on and caught up with Miss Lloyd. She said euphemistically, 'Oh, that's too bad.' We had two miles to go, with my hand in hell all the way. Then the horse had to be tied up. I could hardly walk when I got on to the ground and staggered for first aid.

To make matters worse, the housekeeper observed to the man who dressed my hand, 'Oh God, it's a wonder he doesn't faint!' I trembled with pain while the hand was being dressed. I screwed up my face and stamped and drank enough whisky to make me tight, but the pain was still unendurable.

I tried for sympathy everywhere, but got little. I then drank more and more. My packing was done by a servant to whom I gave pie-eyed instructions. After that, I had a hot shower in a stupor.

Anita was solicitous when she heard about the accident. I moaned with gratitude. Cocktails came and went. Lederer was funnier than ever at dinner.

Afterwards, people seemed in excellent spirits. Even I did a wild and weird dance with Marion, which promptly petered out when Hearst appeared upon the scene. He left, and the fun began again. I executed a tremendous tango with Eileen Percy. We rolled together on the floor amidst screams of joy. My hand was squashed and throbbed like a tom-tom. That awful Eddie Kane, not to be outdone, took my place. I subsided, panting with pain and exhaustion.

Eddie and Eileen now danced a frenzied apache together, making a beeline for a gold, carved chest so priceless that Hearst would not allow a telephone to be on it, nor anyone but the head housekeeper to dust it. The dancers dashed at the forbidden object, opened the lid and jumped inside. On the bottom was a bowl of water to preserve the wood from warping. Splash went Eddie Kane; splash followed Eileen Percy. Marion closed the lid on them, then jumped on it to keep the prisoners inside. The bottom of the chest caved in. Water poured from underneath.

And at that very moment, Hearst most typically came back into the room. He watched the tableau with a deathly white expression.

There was a distinct coolness after that. A chastened group moved on to the terrace to see something of the new Clara Bow film. Then we hurriedly departed to catch our train.

A BRAWL

We dined at the Spanish restaurant *El Cholo*—Anita, Wilson Mizner, Irving Berlin and myself. Wilson and Irving were having a reconciliation. They've been friends for twenty-five years, but lately each thought the other was trying to high-hat him. Anita played the peacemaker; Irving brought along a bottle of Napoleon brandy as a loving cup. The two prodigals were in high spirits: 'Well, you old son of a bitch. Ha, ha! Haw, haw! Oh, you old bastard, you son of a bitch! Haw, haw! Bang! Ha, ha!'

The four of us sat down to dinner in the back parlour of the restaurant and proceeded to devour excellent Mexican foods: soup and beans, tamales, rices and dishes with unknown names. I concentrated on the food, feeling rather out of the conversation. Irving kept leaning across Anita to say, 'Well Willy, you old son of a bitch, do you remember . . .?'

'Ooough! Jesus Christ, you old bastard! You son of a bitch. But I've always liked you, haven't I, you old son of a bitch?'

Anita, very gay, screamed with laughter. The bottle of Napoleon brandy quickly became empty, the profanity more raucous. Wilson broke out in a running sweat, mopped his head and chin with a quivering hand, drew in his breath with a whistle and guffawed more asthmatically than ever.

A young man strolled in, smilingly joined us and shook hands all round. He was drunk. Wilson encouraged him by making jokes. The drunk thought Wilson a hell of a fellow, kept saying, 'You're fine,' never realising how funny Wilson was being about him. The drunk beamed and gazed with glassy eyes. There were occasional awkward silences. Then the razzing continued.

Another glazed drunk appeared. This one seemed a mean hound. He recognized Irving Berlin and at once lapsed into familiarity with, 'Irvie, old fella.'

The first drunk was a nice sort, his enormous mouth stretching

Kairouan

C.B. in Hollywood

in a grin from ear to ear. He wore a yellow overcoat, punctured leather gloves and a hat with a little feather in it. Wilson now made jokes about his clothes. Drunk Number One beamed and again shook hands all round. He leered across the table at the others while pinching my arms and shoulders. 'Oh, you're all fine,' he reiterated.

Wilson had by now become bored with the situation. 'Say look here. We've got to discuss something private. It's about money and we don't want to let strangers in on it. You see, we're squaring a deal; and this little woman wants a twenty-five per cent share, only she didn't do a damned thing for it. So be nice fellows and leave us for a moment.'

'You really mean that? You want to get rid of me? Well, all right. I'll go.' But before going, Drunk Number One insisted on another round of handshakes, during which a new conversation served him as delaying tactics. Drunk Number Two meanwhile sustained his mean-dog look.

Irving took me into a corner for quick consultation on how to get rid of them. But Wilson had already done the damage by encouraging the strays too much. They were, as Wilson put it, 'among friends'.

The friendly drunk now brought out some bonds to show he was a broker. His unfriendly companion, afraid that he might be losing something valuable, shouted, 'Where are those Anaconda Copper Bonds?' 'In my pocket (pronounced *puckert*).' 'Where?' 'In my *puckert*!' 'But where?' 'In my *puckert*!' They shouted at one another in drunken fury. Wilson asked the grinning drunk what his name was. 'Bu-y' (Buddy). And the other? Frank or Gus. 'And you're brothers?' Wilson raised his eyebrows. 'Oh, no, go on, you're kidding. He's not really your brother, is he?' 'Yes.' And then, very quietly. 'Why, don't you like him?'

The whole complexion of the scene altered. The bores were now growling dogs getting ready for a fight. It was ominous.

'Don't be silly,' Wilson soothed. 'I've said nothing. We're among friends. Be sweet now.'

The lurching pair were hot for a fight, their eyes sparkling. Wilson stood up. 'Go home and be quiet. No kidding.' The growling became vicious. Drunk Number Two, who only a

H

moment ago had said, 'Irvie old fella,' abruptly changed his tune. 'Jew!' he shouted at Irving. 'Jew! Dirty Jew!'

Wilson kept stuttering, 'Be sweet now.'

One of the drunks made a rude noise, then said, 'And so much bull to you!' The other shouted to Wilson, 'Sit down!' Both shouted, 'Sit down!'

Old Wilson, his white face pouring with sweat, rose and stood to attention in all his giant height. Anita got up from the table. We all clustered round, weakly advocating, 'Now be quiet.' The restaurant proprietor, a timid little grey-haired man, became grey-faced too. The Mexican waitress stood ashen. The mean hound said, 'It's all right, Buddy. I've got my coat off.' And with that there was a fierce blow aimed at Wilson's face. Happily, the blow went wild. But it was enough to start the mêlée. Wilson, with blood in his eyes, fumbled quickly for a beer bottle and cracked it over the side of Buddy's head. Crash! The glass fell in smithereens.

'Wilson! Stop it!'

A scuffling, then more bottles flew through the air and burst like bombs. The noise was deafening. The drunks sought ammunition in the front part of the restaurant. Wilson, the old tough, stood in the doorway dividing shop and back parlour. His face deathly white and pouring with sweat, his eyes darting out of his head, he threw bottles at the enemy while the enemy responded with other bottles, tumblers and heavy glass water carafes that whizzed through the air past his head and broke in a thousand pieces against the wall.

The proprietor, who had been impotent to stop the fight at the beginning, now stood cowering behind a net curtain. Wilson barked huskily to Irving and me: 'Get her out! Get her out!' But there was no escape for Anita. The back door was locked; the only means of escape seemed to be the main door, from which direction the drunks in their fury now threw anything and everything they could lay hands on. The fight would never cease until we were all dead.

Crash! An earsplitting bang, and the mirror on the wall dropped in splinters. Wilson would surely be killed, or at least have his head gashed open. He roared like a bull. Protecting himself round the doorway, he flung things back in reprisal.

How *would* this end? It seemed useless for the rest of us to join the battle. We were sober, and didn't want to kill the drunks. We only wanted the fight to cease. The drunks, though, were out for blood. Wildly, we tapped on the back windows to attract the chauffeur's attention so that he would send for a copper. The smashing, roaring and shouting went on.

Then, suddenly, the fight stopped: the drunks had mysteriously retreated. We held a frenzied conference. 'Hide the Napoleon brandy in case the police come! Where's the key to the kitchen door?' The ashen proprietor produced the key. Irving and Anita dragged a reluctant Wilson out through the kitchen while I hurriedly paid at least the food bill.[1] The shop was entirely wrecked. No picture remained intact upon the walls; every mirror had been broken: pieces of glass lay strewn about. Beer and water ran down the walls and along the floor.

The drunks were now returning. 'Are those people here yet?' 'No,' I heard the Mexican waitress gabbling, 'they are already gone.' And that's all I heard: for I, too, slipped through the kitchen and joined the others in the car.

The chauffeur, it turned out, had been unable to find a policeman. But all had ended happily. Wilson was unscathed; and none of the drunks, I reported, seemed badly hurt.

Now that we were safely in the car, the whole scene took on a different aspect. 'Really, boys! We all might have landed on the front page,' Anita piped.

We might have, and a choice assortment of names it would have been! We began to laugh hysterically. Wilson of the amazing performance turned to me and said, 'Well, young Beaton, now you've seen the social life of Hollywood!'

February 5th, New York

I went down Broadway to see Adele Astaire at a Negro dance school where she is taking lessons. Adele looked her best in a pair of pale blue drawers that revealed witty legs. She smiled like a little monkey and said, 'Oh, Buddy has taught me such marvellous, new, dirty steps.'

I am staggered each time I see Adele perform. She stabs her pointed toe with delicacy and force. Her dancing has such personality; it is subtle, sophisticated and—to use a word which

---

[1] Irving Berlin settled all damages with the proprietor the next day.

strangely enough does apply to someone so American and modern—dainty.

An atmospheric place, this dance school: a rather 'high' smell of stale sweat and face powder predominated. Gramophones ground away in competition from every room, accompanied by a frenzied tapping of steel-toed shoes. The proprietor toured me round, telling anecdotes about these pupils who had become famous. Many of them still come back to learn new tricks, even though their names are now in lights.

February 6th

Adele said she wouldn't mind if I joined her for a few lessons. Whereat Adele changed into her rehearsal clothes and gaily started to strut as if in her real element. I felt impotent with no control over my feet whatsoever. Even a simple succession of steps became a mountainous difficulty.

I sweated like a bull while a fifteen-year-old Negro boy kept urging, 'Do it again! Do it again!' The merciless little wretch went on doggedly while I continued to try so hard to remember and concentrate with my eyes shut.

I asked Adele about the first visit to London she made with her brother, and she told me how at the beginning they hated it. They got taken out by June and Anita Elson to Babe Barnato's, but then they were invited by the Duke and Duchess of York to a party at Chesterfield House, and they became intimate with the Prince of Wales, Prince George, Lady Louis Mountbatten, Audrey Coats, and all their friends. These extraordinary little hoofers went through the Royal Family like a streak.

Adele is an utterly natural star, and this is a rare phenomenon. She is brilliant in intuitive ways, also looney and childish. For years she had poored over watches and clocks; and not until she was seventeen did she learn to tell the time.

Adele then took me to watch Fred and Marilyn Miller rehearsing a dance on the top of the Ziegfeld theatre building. I had never seen such a display of energy and high spirits. The room re-echoed every sound as they screamed and yelled and stamped and kicked as if they were mad. Fred was excited and chewed gum frenziedly, chewed a bit more, then crunched it with his front teeth as well.

He looked very ashen and pink-eyed, and terribly thin. Miller with a face like a little pig, pink and fat, and mouth sprouting teeth. She is very 'old-fashioned' looking, and has a twangy speaking voice. But I do admit her legs and feet are perfection; her agility is amazing.

I envied these two their hilarious fun, planning their dances and encores, and when the difficult work is done, running through the routines so slickly to the ring of success—success.

February 13th

We intended going to a German talkie but arrived too late. None of the picture palaces on Broadway seemed to have appetising attractions, so we ended up at Minsky's burlesque show.

There was hardly a woman in the audience, apart from Anita. It was a lecherous conglomeration of thugs, 'he-men' and old gagas. On the stage were the toughest, dirtiest lot of comics and showgirls. The jokes were so broad they could scarcely be called *double entendre*. The ladies, exhibiting nipples and navels, shimmied out on an illuminated gangplank. They had blue-bruised legs and arms; they shook their tasselled bottoms. Policemen stood ready to throw out any man who became too lustful and held on to a pair of varicose legs!

There were lots of 'teaser' numbers. With the same chorus repeated over and over, the leading lady coyly and tantalisingly takes off one piece of clothing at a time, then goes offstage until the audience applauds sufficiently to bring her back again. Ultimately, if the applause is overwhelming, she takes her final bow almost in the nude—three leaves!

Some of the 'teasers' were far from young. The leading lady we had seen outside the theatre while buying our tickets. A fat, hennaed old hag in a fur coat, she'd been explaining to the policeman that she had a terrible cold in the head. Now she was strutting over the stage, wearing a small bit of silver fringe over her sex and singing the dirtiest song about her 'artillery' man.

The wow of the evening was Carmen, the belly dancer. I had never seen anything like Carmen's expert orgy. Even the toughs in the audience hooted in embarrassed laughter.

New York, undated

These past months I have gained independence and assurance. If I am left alone, I like it; I take an 'it's spinach-and-to-hell-with-it' attitude. I've taken to chewing gum, having my hair cut short and sitting with my legs wide apart.

Perhaps I've even acquired an easier personality. I've certainly had more success and this was observed by Mrs Moats who remarked that there *was* a challenging look in my eye, and an authority—as if I had just possessed a woman!

Part X

A Country Setting

1930 and 1931

My journal has remained untouched during the past eighteen months or more: not for lack of personal events that have been of great moment to me, in fact just the opposite. All of a sudden, existence seemed stackful of excitement, and so much happening every day, that the next day's activities had started before the diary was even thought of. Now there is a lull let me appraise the last eighteen months.

It was only a year ago last August that, in a flurry of elation and dripping with sweat, I ran down Covent Garden to the publishing firm of Messrs Duckworth. Under my arm was the finished manuscript of my first book. Mr Thomas Balston (to whom I was recommended by the Sitwells) blinked like a barn owl behind opaque glasses, as he bid me catch my breath and have a cup of office tea. He then turned the pages of *The Book of Beauty*.

The manuscript was not a bulky one, in spite of the drawings and photographs with which it was interspersed; yet to me it represented a monumental work. After many weeks spent in the British Museum Library among the sentimental engravings of ladies holding doves as they inspired the poets of their day, I returned home to write my eulogies of their contemporary counterparts. Miss Joseph, a handsome raven-haired Rebecca who became my secretary and boon companion, pounded out my halting or garbled sentences on a portable typewriter. Then I had taken my chapters to Wiltshire to undergo the eagle scrutiny of Edith Olivier, that most kind of all Christian ladies. In her 'long room' (a wooden annexe) we sat on the floor with scissors and paste, reorganising the construction of the book.

Occasionally our industriousness would be interrupted by a visit from a member of the Women's Institute, or an old forester coming for advice. Earlier, Mr A. G. Street the Wiltshire farmer had brought Edith his first work, a novel about high life in Monte Carlo; Edith had tactfully suggested, with excellent results, that, in future, he should write only of the countryside and things he knew about intimately. These diversions were so entertaining that I never chafed if our work was curtailed: no one staying with Edith could but be infected by her lack of self interest, and by her serene enjoyment of life.

Rex, who treated Edith's house as his second home, also exuded this sense of calm; together they created an atmosphere that was idyllic.

At the end of lunch one day, the three of us were sitting at her small round table on the chairs Edith had covered with needle-work pictures of the various rectories in which she had lived her full, if secluded, life. We had eaten trout caught from the river outside the bay-window; we had drunk white wine out of Edith's tall green goblets. After strawberries from her garden, and coffee, we were extolling the glories of Wiltshire. I wondered aloud if I could find a cottage nearby, and if I, too, might not be able to achieve this peace of mind?

'Cottages are scarce,' Edith regretted and suddenly her eyes became brilliant. 'But now I come to think of it, Stephen Tomlin, the sculptor from Swallowcliffe, *did* say he'd seen, while on a walking tour of the downs, a deserted house that had a grotto!' Wild with anticipation at the prospect of anything so romantic and Sitwellian as a grotto, I insisted that Edith abandon scissors and paste and drive Rex and myself in hot pursuit. After many dramatic experiences of losing our way among the downs, we discovered, in an utterly isolated, remote, and almost hidden valley, my *Grands Meaulnes*.

Sleeping among the drooping ilex trees stood a small cluster of cedarwood-coloured brick buildings, elegantly faced with stone. From the moment I saw this haunting, haunted sight, in its aura of lazy beauty, I knew Ashcombe would belong to me.

For several weeks my requests to the landlord to buy his impractical place were ignored. But I persevered. The owner recognised the advantages of having some fool put into livable order his game-keeper's store-house, pheasant hatchery and unused stables. He would let me rent the place, so long as his birds were not disturbed.

Michael Rosenauer, a successful Viennese architect and cherubic-faced friend of Anita Loos, came down to a high-summer's picnic. In this bucolic, out-of-the-world spot, Rosenauer, with his town clothes and cigar rolling in his bared teeth, looked curiously urbane as he mapped out his plans, and bargained with cocksure little Mr Brazier, the tweed-clad builder from Wilton. A sum was named. Scribbling in a sketch book 'Not so much as I feared,' I passed it to Edith; 'Nor me either,' she wrote, and added, 'Hurrah!'

Now flashback to Covent Garden. I mopped my forehead and looked around Mr Balston's office. It was very dark, dry and stale. I knew I did not belong in this serious, scholarly atmosphere; Mr Balston and his likewise black-clad assistant, knew it too. There was something quite haunting about this young assistant. He pervaded a Dickensian misery; for it seemed that, against his will, he was caught in the trap of a publishing firm and would possibly remain for ever. It is extraordinary how quickly one senses a situation, and without ever discussing it knows that it is mutually understood. Anthony Powell,[1] for that was the assistant's name, gave me looks of understanding and made himself friendly, while Mr Balston blinked and turned the pages which my Rebecca had so patiently produced for the fiftieth time from her typewriter.

Perhaps an hour had passed in that dark office in Covent Garden. At last Mr Balston snapped-to the covers of the folder

[1] Who left the office to become the well-known satiric-novelist.

H*

enclosing my puny offspring. He blinked at me some more and smiled, 'It's most entertaining!' I had quite expected him to say it was not quite serious enough for a firm such as his to publish. But instead he added, 'We'll put it in work right away. The proofs will be ready in six weeks.'

With the satisfaction of knowing that the builders were at work at Ashcombe, and the printers on my book, I went off to join Anita in Vienna. Here antiquaries were ransacked for cheap baroque chairs and consoles for my new home. Oliver Messel joined us; and with him a tall, gangling young man, with the face of a charming cod-fish, named Peter Watson. Of all my recently acquired friends, he was to strike the deepest and rarest chord of sympathy. Peter's acute sensibility, subtlety of mind, wry sense of humour and mysterious qualities of charm made him unlike anyone I had known. Not that we took to one another at first sight. To begin with, when we went *en masse* to beer halls and fêtes, we were merely civil. I did not recognize his virtues, and asked Oliver if the newcomer was not a bit of a bore. But one morning, when Peter decided to come out with me on a sight-seeing expedition, and we stood in stiff silence coming down in the hotel lift, he caught sight of me, and I caught sight of him, each glancing surreptitiously at the other in the looking-glass. We burst into laughter, and arm-in-arm walked off into the Vienna side-streets to become the greatest of friends. We stimulated one another. Whereas I gave Peter his first glimpse of a modern painting—a Matisse at the Leicester Galleries—he taught me an appreciation of music. Before meeting him I had heard of the composer Strauss, but had not yet discovered that he could be either, Johann, Richard or Oscar.

Oliver and Peter were going on to Venice, and it did not take much persuasion on their part to make me join them. Here, in the dank alleyways, I foraged for junk and bought for Ashcombe old painted doors and cupboards, and stone ornaments, to be sent home by *Petite Vitesse*.

With a feeling of almost complete contentment, I returned to England to correct proofs and work on my new acquisition. Rex pencilled designs for a doorway, with a pineapple in its broken pediment, for urns for the parapet and a chimney piece for the sitting-room; these were given to a local stone mason. But since bona fide antiques were beyond my financial reach, ingenuity and the Caledonian market had to come to my rescue for the furnishing of the house. Even carpets and curtains cost more than I could afford. Materials were put to uses never intended. 'Animal baize,' as the felt is called which covers pantomime zebras and leopards, provided excellent carpeting, and other theatrical materials, originally invented to last for the run of a play, have to stand the test nobly as curtains and sofa coverings.

The wild winter's evening arrived eventually when Rex, Oliver, Peter and I ventured down the steep chalky hill of the valley to spend the first weekend at Ashcombe. We savoured the chill smells of paint and freshly carpentered wood, combined with the warm smell of calico, new rugs, and crackling log fires. The small habitation, for so long abandoned to its loneliness, suddenly became alive and took on its own personality. It was unlike any other abode, admittedly fantastic and strange with its bright colours and silver trumpery but to me, at any rate, infinitely charming.

Edith Olivier joined us; and together with the cheerful, bucolic creatures who were to work with devotion in house, kitchen and garden, ran out into a wintry holocaust, danced around a bonfire, fell in the mud, and toasted the future in champagne.

Ashcombe became lived in. Imported plants grew in pots, chickens browned and crackled in the unreliable antiquated oven. In addition to the favourite kedgerees, haddock and kipper dishes, we enjoyed the novelty of sweet potatoes and shadroe from America, and the luxuries of brandied fruits and cigars from Fortnums. Lorries, bringing more curious pieces of furniture, were lost in Brontë-esque storms, but finally bumped over the hazardous descent through the downland, churning up the courtyard into a playground of mire.

By degrees the stables became a studio, fashionably decorated white upon white; my bedroom acquired circus murals painted by friends. Whatever decorative folly was perpetrated, the mood of this remote and poetic spot remained unharmed. Ashcombe always retained its time-haunted peacefulness. Of course, the chimneys smoked, but I was happy.

Christmas-time saw the first family party. My father was quite baffled by the décor, and tripped over the dais on which my

223

Carousel bed was poised. Rubbing a sprained ankle, he complained that for his taste the house was too full of booby traps. By degrees my mother, forgetting Ashcombe's impracticabilities and its remoteness, made excellent suggestions for next summer in the garden; while Aunt Jessie, with eyes twinkling, oohed and ahed to my heart's delight.

The *Beauty* book appeared: although it ignited perhaps less of a blaze than I had hoped, Lady Cunard added to the conflagration by throwing her copy into the fire. Her luncheon guests were astonished to watch her thrusting a poker through the burning covers as she exclaimed in a high canary squeak, 'He calls me a hostess, that shows he's a low fellow!'

In the New Year Peter Watson took the opportunity to make his first trip to America by coming with me on an elaborate journey than encompassed most of the great sights of that vast continent. I soon began to be envious when Marjorie and other friends liked Peter more than they did me. We went together to applaud the Astaires, bought records, listened to opera, concerts, and dance bands in Harlem.

Followed a complicated itinerary of train journeys during which Peter was always beating me at backgammon, and keeping me guessing. We were impressed by the treasures in the museums of the big cities, enjoyed the lazy atmosphere of the southern states, and bathed in the winter sunshine of the Bahamas. In Haiti, more haunting than any voodoo, was the Negro Emperor Christophe's citadel built by slave labour on the top of the mountain. As a monument to megalomania it is only comparable to the Pyramids.

From Havana, where I first saw orchids growing in a tree, we sailed, to arrive, severely sun-scorched, at Vera Cruz. Then by a slow wooden train a spiral ascent through tropical lushness to Mexico City. The small German *pension* was preposterously called the Hotel Ritz, and smelled of lignum-vitae wood-panelling. It was the base from which expeditions were made to Churrigueresque churches coarsely carved and tiled with gilt gingerbread madonnas; the bazaars, vivid with poison-coloured masks and paper flowers; to Cuernavaca, Taxco, and Puebla.

When I returned to England, Nancy and Baba, with Peter (who had returned earlier), met me at Southampton. We all drove to Ashcombe, where spring was burgeoning. In the bath-room, I heard Baba saying to Nancy that Peter and I now talked so like one another that we were indistinguishable on the tele-phone. Reggie, happily ensconced in the Flying Corps, was stationed nearby at Andover. He was a bit worried that his bad headaches might interfere with his career, but otherwise seemed to be thrilled with his new life, though we found the heartiness of some of his fellow officers whom he would bring over *en masse* was a bit jarring to the rather special atmosphere.

Ashcombe had become my chief interest. I worked hard at this pleasure, planning with Noble, the gardener, the new terraces and orchard, taking measurements, and scouring the antique shops of adjoining counties. By degrees another room was finished, but there was always more to be done.

Each Friday I would motor from London, at breakneck speed, with further additions to the house. The small Ford became almost invisible under its load of wooden statues, bird cages, books, American magazines, hook rugs, gramophone records and boxes of flowers from Covent Garden.

More guests than there was room for would arrive on Satur-day, to walk for miles in the wild, uninhabited remoteness of the downs, or lie on the lawns surrounded by pigeons and scrap albums. After dinner there were elaborate entertainments, with Oliver Messel, Oggie Lynn,[1] or John Sutro as star cabaret turns. The large neighbouring family from Ferne House, over the hill, were our long-suffering audience while, till early morning, we continued our charades with their endlessly resourceful changes of costume improvised from the depths of the dressing-up chest.

Lord Berners had become a habitué of Ashcombe. Gerald could compose music, write novels, and paint in the manner of Corot. He was also a natural eccentric and practical joker, with the motto 'Amusement First' and telegraphic address 'Neighbourtease.'

PAVLIK TCHELITCHEW

It was while staying with Gerald Berners in his house overlooking the Forum that I saw the apricot light, clear skies and parasol pines of Rome for the first time. Rome does not take strangers to its bosom, and the malice of society in the eternal city was a bit alarming, but painting expeditions, the panoply surrounding the church, Firbankian intrigues, and the eccentrics of the English Tea Room were all part of the general enjoyment. En route for home there was a three-week stop-off in Paris. This coincided with Edward James's controversial new season of ballet, with Kurt Weill writing music for 'The Seven Deadly Sins' and Lotte Lenya rasping it out: also Pavlik Tchelitchew, the Russian painter designing transparent scenery for 'Errante'.

Tchelitchew at first intimidated me (he could be devastating in his disapproval) but soon cast an almost hypnotic influence over me, and under his spell my photographs became 'neoromantic'.

One particular evening he exercised himself on a variety of sacred and profane subjects. He started with colour. Grey: certain greys were gritty and dry to him. Mantegna's colours are so dry he feels they pop and crack, giving the spectator the feeling of being able to break off with equal ease the drapery, the mountains, or Christ's feet and legs.

---

[1] Olga Lynn, a diminutive concert singer, whose company was so sought after by those in search of amusement that social success impaired her career as a serious artist.

With his histrionic brilliance Pavlik makes even the simplest anecdote a marvel. He whispers and then shouts; he becomes alternately a bull or a child.

THE FORVM

Pavlik rehashed an argument with Virgil Thomson about music. V.T. said the only noise that frightened people today was a siren. Pavlik objected. 'Some sensitive people are frightened by the flutter of a falling piece of paper, the whisper of a breeze through a window.'

He tells how most people (if no one is around) will touch the private parts of statues in the museum; and in consequence these parts have continually to be washed! He embroiders on this assertion, relating an encounter with Etienne de Beaumont among the statues—all the more exciting an adventure because nothing happens. He conjured up a bad picture in some remote museum, painting it with a few deft verbal strokes that endow it with imaginative immortality.

227

Pavlik's imitation of Klessinskaya in her heyday as ballerina and Czar's darling was accompanied by many twirls and arm flourishes. The subject transports him: he takes to his feet and executes several elaborate arabesques. The impression is that of a bluebottle—darting, resting, then off again on its tormenting flight. And this bluebottle was dressed as follows (Pavlik evoked the costume with gestures): a tutu made of thousands of yards of the most expensive pink silk tulle; over this, black lace; then a bitter-almond-green satin corsage, with a huge pink rose at the breast; neck and chest a dazzle of diamonds, ears heavy with enormous cabochons, elaborately coiffed head sprouting black and white aigrets. It was a performance of sublime ridiculousness. But so intense and successful was his determination to conjure up this phenomenon that the monk-like Slav transcended his outward appearance and, in fact, *became* this pampered esoteric plaything of a forgotten age.

It was during this visit, despite the danger of being considered disloyal, that I first became a devoted admirer of Pavlik's great rival Christian Bérard. From the moment we met Bébé gave me his open hand. When George Huene took me to see Jean Cocteau smoking opium I considered that adult life could reach no higher.

FIRST BALLET

My former disappointment and bitterness at not having worked for Cochran had long since been forgotten; now once more he approached me: this time, the offer to decorate a ballet Osbert had written upon a sheet of Renishaw Hall writing paper—was definite. The subject of the work involved the love complications at an Edwardian pheasant shoot. Willie Walton had composed the perversely lyrical music—and this was to be the first of many collaborations with Frederick Ashton.

Over lunch in a Soho restaurant Fred and I discussed the proposed sets and the costumes, and used the menu for pencilled suggestions. More menus were called for. Before the hors d'oeuvres had been cleared, Fred remarked somewhat wryly, 'You have finished your work—it has taken twenty minutes. I still have all mine to do.' His face then crinkled into that wonderfully disarming laugh.

A few weeks later, the stage curtains parted to reveal my first living-picture in the theatre. It was a moment of exaltation for which the long wait had been well worth while.

May 17th 1931, London

I had a pleasant afternoon at Frank Dobson's studio, sitting for my almost completed bust. It doesn't look anything like me, but I didn't say so. Afterwards I pottered about among the discarded plaster casts, unearthing heads of Tallulah, Osbert and Lopokova.

OSBERT'S HEAD IN DOBSONS STUDIO

Out on the street, I thought for a moment of walking home in the fine spring weather. But an empty taxi rolled by; and instinctively I put up my hand to hail it. I am glad I did: otherwise I should never have obtained a glimpse, after all this time, of my once great friend, Boy le Bas.

For many years Boy and I were inseparable. At Cambridge I saw him every day and, more often than not, *all* day. I liked and admired Boy; I was more at ease with him than with any other friend I've ever had. Yet, when he left Cambridge, he went more or less completely out of my life. Boy turned 'earnest'. He lived away from his rich family; he never 'dressed' or went to parties. He avoided good restaurants, eating in a garret in Soho.

229

I suppose it was only natural for Boy to avoid me, too. Slowly he dropped me altogether, never answering my letters. Once in a while I still wrote to him, thinking that, even if he despised my dilettante existence, he must surely be interested to see me again after such a lengthy gap. We'd been rare friends—stimulating one another's efforts, saying funny things together. But now, he didn't seem curious.

From the taxi window, I spied him walking with a fellow art student. He looked just the same, except that he had grown a beard and his clothes were dirty. The taxi bowled past before I could gather my wits. I must stop and have a word with Boy. I tapped on the window and told the driver to go back. We circled, drawing up close.

I remembered that Boy no longer liked being called Boy, so I shouted, 'le Bas! le Bas!'

He turned round, baffled, speechless and so nervy that I thought any minute he would bolt away. He seemed unfriendly: when I put my hand out, he hesitated before shaking it.

Hastily, I made conversation about his painting. He replied in a voice that had changed to a deep, dull tone: 'I've nothing to show. It's a slow business.' He laughed a hearty, mirthless laugh. I thought it might turn into the old humorous laugh, but it didn't.

Boy asked no questions about me or my family. I began to feel embarrassed. I had heard Mrs le Bas was ill and now asked, 'How is your mother?'

'Oh, she's definitely on the road to recovery. But she's still a bundle of nerves. Yes, a bundle of nerves.' He nodded his head like a professor. Several more lame sentences were exchanged. It seemed incredible. I was talking to a completely different person. Gone were the understanding, the sympathy, the special sense of humour we had once shared. Yet if only for old times' sake, I wanted to ask a hundred questions. Did he ever see anyone from his former life? Did he resent that life so terribly? Why did he resent me? I wanted him to say what he thought of me now today, of my appearance and manner. I wanted anything but for him to remain so aloof and hostile.

'Where are you living?' I persisted.

'Oh, round about Soho. That part.'

It was a mortifying encounter. There was something shocking about the completeness with which he had interred his old self. I heard this stranger saying, 'Well, whenever I have any painting worth seeing, I'll let you know.'

That was my cue for departure. I tapped on the window to the driver. Boy sloughed me off and went on with his unintroduced friend.

Perhaps the whole incident wouldn't have meant so much to me if it weren't for the haunting memory of that other Boy. Where was the intelligence and charm? Where was his sense of the ridiculous? He might be an accomplished painter, but did he have to acquire such colourless sobriety?

Or was it my fault? Do I see myself as others see me? Did I strike Boy as being ridiculous, superficial? Perhaps I am, but I have my serious moments. Does Boy think that art and levity are incompatible? Whatever, I felt that our meeting had been tragic. I supposed it was the last time we should cross paths.

Part XI

North Africa

1931

George Hoyningen-Huene invited me to his newly acquired property in Tunisia. Huene, a pupil of Steichen, that grand old monster of the camera, was one of the photographers whose work I most admired. Whenever I visited him in Paris he had always been generous with his encouragement of my work. On the following trip he helped me to take photographs of 'places and things' rather than of people. Before this, I had been satisfied to take snapshot 'views'. Following in Huene's steps, I started to make, out of the life around me, pictures that attempted to be interesting as compositions, to bring a point of view to the subject, and, if possible to make a comment. To George my thanks are proffered for adding this additional pleasure to travel and an extra facet to my photographic career.

I was inspired to another new enthusiasm: journeys to exotic and romantic lands.

TUNISIA

Hammarmet
We were unpacking our trunks on arrival at George's house here,

when a heavily burnoosed effigy appeared at the grilled window and resulted in being the old Comte Max Foy. He had a coif of white hair, a parrot's face and the declamatory gesture of a classical French actor. Also he had plans for an immediate trip into the dessert.

For several days the expedition was postponed, but finally we started; I, with the aged and impatient Count in his small car; the two Georges[1] following in a vast Queen Mary limousine. 'That was an old Roman fort—' I looked dutifully, and felt self-conscious as I smiled politely. We passed kilometre after kilometre of flat waste land, with distant mountains like the temperature chart of an invalid. An occasional Arab rode his donkey and led a few goats, or a camel ate spiky cacti as though it were enjoying a delicate salad. These would be the only exclamation marks. We came to a lake with water like oil.

Then suddenly, with the sunset, the journey was justified! I lost all shreds of self-consciousness in my sudden enthusiasm. As the sun lowered itself towards the ever distant mountains, the sky became a symphony of unimaginable brilliance.

Leonardo used to see pictures in the uneven surfaces of old walls, in roughly plastered ceilings and crackled paint. It did not need his imagination to recognise the marvellous illustrations projected above. Imperceptibly changing as we watched were scenes of the Apocalypse, of chariot races with Olympian charging horses, kings and emperors sitting in judgement on thrones, mysteriously gesticulating at the top of flights of stairs or in fiery molten caves. Enormous profiles of angels and animals now melted into raging torrents and tempestuous seas and became part of Shakespeare's *Tempest*.

Generally the sky forms only a small part of the world one sees from day to day, but here the earth was as flat as a gramophone record, and one felt oneself to be part of the burning heavens.

As the sun was meeting the horizon we arrived at Kairouan. The dying light flushed with rose the marshmallow cupolas and minarets. Then all turned to a glittering night-scene. An indigo sky was spangled with stars, while, beneath in the market, torches and flares sparkled on arrays of painted sweetmeats,

---

[1] The second George being George Sebastian, a Rumanian neighbour who had built himself a beautiful Moorish house with colonnaded swimming pool.

miniature mountains of corn and cereals, and the fruit stalls, garlanded with swags of oranges, cut with the fresh leaves growing on the stalks.

We marvelled at the great mosque: we wandered down mysterious streets overhung with pepper trees, or past alleyways, dimly lit doorways or dark hovels. We sat in an arcaded café decorated with odd tinsel pictures and glass scenes from *Othello*. Birdcages hung from the red and blue striped ceiling; and a mother o' pearl gramophone, with brass horn, played raucous Eastern music, with screeching voices agonisingly shrill.

The crescent moon still shone bright when next morning we were called before dawn. We hoped, with good fortune on our side, to arrive at Tozeur before nightfall. The sky gradually lightened through the delicate filigree of the olive trees and *faux poivriers*, homes for waking birds.

Groups of Arabs, squatting forlornly near their camels, were waiting for the sun to rise before burying their dead. The corpse, shrouded in a sheet, lay on the ground or was stiffly jerked along tied to the camel's back.

Once again, in a desert landscape, we passed muffled women in dark blue with tattooed make-up and the stumbling grace of Tanagra figurines. Arabs jogged along on bird-delicate footed long-eared donkeys, their wide-eyed Bedouin children looking out from black curls. It seemed odd to see a solitary woman, surrounded by infinite miles of aridity, thrashing with full force and factory-vigour at the coarse tufts of grass. It would come as a shock to see a human being walking in the empty vastness with the jostling fervour of a woman shopping for bargains. Yet these solitary pedestrians will spur themselves on for two days in order to sell a chicken; sometimes hiking for three months without stopping, except to rest at night under a flimsy banket, with only a tuft of coarse alfalfa grass for protection.

My companion, the venerable Count, by now, had proved an entertaining conversationalist. Crafty and humorous, age had given him a balance which his little car lacked. Over pits, boulders, cracks and holes, the Count drove his 'little Jade'; the harder we bounded the more the old Count cackled with amusement. Occasionally he had to drive over ground that looked impassable.

234

Our first stop was at Sbeitla to see the Roman ruins which comprise the greater part of three temples in almost perfect condition, made of a stone that is saffron coloured. Cacti sprouted wildly from the cornice of a triumphal arch. Very dramatic.

On—on—on. We must cross a certain river before nightfall or we would not find the way. We passed a stray herd of camels, They were pregnant and could not be used for carrying. In our headlights they looked flat as made of cardboard; desert birds were big and bright, and scurrying mice and rats flew across our path. At last the twinkling lights of our goal. Groups in dirty white huddled round a lamp, which dramatises the crude but beautiful honeycomb brickwork of the city.

REX WHISTLER'S DESIGNS FOR ASHCOMBE DOOR & URN.

The cries of the Arabs being called to prayer woke us before daylight. Soon the square of my window became violet blue, and we prepared for a five hour expedition through the desert to El Oued. A special vehicle, which is necessary to navigate the high sand dunes, arrived, looking like an enormous caterpillar, or a prehistoric car once owned by Lord Lonsdale. Indeed, the Comte Max resembled the sporting earl as he sat aloft, wearing a large white panama hat and scarlet burnous. The caterpillar had eight wheels, and, after we had navigated some precipitous mountains of sand we realised they were all of them necessary.

One marvelled that the sand was combed with so many varying textures, as if an army of immaculate gardeners had been at work with rakes of every size. Gradually the undulations became more gentle and we then saw the non-existing lakes, rivers, minarets and towers of a mirage. It gave one a somewhat uncanny sensation. One realised how easily parched travellers had gone on to their doom in an effort to arrive at this illusory haven.

Eventually the mirage evaporated, and once more we travelled through a flatness like a pretrified sea. At last the mirage became reality: a Saharan Nights dream cluster of minarets, delicately plumaged palmettoes like spurting land-fireworks, proved that we had reached the oasis of El Oued.

When our caterpillar came to a halt, we found ourselves in a pale biscuit-coloured world: the carefully sifted sand beneath our feet, the towers and domes, even the dogs and the sand-fox with big ears, were all monochrome. The entire population seemed to greet us: little children ran out with infants on their backs.

We immediately picked as our guide, from a sea of turbanned faces, a boy who could not have been more than ten years old. Yet his manner was mature and calm, as he spoke with a delightful French accent. At once, with immense dignity and charm, he embarked upon a tour of the town. He showed us the synagogue, with unbelievably old men trembling at prayer; the big mosque, with cross-legged groups singing in euphoric rhythms: the silent groups reclining in the market square. In a dimly lit vault, with a low wall running round the room, sat soldiers in red fezzes. With her pet goat beside her sat an old, half-blind Madam. Bundled together were the whores, like a flock of tropical birds with their heavily painted faces, barbaric jewellery and elaborate costumes.

One Jezebel, the most striking, sat motionless with calm dignity holding in her hennaed hands a heavy silver key. This key would open the room, large enough only for a bed and brass tray of tea, to which she would take one of the soldiers when he had a mind to invite her to do so. With high Chinese cheekbones, a long oval yellow face and receding chin she was attired in the most sophisticated taste of dark blues and white with silver ornaments.

There was something haunting and sinister about the quietness of this waiting-room; no one talked, or appeared to pay any attention to anyone else, until suddenly one of the soldiers would amble off towards one of the silently smoking women, to dis-

Tunisian Woman

appear with her in her cell. Madam and her goat paid no attention.

Early next morning, George Huene and I wandered to the oasis. It is one of nature's most extraordinary phenomena that in the centre of a desert-barrenness, there should suddenly be crystal pools, a fertile garden of emerald grasses and silver olive

237

trees. The huge bursting dates looked appetising hanging on their orange coloured sticks. Monkey-like Arab boys ran almost vertically up the palm trunks to cut heavy bunches of fruit from among the motionless plumes of grey and blue spikes. Older Arabs squatted below, as they washed the fruit, taking from them the stones which they then fed to the camels. Here, in this bowl of palm trees, the ears were filled with the liquid chirruping of birds: the grey skylarks with tufted crests, the hoopoes, tortorelles (turtle doves) and the petulant twitter of frisking sparrows.

Later our small guide conducted us on a return visit to the Chinese Ouled Naïl. At our approach, dogs barked, the houris screamed with surprise at daytime visitors, and when we produced our cameras they ran behind curtains. Our ten-year-old guide then explained to the Madam in man-of-the-world fashion that we did not want to go to bed with the residents, but would pay to take their photographs. In answer the women demanded twenty francs for each snap—this seemed excessive, for they allow people to sleep with them for two francs! The boy squatted on the floor and haggled in our interests. At last he prevailed upon our favourite to pose for a drawing. She sat motionless, lids lowered as though in a trance, on her small bed with out-splayed legs like an odalisque by Matisse. The other whores crowded round excitedly to watch the pencil strokes. When the sketch was finished, the others squawked that they too should have a portrait. The Chinese favourite was about to relent and allow herself to be photographed when all the other inmates screamed in protest.

When the time came for the four travellers to make the return journey to Hammarmet, there were last minute delays. The caterpillar-car must be overhauled. So I wandered off by myself down some stone-coloured alleyways and labyrinths, looking for the last time at my favourite sights.

MOROCCO

Tangier, undated

The first sight of Tangier was of a sugary mass of white cubes sloping up from the sea to a turquoise sky. As David Herbert and I walked through the walled streets to the Sultan's palace in the Arab quarter. We agreed that it matters little that modern buildings have been erected among the old moorish shops and walls. The whole town has a bleached uniformity.

238

In the main market place, many white-blanketed figures shuffled about, while others bent over to inspect incongruous bits of rubbish, old nails, dried snakes and bicycle clips laid out on the ground. An Arab boy walked down a steep path against a curdled wall, carrying on his head an enormous basket of flowers. He looked, from the distance, as though he were wearing an Edwardian lady's elaborate hat. Under the gnarled, clean silver trees,

Moroccan group

old women sat beneath vast straw hats, patiently waiting to get rid of blue irises and feathery mimosa.

The Moroccan year passes in seasons of flowers. All the English spring blossoms are here as well as the summer ones; roses of unfamiliar species tumble over balconies in pillowy profusion.

We furnished our house in the Casbah with junk from the market (gaudily effective materials made curtains and covers), and bought potted azaleas with which to decorate our white-walled garden. While I remained on the roof of our house in the shade of a fig tree working on the illustrations for a book, David stood on the parapet and described scenes taking place in the square below. A shipload of English tourists has arrived. They scream with hysterical horror at the snake charmer, who does his stunt much too long. The French boat is in. Then it is Friday. The Governor goes to his mosque to pray, amid the strains of the National Anthem tootled by red uniformed, white turbanned guards. Again it is Friday; again the Governor arrives. Fridays come around too quickly. On Thursday, the place is filled with sorrowful women in white, carrying baskets of food as presents for their children in the small boys' prison opposite. One old lady finds the pull up the hill too much for her. She has not allowed enough time for the ascent. The clock strikes three; the guards locks the door against her as she sits down and cries.

On the postcards that I sent home I wrote that we were situated between the prison and the madhouse. One night, we heard that two murderers had escaped. It was then we began to realise that some of the cries that we imagined came from bread- or fruit-sellers were those of the lunatics next door. Only after three weeks did David tell me about the four madmen shut in a cell so small that one with a wooden leg has had a hole bored to allow him to stretch it out. Throughout the night, I listened now to the tormented wails. Often they awoke me with a start. Towards dawn, one madman sang with great force, a prelude of infinite sadness to the sunrise.

A small tour has been planned. On our way to Fez the motor car runs through a long tunnel of pepper trees, filled with birds so small that only songs and squeaks reveal their presence. The landscape is cosily tranquil, with distant herds grazing on lush, velvety slopes. Greece in spring must be like this, with cascades of ilex trees and groves of olives. Wild flowers, growing at the roadside like carefully planned borders, pungently scent the air.

The ancient town of Fez makes up for the ugliness of its modern quarter. Our initial tour took us through honeycombed passages that offered surprising sights. Through an archway we caught a sudden *tableau vivant* of ten Negroes, black as the black world of charcoal and charcoal dust that surrounded them. All that was white was in their eyes. In a small courtyard, a gushing torrent, pumped from a well, splashed on to a group busily washing the hides of sheep. A child of three looked like a miniature woman in a bustle improvized from an apron. She carried a long platter of bread cakes on her coconut-small head.

The entire town of Fez has tall, sand-coloured walls and green-tiled roofs. Often overhanging houses meet one another in mid-air. They are propped up with struts of huge beams, making a dark tunnel for the current of people below. Some of the passages are fantastically narrow, and so dark that strangers have to grope their way. Yet donkeys and mules pass through the tightly wedged crowds with never an accident.

We were lucky enough to find the venerable Scottish missionary, Miss Denison, at home. One of the great characters of Fez, she lives in a doll's house decorated like the lodgekeeper's quarters of any country mansion in England. Outwardly, her existence might seem to be that of any retired old nannie. Yet Miss D., who must be pushing eighty, is up at five a.m., and by six begins dispensing medicines to the natives. This very morning she had tended over a hundred and twenty people. She reads a few prayers, sings a hymn, and then doles out prescriptions from her dispensary of closely packed bottles lining the wall.

Miss Denison is a small, bent, grey-haired woman. This evening she wore a knitted jersey and skirt, but generally she dons native costume. She knows the language perfectly, having lived here for forty-five years. When she arrived in Fez, there were no 'conveniences', and it was a lengthy business of many weeks to get from one nearby town to another. 'There were seven of us to begin with,' she explains. 'But the others have all passed on now.' The dead included a dear friend with whom she had shared this house for thirty years.

I thought Miss D. quite obviously a contented, even happy person. She herself is convinced that her life is an enviable one, though to a stranger from Europe it seems spartan. Still, this is home to her; England now is a place to visit only every ten years.

After a dinner of unexpected exotic dishes, we watched the whores dance in the *quartier réserve*, and fell under the spell of the beauty of some of the young girls. Their faces were like gazelles; their eyes, glistening with excitement and belladonna, seemed like the eyes of strange birds. Their pastel-coloured dresses were encrusted with sparkling butterflies. And the *schlur* dancers, cracking their naked feet on the tiled floors with gunlike reports, added a weird aura to the scene. Outside, in the dark of the night, we caught hurried glimpses of beautiful and mysterious faces.

Part XII

Ashcombe

1931

Ashcombe was always prey to the elements. Sequestered during the lazy idylls of summer, the small buildings and garden would bear the full force of the gales that lashed across the bleak downland in winter, and become like a small ship tossed in an angry ocean. Even a heavy rainfall could make an ascent in a motor up the steep slippery hill of chalk into an adventure. Often terrified dinner guests would return, an hour after they had made their adieux, having left their motor broadside across the hill or overhanging a precipice, to beg a bed for the night until, with daylight, help could come, and they could be towed up the hill. A fallen tree or snow drift made the place impregnable sometimes for a week on end.

Perhaps for the very reason that Ashcombe was such a difficult place to reach I enjoyed the challenge, for an occasion, of peopling it with multitudes of surprised guests.

Occasionally Ashcombe would be the scene of a mammoth fancy dress gala with special buses, with chained wheels, to do a funicular service. The most elaborate was a fête champêtre, given with Michael

Duff as co-host, when a perversely sophisticated piece of rusticity was staged. The decorations came from Milan and Paris, the guests from all over the world. The fact that six weeks were spent organising the event was proof that, in comparison with my later life, professional work did not tax me too much.

A corner at Ashcombe

But although, on occasion, the house would be overcrowded with guests, yet much of the time was spent there alone. For the first time in my life I would feel free to do whatever I wanted at any given time without being an inconvenience to others. During these green years at Ashcombe I enjoyed experimenting with time. I would often wake *myself up so as to be about when dawn was breaking over the inter-locking hills. Sometimes I would go alone for midnight walks, or remain up all night reading, playing the gramophone, or turning out cupboards. In the small sitting-room I would listen to the owls outside the windows, and to the vicious jungle sounds of animals killing or fighting in the dark. I would jump with fright when, after the long day, the furniture popped or creaked in the warmth, the coals re-arranged themselves in the hearth, or a flower changed its position in a vase. But remote and wild as the place was, I never had a feeling of loneliness, or of danger.*

ASHCOMBE, TOLLARD ROYAL, WILTSHIRE

May 1931

There is always excitement on returning to Ashcombe. Today the grass had been cut and tidied. There were good imitations of sweeping lawns. The horse and cart were carrying away soft green mounds of mowings. Staves and rakes lay about, adding to a Gainsborough scene.

I lay, in a haze of peace on the lawn, watching the new doves unloosed from their temporary house, enjoying to the fullest the first real day of summer. Every imaginable kind of bird seemed to be singing. I dozed in the boiling sun, dimly aware of great busyness around me with the gardener and his boy trimming and tidying.

I listened vaguely to the clop and brittle scraping of earthen-ware pots being moved about on the cobblestones.

I wandered to the greenhouse to enjoy the humid scent of warmth and nurtured growth. Carefully tended shoots grew in potted rows; flaking rubble lay underfoot. There were strands of bass, and an empty, chalky water bucket.

Down by the lily pond, elder flower petals, looking like ver-micelli, had been wafted on to the surface of the water. Self-sown plants sprouted in the chinks of the stone walls of the terrace. One plant looked like an artichoke; old ladies use it to make an ointment for healing purposes.

Noble, the gardener, explained that the plaster for repairing the walls was only chalk and water, so that recently the wall fell down and he and Ry[1] had a terrible time getting the mess

---

[1] His wife who worked as cook in the kitchen.

I

cleared up. Six and a half barrow loads it was. Noble says Joannie, the child, fell into the lily pond. They were counting the lily buds when she went right under.

Bees droned, a thousand rooks cawed and the thrushes chortled as they settled down for the night. In long summer evenings, the sun does not disappear until nearly ten o'clock. Shadows become elongated. The trees do not stir, are still bright green in the twilight.

I remember particularly vividly a late summer party at Ashcombe. All preparations made, I walked slowly up the valley, hoping to meet the first guests at the top of the downs. I sat on a mound and waited. From my mossy vantage point, the view of rolling hillocks and avalanches of woods for miles around was saddeningly beautiful. Innumerable rabbits appeared. A deer peered from a thicket. Birds of almost every variety swooped across the wooded canyon.

Chalk stones whirled under the wheels of the motors. The guests at last! Feminine laughter. High spirits, high hopes. 'Let's get out here and all walk down together!'

After dinner that night writing games were played by the firelight in the studio. Then drawing games; Heads, Bodies and Legs; or Titles and Pictures. Rex, of course, excelled at this. The others were apt to become pornographic.

Peter arrived customarily late, and prowled around surreptitiously before making his presence known. Then the women trooped off to bed with the evening's jokes and lighted candles, Nancy inaugurating the new Marie Antoinette room improvised in the barn.

Peter and I changed our shoes, deciding to have a late moonlight walk on the downs. It was four o'clock before we returned. We foraged in the dark for food. 'What about a bit of this Camembert!' But we ate ginger cake.

June

Alice Astor,[1] Freddie Ashton and Ivan Moffat arrived to stay another weekend.

Freddie entered the sitting-room, cocked an eye at the chimney piece formed in tiers with a potted geranium on each level and

[1] Later Alice von Hofmannsthal.

suggested, 'You ought to have a ladder or staircase placed along-side that chimney: leading up to an unknown room.' It was a ridiculous idea, but full of fancy, pictorially justified.

Later, Freddie entertained us with brilliant, spontaneous imitations, each a choreographic gem in itself. He is a born mimic, relying on gesture to create a devastating caricature of a person or situation. We sat amazed as he ran through a repertory from Sir Thomas Beecham to an Edwardian lady and Sarah Bernhardt. This display was deft, professional, done without shyness or blunder. His sure hands created improvised effects from whatever his eye lighted upon, with the certitude that only an artist can possess. The lid of a coal scuttle served many purposes, becoming a picture hat, then a garden basket in which the Edwardian horticulturist gathered her specimen flowers.

The Bernhardt impersonation was a cameo of one of the actress's stage *tours de force*, during which she acted a dramatic scene while arranging an elaborate bouquet of flowers in a vase without even looking. Her back to the public but head turned towards the arc lights, she selected each bloom, placed it with careful precision until the arrangement was finished, then stepped back with grandiose gesture to admire the effect. The audience applauded wildly.

Freddie's performance prompted Ivan to discuss how much children sensed of everything that was happening. No doubt Freddie never actually *saw* Bernardt arranging those flowers, but even in his perambulator he must instinctively have known she was doing it and that the audience would applaud. Just so, Ivan at the age of three knew that his mother, pouting and frowning and moaning, was only pretending to concentrate for his benefit. It is true that all children seem astonishingly intuitive, and will automatically be aware, even at a distance, that things about which they should be ignorant are being discussed.

Freddie said he considered that he had been living all his adult life on investments from boyhood. In illustration of this, he was able to convey with exceptional *éclat* the romance that some Brazilian woman had had for him in his youth, when he lived in South America. He recalled how a certain disdainful woman had behaved after being given the honour of dancing with the Kaiser. He mimed the way this same woman made conversation with the British Minister at a garden party in

Buenos Aires, and how she turned her head beautifully for the waiting photographer. He also described the stance of Edwardian beauties, their heads held high, their chins proffered slantwards to reveal to perfection the line of neck and throat.

EDITH OLIVIER

The remarkable Edith Olivier has left Ashcombe after a visit of three days. It gave me an opportunity to see her at her unusual best. So often we meet when surrounded by many people, but her qualities are not to be enjoyed in a crowd.

Edith Olivier

Edith is sixty-three, maybe more. Rex and I treat her as a contemporary. Sometimes it seems inconceivable that, from the vicarage in Wilton this pennilesss spinster should create such ripples. Her energy and vitality are unlimited. She can talk or listen intently all day; she relates long stories with heroic gusto;

she is witty and full of jokes. At night, she retires to read three books and write a detailed journal. Next morning, she re-appears as fresh as ever.

But it is, above all, Edith's understanding qualities that make her a boon to those who write or create in the other arts, as well as to simple country folk. She has infinite sympathy. Everyone goes to her with troubles, knowing she can be trusted implicitly. Her advice is always wise and easy.

I love Edith more than almost any friend I have. If she were to die, no one could fill the breach.

August

Just as I seldom sink to my knees in prayer save when unhappiness overcomes me, so my pen is lifted to paper only when the mood is sad. These scraps would give a picture of inordinate gloom to anyone judging my existence from them. Perhaps I concentrate too hard on an unrequited love affair, on my failings and short-comings. Yet in so many ways my existence is enviable: I do not have to think of money, which is the ultimate in luxury. Great riches will never be mine, but enough is earned to do un-hampered most of the things I like. I work hard, yet with my own schedule; it is often difficult to find time to get a haircut or buy new shirts.

Meanwhile this past week has been a good week, probably the best I remember having spent at Ashcombe. There has been an Italian-blue, cloudless sky. The sun pours down on to this roman-tic, melancholy spot. The summer noises are soothing—hand-pump drawing water, doves throttling, and metallic cooing of lawn mower. Indoors, the house has brimmed with sunlight and reflections from prismatic glass; friends around the table have offered laughter and wit.

And I have even had an interesting lunch with someone else I believe I am rather in love with.

THE DUCHESS OF HAMILTON'S TEA PARTY

December

Tea at my nearest neighbours: over the hill in the cold wet darkness to Ferne House.

249

Margaret Drummond-Hay is golden-haired, with love-in-the-mist eyes and russet cheeks. She has masses of equally healthy-looking giants for brothers. They troop over to me for charades on Saturday evenings, and we often ride together on the downs. Margaret has even introduced me to the pleasures of the Hunt.

Today's invitation was from the mother (whom I had never met) of these athletic, God-like creatures. I had heard that her husband, the Duke, was a cripple, that he had been paralysed after falling from the mast of a ship. I knew well of the Duchess being a rabid humanitarian and anti-vivisectionist, and that she had turned Ferne into a sort of dog's home. In fact, any stray that finds its way through these remote Wiltshire lanes to this ugly Victorian mansion, whether it be a human refugee, discarded pet bird, donkey, monkey, or mongrel is sure of a welcome.

Today the school-like dining-room was alive with children and dogs. What with all the young sons and daughters of the house, and their pets, and with the addition of many guests of all denominations, the floor seemed to be a sea of moving limbs and paws. Children, on all fours, scrambled under tables, together with the dogs and cats who gnawed at the remains from table and filled in every cubic inch of space. I sat next to the Duchess, a tall woman of independent character rather than of the classical beauty unexpectedly apparent in her children. She was dressed in white summer clothes as is her custom throughout the year. It is her perpetual expression of mourning for one of her young children who died tragically.

We tried to talk about books, but our attempts at conversation were constantly interrupted by animals and children of various sizes and shapes.

At last we found ourselves marshalled into the drawing-room, where a spindly Christmas tree stood decorated with tinsel toys and illuminated by coloured bulbs. Soon the village children from Berwick St John trooped in by invitation—fifty or sixty of them standing like a military unit. They had large heads, pale, weedy complexions, and goggle eyes. An overfat schoolmaster, crimson in the face, conducted a hymn while his minions sang with only a remote interest in the proceedings.

The Duchess stood to attention surrounded by many ugly, grey-haired women, including a few deaf mutes. The village children, puny and unattractive, made a startling contrast to the healthy ducal offspring.

Her Grace then spoke a few words, welcoming the local children and giving them a dissertation on the advantages of country over city. Each leaf, she explained, was different in the country. There were many things to watch; they must appreciate and preserve its rustic joys.

One boy was asked the main difference between town and country and ruggedly replied, 'Oi think the moine difference is that in the cities there is so much dust and doirt and muck. In the country, the air is different and there are flewers.'

'Quite right, that is excellent.' The Duchess seemed a stalking crane in her off-white flannel skirt, socks and gym shoes. Finally she excoriated those who are cruel to the animals. 'Above all you must be kind to birds.'

The children were then encouraged to give bird calls for Father Christmas. They moved joylessly into the pitchpine panelled hall and intoned at the top of their melancholy screechy voices. After delays, and hitches and whispered commands from the family, and repeated shouts in unison from the children, Father Christmas materialised in the form of the Duke who was wheeled on to the scene by Geordie, his stalwart son. The Duke was dressed in red flannel with hood and a wig of white cotton wool. The children were told to line up in order of their ages. Those who were twelve years old must head the procession and be given a present.

A few mumbled words, then the village children were given orders to troop as a platoon into the frigid drawing-room. Each child took an orange and an apple from fruit-filled Tate sugar boxes placed near the door.

Everyone waited: grey-haired women, deaf mutes, refugee cats and dogs, and children of all ages. Then the lights went out; a few of the smaller village children began to whimper. The ducal grandchildren crawled in and out of legs, human and animal, while outside the French windows their handsome parents, could be seen for a flash or two, as they ran in the stormy darkness with matches and beacons. Suddenly a Catherine wheel hissed; then in the rain appeared a shower of 'golden rain'; squibs popped; jumping crackers exploded on the wet ground; chinese crackers went off in a series of half-hearted reports.

The whimpering village children now burst into screams of alarm. Terrified of the darkness and the noise, they howled, bellowed, shrieked with each new explosion. Babies cried, dogs barked, oranges and apples rolled on the floor. From exploding rockets blinding flashes revealed a maggot-crawling mass of panicking children and dogs. The hysteria reached a terrifying crescendo when a spurting, spluttering 'sparkler' came flying indoors.

February

Where do the weeks go? They seem to hurry by even quicker than the days or the hours. It is the immediate future that holds such store, and that keeps our enthusiasms so active. If we had time to realise how quickly the unknown becomes the known, the future the present, and the present the past—should we then perhaps take a calmer view of the weeks and minimise our activity? Then maybe one would have time to consider the real significance of all those meetings, those jobs, those pleasures.

Part XIII

America Again

1932

March 1932

Now, as I write this, I am in America again. My New York winter has been spent at the Waldorf, in a tower suite which I have filled with tripe in an attempt to destroy its impersonal 'good taste'-type of decoration.

There were relays of activity with the Winston Churchills, and their rumbustious family, staying on the floor below. A stop was put to this when Churchill got knocked down and very nearly killed by a taxicab. I saw a lot of Tilly,[1] did drawings of nudes with the Bismarcks[2] and listened to Toscanini concerts.

If I were to criticise my existence, it would merely be that it has become more or less predictable, whereas before I never knew what was forthcoming. I suppose that happens as the years form a pattern of living. Or is it that I have fallen into a rut?

[1] Tilly Losch.
[2] Jack and Yorck Ruppert von Bismarck, German born artists currently successful in New York. She is the Berlin Marie-Laurencin, he with his murals comprising mirror and concrete.

I*

GRETA GARBO

Hollywood

Once more I arrived in this arc-lit, slightly macabre suburbia. By now, I was no longer a stranger, and could call friends with whom I felt at home. I became absorbed in their tales of the film industry. The conversation always seemed to revert to Garbo; her hermit-like independence, her unconventionality in this most conventional of all worlds.

For years now Garbo had become quite an obsession with me. Her screen image haunted me. I collected her every published photograph, and now in a valiant, though doomed, attempt to take my own pictures of her, pestered Howard Strickling of the MGM Publicity staff. Instead of flatly discouraging me, he held out hopes. She had gone to the mountains to get some rest, but was due back tomorrow. . . . Meanwhile, Miss Shearer was offered on a plate, or Miss Crawford. . . .

Piecing together the various pieces of the Garbo jigsaw my curiosity grew in intensity. I gleaned: this living legend is unattainable. No advice or pressure would be of avail; she could never be won over by flattery; other people's fame means as little to her as her own. She dislikes all and every kind of publicity. Each week her fan mail is taken unread into her garden and burnt. She depises the symbol of sex for which she is cast in films, resents the part she plays, and considers the producers barbarically ignorant. Neither is she interested in the way she photographs. 'What difference does it make if the photographs are the best I'll ever have taken?' she answers the baffled Mr Strickling. As soon as shooting on a picture is finished, Garbo disappears. The studio is often in despair as to how to contact her in case of retakes or an emergency, 'I go into the mountains. I have no address—leave a message in a certain tree, and I will go and look for it.'

Her Nordic blood may be a reason for her tendency towards morbidity, and being so highly strung, together with her sadness at finding herself in a trap, she periodically gives way to bouts of complete despair. It is then that she locks herself up without seeing even her maid for days; for two years no one crossed the threshold of her home.

But, when she is happy, she is childishly uninhibited, walking on chairs and tables, climbing trees and hanging from the branches

254

She enjoys reciting fragments of poetry and mystical catch phrases, and uses romantic similes: 'The moon's face tonight is soft, like moss with white violets in it.' Her humour can be ironic. She is secretly amused at her way of knowingly mystifying the officials at the studio. Once when shopping at her favourite 'Army and Navy Store' in Los Angeles, she discovered a one-piece undergarment in thickest wool, with long legs and sleeves, that is known throughout the United States. One day at the studio, feeling cold, she wore this garment under her vaporous evening dress. When the startled director asked her what she was wearing, her periwinkle eyes stared into the half distance as she answered, 'a union suit'.

My chances of capturing the butterfly were becoming more slender each day. Yes Garbo had returned, and had been busy on some retakes, but these were now about to come to an end. I was resigning myself to leaving Hollywood with my mission un-completed. Funds were running rather low, and Howard Strick-ling's prevarications became exhausting.

However, when an English couple, Eddie Goulding, the director, and his wife, the former ballroom dancer, Marjorie Moss, suggested my leaving the hotel and coming to their house for a few days, the invitation was accepted with alacrity—particularly since Eddie had directed Garbo in *Grand Hotel*, and was one of the few people she visited at weekends. 'We never know if we should expect her, but she generally rings up at the last moment to ask if she can come along for cold Sunday supper.'

My turret bedroom was reached by circular steps, in this typical 'Spanish-type' mansion. Marjorie mothered me in her disarming nasal voice, which sounded particularly Cockney in Hollywood: Eddie was entertaining in his exaggerated British bull-dog bass. I drove a hired car to the various studios and to the 'Army and Navy Stores'. Here was a treasure trove of men's clothing that could be worn with impunity only in Holly-wood or at Ashcombe. I bought vast quantities, at almost negligible cost, of football vests, exotic footgear, the scantiest shorts in all colours and in white sharkskin; I could not resist one particularly beautiful white kid jacket.

Sunday arrived, my last day before returning home via San Francisco. Would Garbo 'drop in', and would I be included in the spontaneous party? Yes, she *had* telephoned, but she didn't want to meet me. She usually hid from English people, and she said, 'He talks to newspapers'. Crushed with defeat and dejection, I tried to telephone a mutual friend; if it was not permitted to pass the evening talking to Garbo, then it could be spent talking *about* her. The friend was out. The call was repeated all the afternoon. So I slept. I woke. Still no reply from the mutual; and, for want of anything better to do, I took a long hot bath. I dressed myself, choosing to wear, for the first time, the pristine white kid coat, the sharkskin shorts, and new white shoes and socks.

Then I looked out of the window. In the garden below my host and hostess were gossiping. With them was a visitor. Garbo was sitting cross-legged on a white garden seat, smoking a cigarette held high in two definite fingers. I could not hear their conversation, but the Gouldings seemed animated, and Garbo wore a sort of Olympian smile with quizzically raised eyebrows and lowered lids.

Garbo, too, was all in white, wearing a thick woollen sweater, shorts, and half an eggshell on her back-scraped hair. Her waxen complexion and her thighs were sunburnt to a rich biscuit colour.

If a unicorn had suddenly appeared in the late afternoon light of this ugly, ordinary garden, I could have been neither more surprised nor more amazed by the beauty of this exotic creature.

I dared not remain a peeping Tom. As I stood away from the window, my heart was thumping. Eventually I must have come out of my trance, for I quietly made my way down the turret-staircase in order, once more, to try the same damned telephone number.

When I catwalked into the drawing-room, I found that the trio had already come indoors and were sitting on a sofa with glasses in their hands. Somewhat breathy with surprise, I gasped 'Oh! Sorry,' turned about on my heels and sharply left the room. Half-way up the stairs, I heard Marjorie's Cockney voice tinklingly bidding me to come down and join them. This time I walked across the drawing-room on air.

I was overcome by stagefright when the introduction was made, but finding myself confronted by such an understanding smile, something so sympathetic and encouragingly helpful, I was able to continue to breathe. A deep, familiar voice cooed at me, and bade me sit by her on a leather pouf.

The situation became even more piquant when the voice showered me with compliments, 'But you're so yorng? How do you stay so yorng? Are you like one of those people that never grow up? I know a man who is fifty who still looks so yorng; and you're so white. If only I could draw you like that.' I held on to her hands.

The voice continued, 'You're so beautiful.' 'But *you're* so beautiful,' was my lame reply. 'No, you should never return a compliment.' This was a moment of danger. But after a flicker of displeasure passed across those brows, my solecism was forgiven. It was accepted—while a huge tumbler of orange juice' and champagne was proffered by Marjorie. It tasted like nectar.

Even if Garbo would not allow me to give vent to eulogies I could now drink in every detail of her beauty. This marvellous gay creature had the sadness of Debureau, the clown—a resemblance accentuated by her pale face, her deep-set darkened eyelids, and skull cap. There was an incredible sensitivity about the modelling of the nose, as if she were able to savour exquisite perfumes too subtle for other human being to enjoy. Her lips, bereft of lipstick, were like polished shells, and when she gave her big generous smile, her teeth showed square and shining.

Conversation then continued without any of the polite preliminaries of strangers. We talked nonsense as if we had known one another forever. 'In short, these are the nicest Indian shoes I have ever seen in my life, and I have not seen many! But are we dressmakers that we talk of clothes?'

The Gouldings must have been surprised to find that, from now on, they hardly existed in the presence of their guests. Yet they were not resentful. And although I could never be grateful enough to them for bringing about this meeting, how could they now be paid more than desultory deference?

Garbo told us about her coloured-maid, whose husband had cold feet at night. The maid undresses in the dark. She described a woman who had an oversize Adam's apple, and how some men have such big 'Ardumms arppless' that they go up and down when they swallow. 'Oh, it's pathetic; how can you laugh at human beings?'

We all moved to the bar for more nectar. On the way Garbo

257

and I crab-walked with arms round each other's waists, and much friendly hand squeezing. She pervaded a scent of new-mown hay, and of freshly-washed children. 'Show Greta your hands,' Marjorie piped. My hands were carefully scrutinised. Garbo said hers were kitchenette hands and laughed, 'I play the most sophisticated women without a manicure.'

We all drank a great deal of this cold, refreshing, very intoxicating drink. Garbo was inspired to hop about the room gesticulating and giving spontaneous impersonations of grandiose actresses, quoting snatches of poetry or prose that came into her head.

A huge vase of yellow roses freshly sprayed with water had been placed on the bar. 'Oh, who put the dew on them?' Garbo picked a rose and kissed it, fingered it with an infinite variety of caresses and raised it above her head. As she looked up at it, she intoned, 'A rose that lives and dies and never again returns.' Suddenly with wild eyes and a deep look of astonishment she asked, in her hushed 'mystery' voice, 'How is one to know?' She supplied the answer, '*je ne sais pas*,' then burst into laughter apologising for her accent. 'Oh, my poor few words that I know of French!' Then like a celestial parrot she repeated, 'For thee and thine' (pronounced with a thick Scandinavian 'Th'); and the German for silk shirt.

We were bidden by Marjorie to partake of the collation appetisingly laid out in the enforced absence of the servants. 'Och! Lobster Americaine!' The spontaneous picnic was applauded. The parrot kept repeating the words 'Lobster Americaine' and made them sound extremely comic. She helped me to lettuce. 'I'm no *hausfrau*,' she said, but did an imitation of a dainty lady with little finger perched in air; this dainty lady then started to embroider a table napkin, before becoming extremely interested in the sex of two cold chickens.

We all ate enormously. Talking of the food of different countries it became apparent that Garbo has a highly sensitised palate, with an uncanny instinct for the most sophisticated tastes.

Suddenly something untoward has happened. The air is electric. Eddie is severely reprimanded. It seems he has said something insensitive, and unsuitable. Garbo has a rooted dislike of 'loose language'—slang such as 'honey' or 'swell'—and cannot understand educated people wanting to talk like the electrician

258

and the 'prop' man. Worst of all to her are schoolboy jokes,
particularly those to do with the posterior portions of the
anatomy. Eddie has idiotically proclaimed that if Garbo didn't do
his bidding as director he'd turn her upside down and give her a
smacking where she sits upon. Fortunately this tiff quickly passed
off and Garbo was asked if she would like to go upstairs and see
my photographs of Ashcombe where I wished she would come
and live for ever. The parrot replied, 'Absolutely Adolphe.'

'Are you happy?' she asked.
'Yes.'
'It's so easy to say Yes.'
'And you?'
She sighed. 'Tomorrow I got to work with a lot of people who
are dead. It's so sad. I'm an onlooker. I've passed being active in
life. It's not a question of time and age—but it's just what you are
yourself. One doesn't do the things one doesn't want to do.'

Twilight had passed; the curtain breezed in by the window.
'Is that a ghost? Ssh!' We ran downstairs and the hilarity continued. We all danced to the 'rardio'. Garbo in imitation of
Douglas Fairbanks swung from the cross beam and Spanish
rafters. Marjorie, as light as thistledown, did a ballroom dance.
Then in turn we did improvisations to Strauss waltzes, Rach-
maninoff, *The Lost Chord* and *Wunderbar*. Garbo, as a policeman,
arrested me for some importunity. The lights were turned out
and our bacchanalia became wilder in the firelight.

Suddenly the dream was over. It was time for Garbo to leave.
It was very late, daylight had reappeared, and she had to be
at the studio in a few hours. She was at the wheel in a rather
shabby, big motor car. We put our hands through the windows.
I was due to leave California, but if she would see me again, I
would stay. 'Can't I come and eat spinach with you tomorrow—
no today—at the studio at the lunch interval?' 'No.' Surely this
cannot be the end? Shall we never meet again? Will we be able to
communicate in some way? In desperation I seized hold of a
feather duster with a long handle, a curious object that was lying
by her side. 'Can I keep this as a memento?'
'No.'
'Then this is Goodbye?'
'Yes, I'm afraid so. *C'est la vie*!'

The Gouldings were rather too baffled by the evening to talk about it. I could hardly believe what had happened. The only concrete proof was the yellow rose which she had kissed, and which I now took up the turret stairs to keep pressed between the pages of my diary.

Mrs Patrick Campbell and Moonbeam

Nancy arrives with my Father for her wedding

The Windsor wedding

Christian Bérard painting the cover portrait of C.B.

Part XIV

Looking Back

1933, 1934 and 1935

September 1933, London

Looking back on this year, the most important event was Nancy's wedding. Her fiancé Hugh[1] has pale blue Hanoverian eyes and clipped speech and brusque manner; and at first it was difficult to get used to the idea of his being a member of the family. And now Baba is engaged to be married to Alec Hambro and life begins to empty for my parents since Reggie seldom gets leave from the Flying Corps (thank heavens he seems to have found his niche in the air!) I will have to try and supply more fun for them.

REGGIE

October 16th, London

This evening, at eleven o'clock Reggie was killed by an underground train.

It had been a pleasant enough day. I puttered the morning

[1] Sir Hugh Smiley.

away, answering letters, sending off photographs and doing odd jobs. At lunch, I told Christabel McLaren that Nancy was going to have a child. Christabel then confided with great amusement, 'I'm forty-five and I'm going to have another baby, too.'

In the afternoon, I went riding in Richmond Park with Peter. Then there was Sybil Colefax's dinner party for Mona Williams. And, after a night club, I took Doris home.

When I returned very late, there was still a light in the hall. Who could be up at this hour? I found Baba waiting in the glare of the yellow Italian lamp. She looked pale, her skin shiny. She said, 'I'm glad you've come in at last. Reggie has had an accident. He's been killed.'

I felt sinisterly unmoved. I listened calmly while Baba related what she knew. Mummie and Daddy had been wakened after midnight by a reporter from the *Daily Mail*. In fact, Mum had wakened with such a start at the sound of gruff voices below that, in snatching for the electric light, she knocked it over. The reporter confided to Baba that Reggie was dead. In front of Mummie, he simply said there had been an accident. Daddy, accompanied by Manley[1], hurried off to the hospital to identify the body. But now Mum knew the truth.

My first regret was that I had paid so little attention to Reggie for such a long time. I'd been off-hand and busy; and since we had little in common, I seldom even saw him. The last time was yesterday (today I'd only heard him calling for Manley). I'd been opening and reading letters, taking little notice of his questions as he hovered about the desk.

I said, 'I do feel badly about not being nicer to him.'

Baba replied, 'Reggie was so different from the rest of us.'

We stood in the hall, talking emptily. I couldn't believe that I felt so unmoved. Then poor Mummie came down the stairs, weeping bitterly. Her face was distorted from crying.

'Oh dear, oh dear, the poor boy.' Mum kept blaming herself, overwhelmed with remorse for having scolded him last week because he went out too much. At the same time, she felt guilty for having let him go out again tonight: 'Oh, if I had only made him stay in! He was here to lunch, and afterwards he went out. We passed on the stairs and I never saw him again.' She broke down in another flood of tears.

---

[1] The family butler-factotum.

I went upstairs to see Daddy. He lay in bed, unable to sleep. Some of his false teeth were out. The blankets looked rough and unattractive. Daddy wasn't weeping, yet seemed incapable of taking in the situation. He coughed a lot, explaining all over again about the accident. He said that, when he had identified the body, Reggie looked calm in spite of gashes cut on his face. He had apparently fallen in front of a train and been dragged along.

I thought, 'Dear Daddy, what a nightmare ordeal for you. Reggie was your favourite son; you'd been such friends.'

Baba and I went on talking for some time afterwards. Then I wrote this diary entry, sitting cold-bloodedly calm in bed.

I am thinking now of all the days Reggie and I spent together. We grew up in great intimacy, fighting a lot but really devoted. It was only later that we drifted apart. I felt shy of him as a grown-up. When he joined the Flying Corps and made new friends, we had few interests in common.

Now that I am less surprised at the terrible news and my horrifying reaction to it, I begin to feel the emotion and the reality. I begin to realise that I won't ever again hear Reggie calling Becky, telephoning to young ladies or talking to Manley in a plummy voice.

I feel full of regret and guilt for having been so selfish, for not trying to enter into his world.

Recently, I noticed how much less hairy Reggie's hands were than mine. I think of his wristwatch and his fingernails. . . .

October 17th

I awoke early. Nancy had to be telephoned before she read the newspapers: in her present 'condition' she must not have any unnecessary shock.

Time moved slowly. Reports of the accident in newsprint convinced me of the undeniable fact. Mummie lay in bed, a quivering, weeping pulp. She'd been unable to sleep for a minute. Her head ached, her teeth and cheeks ached. I felt desperately sorry for her. I began now to react myself. A lump gathered in my throat. My eyes swelled. I could not keep back a stream of tears, wept quietly over breakfast while Daddy remained calm.

October 19th, Ashcombe

It is all over. I'll try to write about the events of the past three days, which seem like so many weeks.

Hardly ever in my life have I wanted the clock to move more quickly. At every moment, I kept waiting impatiently for the next thing to happen.

Where had Reggie been? It was necessary to get on the telephone and discover his whereabouts on Wednesday evening. He had left the Dennis Bradley cocktail party with two men. Each was contacted in turn, but could give no news, except to say that Reggie hadn't been tight and seemed in good spirits.

Daddy went off to hear the details of the accident. I taxied to Dennis Bradley's and back, but Dennis had little to tell me about Reggie's last movements. Telegrams and letters began to arrive. I answered each as soon as it came. The morning was still young, yet so much had happened since seven-thirty; indeed, since Reggie's death barely twelve hours previously.

I heard the click of a car door outside. Manley announced the Smileys. Nancy and I wept on one another's shoulders. Somehow I tried to work with Miss Joseph on an article. It was impossible to concentrate. Then Daddy returned, but could give us no further details except to say there would be an inquest on Friday morning.

The afternoon and evening papers began to appear, with photographs of Reggie in them. Time crawled. The house seemed cold as I wandered from room to room. The doctor came to see Mummie. I, too, went to bed, where it was warmer. I tried to get on with the article but failed. At dinner, Baba showed no emotion; Daddy continued to remain calm.

The night was bad for Mummie, who shook in all her limbs. Her hands trembled like an old lady's. Aunt Cada kept watch by her.

Next morning, Daddy and I arrived early for the inquest. We waited anxiously, making attempts at conversation with those who were to appear—the Bradleys, Jeanne Stourton, a Captain Spencer and Mrs O'Brien, who was one of Reggie's best friends.

Mrs O'Brien spoke of Reggie's eye trouble and continuous 'blackouts', as he called them. Reggie had had one only last weekend in her drawing-room. And, in fact, on Wednesday morning at home, just twelve hours before he died, he'd had another on his way out of the bath, coming a 'purler' on the bathroom floor. That surely was what must have happened while he waited for an underground train home. Reggie would have been the least likely person to kill himself. He'd never been depressed, always bubbling with high spirits and taking life so easily. He never worried or thought of any time but the present.

The Coroner's Court was cold and dreary. We sat on benches of orange-stained wood. Our anxiety became even more prolonged, as we had at first to listen to another case concerning a young labourer who, for no reason but that he was 'tired of life', had hanged himself from a tree. The victim had left a good-bye letter of explanation to his parents. The coroner went calmly and logically through these facts, in a cold voice. Dispassionately he announced the verdict: 'Suicide while of unsound mind.'

At last it was our turn. Daddy took the witness stand, answering formal questions about the 'deceased man'.

The coroner asked, 'Did he enjoy his life in the Flying Corps?'

Daddy, as though his life depended on the answer, replied fervently and poignantly, 'He loved it.' The words gave me an abrupt shock. After so much formality and lack of emotion, we were now participating in a human tragedy.

Daddy did his piece beautifully, clearly, quickly and dramatically. I felt proud of him, as the strain must have been enormous.

A doctor was now called. Yes, he had examined the corpse. Death had been instantaneous, from multiple causes. No alcohol was found in the stomach. A long list of injuries was now read out. No part of the body, it seems, had been spared.

The engine driver testified. 'At eleven o'clock I was driving my train into Piccadilly Station. About seventy yards from the tunnel opening stood a man without a hat. He was about a yard from the edge of the platform, looking straight in front of him across the tracks. As I came within a few feet of him, he raised his hands to his head and dived in front of the train.'

My blood ran cold. The coroner went on implacably, 'Do you think this man fell, or do you think he deliberately jumped in front of the train?'

'I think it was deliberate.'

'And where was the body found?'

'Under the third carriage on the far side of the line.'

Things looked black for us. I prayed for a verdict of 'accidental death'.

Daddy called his witnesses. Bradley said, 'Reggie was gay, in good spirits.' Spencer told of the blackout and fall in the bathroom that morning. Jeanne Stourton spoke of how she had planned future dates with Reggie. It now seemed possible, indeed there was a half and half chance, that in spite of the train driver's evidence the verdict would be open.

Each word was a year, each sentence a decade while the coroner impartially summed up. I thought him insufferably in-human as he kept referring to 'this man'. How could Reggie be put in the category of 'this man'? How could my younger brother, who went off in the train to St Cyprian's with me, who was so happy on our childhood holiday at Arley, who fell out of the hammock when I swung him too high, who played cricket and tennis with such flair, who taught me how to drive, who had a mysterious sense of humour, who for all his outward heartiness was a subtle enigma—how could Reggie ever be called 'this man'?

The coroner concluded, 'Although this man was content with his life and in good spirits, yet like many men today he apparently took that life for no apparent reason. In this case, I am convinced that this man had been worrying in secret about his eyesight. Indeed, what could be more important to someone in the Flying Corps? Suddenly an impulse had overtaken him to get rid of his troubles. And so, acting while of unsound mind, he killed himself.'

It was all over. There could be no repeal of the verdict. Useless to worry now about not having had a solicitor to appear for us. This impossible verdict must be accepted, but how were we to face Mummie and tell her the news? It would have been a com-fort to bring home a verdict of 'accidental'. A judgment of suicide could only crown her misery and despair.

Daddy had to leave for the City. I returned to confront Mummie. I have never hated a scene more in my life. I stopped outside her door, wishing so much that this had not been neces-sary. We had already called the doctor, in case it would be better to give her some soothing injection. But Mummie, perhaps through sheer exhaustion, seemed calmer as I went in to her. I gazed at her colourless, unalive face on the pillow.

'Do tell me what they said,' she pleaded.

In the softest way possible, I related the events of the inquest. Her eyes lit up for a second's agony; she raised her head and cried, 'Oh, but it's too awful!'

The whole disaster struck me now as some incongruous nightmare. It was unlike anything that could possibly happen to us. If anyone in the family were ever to have been tempted to suicide, then why not me? Yet, despairing as I have been at times, such thoughts never really entered my mind. The others, Reggie in particular, couldn't have been more normal. It was nothing short of impossible that it should be *his* face in the papers under 'killed by a train'. It was an absurd unreality that *he* should be the 'Flying Officer' on the placards. Such tragedies happened to other people, never to one's own family. What error of fate could overnight have overwhelmed us like this? How inconceivable that *we* should be the ones about whose trouble everyone in London was reading over the breakfast table.

In the drawing-room a trail of wreaths had begun to arrive for the coffin. I cried when I read the names and a further batch of sympathy letters.

I lay in bed uneasily. It took a long time to go to sleep. I remembered Reggie's heavy tread on his way up to his bedroom; his calling Manley and his rather breathless, 'Becka, Becka, Beck, Beck,' to the dog. I kept seeing Reggie's fresh, clear-cut features, his good nose, his eagle, lidless eyes so direct yet soft in their gaze, his forehead wrinkled in surprise.

This morning (Saturday) was the funeral. More flowers arrived, including a sheaf of lilies I had sent. Hesitantly, I wrote a last message to Reggie on the accompanying card. The flowers were somehow ugly, and they didn't seem to smell.

Mummie was up from bed, weeping dejectedly as she waited in her bedroom for the funeral to begin. Nancy and Baba looked unaccustomedly pale without make-up. They sat on the arms of Mummie's chair. Everyone looked strange in black.

Time now to go to the church opposite for the service. The wreaths had already been taken across. I was sent to tell Mum to come down. I tried to say casually, 'I think we ought to be going.'

As we descended the cold staircase, I turned slightly and noticed my mother had on black satin shoes rather frayed at the toes. The coffin preceded us to the church. We walked up the aisle, Mum very bent with tears pouring down her face. She cried throughout the service.

The coffin looked solid and shiny. I couldn't believe anyone lay inside it, least of all Reggie. The black-beetle pall bearers staggered under the load as they made their way down the aisle. We followed, the family and Reggie's best friends—Raymond, Mrs O'Brien, Ninnie, Manley, Miss Joseph, Lady Chichester, relations and a few men I did not know and scarcely saw.

Outside there were painful kisses, silent handshakes. Nancy and Baba had faces swollen red with tears. Daddy and I drove silently to Hampstead cemetery. On the way, I watched to see which of the passers-by took off their hats as the hearse moved along. I noticed what a lot of people had cigarettes in their mouths.

The sun shone. We gathered around the open grave, watching the coffin lowered slowly into the vault as the last prayer was said. Only now did my father burst into tears. He tried to hide his face with his hat; he trembled and quivered. I was howling. Someone held my arm very tight.

After a few necessary words to relations and friends, we drove home. On the way, Daddy brought out his watch. 'Twenty minutes to twelve. That didn't take very long,' he said.

The drawing-room looked like a scene in a Pirandello play, with so many flowers and everyone wearing black. There was sherry and brandy on the side table. No one spoke much.

January 14th 1934

A new year and another birthday. I am thirty now. My line of being young, inconsequent and all that, will not be possible any longer. Yet it's hard for me to realise my age. Still thinking of myself as being twenty, it is a shock to see school contemporaries going slightly bald or grey, settled down stolidly to uneventful domestic lives.

CHRISTMAS AT ASHCOMBE, 1935

Our Christmas dinner wasn't really festive. The three of us—Mummie, Daddy and myself—sat down in no spirit of gladness.

We made small effort to feel gay, though the bottle of champagne engendered a certain self-conscious levity. And my father, as he has done each Christmas Day ever since I can remember, raised his glass to my mother: 'Well, Mrs Beaton, thirty-one years ago today we drew up this contract. Now, is this to be continued for another seven, fourteen or twenty-one years?'

My mother sadly and earnestly replied, 'I shan't be here for another seven years.'

'But you're too late,' my father jested. 'You should have given notice before.' It was a nice way of overcoming Mummie's morbidity.

I sat feeling caddish at my inability to rise to the occasion. But try as I would, I could not add stimulus to fragmentary conversations that died as soon as they were born.

At any rate, this Christmas dinner was less poignantly dramatic than last year's. At that time, we had not got accustomed to family losses: it was Nancy's first Christmas of wedded life: Reggie lay but recently in a cold, granite grave. There had been forced jollity, and a sad moment when glasses were raised to 'absent friends'. That walrus buffoon, Uncle Wilfred, had insisted on making his joke, 'Yes, let's drink to absent-minded friends.'

Now Christmas is over. My father returns to London tomorrow: to a hotel, to an office where there is nothing of any importance to be done at all.

CONVALESCING

Newton Ferrers: Callington

States of health play curious tricks with one's sense of time. I have been here in the Cornish countryside for the past four days, recuperating from an appendicitis operation as the guest of Bertie and Diane Abdy. I ought now to be stronger after so much sleep and quiet. Yet I am unable to remember how I felt when I arrived, just as I have quickly become incapable of differentiating one day from another. Time flies as never before. I sleep so much that it gives me a headache. I am drugged from too much sleep, but have been unable to keep awake.

Initiative not only lags, it is totally lacking. I read little, in spite of my intention to read a great deal. I have not drawn, nor

have I stuck any pictures in my album, nor have I written any
thing but the shortest notes in lieu of correspondence. Waking
hours seem to be devoted to eating delicious food, looking at
picture books and talking ceaselessly with Diane. We compare our
illnesses and their attending consequences; we talk about painting,
about furniture and decoration, everything pleasant.

Diane is the most articulate companion. Such a varied and
brilliant use of words is rare.

Bertie, too, infects me with his enthusiasms. I would willingly
put myself under his tutelage and learn a great deal more than I
know about art or—perhaps more important—the art of living
itself. Both he and Diane make me realise how incompetent and
sluggish I am in the practise of this art. Ordinarily, life rushes
by in a whirl of unconsciousness. I drug myself against reality by
plunging into work and engagements, without allowing myself
time to be aware of anything beyond my immediate interests.
I am like a horse with blinkers on.

'What is this life if, full of care, we have no time to stand and
stare?' But I mingle with too many people; I'm dazed by too
many lights. My sketches are too quick, my articles too quick-
fire, my photographs too many. Crowded weeks give place to
others, while I labour under the delusion that I am living more
vitally than if I sat down by a pool and just looked at some goldfish.

Yet even my play and pleasure are hurried. I am at best able
to appreciate only certain superficial forms of beauty and sensual
delights. By contrast I think of someone like Peter Watson, who
has joined me here at the Abdy's to motor me home. Peter feels
himself inwardly to be an inferior human being. He practises no
art, but I think him a very extraordinary person. If we are meant
to live life fully, then surely he is one of the few people who
know how to do this. Just being in his company affords an odd
stimulus. He puts me on my mettle, makes me strive to inspirit
him as much as he does me. As an observer, he is so incredibly
sensitive and acute that it opens my eyes to many subtleties. Peter
is the best person at the art of living I know. I wish I had some of
his gifts.

HAZEL LAVERY

One of the biggest stars in my adolescence was Hazel Lavery.[1]

[1] The Chicago-born wife of Royal Academy painter Sir John Lavery.

She looked like a Luini madonna—skin of alabaster, hair aflame, eyes huge as a hare's and rabbit nostrils.

Hazel's life was the apex of all worldly delights. Painters forever painted her; photographers squeezed their bulbs, and everybody gossiped. She moved in an aura of romance; she was in the swing. She posed as Botticelli's *Primavera*, as Lady Hamilton, as a society woman in velvets, leopard skin and gold embroidery. Did Pavlova give a society garden party? Then Hazel would be snapped talking to Bernard Shaw.

On her private life she showered the extravagance of an artist. Had Hazel returned from Morocco? Then she brought a little coloured boy back with her. Wearing a turban, he trundled in with coffee to a dining-table aglow from crimson glass and columbines in vases. Did Hazel always wear mauve orchids? They were sent by an anonymous lover.

Now dear Hazel Lavery is dead. Not only has one of my first and favoured stars ceased to shine, but I have lost a true and sympathetic friend. When I started my career, Hazel was one of the first to overwhelm me with encouragement and kindness. She did all she could to help me. She sent notes, drawings, criticisms and suggestions. She sympathised with my despairs.

In her glory, Hazel was a witty companion overflowing with affection and happiness. She'd been a person after my own heart; a great player of make-believe. Without affecting grandeur, she enjoyed creating a good theatrical effect. No Cartier's for her: she could not afford it, and in any case preferred paste jewels. Her clothes were generally concocted by herself and her maid. She would appear in public faultlessly wearing organdie frills and a picture hat she had pinned together. The result was in the best picturesque style. When she went to Courts, she wore Prince-of-Wales feathers on the front of her head. Often she met with failure in these home-made efforts. Once she became so irritated that she burnt a fur muff.

Hazel had artistic talent. She drew expertly but never concentrated long enough on her work. She could not bear to become tired or dirty. As soon as her hands were smudged with pencil or charcoal, she must give up. She was a charming, feminine amateur.

The past years were sad. From a plump and stocky beauty still flawless of face, she gradually changed into a haggard wraith.

271

She knew she was ill, and her illness made her restless and hysterical. She became 'poor Hazel'. She had always talked too much—of her young beaux and of Michael Collins, of Lady Colefax and Lady Cunard and Lady Castlerosse. But now she refused to allow a conversation to take its natural course.

Poor Hazel has been laid in her coffin and taken to Kensal Rise Cemetery. A living spirit has become a thing of the past. Those who loved her will perhaps make a legend of her, decorating her memory with the tuberoses, orchids and crimson roses that she surrounded herself with in life. But soon and inevitably, even these dearest friends will be busy going out to lunch with someone else.

THE END OF SUSSEX GARDENS

I wasn't well enough to be there for the sorting and packing, but went this afternoon for a last visit to the address that has so long been ours: 61 Sussex Gardens.

The house is ripped bare now. Packing cases are strewn everywhere; and with the curtains down, it looks forlorn, stark. There are dirty shadows on the wall where pictures used to hang. And so many memories that have been lost beneath the untidy accumulation of years come suddenly to light. I am reminded with a stab of long-forgotten incidents.

The house was always a cold one. For that reason, I bore it a grudge in winter. But I'd been fond of it, too. It represented an exciting, eventful period of our lives. When we first arrived, I had great fun trying to make it appear as grand as we could afford. It was my ambition to make each room look like a stage set—the drawing-room fashionably apple-green and gold, Nancy's and Baba's bedroom Marie-Laurencin pink and blue, and my room a circus of many colours. Even today, I like the look of that circus.

My photographic career thrived in this house. From here I had my first exhibition. Through this letter box the first press cuttings arrived. From here I set out on my virgin trip to America, and returned to find a fresh-faced family. It was the first time I had seen them in many months, and I remember thinking their blue eyes looked strangely cat-like, piercing.

Here, first Nancy and then Baba became grown-up, shouting

excitedly over the banisters, 'Telephone! Photographs! Hurry!'
Becky, the dog, barked every time the postman made a delivery.
Manley slid down the banisters the quicker to open the front door.
Once, he answered the summons to find Sacheverell Sitwell
standing there. It was said that Manley bade him peremptorily
to 'go to the back door, Sonnie'. But this Sitwell family joke
would not have been based on fact. For Manley was a marvel of
tact and industry, coping with assorted messages and calls for my
parents, Reggie, Nancy, Baba, and myself. Manley had an uncanny instinct about whom one wished to speak to. At times he
was guarded: 'I'll see if he has left yet.' But he always knew I
would speak to Mr Watson.

In this house, every morning at ten o'clock, Miss Joseph
arrived to help me through the technicalities of the day. I would
come down to morning coffee in my dressing gown. Business
started with the morning letters and kept up at a fever pitch.

Coming home late at night, I would unlock the door to the
familiar Italian light giving an orange glow in the hall. If everyone
was in, I clicked off the lantern and found my way upstairs in the
dark. Exhaustedly, I fell asleep as soon as my head touched the
pillow on my narrow four poster bed.

One day, while I was in the drawing-room taking a photograph of a baroque wood pedestal filled with flowers, my mother
told me that Baba was going to marry Alec Hambro. Weddings
are contagious. Within a week, Nancy was also engaged.

Then came that terrible night when Baba was waiting up for
me. By the glow of the orange light she told me that Reggie had
been killed. The house knew death: black scenes and wreaths
stretching from the conservatory through to the drawing-room.

Marriages, death, parties, career, friends, dramatic telephone
conversations, jokes, laughter—general experiences, but unique
for each and every person. I wonder if 61 Sussex Gardens can
entirely cast off our memories just because it is an inanimate
thing?

Part XV

The Gallic Influence

1935

Ever since my father treated my brother and me to a holiday from a holiday, and first took us across the Channel from our rented house in Folkestone, a visit to Paris has been considered the ultimate in pleasure.

As the years have passed, Paris has become ever more significant. Invariably, a few moments after arrival, the light in the sky becomes more varied, and one's surroundings are seen with a fresh eye. The way that the loaves of bread are laid out in a shop window, a curtain tied back, or the fusion of two colours, give one a stimulus. After two days, my anonymous hotel is filled with new names, catalogues, pictures of things which show the way towards undiscovered tracks.

The French are said to be inhospitable: Yet, if so, how was it that if I made known my arrival to Christian Bérard, Marie Louise Bousquet, or a couple of other friends, I would forthwith be given the keys to whatever part of the city it interested me to see?

274

Paris artists and writers seem to have infinite leisure so that one never has the impression of interrupting the tenor of their day or night. Colette had covered reams of blue stationery with enormous calligraphic scrolls with the choice of a dozen fountain pens at her elbow, when she cheerfully cleared away her tray to

give full attention to her visitor. Likewise Gide was content to ignore the ringing of the doorbell while he allowed me to spend a morning in his company.

When first I met Picasso, he greeted me in his quiet dignified manner, with a twinkle of liquid amusement in his brilliant eyes. It somewhat surprised me to see him wearing the most conventional and elegant of blue suits, with a white shirt. On first sight his surroundings struck me as being like that of a typical doctor's waiting room. The current fashion of stripped panelling, whitened woods and vague baroqueries was so universal that these plain walls and bold mahogany furniture came as a disappointment. But by degrees I acquired a new vision and noticed that every piece of furniture was of eclectic simplicity. Noticing my growing enthusiasm he demonstrated the ingenious craftsmanship of the various pieces; how a low stool turned into a pair of steps, or a desk possessed hidden levers, drawers, and lids, and that the curious objects on tables and chimney piece had been made from matchboxes, by piecing together pieces of menus, lottery tickets and playing cards, or part of a leather bicycle seat.

Surely it was a privilege to be given a secret glimpse of his seldom used salon? Shutters were thrown wide to reveal a white pannelled room stacked with vast portraits of his wife, some like Ingres, others Cubistic. The large armchairs were covered in white linen. Suddenly Picasso indulged in a piece of legerdemain as he danced towards one of the chairs and in a bold gesture ripped off its cover to disclose a shining conch-shell of orange. One by one he threw off other covers to reveal chairs upholstered in brilliant satins that somehow reminded me of those sugared cushion-sweets of one's childhood. With a flick of his arm he conjured up a hot-yellow conch: then another butcher blue. Yet another crimson, and now an emerald green, Picasso's eyes flashed with excited enjoyment as each new colour appeared. These were the real colours of Spain, bold, unconforming and startling. It gave me an indication of a whole taste of which I had never before been conscious.

A DAY IN PARIS

Summer 1935

Tilly Losch asked me to help her with her costume for the Oriental Ball. It soon became my work of the morning. Endless telephoning. What is the address of the woman who is so good at make-up? Daisy would know but is out. Iya knows it. Iya is away. Boris would know, or Natasha, or Nabokoff.

We then went in search, and at last found, near the Musée Grévin, that curious little circus shop called Poupineau. Here we revelled in the glories of spangle and tinsel.

Tilly has a smouldering, Slavic face. In costume as an *ouled naïl*, her appearance becomes barbarically *fatale*. Unfortunately she is completely helpless—either lazy and spoilt or else clever at getting things done for her. After creating her costume the whole morning I said, 'Now you are complete. All you have to do for the Ball is glue a sequin between your brows.' Tilly whimpered,

'But how can I do that? Won't you come to the hotel and bring some glue?'

Lunch *chez* Noailles was not at all what I had expected. I imagined that the two children, Marie Laure and myself would sit rather embarrassedly discussing generalities and veering towards our mutual object of affection. But no, it proved to be a lunch party *manqué*, with an empty place for the hostess. Just before lunch, Marie Laure received news that René Crevel had attempted suicide and she rushed off to his bedside in the hospital.

All day long the telephone buzzed. Harassed conversation alternated between the dying man and tomorrow's costume ball. '*C'est effroyable! O, ma robe, c'est une merveille! Pauvre petit garçon. O, ma robe!*' There was a scene at Karinska's emporium in the afternoon, with everyone turning up for a minute to try on a turban and discuss the unhappy news.

Later in the evening, in Bébé's cluttered room at the First Hotel everyone talked of René. Tony Ganderillas arrived from the hospital, panting for a palliative. This *would* happen just as he came to Paris for a few days' holiday. 'It is too much. I've been through this too many times before. All my friends commit suicide.'

Later, at Marie Blanche de Polignac's, we heard that the attempted suicide had succeeded: after dying all day long, René eventually expired.

In spite of the tragedy, the evening turned out to be just the sort I like best. The two Polignacs, Bébé, Boris[1] and I sat down to a rare dinner. There was lamb cooked in maize, so delicious that I could not believe such things existed. The sauces were unbelievable, the atmosphere of the house equally sympathetic. Bébé's murals, influenced by Raphael, in the dining-room are his best things. We looked at the lovely, loved collection of Madame Lanvin[2]—Renoirs, Degas, Stephens and ravishing small Boldinis. We talked of the solid charm of English country houses, browsed through snapshot albums, admired the pretty objects throughout the house.

The others went off to a party at the British Embassy, and for the rest of the evening I was with Bébé. We stopped at Maxim's, talked of Marie Laure, were charmingly interrupted by Figgi

---

[1] Boris Kochno, Producer of Ballets for Diaghilev.
[2] Marie Blanche de Polignac's mother, living in the same house.

Ralli and Igor Markevitch. Then, back to the First Hotel until four o'clock in the morning. Bébé smoked and talked with the avidness of a haunted creature, desperate to rid himself of some devil. 'You do like me, Cecil, don't you?' My reply was such a relief that it went through him like an electric shock. 'That's over. Good! Now we continue.'

Bébé's sensitivity and intensity are beyond compare. He talked inspiredly of his hobbies of collecting—*objets d'art*, terra cottas, rare books—and of reading the cheapest American magazines, devouring the detailed lives of movie stars. He praised Eduard Bourdet for being such a gentle and inspiring collaborator in the theatre and we both eulogised the photographs of Cartier Bresson. Bébé also talked of Boris, while Boris slept. It seems that Boris, about to organise a new ballet season, hadn't turned up for an important date with Markevitch and Dali. Bébé loves Boris, but minds very much that, in details, Boris is disorderly and late, throwing away so many of his important chances.

I haven't known Bébé for long, but I already understand him. I love him for the rocklike character that fundamentally, and in spite of all his superficial nonsenses, he really is.

JEAN COCTEAU

Spring 1936

Jean lives at the Castile, which is visible from my hotel room. As a result of a telephone call, we waved towels and handkerchiefs at one another from our balconies.

After this semaphore, he became ill. For several days he could not sleep, eat or smoke opium. His throat was completely constricted. At last someone puffed opium smoke into his mouth; and like a galvanised corpse he staggered from his bed, and gave a virtuoso performance that was full of ideas, wit and poetry.

Looking like cheese, Jean came out to the ruins of the Paris Exhibition to be photographed. It was very cold. His nose turned purple, making the rest of the face seem even more grey, green and yellow. But the low temperature did not chill his volubility. Indeed, I could hardly persuade him to stop talking long enough for exposures to be made.

Like all ruins, this discarded playground is strange and very romantic.

Jean is having a hard time: his recently completed play was rejected by Jouvet and Bourdet. Jean feels all France to be against him, rails that he alone has not succumbed to the perils of cheap success and vulgarity.

As for the play, it is said to be unlike anything else he has written. No metaphysical characters, just five members of an ordinary family. It is only their wickedness, viciousness and

Cocteau

meanness that make them appear extraordinary. Marcel,[1] to whom Jean read the play, was so horrified that his face swelled and broke out in spots. Glenway Westcott heard it the next night. He told me the audience would roll in the aisles; but he thought the play eminently actable and translatable into German and English—a thoroughly well-constructed piece of work in the Bernstein manner.

[1] Marcel Khill.

I should like to make a catalogue of Jean's qualities and characteristics.

Where to begin? His physical appearance: a fakir-thin body is held up by legs as thin as a sparrow's; yet curiously, he has flat feet. His hands seem so brittle you are afraid a sharp blow may crack them off. The fingers taper, can bend backwards. The nails are discoloured and slightly dirty (a sign of the dope addict's *laisser-aller*). As with most artists, the eyes communicate their owner's deepest secrets. As silent as Jean's mouth is talkative, the dilated pupils of his bulging fishy eyes, anguished and tortured, aghast and helpless, seem to be looking into another existence.

Charm, childish exuberance and longing to please are Jean's greatest personality assets. He is completely unself-conscious during conversation, chuckling with an infectious gaiety. Sometimes he will nervously thump his listener's chest and shoulders as though to assure himself of riveted attention.

Famous are Jean's annihilating descriptions of people with whom he is displeased. 'When that ballerina misses a step,' he exclaims acidly, 'she creates the same embarrassing effect on her audience as an old woman who bends down to pick up something and lets off a loud report.'

Jean's surroundings are a typical reflection of his personality. There is a tingling aliveness about his room. Even the bad photograph of Daisy Fellowes is now justified, for he has cut it to make her look like a bird and has stuck real feathers on her. Black drawing boards are covered with chalk scribblings—his engagements, random drawings or ideas. There are plaster heads decorated with wax tears.

In spite of the darkness of Jean's room, it has comfort and great organization. A high desk serves for drawing; a bedside table holds equipment for smoking. Neat files of letters and photographs in portfolios permit him to find things quickly. His india rubber is never lost. In evidence are the drawings, always displaying an easy flow of line and imagination. Two sailors playing games with one another suggest the celestial regions to which lust can be elevated. (A more earthy illustration is provided by the indecent postcards strewn about.)

If a stranger looks at the objects in the room, he will perhaps guess Jean's unhappy side—the great disasters, the personal tragedy of being abandoned by lovers. There is a lurking sentimentality in the crimson wools, a death-like aura about the life masks of his head and hands, a secretly depressing claustrophobia in this atmosphere redolent of the seminal smell of opium.

But Jean himself is unmistakeably alive, frenziedly so. No one can doubt his supreme intelligence, wit and authority. When the master expresses himself, it is always a very special performance, matinee or evening. Nor is he showing off; rather, he merely discourses with his disciples.

It is interesting when an artist has sufficient strength of personality to be *outré*, yet accepted by the most conservative elements of society.

GERTRUDE STEIN AND ALICE TOKLAS

Paris

This afternoon I went to see Gertrude Stein in her new apartment on the Rue Christine.

Oddly, I had never imagined Miss Stein's apartment would be so impressive, though there was no reason to believe otherwise: whenever we met, I'd always been particularly struck with her sense and taste. Here now was the expression of a *goût impeccable*. Tall ceilings, panelled walls and high windows delighted the eye. Each piece of furniture seemed solid and beautiful in design. There was no *chichi* or vulgarity anywhere. The Misses Stein and Toklas live like Biblical royalty: simply, yet in complete luxury.

A well-scrubbed, apple-cheeked maid opened the door. Miss Toklas was sewing in her bedroom. She did not move, determined to spend the afternoon there. This plan succeeded admirably, except when explanations were necessary to a workman who had come to mend a latch.

Miss Stein took me on a tour of inspection. I noticed her low-heeled brown shoes, as highly polished as the furniture in the various rooms. 'This,' she gestured, 'is where we have some of our pictures.' Over the fireplace was an enormous portrait of a woman by Cézanne. Hung in front of a huge looking-glass was a full-length Picasso nude; while his portrait of Gertrude Stein occupied the space above a beautiful brown and gold cabinet, its colours reflecting those of the painting.

A few unique objects were displayed: a portrait of Voltaire

done with pin-pricks, a china cherub fallen asleep with his head resting on a skull. Cut azaleas were in bowls; bluebells sprouted from earthenware vases. The copybooks in which Miss Stein writes all her works had been placed in orderly readiness. Fuss, bother and discomfort seemed eliminated from an apartment whose great strength resides in its uniformity.

The curtains were made of glazed white linen with a waxy, dotted-leaf motif. Ubiquitous brown carpets and brown wood furniture with brass ornamentation created a bold background for the petit-point chairs, embroidered by Miss Toklas from designs Picasso had drawn on to the canvas.

Miss Stein showed me the paintings of Francis Rose. It was the first time I had seen any. Pavlik turns Mantegna-grey at the mention of his name. To him, Francis Rose and his work are the last word in something-or-other. Here, hung in a gallery, were about forty of his canvasses. Most salient is a heavy, pregnant gloom and fatality. Rose seems to have absorbed from all the big painters, yet with no slavish eclecticism.

When I asked Miss Stein about him, she told her story with Steinian simplicity. 'Well, his mother was French, his father a baronet, he is about twenty-seven years old, with very pretty ways and gentle manners. He was brought up in Paris, came under the influence of Cocteau and that *galère*. He painted, painted, painted. It's the only thing that interested him. Then he fell in with this American fraud, lost the greater part of his money and is now in America painting hard all the time. It is a typical English story.'

We looked at portfolios full of Rose's drawings: cross-sections of the brain; detailed lines of the hand.

We discussed other painters. Miss Stein thinks Pavlik is an illustrator, that he possesses no aesthetic sense. She likes Picabia (whom I have hated) for his tireless search to find a new dimension in space.

Juan Gris is another of Stein's masters. When she lives with pictures that continue to be good, then she knows they are great. 'There's no doubt about it. There are no ifs and ands. If I live with a man I know so. There's no *parti pris*. It's just definite, and Juan is great.'

Gertrude held on to Pepé, the dog, standing against the blue and white wallpaper depicting pigeons on the grass, alas.

I photographed also Toklas at her sewing. Determined not to talk this afternoon she nodded by way of understanding and said, 'Interior'.

ERWIN BLUMENFELD

Paris

It was difficult to find the studio of Erwin Blumenfeld, the photographer whose work has intrigued me during the last few months. I crept along a pitch-black corridor. Then my eyes gradually became accustomed to the dark, and I noticed a crack of light coming from under a door. I knocked and was ushered in.

Somehow I had expected a young man. But Blumenfeld turned out to be a middle-aged, huge-nosed Dutchman, like a gay and evil spirit in a Bosch painting.

Without preliminaries, he showed me the photograph of an early African war god. 'Is it not extraordinary? Is it not extraordinary in taste?'

The god was, indeed, a remarkable object. But his other photographs were what I particularly liked. These, in fact, seemed revelations—the work of a photographer totally uninfluenced by others. Blumenfeld has a fresh, clean mind. It is wrong and disgraceful that his photographs never fetch much money. With three children to support, he remains poor. But Blumenfeld's merit as an artist lies in the fact that he is incapable of compromise.

He showed me a series of nudes—women lying with wet draperies covering them, like sculptured figures of the French Renaissance. He has taken many photographs of medieval sculptures and tapestries, interpreting them with a new vision which make the pictures works of art in themselves. He showed me prints of cathedrals and cathedral details, treated with a new eye. There was a trick photograph of his son, that had the poignance of an early Ronault.

Sometimes I come across a photographer whose work I like, though his personality proves to be a blank (De Meyer was a colossal disappointment). But this little gnome has the appeal of only a genuine artist. I found myself forgetting the hours as we browsed about a bare attic studio amid a mess of cigarette stubs and electric wires. Enlargements on the walls included distortions of nudes mingled with old fashioned still lives; pale, romantic prints of apple trees in blossom alternated with ivy grots and broken steps in an overgrown garden. Nudes of witch-like hags contrasted with shadows of young nudes seen through muslin screens. One picture showed the photographer himself lying half under the bath water, with the visible part of his body reflected by the water's surface.

'Do you mean to tell me you don't do your own technical work?' Blumenfeld turned a full Dutch disbelief on my candid admission.

'I used to, years ago. But now I don't have the time. Besides, there are others who do it so much better.'

'You don't develop, you don't enlarge? For me, when I have taken the picture, the technical work is the greatest joy. I have such will power, such belief that the pictures must come out as I hope. Even if they were washed in water instead of developer, I think they would gradually appear in the basins. To me, the greatest magic of this century is in the dark room.'

After three hours, I tore myself away. Glenway had been waiting half an hour for me at the hotel. My arms were full of an assortment of Blumenfeld's pictures, which I'll send to *Vogue*. They will be fools in my eyes if they do not use him.

MADAME ERRAZURIZ

Paris

Mme Errazuriz is now a very old woman, making it impossible to engage in connected conversation. But one can see how blazingly lovely she must have been when Helleu, Sargent, Boldini and others painted this Chilean innovator at the turn of the century.

We made attempts to talk, while Mme E. ate a sandwich. Alas, the bread sagged, dropping by slow degrees from mouth to chin, from chin to chest, from chest to floor. It was only when I admired a porcelain pot decorated with twigs and leaves that she responded. Taking up the cream-crackled pot and holding it in her trembling hands firmly, lovingly, she said with fire, 'I've never liked anything so much as this little pot. Isn't it beautiful? Isn't it a most beautiful pot?'

Mme E.'s house looks on to Etienne de Beaumont's court.

Gazing out of the window, I could see a small child chasing pigeons.

We sauntered through rooms furnished with the same stark taste that characterises Picasso and Gertrude Stein. The floors are polished and bare; furniture is bold and there is much brass. Panelled walls have been painted a French grey. A bunch of tightly packed peonies, in a glass goblet on a brass table, should have been painted by Manet. The curtains were made of sprigged white muslin. Huge abstract pictures by Picasso hung on the walls. Every object on the tea table seemed likewise beautiful and simple—the great glass jar of marmalade, the champagne beakers and the brass-ended wooden trays.

Madame Errazuriz's lodge-house is small, simple and in no way spectacular. But for those who can recognise such things, the taste is the height of luxury. There is a whole moral tale to be derived from this microcosm. This woman's surroundings have reflected the same uncompromising and sophisticated sparseness for more than half a century. Plush and panache have come and gone, but the empty richness that startled *fin de siècle* eyes, and made Picasso realise he had found a kindred spirit, is still the triumphant expression of an abiding strength.

Part XVI

Griefs and Laughter

1935

August 1935

Two idyllic days have been spent in Alsace, replenishing one's
spirit by enjoying the tender green vineyards, Romanesque
churches, museums and these tortured, torturing masterpieces, the
Grunewalds at Colmar. The great altar piece of the Crucifixion
is painted in the colours that appear when copper is thrown into a
furnace. The stark reality of the agony, the physical putrefaction
and emotional misery of all concerned, is portrayed with a
German metallic precision that delights in sparing us no pain.
Yet the effect is of a hitherto unknown beauty. For the replenish-
ment of the body there were gourmet's foods; and it seemed as if
wine was being discovered for the first time. Accommodation
had been provided at a chateau owned by some friends of
Nicholas,[1] and the atmosphere was agreeable. The terraced
gardens smelled particularly beautiful at night, with banks of
tobacco flowers.

[1] Nicholas Nabokoff, the composer.

286

Always to be heard was the gaiety of many children. On the night of our departure, they treated us to a special performance. The barn had been lighted by paper lanterns surrounded with vine leaves. The *décors* seemed all the more impressive for their lack of elaboration. Surprisingly, the children's plays proved completely surrealist, death and horror always recurring.

Then, after a night journey to Salzburg, came the excitement of arriving at Schloss Kammer, on the edge of Lake Kammer. In this somewhat uncanny, mountainous landscape, an enormous quantity of curious people have gathered to create a world of their own under the aegis of Alice von Hofmannsthal and Eleanor Mendelssohn, who with their families share the castle.

Kammer has a strong personality—ruthless sometimes morbid. However much Alice may redecorate the rooms or alter the construction of house and gardens, the atmosphere remains unchanged. Sometimes a shadow falls over the gayest parties. Guests find themselves miserable and never return. Others, like myself, are stimulated for a while. But however much one has enjoyed a visit, it is always as though a cloud has lifted when one leaves.

This summer the castle became a sort of kindergarten for extraordinary grown-ups; long, hilarious discussions; incongruous groups for lunch, for tea, for swimming, for sightseeing. We rode and went shooting in the mountains. At night on the lake, we ate gay dinners on rafts by torchlight, with music provided from adjoining barques.

Apart from the superficial gaiety, jealous intrigue and romantic complications flourished. Scarcely a day but provides a dozen situations for a play, or material for a novel. Lawyers create dramatic scenes to keep X or Y from buying up part of the castle. Complete strangers arrive to stay, and only after two or three days does Eleanor get around to asking their names. Guests arrive in hoards to find neither host nor hostess. The wife of a composer, upon being expelled from the castle, flounced out rudely exhibiting her behind.

Raimund, a power-station of energy, laughingly relates that Alice must cope with three vans full of furniture just arrived from America. The shipment has already crossed the Atlantic three times. One of the tables, intended for her London house, didn't fit; and so it was sent back to Rhinebeck, but there they decided it could go well in Schloss Kammer. Now Alice is being kind to the customs appraisers, shaking hands and saying, 'Guten Tag', and seeing that they are forthwith made drunk on the local wine.

'Alice has a new wheeze,' Raimund confides. 'It is telephone shopping. The other day, while several people were gathered in her bedroom, she took up the telephone and acquired more furniture, including some painted peasant tables and cupboards, circa 1790. "Hullo," says Alice, "have you something with birds painted on it?" A pause, while the man in the antique shop hunts around. Then he comes back and says, "No, but we have a pretty chest with deer on the drawers."'

Margot Oxford motored over to lunch today. She talked about 'her queen', her Alexandra. Alexandra was so *beautiful*, so interested in people and not a bit stuck up. When it was time for Margot to settle down to the business of an autobiography, she sent a letter to 'her Alexandra' asking for permission to write about their friendship. In reply came a telegram saying, 'Of course, any damn thing you like. Love A.'

Margot's mind is as alive and alert as that of Ivan Moffat, the youngest guest at the Schloss But she boasts the advantage that only older persons have—experience. And she can say, as only more mature people do, exactly what is on her mind. Margot will never do anything she doesn't wish; her mind cannot be exhausted by complicated half-truths. On leaving, she turned to her host with a candid, 'It's been most enjoyable. Thank you, sweet Raimund. Please ask me a little more often.' The diminutive shaved off any rudeness, while the tragedy of age and the cleverness remained.

FRITZI MASSARY AND LILY ELSIE

Fritzi Massary, in her heyday as a musical comedy actress in Berlin and Vienna, is staying nearby on the edge of the Lake. Fritzi is now recovering from the shock of Hitler and her husband's death. When she visited us today, I saw at first a scrawny, wrinkled little wretch. But she has such metallic spring and quickly exerted a personality so witty and alluring that I soon became her abject admirer.

When she sang 'Joseph, oh Joseph' and other songs from

288

Köningen and *Pompadour* for us in the courtyard, without accompaniment except the barking of dogs, we were all in raptures.

Later I asked her if she knew her English counterpart Lily Elsie, our 'Merry Widow'. And in English, which she is learning to speak now, she told the following story (so well that both David and I were moved to hug her matchstick shoulders).

Fritzi Massary came to London a year ago, at which time she lunched with some people called Marks in their Hampstead house. Six women were present; and, as a result of the typically casual English fault that makes hosts forget to introduce their guests, neither Fritzi nor the lady sitting next to her knew who the other was.

Both maintained silence for a spell: they had nothing to talk about, and breaking the ice proved difficult. At last the neighbour, ladylike, straight and fair, broached the subject of the theatre. Fritzi responded to the cue, observing that only once had she seen any outstanding personality on the English stage. It was in *The Dollar Princess*; and the lady was Lily Elsie. To which her neighbour replied quietly, 'I am Lily Elsie.'

They talked more of the theatre. Lily Elsie explained that she lost her singing voice some time ago, and an occasional return in straight plays had not been markedy successful. Now she was no longer interested in the theatre; she did not like the change that had come over today's entertainments. In *her* heyday, operetta had been so alive, Strauss and Lehar tunes so full of melody. She'd been too busy to travel much abroad and see the musical comedies. But in Germany she once saw the only person she thought a wonderful musical comedy heroine—Fritzi Massary. Fritzi Massary smiled and said, 'I am sorry, but I am Fritzi Massary.' The two women wept.

Ivan talked about the peculiar fact that in Salzburg and Central Europe, the out-of-doors gives an indoor impression. No tree stirs. The leaves of the lowest branches may twitch a little, but top foliage is completely stationary. Façades of houses seem so flat they look like cardboard cutouts. All is a toy representation. Here, the river looks unreal, as though the machinery had been turned on too quickly; the water flows too fast to be true.

Yet this timeless Hansel-and-Gretel quality constitutes one of the great charms of being at the Schloss.

289

Nicholas Nabokoff arrived belatedly from Alsace, his vitality unsurpassed. Most people stagger off a night train incapable of
speech for a while. But the journey had been like champagne to
Nicolas. He bubbled now with great effervescence. In the early
mornings, before the rest of the household had stirred, he would
come into my room while I was having breakfast and read me
the lectures on music that he planned to give during the winter at
Wells College in New York . . . or perhaps I would find some
morning's letter interesting enough to read to him. This following
was a typical periodic scolding that I received this morning from
Pavlik. 'How trivial and boring is the life of the *monde*! What
does it mean? A bunch of whores and bitches, with or without
money, with or without taste, with or without sexes. The *monde*
has no eyes to see, no nose for smelling, ears for hearing only
those things it wants to. It is difficult to make you feel my feelings,
because you like too much this kind of life and people, and they
appeal to your imagination. But I really only have contempt, for
they are milk reduced to water. The tragic thing is that they can
eat us up if we give them a chance, because amusement is queen,
and everything must go into the arena. I think you must have
a charming time at Kammer. I do like Raimund very much. He
has something very lyric about him profoundly, and I do admire
the beauty of Alice which she ignores and does nothing about. It
is the beauty of an Hindu, or a Spanish dancer, or a gypsy—
and something of a Persian Queen. Why am I fascinated by human
appearances? I really do like people, and I admire their beauty in
spite of everything.'

MY FATHER

August 24th 1936

It was on one of these mornings that the breakfast tray brought
with it a fatal telegram: 'Daddy gravely ill. Come.' In a flash,
everything changed. My mood, my life, the colour of the room,
the significance of everything altered.

Since I was very small, I had always wondered what would
happen if one of my parents died. The mere contemplation of
such an event brought tears to my eyes. Now it had materialised
in absentia, and it hurt sufficiently for me to cry.

In a few minutes I got through to London on the telephone.

My mother was suffering greatly, and wailed hysterically for me to come. My father had died of a heart attack at dawn.

More details I did not learn for a long while; it proved impossible to fly back to England at once. I was motored furiously to Munich, but arrived half an hour after the last plane of the day had left. I waited in an agony of idleness, impotent to move until the morrow's plane took me back to scenes that needed much courage to face.

My poor mother! After almost thirty-five years of married life, the blow would be bitter. It was especially hard that none of her children should be with her; but the doctor had told us that all was going as well as could be expected. We had gone on holidays, leaving only a temporary servant at home.

What scenes were being enacted at home? The gnawing uncertainty gave my imagination full play.

Yet abstract misery and querulousness combined to produce a sort of waking dream. I decided that activity would be helpful. I ate enormously at the Walterspiel, thinking irrelevantly that it must be the best restaurant in the world. I then went to see the Greek and Roman sculptures in the museum, and in the evening took myself to the rococo Residentz Theatre for an excellent presentation of Mozart's *Die Entführung aus dem Serail*.

I slept badly. The anxiety of a dawn call kept me on edge. But to my relief, I was alerted at the correct time and managed to catch the aeroplane.

I no longer have a father alive. My father is dead. My father died at five o'clock in the morning.

All this sounds as nothing. It is read in the newspaper every day; it happens every day. The special significance is for me and my family. It means that I will no longer see Papa return from having taken the dog for a walk, coming in all bowed and then looking up with kind, bright eyes. No longer will he sit at his desk like a formal child, feet side by side (in later years they were seldom crossed). He will never play patience again, nor will his advice be asked in moments of emergency over technicalities, money, rents or politics.

My father had been ill off and on for the past two years, and had suffered two previous attacks of thrombosis. I remembered one early dawn when my mother rushed wildly into my room, eyes blazing and hair distraught. On that occasion, she'd been unable to open the patent catch on the tin of pastilles used to alleviate his breathing difficulties.

Once more, Mum had been awakened in the night by a tapping on the door. She rushed to Daddy's assistance but was too late to help. There had been no pain this time. A weakness simply overcame him. Powerless to talk, he stared in front of him, then fell sideways on to the pillow as though dropping off to sleep. The difference was that he would never wake up again.

And that was death . . . nothing horrifying, nothing to make children quake and have nightmares about. The horrifying part was the consequences. Two ghouls in nurses' clothes arrived to prepare the body. (What did they have to do to make the body suitable for a coffin?) The ghouls and the insect corps of undertakers: these are death's frightening adjuncts. But my father's death was not terrible in itself. It came as a quiet end to a quiet life.

That life had been entirely honourable. It had also ended as something of a failure from a worldly point of view. Yet in his youth, he'd had real interests—sports, the theatre. His father had been wealthy; life had been full of promise, with a good business to fall heir to. He made a happy marriage to a beautiful woman; he had four children. How could he have foreseen that the 1914 war would end the old world he had known and bring about such radical changes? His business became more and more old-fashioned, the losses heavy. His children grew up to have tastes other than his own, to become almost strangers to him. His hobbies and interests dwindled. He became too infirm to play tennis, to ride or play cricket. He had no social distractions; and since he read little, his old age must have been sadly lonely.

The harsh thing about the death of a parent is that it destroys one of the cornerstones of one's life. A precious link with happy childhood memories is broken. Every evening in the nursery, bubbling over with cupboard love, I cherished Daddy's return home. He brought with him the *Evening Standard*, and that newspaper contained the Bessie Ascough fashion drawing which I was so eager to colour. It was my father who first took me to the theatre; who gave me pocket money, who made sacrifices so that I might be sent to a good school and be given the best opportunity. He liked to be host, especially if the guests were 'under-dogs'. He seemed at his gayest then, especially on the occasions of enormous impromptu dinners at home for his club cricketers. He did imitations of Hawtrey, Tree, Irving and other leading actors of the day.

Still, I cannot be insincere. The warm memories I have of him, the devotion I always felt, were not unmingled with a great sense of estrangement. We had little in common; even though I feel now that it might have been much better if, in more ways than one, I *had* closely resembled him.

It is difficult for me to write about my father without becoming sentimental after the fact. But I will try to describe his traits of character, which have become indelible with the years.

He was a man—a one-hundred-per-cent gentleman. Such a phrase is apt to provoke laughter or sneers nowadays. But it entirely befits him. He was incredibly fair, the most just person I have ever known. Seldom did he seem influenced by personal prejudice. This attitude he had perhaps acquired in his youth on the playing fields of a lost England. In those days, sports were a serious recommendation for life. My father's prowess at sculling augured well; he learned his ethics from the cider, ginger ale and raw-wood smell of the cricket pavilions.

As is often the case in a man's more resilient years, his youth had been gay and successful. He was debonair, wore a large rose in his buttonhole, went out to dances until late at night. He acted the lead in amateur plays. It was in *A Bunch of Violets* that my mother first saw him.

My father's histrionic flair showed itself, too, in little touches of fantasy. His jokes were odd, his after-dinner speeches witty. His attitude towards household pets was whimsical, and his letters to children elaborately humorous. (Once, while in America, he wrote a long letter to me, addressing me as Ginger-Top Fizzgig Marmaduke Beaton. I was nine months old!)

Yet my father remained an extremely simple person—direct, sincere, not easily gullible but quite naïve. He disliked 'flash' brilliance and sophistication. His temper, generally even, became terrifying when aroused; and nothing aroused it more quickly than such a womanly artifice as painted lips.

My father had no small talk, boasted no easy knack of friendship. Even with his brothers he would talk as if they were comparative strangers, though this was perhaps a family idiosyncrasy.

He felt more at ease with intellectual and social inferiors, would go to great lengths to please them: 'Let's ask so-and-so to dinner. I know he would appreciate it.' By contrast, he seemed surprised and disarmed when people liked *him* or were amused and interested in *him*. To our eternal shame, his own family seldom gave him much of a chance to shine in later life (the brutality of family opinion can be murderous).

Father was exceptionally compassionate. It made him generous to others when he shunned extravagance for himself. In later years, after business became worse, he gave up even the modest self-indulgence of cigars. Yet never for a moment were charitable subscriptions cancelled. And if Nancy's or Baba's wedding entailed an outlay, he paid out of all proportion to what he could afford.

Often we were unaware of how seriously matters stood, since pride forbade him to confide his troubles. Instead of moaning poverty, he quietly found excuses for dropping his hobbies. Scotland, which he loved, and even the theatre, became extravagances beyond his purse. His clothes became rather shabby.

The crowning blow was Reggie's death. Of his sons, Reggie was the favourite. The two understood one another; they were kindred spirits. Indeed, with Reggie gone, life held little meaning for him, in spite of Mummie's kind and close concern for his cares. The timber business now became totally non-existent. A baffled resignation set in.

Partly, Daddy's tragedy stemmed from a staunch rigidity. He had always been slow, methodical. He did not change with the times. As for success, he never mentioned it. I think he even mistrusted it. When I returned from America with incredible stories of the fancy prices my work had begun to fetch, he responded dubiously: 'It sounds all right, but is it?'

Looking backwards, I am inclined to think my father was wise. I realise that restless invention and quick-fire creativity leave something to be desired. An uncle at the funeral said, 'Wull, wull, you've lost a good father.' Good he was. In spite of, or perhaps because of his failures, I respect his life. I respect him for never having taken short cuts; for accepting his luck, both good and bad, with the equanimity of a man. In comparison to him, I feel small.

HUNGARY

Late September

Mum was with Nancy and Hugh at their home in the country. I felt too depressed to stay alone in London in the empty flat. Gladly I accepted David's[1] suggestion to join him on a motor trip through Hungary and Dalmatia. My spirits rose under his buoyant influence.

On the way from Austria into Hungary, we stopped for lunch at a little *Gasthaus*. The radio played relays of Italian opera and German tangos. Then, abruptly, a vast Hungarian gypsy orchestra paved the way to our goal—Budapest. Never has music seemed livelier or more emotional.

As we sped on, the countryside changed. It became wilder, less like a child's storybook illustration. Villages seemed Oriental, with low, bold Russian doorways.

Our approach to Budapest was made more dramatic by a bad skid. I was at the wheel. Unbeknownst to us, the car tyres had been worn treadless. Now, on a hill damp with rain, the wheels started sliding over the surface of the road. I lost control. Worse: I lost my head as well, waiting for the crash while David leaped into the breach, put the car out of gear and twisted the steering wheel. The machine turned in circles, crashed down a tree and ended nose upwards in a ditch.

By the time we staggered to our beds at dawn, we felt as though we'd already spent a week sightseeing and living in Budapest. Many impressions had been gathered. A letter of introduction provided us with a willing escort, who promptly guided two eager foreigners and showed them every aspect of night life. We ate Hungarian food in enormous quantities including a kind of salmon-trout from Lake Balaton. Gypsy orchestras serenaded us. In the huge inferno-nightclub *Arizona*, spectacle vyed with spectacle. There were revolving dance floors and a cabaret that went on from ten o'clock until three in the morning. The walls had breathing shells; balconies suddenly shot ceilingwards on the trunk of a palm tree; stars flashed and chorus girls, suspended by their teeth, twirled at the end of ropes. To Miss Arizona, once a beauty and now the singer-wife of the proprietor, were allotted

---

[1] The Hon. David Herbert.

the big 'production numbers'. Her entrances were spectacular accompanied by every variety of dog, or riding an elephant.

In the days that followed, we were seldom idle. We swam in swimming baths with artificial waves. In the museums we admired German primitives, Grecos, and pre-Christian gold. We goggled at the architecture of fantastic buildings, including some without antecedent or precedent—the Sunlight Insurance Company's home, for example. Even the Empire furnishings of the prime minister's palace seemed good, clean, Ruritanian fun.

One Sunday we went to a country village to see the peasants in their Sunday-best costumes. Passing fields of sugar cane we came to a wild plain and halted for a religious procession. The Madonna, heavily encrusted within a gold frame, was held aloft by girls in gaudy crinolines and tinsel head-dresses.

The scene, on arrival at our destination just as church service was ending, was spectacular. A group of fancy-clad people stood in the town square. The colours were startlingly unusual, and of a brilliance to dazzle the eye. But even the most vivid costumes were overpowered by the beauty of the old women in black, who idled gossiping by the church walls.

The village girls showered us with attention. They ran like so many parakeets in all directions, showing the way to buy this and that, to drink, to dance. We drank; a five-piece orchestra played for us while we ate. Their music was of a melodious sadness and full-hearted yearning. The special flute which is played in this region produces a sound that seems to express the essence of lovelorn emotion. Zither and xylophone added plaintive and percussive variation to the ensemble.

At twilight, several of the brightly-coloured bird-girls brought us to their home. In the lamplight we joined in the dancing of the *Czardas*.

DUBROVNIK

It is evening. But the heat of the day's sun is retained by the dove-coloured stone walls of this fortified town. The whole populace comes out to walk up and down in the perfumed, soft air. Eyes are keen for love. Nowhere else are regards so lingering, so impatiently amorous. Groups cluster round the giant telescope, through which the huge stars become even bigger. Cafés are filled, gypsy orchestras play. We sit in the Weinstube drinking white wine and enjoying thin wafers of raw ham.

Dubrovnik is like a rural Venice, replete with delicately chiselled carvings on cornice, lintel and balustrade, with its own Doge's Palace, domed cathedral and flocks of pigeons. Unlike Venice, it has trees. Unlike Venice, it has been built upon high rocks, with a spectacular mountain back-drop adding intimacy.

From the moment of entering Dubrovnik's high medieval walls, repaired by Viollet le Duc, we fell under the spell of this curious town, comprising a jumble of architecture of so many periods. Here, far from his home, a medieval statue of Knight Roland stands against a floreated church that might be part of baroque Oxford. The market square, bright with vegetables and fruit, is mainly of the seventeenth century; though an eighteenth-century poet sculpted in the nineteenth century presides behind green railings, a pigeon perched on his curled wig.

There is no end to sightseeing. The town may be circled from the summit of its stone walls. Dominican and Franciscan monasteries rival each other in delicacy of carved detail. Here can be found the oldest apothecary in the world, with Aesculapius in stone among his vessels and books.

Rome has its fountains; Dubrovnik has its fountains, also many churches with, alas, exteriors more impressive than interiors. Similarly, the houses of a decadent nobility still belong in the family, but only a shell remains. Furniture was ransomed for ready money, chairs sold to pay for a new ball dress. Now all that is left are gold-engraved glasses from which we receive the hospitality of local red wine. Out in the garden, columns and cypresses have become overgrown. But the view remains unspoilt, with the mountains cyclamen-coloured in the late afternoon. And at sunset, the Adriatic undergoes a sea-change, turning from brilliant blue to yellow and pink.

Dubrovnik's people wear simple costumes of beautiful form, the women with head-dresses immaculately white. Waists are small, skirts voluminous. The men wear Turkish trousers with embroidered waistcoats and fezzes. A few prefer curious caps which look like half a huge eggshell; German tourists delight to wear them.

The local citizens are happily uncurious. They never stare at visitors, however strange their appearance. Vague and unmindful, Dubrovnik's populace is apt not to look twice at Queen Marie of Roumania wearing a motor helmet and driving through a cloud of pigeons.

For so small a place, Dubrovnik seems rich in rare personalities. The poverty-stricken nobility and others provide some great characters; like Miranda da Gozzi who has never left the confines of its walls, yet speaks several languages and knows much of outside affairs. Many of the townspeople show evidence of an antique past. The male prostitute looks like a Roman senator. The lame tailor comes alive from a fifth-century Greek carving. The Moslem who proffers ikons and brocades in an Oriental parlour looks as though he had been installed there since the time of Darius.

Part XVII

Royal Romance

1935 and 1936

MRS SIMPSON

Autumn 1935

Though nothing about Mrs Simpson appears in the English papers, her name seems never to be off people's lips. For those who enjoy gossip she is a particular treat. The sound of her name implies secrecy, royalty, and being in-the-know. As a topic she has become a mania, so much so that her name is banned in many houses to allow breathing space for other topics.

Five years ago I met Mrs Simpson in a box with some Americans at the Three Arts Club Ball. Present were Thelma Furness, her sister, Mrs Gloria Vanderbilt, and a lot of other people. Mrs Simpson was introduced as being a vague relation to me by marriage; her husband, Ernest Simpson, being the brother of Mrs Smiley.[1] Mrs Simpson seemed somewhat brawny and raw-boned in her sapphire-blue velvet. Her voice had a high nasal twang.

[1] Mrs Kerr Smiley, the aunt of my brother-in-law, Sir Hugh Smiley: quite a distant relationship!

About a year ago, I had an opportunity to renew acquaintance with Mrs Simpson. I liked her immensely. I found her bright and witty, improved in looks and chic.

Today she is sought after as the probable wife of the King. Even the old Edwardians receive her, if she happens to be free to accept their invitations. American newspapers have already announced the engagement, and in the highest court circles there is great consternation. It is said that Queen Mary weeps continuously.

I am taking bets that the marriage will not happen this year.

Now I was to photograph her. Mrs Simpson was punctual, arriving at my studio rather shyly (although she has acquired considerable assurance since the recent developments).

She had scarcely arrived when the telephone rang for her. It seems that incessant callers make demands upon her all the time. 'Will you lunch?' 'May I come in for a cocktail?' To accept all this lionising requires careful arranging, which she manages well. She has learned how to keep people at a distance: 'Wait till I get home and look at my book.' 'My secretary will give you a ring in the morning.' Her voice seemed quieter.

Our photographic sitting was not particularly eventful, except that I found it difficult to avoid making remarks which might be miscontrued. For instance, as background I suggested scrolls of ermine pinned on a white cloth. She immediately responded with, 'Don't do anything connected with the Coronation for me. I want none of that now.' And again, when I asked her to lower her chin 'as though bowing', the unfortunate simile caused her to look sharply at me.

Whatever fantastic changes have taken place in Mrs Simpson's life, she has obviously suffered. There is a sad look to be seen in her eyes. The camera was not blind to this. We worked well together for a long time, and made a date so that I could do some drawings.

Two afternoons later, I went to her house in Regent's Park, bringing my sketching paraphernalia and the proofs of the recent photographs. There was a policeman at the end of the road; but then, there generally is in most London streets. The house has been rented furnished, but has a few temporary additions by Syrie Maugham, and Mrs Spry contributes her arrangements of expensive flowers mixed with bark and local weeds. This day Mrs Simpson looked immaculate, soignée and fresh as a young girl. Her skin was as bright and smooth as the inside of a shell, her hair so sleek she might have been Chinese.

The afternoon was successful, in spite of the fact that none of my sketches quite came off. Mrs Simpson proved an exceptionally difficult woman to draw. I found nothing facile to catch hold of and soon discovered that even the slightest impression was devilishly difficult. Still, we had a lot of fun, discussing London and various personalities we knew in common.

She spoke amusingly, in staccato sentences punctuated by explosive bursts of laughter that lit up her face with great gaiety and made her eyebrows look attractively surprised.

I worked while she talked. Mrs Simpson glanced about the pale white and olive green drawing-room. 'I would do more with this place if I were staying here longer. But I've only got it for such a short time more.'

Suddenly I asked, 'Where will you go for the Coronation? A flat again?'

'A flat is much easier to run,' she considered. 'This is so far away. I'd like Claridge's, but there is the disadvantage of public exits.'

I said, 'But in any case, wherever you are, I should think there'll be crowds of Americans waiting outside for a look-see. That is, if I know anything from my American papers.' Then I hazarded, 'Do you realise how much people talk about you? Do you know that as a topic I have banned you?'

'Yes. Yes.'

From that moment onwards, there was practically nothing we did not discuss. She said, 'After this, I think I must call you Cecil. And I don't want you to call me by that name of Mrs Simpson, which the American yellow press has made me loathe.'

Yes, her private life had been taken away from her. People stared and hung about all the time. The King minded greatly for her sake. And what absolute nonsense all this was about marriage. How could English people be so silly? They hadn't gossiped before the American newspapers got hold of it. There was no question of marriage.

I said, 'I've made bets against it. But maybe you'll ruin me.'

She replied, 'No. I expect I'll be very poor and you'll clean up.'

We then discussed the possibility of my photographing the King. Wallis said, 'You mustn't put any background in, he'd hate it.' At which the door opened and the butler announced, 'His Majesty.'

Wallis gave a caw of surprise. 'Oh sirrr,' she drawled, 'we were just talking about you. Oh, you've got what the *Daily Express* calls your coif today, sirr.'

The King, in bright spirits and not nervous at all, laughed and examined my photographic proofs laid out on the sofa. Quickly he gave his definite opinion as to which were good and which were not.

Jokes and laughter ensued. 'I like this,' the King commented; 'that one, too. In fact, all these are good. I want the lot.'

'Oh, sir, wouldn't that be too much of a Wallis collection?'

'Ha, ha!' And we all laughed.

'No, I don't think Cecil likes this one, sir. It's hard, like granite.'

His Majesty repeated several times, 'Funny kind of granite.'

'Now, sir, won't you sit down and have a drink? Let Cecil do a quick drawing of your profile.'

In a trice the King, holding a whisky and soda, was sitting *en profile* and talking of the events of the day as reported in the *Evening News*—the Spanish revolution, unemployment in South Wales, Mr Ernest Brown's incessant quotations from the Bible.

The King has an enormous store of general knowledge. He never forgets names, remembers statistics. He knows, too, the average man's tastes and inclinations, is himself a kind of average man *par excellence*. He will be a very popular King, as one instinctively respects him.

Quips and sallies were rather broad. The King observed that Ataturk must have taken his title as President of Turkey from the American 'Attaboy'. But, however trite his humour, he betrayed no interest in gossip or personalities.

We were shown the snapshots of the Nahlin cruise along the Dalmatian coast, with both the King and Wallis wearing shorts. 'That's sweet, isn't it? That's Corcula or however you pronounce it. And that's when we came ashore in Turkey. We weren't announced, but they all came down to greet us. Do you remember it? It was swell.'

Into this atmosphere came Wallis' aunt, lately arrived in England. She added to the general wisecracking, relating the story of her boat trip (during which, as Wallis had earlier told me, she listened to people talking about the pros and cons of the King's possible marriage to her niece)'

A silver tray was brought in. On it were eight different varieties of hot *hors d'oeuvres,* also green grapes stuffed with cream cheese. The King talked very fast, darted around the room, rang bells, busily untied parcels with red, slightly horny hands that looked surprisingly like a mechanic's. He had a bad cold and wore a heavy silk jersey. Wallis' eyes sparkled; her brows lifted in mock-pain; her mouth turned down at the corners as she laughed. The aunt sat back quipping.

At last the King (like a child whose before-dinner play hour had come to an end) was told that we must all go. Wallis, who had only a few minutes to dress for Emerald Cunard's dinner, was already beginning to unbutton her dress.

Winter, New York

I watched and listened to old Mrs Vanderbilt, the Queen of New York. Towards the end of lunch she told me how upset she was about the King's abdication. First, she produced a small bag. Then, from inside, she whisked the wherewithal to make her nose clown-white. Ridiculously, she began covering her entire face with ugly blobs of powder. The chin received another heavy patch. During the story-telling, by dint of gradual smoothing away, a natural face slowly appeared from under its heavy coating. 'Oh, I can't tell you how I have suffered! I can't tell you what that family means to me. I was the first person to be received by the late King after his illness. I was summoned to tea with Their Majesties and we talked and talked and talked. I kept waiting to be dismissed. But no, we talked until I began to get a little faint. My head drooped; I said, "Ma'am, am I not keeping you? Must I not go?" And the Queen said, "Oh no, if you *have* to go that is different, but if you can, please stay." And do you know, I had arrived at the Palace at five o'clock and by the time I left it was—six o'clock. Oh, they've been so wonderful to me. I could lay down my life for that family.'

A VISIT TO WALLIS SIMPSON AT CHÂTEAU CANDÉ

Spring 1937, Paris

I meant to take the train to Touraine, thus offering myself the enjoyment of reading *Le dernier des Villavides*. But the day proved too beautiful, with spring far advanced. I motored instead, feeling more than compensated by a countryside blossoming with lilac, fruit trees and chestnut. I also saw Chartres for the first time; and the Palace at Blois and a few chateaux along the Loire.

Château Candé is situated on high, commanding a view of miles of green country. Tall poplars and willows grow in platoons. The Chateau itself, begun in the sixteenth century, has seen many subsequent additions in the intervening years. It is feudal and rather ugly, with high towers, pointed turrets and heavily embellished Gothic doorways. But the house is run with a modern luxurious comfort that would make a Long Island millionaire envious.

I arrived to find Wallis looking rested after her long incarceration here. Mr and Mrs Herman Rogers and Mme Bedaux joined us. All were thirsting for news of the outside world. To the accompaniment of cocktails, chatter was of people and clothes and the 'Buick of which you've read so much.' Then it was late, and time to change.

My rooms were Empire, decorated in striped satin. From the bathroom, with its sunken bath, came clouds of red carnation scent.

A footman waited to conduct me to the underground vault where dinner was to be served. Hams and salami sausages hung from hooks in the ceiling. In dim candlelight we were royally waited on by a solicitous butler (who really overdid his act) and three footmen. The chef used to be with the Duke of Alba, who must have regretted letting him go. There was a superb variety of wines, and everyone's spirits rose.

The women had dressed to the nines, all in reds. Wallis sported a new jewel in the form of two huge quills, one set with diamonds, the other with rubies. Her dress showed to advantage an incredibly narrow figure, narrower since the abdication.

The atmosphere was one of suppressed excitement. Rogers said that though the worst was over, the strain on Wallis became greater as the wedding day approached. Her divorce goes through this week; and after the Coronation, they will undoubtedly be married without further delay. Still, no mention could be made of the date or details.

After dinner we went across a courtyard to a games pavilion. Billiards ensued, then were abandoned for conversation. At midnight the Rogers said goodnight, leaving Wallis and me to talk in full earnest until nearly dawn.

I was struck by the clarity and vitality of her mind. When at last I went to bed, I realised that she not only had individuality and personality, but was a very strong force as well. She may have limitations, she may be politically ignorant and aesthetically untutored; but she knows a great deal about life.

Some people maintain that Wallis obviously possesses little insight into British character and customs. Certainly I got the impression that she has been taken as much by surprise by recent events as anyone else. Though her divorce proceedings had already begun, I don't believe she had any clear intentions of marriage. If the King ever said to her, 'What about your wearing that little crown?' she more than likely laughed and replied, 'Let's talk about it after your Coronation.'

Of the abdication, she told me she had known less than anybody. It had been impossible to talk freely with the ex-King on the telephone, as the wires were constantly tapped. But two things, she confided, had not been generally known. One was that the ex-King had told Mr Baldwin he would be willing to let the matter of his marriage hang fire, to be discussed again six months after his Coronation. Secondly, during the entire period of these discussions, Mr Baldwin held in his possession papers which had been signed by Wallis, to the effect that she was willing to stop divorce proceedings against her husband.

It wasn't just tactfulness, I am sure, that prevented Wallis from airing any grievance she might have against Mr Baldwin or the so-called friends who 'welshed' on her when the situation altered. She said, 'It has only shown me *who* among my friends *are* my friends.' She is bitter towards no one.

As for her future, she seems determined that she and the Duke will 'work things out'. Obviously she has great admiration for his character and his vitality; she loves him though I feel she is not *in* love with him. In any case, she has a great responsibility in looking after someone who is temperamentally polar to her but yet relies entirely upon her.

Our conversation in the abstract was most interesting. I became sleepy and soft from time to time, perhaps saying things without careful consideration. Thereupon, Wallis, quick as a flash, would contradict or challenge me, observing, 'No, I don't agree with you. I've always found that in life people may be given this but they do that.'

She twisted and twirled her rugged hands. She laughed a square laugh, protruded her lower lip. Her eyes were excessively bright, slightly froglike, also wistful.

Candidly, she concluded that she had always been much alone in her life. Perhaps this isolation helped her now. She confessed that it had been difficult for her not to give way and hang herself on one of the many pairs of antlers in the room in which we sat. But her control surprised her. She was, she said, very like a man in many ways; she has few woman friends, and Katherine Rogers, the most intimate among them, has likewise, I think, a man's mentality. Yes, both the Rogers had been wonderful friends and had borne the brunt of her hysterics; but a great deal of her time had none the less been spent by herself in her bedroom.

The next morning, Sunday, was given over to preparations for the photography. A manicurist and hairdresser arrived from Paris. Her hair was set in a new way, with waves flowing up instead of down.

After lunch, our camera session started with 'romantic' pictures in the shade of sunlit trees, where the thick grass was covered by daisies. A greyhound came in useful, together with bunches of gorse and broom. Wallis was terrified of treading in the long grass where her dog, Slippers, had recently been fatally bitten by a viper, but tread she did.

The photography went on for many hours. Birds sang; conditions, and settings and organdie dresses were ideal. We mounted a Gothic turret to Wallis's bedroom, where the *boiseries* made a good background, for a succession of clothes which were put on and off with the speed of a quick change artist. Jewellery was produced in unostentatious driblets. It impressed me to see some big historic stones, including a pair of diamond pear-shaped clips the size of pigeons' eggs. Wallis, helpful and serious, purposely dropped her usual badinage.

306

On the desk, dressing table and bedside table were informal pictures of the Duke, signed 'To Wallis-David.' Over a number of these pictures hung little enamel or palm crosses.

Regularly, like the chimes of a clock, the telephone rings: at seven o'clock and again at ten. For the Duke still enjoys his long telephone conversations. At frequent intervals the press also rang up to make inquiries. Wallis seemed to be at pains to please them. She continually remarked to whoever answered, 'Be careful to be nice: So-and-So is very important.' Once we laughed when someone asked for proof that Mrs Simpson was really there, as a report published in America had authenticated her return to Baltimore!

After dinner, Rogers showed a series of cine-Kodak films which he had taken intermittently since 1924.

The first setting was China, at a time when Wallis had again been staying with the Rogers during six months of divorce proceedings against Spencer. The women wearing knee-length dresses and boudoir caps or bandages on their foreheads and gambolled and laughed coyly. The men were in immensely tight trousers and high collars. In one sequence Wallis hilariously kissed Rogers, laughed into the camera and then continued her attack.

There were scenes at the races, also intimate glimpses of the English colony with Wallis, as ever, the life and soul of the gatherings. She seemed much less individual then, her hair thicker, her head bigger, her body fatter.

This was followed by glimpses of the Simpson-Rogers friendship with the Prince of Wales and future King. They appeared, a jovial group, in Budapest and Vienna. In the south of France, they splashed and frisked in a turquoise sea. They picnicked on rocks, snapped one another, rowed in collapsible boats, ate lunch.

Then came the 'Nahlin' cruise, showing the Royal party steadfastly roughing it at sea. The King, with Wallis at his side, went round asking questions of the crew, of anybody and everybody. He seemed a wizened little boy, distinguished by untidy golden hair and a brown, naked back.

But an unique film showed the Simpson-Rogers visit to Balmoral. Here, against the Highland setting, more candid shots of the turreted castle, which caught the King demonstrating to his guests an Austrian game by shooting some kind of arrow through the air. Lord Louis Mountbatten tried after him, then the Duke of Kent. They fared badly, making everyone laugh. As they sat on the terrace waiting for lunch, the ladies looked untidy and relaxed. The Duchess of Sunderland seemed enormous in a dowdy hat; Mollie Buccleugh was made to look very squat in tartans. Neither Mary Marlborough nor a begoggled Edwina Mountbatten were flattered by the camera; only the Duchess of Kent looked romantic with her hair untidily blowing and tied with a baby bow of ribbon. Every few feet of film, the King appeared with Wallis. She looked very different from the others, neat and towny in smart clothes and a black felt hat. In the background, the Rogers laughed and ran round in circles.

One sequence showed the King in a huge hood and cloak, lying in wait on the moors. He munched an apple, asked questions of the old retainers, helped the stalkers to put the victim deer on the pony's back. . . .

After Rogers' cine-Kodak, we discussed the 'stills' I had taken earlier in the day. There were enquiries as to the proper use of these pictures. Some must be allowed to the general press, for Wallis has got used to her publicity now.

We exchanged goodnights, and the weekend was over. It has given me much to muse upon. The Rogers, I concluded, are nice—but in spite of being wary, not very intelligent and apt to be fooled. Still, they're loyal friends. Wallis appreciates this, and throughout her success she has always insisted on the Rogers being included in social invitations.

Next morning, the over-solicitous butler and footmen were lined up at the door to salute my departure. I concluded that, for Mrs Simpson, events might have been worse. If she has not been fated to wear a crown, she is still loved by an abdicated King and will soon be married to him. It won't be so bad to be called the Duchess of Windsor.

PRE-PHOTOGRAPHING THE WEDDING OF THE DUKE OF WINDSOR AND MRS SIMPSON

June 3rd

I took a very early train to Tours. When I arrived at the chateau, swarms of journalists and their vans and motorcycles waited outside the gates.

Gertrude Stein and Alice B. Toklas in the garden at Billignin

Guests waving goodbye to Toscanini at Kammer

Mrs Spry and her assistant Miss Pirie, two laden Ganymedes, calmly went about their business of decorating the whole chateau with magnificent mountains of mixed flowers. Rogers with his typewritten lists busily handled the telephone, and the press.

Wallis hovered about in yellow, slightly more businesslike than usual; with her face showing the strain: she looked far from her best. The Duke, by contrast, seemed radiant—his hair ruffled gold, his complexion clear and sunburnt, his blue eyes transparent with excitement. Marriage in Westminster Abbey should have been his birthright yet now he beamed contentedly at the impromptu wedding arrangements set up in the music room. The piano had been taken out; and thirty-two chairs placed in the room. Wallis inquired, 'We don't have to shake hands with everybardee, doo weeh?'

A car drove up. Great consternation and activity were occasioned by the arrival of the clergyman who (out of the blue and at the eleventh hour) had volunteered to marry the loving pair. This obscure Darlington vicar had felt it an injustice that the Duke should be denied a religious ceremony, and sent through the post a letter to that effect. As with all the other letters, it was personally opened by the Duke. And so, out of provincial obscurity, a vicar had been hied to Chateau Candé to be the centre of world interest.

The Duke was interested in everything he had to say, and spent much time discussing arrangements with him.

Now the clergyman wanted an altar, of course. The chateau was scoured for a suitable table. 'What about the one with the drinks on it, or the chest from the hall?' In the confusion someone knocked over an Italian lamp and cracked it. The Duke became greatly perturbed, and tried forthwith to mend it.

At length the chest from the hall was chosen. It promised to be just the thing: a heavily carved, vastly ornate affair of no particular period, with a row of fat caryatids holding up bogus Renaissance carving.

Wallis, rather harrassed but not too harrassed to laugh, wondered about an altar cloth. Pointing to the caryatids, she drawled, 'We must have something to cover up that row of extra women!'

'Oh, I've got a tea cloth,' Wallis suddenly exclaimed.

The tea cloth was produced from the bottom of an already-

L

packed linen trunk. Wallis's Cockney maid, furious at having to unpack the trunk, whined, 'If it's as much trouble as this getting married, I'm sure I'll never go through with it myself.'

Wallis explained, 'I couldn't let the poor girl be put off matrimony for life. I felt duty-bound to say, "Oh, it isn't always as bad as this—only if you're marrying the ex-King of England!"'

The altar cloth was spread. Mr Allen, the solicitor, a rather sheepish expression on his face, trooped in with two heavy candlesticks to be placed on the altar.

Wallis remonstrated, 'Hey, you can't put those out: we want them for the dinner table tonight.'

More flowers were brought in. Mrs Spry, robin-like in a picture hat and overalls, sentimentally broke off a branch of laurel: 'I'm going to make the flowers as beautiful as I can. I'm so glad they've both got what they want with this religious ceremony. I'd do anything for her. I adore her. So did all my girls when they arranged flowers for her in her Regent's Park house and didn't know who she was.'

The parson now allowed the photography to begin without further delay. The electricians had fixed up the lights in Wallis's bedroom, and we started with pictures of the Duke alone. He turned himself into a pliable, easy-to-pose subject, doing his best to make things less difficult. The only taboo: he would not allow himself to be photographed on the right side of his face, preferring the left as it showed the parting in his hair. Though somewhat wrinkled, he still seemed essentially young for all his forty-three years. His expression, though intent, was essentially sad, tragic eyes overruling the impertinent tilt of his nose. Those eyes, fiercely blue, do not seem to focus properly, and one is somewhat lower than the other.

Photographing the bridal couple together proved more elusive. It developed that nowhere in the chateau was there a crucifix to place upon the improvised altar. The British Embassy in Paris must get one; which meant that the Duke himself had to telephone to Lloyd Thomas about the matter. Wallis, wearing a black dress and her huge diamond pear clips, was meanwhile waiting impatiently to be photographed with him. She became perturbed at the delay. The Cockney maid telephoned to his room: 'Is that your Royal Highness? Well, will you please come down right away?' When he finally did appear, Wallis let him see she was annoyed. After a preliminary argument he apologised. Then the two sat hip to hip on the pouf, his far hand round her waist while I clicked away.

There was a lunch interval before we settled down to taking pictures in the wedding vestments. The other guests on hand were whisked off to a restaurant in some neighbouring town by M Bedaux—a strategy designed to get them out of the way. Our own meal was served out on the terrace under the trees. The Duke never eats much lunch, but today had strawberries and cream while Wallis, Rogers, Dudley Forwood the equerry, and myself ate curried eggs and rice, kidneys and other dishes.

At the beginning of lunch, Wallis asked that the large sunshade on the terrace be lowered. The Duke rose from the table to do it himself. Footmen hovered impotently as he called, 'Is this the right height? Six inches lower?'

Lunch conversation was light and witty. At times the Duke roared and wrinkled up his face so that it looked like last year's apple.

Then he went off to change into his morning coat.

Upstairs, in the bathroom-dressing-room, hung Wallis's hard blue wedding dress. On a stand by the window was her hat, of matching feathers with a tulle halo effect.

With Wallis in costume, we were now ready to take the wedding pictures. 'Oh, so this is the great dress? Well, it's lovely, very pretty,' admired the Duke.

To avoid possible sightseers with telescopic lenses, we had to confine ourselves to certain shielded parts of the house. The most successful pictures were those taken on the steps and terrace of the medieval porch.

As misfortune would have it, Forwood brought some bad news just as the bridal couple posed at a turret window. Through the lens I saw the Duke become worried, frowning and contorting his face until he looked as tortured as a German gargoyle. Wallis, too, seemed troubled. The Duke opined, 'That's one point I will stick to. I'm certainly going to have my way on that. After all, I *am* English!'

It was painful. I couldn't very well interrupt and say, 'Please look pleasant.' I took several unflattering but illuminating pictures. Then the mood changed for the better again, as Wallis suggested, 'Let's remember now, we're having our pictures taken.'

The sun poured down beneficently. I was glad to be getting what I knew would be good results, since the day's earlier efforts hadn't augured well. But at last there was no excuse to go on; and so the bridal pair changed their clothes.

The Duke reappeared in a bright blue suit that made his complexion even more rubicund, his hair more flaxen. The latest batch of mail was carried across the lawns to him. Great joke: 'Old Carter with the mail.' I took pictures of the Duke with Carter and the mail tray piled high, every letter bearing the Duke's profile.

Wallis decided to rest. I wandered about the house. Another photographer, who formerly worked for Vandyk, had taken a few shots when my sitting was over. The Duke and Wallis laughed, as he was old-fashioned and chose the darkest, most over-ornamented room in the house to feature them, standing bolt upright against an enormous fireplace. This photographer now came up to me and gave me his card, saying he knew no reason why there should be enmity between rivals. I looked on him with condescending superciliousness. Later, I had reason to think differently.

The guests came back for tea, staggering after their enormous lunch. Baba Metcalfe confided to me her quiet amazement at the Duke's unalloyed high spirits. He had made no mention of England or his family (and I said nothing of the momentary pique at the turret window). But, even as Baba spoke, the Duke seemed once more preoccupied with things other than at hand. He stood on the lawn with his back to us, head lowered while he stared into space. He stood still long enough for me to click the camera for an introspective photograph. Beyond him the dogs wandered about, ignored for the day—the greyhound, the saluki, the endless cairns.

Tea was on now. Wallis's Aunt Bessie officiated. The Duke talked earnestly to the parson. The Metcalfes looked calm; Sir Walter Monckton smiled nicely; Allen wore a grave air. Rogers admitted that he had a headache and was in a bad temper, though his Press announcements were about at an end. Mme Bedaux persisted in saying inconsequential things. She has been staying in the same house with the Duke for weeks; yet this morning she greeted him with a fatuous bob of the head, 'Nice to see you again.' M Bedaux hovered about.

Forwood seemed pooped but alert. He confided to me how deeply hurt the Duke was because certain of his personal friends had not materialised for the wedding.

It was soon time for me to be leaving, with the suitcase I had packed in case they relented and allowed me to stay for the wedding tomorrow. But that proved impossible. Only four representatives of the press had been invited; and I could scarcely be permitted to stay when so many intimates had been excluded.

On leaving I kissed Wallis goodbye: not because she encouraged me to, but I felt moved by all that was happening.

I came away with photographs that, had they been for sale in the open market, would have commanded a fancy price. With the *Queen Mary* sailing tonight, prints would arrive in America a whole week before the press photographs tomorrow. One agent told me that fifteen hundred pounds had been paid for the first Coronation pictures; and these were of equal historical interest. But my *Vogue* contract precludes such negotiations. The bulk of my work was exclusive to them. However, Mrs Chase had agreed that any photographs that *Vogue* did not want could be given to the general press.

This called for a certain celerity. I was pent-up in the train coming back to Paris. By the time I grabbed the aeroplane to London early the next morning, I fancied myself being presented with a cheque that would enable me to clap a new roof on the studio at Ashcombe; the rough chalk road down the valley could be made navigable; I'd give presents to my mother and all my friends.

Still counting chickens, I landed at Northolt and rushed to a conference with *Vogue*. But even as Miss Joseph, at home, was bargaining with the press about the price of pictures I might or might not have left, surprise overtook us. There was already a large photograph in the *Evening Standard* of the Duke and Duchess of Windsor standing bolt upright against an enormous fireplace in a dark, over-ornamented room. The old-fashioned photographer had seized the day! His effort was already being radioed to the USA, with prints on board the *Queen Mary*. I felt like a hare outrun by a tortoise.

Part XVIII

An English Summer

1937

May 1937, London

Today has been a typical day. The telephone wakened me at an ungodly hour. It was Peter, wanting me to go riding with him in Richmond Park. Exhilarated I returned by eleven o'clock to work like a fiend at my desk; an article, correspondence, bills before Daisy[1] arrived to be photographed. She looked so perversely alluring that something unconventional had to be done. She was game to materialise from a shell: a conch Venus.

Then off to the back of the stage at Covent Garden for a rehearsal of *Turandot*. Goeffrey Toye showed me the workings of the various stages and technicalities.

At the Chelsea flower show, the remarks of the crowd were the soul of England speaking. I bought clematis and tobacco plants for Ashcombe; Peter admired the arrangements of vegetables in pyramids.

Tea at Daphne Weymouth's new house. I swung the children above my head, around my waist and under my legs.

[1] The Hon. Mrs Reginald Fellowes.

314

A quiet dinner at Sybil Colefax's, followed by Tallulah's Walpurgis night. Marian Harris, mad as a march hare, sang. Tallulah danced frenziedly, throwing herself about in a mad apache dance with Napier Alington. After he left, she wept and bemoaned the fact that he had never married her. Then she threw off all her clothes, performing what she called 'Chinese classical dances'. In the midst of these outrageous situations, one had reluctantly to drag oneself away.

LUNCH WITH STEPHEN TENNANT

Stephen Tennant has come back into circulation again after a long illness in Switzerland. He has not only recovered physically, but seems mentally many years younger as well. His mind is as alert and unexpected as ever.

I remember Stephen's stepfather saying that he should not draw, as he had a talent for writing. Certainly his language is exceptional; and he can always find the exact, telling word. Arriving late for a lunch appointment with Sir Charles Ritchie, he proffered a bunch of delphiniums saying, 'Such a forgiving blue!' But Lord Grey's assessment was only half right, for Stephen's drawings are also remarkable. He can unflinchingly undertake great feats of endurance with pen and pencil.

The above was provoked by a recent glimpse of our *rara avis* when he gave a lunch party at Wilsford. Since Lady Grey's death, the house has been entirely redecorated, to a bizarrely gay effect. Instead of dark oak and morris chintz, ice-cream colours prevail. There are typical flights of fancy: the old oak staircase whitened and hung with fishnets and cork; petals strewn on a pink carpet; gilded shells fixed to ceilings; revolving postcard stands; bunches of artificial flowers strewn on cushions; clumps of coral and pearl.

About six women and myself turned up for lunch. Lady Violet Bonham Carter served as an ideal foil for the host. Her head is suggestive of an Etruscan frieze and she talks in the manner common to Bloomsbury intellectuals, shuts her eyes and sways her shoulders to and fro. With her, Stephen assumes a hard, dry, annihilatingly cold voice. It means he is choosing his words with special care. Together, they describe the various cries of birds. One bird (I forget which) has a startled somnambulist's cry.

The lunch seemed typical of Stephen. Punch was served—a

mixture that looked like melted jewellery and matched the vermilion flowers on the table. The food was very highly coloured, *chaudfroid* of chicken decorated with circus designs, many sweets and cut-up fruits. Stephen, anxious to please, amused us no end with his qualms. While we waited interminably for the first course, he observed that a Sleeping-Beauty coma must suddenly have come over everybody in his kitchens.

Our host expatiated on the books he had been reading. Of late, he had confined himself to Flaubert, Balzac, Proust and Verlaine. We then looked at scrapbooks of old photographs, and he rhapsodised suitable texts. Some very ordinary pictures of Garbo were brought to life by apt ecstasies. In a breathless voice: 'Look! Look at the beauty of that! It's the aurora borealis. She's not a cinema star: she's something much greater. As E. M. Forster said, "She is that rare exception, an occasion when the vast public unanimously approves of what is truly magnificent." Think of it: three continents worship her to the last man. And this: it has the tragic quality of a child. Here's another picture—rugged, almost rude with insolent health. And again, how infinitely pathetic.'

A BALL AT DITCHLEY

Twilight is the most heart-yearning time of day. This evening it was uncannily beautiful—the trees wrapped in a slight haze of blue, the corn long and lilting, the cows stuck stationary amid daisies and buttercups, as if placed there for the effect.

We were in the right mood for the ball that had been planned for us at Ditchley, and here it was: an enormous eighteenth-century doll's house of honey-coloured stone, as brightly lit from without as within. Through the tall windows the gold ceilings and chandeliers sparkled. Canopied beds could be glimpsed upstairs; the great front door stood open to the stream of guests and the balmy velvet evening. Yellow roses tumbled over the balustrades at the entrance steps. Every detail had been carefully thought out. I hardly knew anything of my host and hostess, but automatically warmed to them for this treat.

Diana and I explored from room to room, admiring the fine taste of the Kent furniture, plaster swags, painted ceilings and chinoiserie carvings on the brocade. Especially for this evening, pink, blue and yellow flowers burgeoned from gold urns. The heads of peonies were architecturally massed in solid cone formation.

The tent for dancing had been decorated by Oliver with garlands of Empire leaves. Fantastically dressed plaster heads were swathed in brilliant Boldini wisps of tulle. In the surrounding floodlit gardens, water and fire were reconciled as fountains played through the fireworks display.

All the women had been asked to wear red and white. Caroline Paget looked the most beautiful storybook princess of all. Her escort, a white-faced, shy but proud Rex Whistler, had designed her a dress of scarlet and white stripes, the bodice thickly encrusted with white flowers.

Nothing could have been more rustic or poetic, except perhaps for another young couple who might have been painted by Rex as a fairy tale illustration. Valerian Wellesley, with heavy-lidded eyes, fair hair, fair eyelashes and moustache, looked a prince disguised as a footman as he waltzed by in his dark-green hunting coat and brass buttons. His Hans Andersen partner, in the person of Patricia Douglas, wore a meagre dress of pleated white chiffon, her hair straight as a page boy's. She looked so white, frail and delicate that I felt she might vanish at any moment. I followed her about, out on to the terrace, wondering if she were not a creation of the moonlight.

REX WHISTLER

September, London

Dinner with Rex. There could scarcely be a nicer way of spending time. More than any among all my friends, Rex has an aura which improves the more you are with him and the older he becomes. His sense of repose, no doubt, springs from an unruffled, poetic and calm interior world. Rex has a tawny elegance; though he may sum up contemporary situations and passing foibles with understanding and wit, his atmosphere is nevertheless that of an older man of another century.

Perhaps this anachronistic solidity is the very reason for Rex's being more laurel-crowned than almost any young painter today, especially by the older generation of cultured aristocrats. And recognition has come to him in spite of his putting every obstacle

L*

in its way: Rex makes himself almost impregnable, hardly ever answering letters or the telephone.

I called for him at Brook House. He was exhausted, looking very grey and white as he worked on the grey and silver decorations of landscape and motifs for Edwina Mountbatten's boudoir. I didn't envy him. The prospect of having to complete the details he has already mapped out for himself would fill me with despair.

It was only after he had eaten a little and drunk a lot that Rex felt able to expand. He then regaled me with characteristic personal descriptions of his weekend stay with the King and Queen at Balmoral.

His great interest, quite naturally, had been in the objects, furnishings and gardens of the castle. All seemed a blazing brightness of colour. Hundreds of vases held Victorian bouquets of flowers that had been freshly and brilliantly arranged. Bright gilt clocks, glass-domed *objets d'art* and albums abounded. The carpets were brilliant flowered or plaid.

The garden struck Rex as being peculiarly fantastic, with many leaden statues of John Brown, of stags, deer and dogs. The emerald-green lawns were studded with Wellingtonias, each planted by some illustrious name.

In preparation for the royal event, Rex had borrowed a wristwatch so that he could be on time for meals. But the equerries proved indefatigable, tapping on the door to announce, 'It'll be all right if you come down in five minutes' time.'

The hours had been long. Everyone came down for breakfast at eight o'clock or eight-thirty (I forget which). This in spite of the fact that, on the night of the Ghillies Ball, no one went to bed until three in the morning.

The Ghillies Ball was held in an enormous Gothic hall. Here they danced ceaselessly throughout the night. The King and Queen jigged with great abandon. The Queen ducked under huge ghillies' arms in the various complications of the reels. Pipes squealed, people hooted and laughed. The complicated footwork of the prancing men was displayed to advantage by virtue of their spats. Even old Princess Marie Louise twinkled her toes by the hour. Rex commented on how surprisingly independent and assured all the Scots were, communicating a staunch feeling of being as good as anybody, unsurpassed by no man.

Part XIX

Manhattan Rhythm

1937 and 1938

Photography, bringing its quick results and quick returns, suited the staccato mood of these years and absorbed much of the time. I spent a part of each winter in Manhattan.

Hence the following:

THE LINE-UP

New York, 1937

Esmond O'Brien[1] arranged for me to see the line-up at police headquarters. When I arrived, Inspector Donovan rather stunned me by saying, 'Mr O'Brien has asked us to look for you. Who in hell is Mr O'Brien?' At any rate, I was allowed to take my place among the gold-badged detectives.

[1] A delightful Irishman-about-town, son of Judge Morgan J. O'Brien of the Supreme Court and brother of Judge Kenneth O'Brien.

Last night's haul of arrests was brought on to a glaringly lit stage. From the front row of the stalls the director pulled them to attention. 'Turn your face towards the microphone. Take your hands out of your pockets.' In turn each man must be scrutinised with his hat on and off. One fellow tugged at the felt brim and pulled it way down on to an eye—tough guy. Another wore his on the back of the head—nonchalant charm. Others clapped their headgear straight on top of the pate, making them look slightly ridiculous.

Tics and nervous gestures abounded. Several suspects pulled at their lapels. Many twisted fingers, averted their gaze, or in babyish fashion lowered heads and eyelids.

An interrogator then asked, into a microphone, each in turn just the question they least wanted to answer. 'Sam Katzenplattinger, you were arrested at the Brentford Height subway stop. Is it true that you put your hand in the pocket of a man asleep on the bench in the subway, and extracted the sum of three dollars and fifty cetns?'

'Nope.' Reply was monosyllabic in most cases.

The majority seemed hardened toughs, but there were a few pathetic youngsters who did not seem to be rogues but had got caught out in some mischief that proved to be reason for arrest. One handsome Italian stood to attention side by side with his caricature of a buddy: a wizened and attenuated dwarf. 'You two were found in a shop at 189th Street and Broadway. How did you get in? Did you force the door? Did you break a window?'

'We wasn't doin' nothin'. We was sleepin' there. When we wanted to get out the place was locked.'

'Have you been arrested before?'

'Yep, but it didn't amount to nothin'.'

A fat business man, respectably dressed as a grey owl, was supposed to have embezzled a lot of money. A blonde girl who looked like Lilian Gish found herself accused of acquiring goods from a Fifth Avenue store. This was the second time she had done so. Her previous arrests embraced such innocent activities as pickpocketing and forgery. In all, seventeen counts had been lodged against her. During the questioning, she kept flicking imaginary specks of fluff from her costume and superciliously refused to answer.

Most incongruous was a quartet of toughs who had held up someone in a restaurant, as a result of which an inspector was shot. Completely correlated in appearance, they made an almost perfect contrast.

The next turn was provided by a trio of weaklings who had robbed a cigarette machine. Then an oyster-eyed, scarred gentleman shared the limelight with an old lady in an astrakhan coat and a red-headed whore. They all disclaimed knowledge of one another but were suspected of stealing clothing and driving away with it in a stolen car. Some Negroes who had hitch-hiked to New York from Carolina were accused of minor offences. The worst looking villain in the whole macabre vaudeville entertainment had already spent many years in Sing Sing for the rape of a seventeen year old girl.

The audience of detectives seemed greatly amused by the morning's programme. At first I thought them callous, then reasoned that since this was a daily routine, the horror doubtless wore off in time. In order to preserve a certain carefree joviality they were obliged to take things less seriously.

As a result of this morning's drama, I have begun to think of the obvious fact that fugitives from the line-up must continuously be in our midst. The woman in the astrakhan coat, for instance, looked like any old bird one might see in a picture gallery on 57th Street. The young boys who had been held for assault were the same ones who deliver my laundry, etc. Inspector Donovan even looked at *me* with a hopeful eye.

THE AUTOMAT

There is no place to rival New York for hospitality—at least, not for an English Duchess. Loelia Westminster has had the pickings to herself this winter and enjoyed a whirl. But, as most of the people ready to give her a whirl are anxious to be seen whirling her, she has only been exposed to a limited area of New York. So, instead of taking her to the inevitable Colony for lunch, we decided that the Broadway Automat might be an interesting change. Loelia, Myrtle Kellet and I set forth full of expectations.

The unreality of the *machine infernale* was as fascinating as ever. In coops behind glass, inhuman sandwiches wrapped in transparent paper awaited inhuman eaters. For a nickel, a mince pie became one's own. In the slot goes the nickel. Click, the alumin-ium plate glass window opens; sesame, the dish is yours.

A tableau of foods is available. Pineapple and grapefruit are cradled in a bed of cracked ice; boiling kidneys, Boston baked beans, lamb stew, primrose yellow salads, cool and crisp, are tempting to the eye. In other restaurants names conjure up dishes that when brought to you, are a disappointment. Here you see what you eat beforehand. And it is a distinct advantage to pay for the meal in advance. By the time one is ready to leave, there is no bill. One walks out with the odd feeling that the meal has been free.

Loelia and Myrtle were vastly entertained. They seemed bliss-fully unconscious of not fitting in with scurrying clerks and truck drivers, who were enjoying a fast feast for thirty cents.

The Revolution intruded, however, in the form of one sharp rebuff. The place was crowded, with hardly a free seat to be had. Spotting an empty table I pounced on it, hoping to establish squatter's rights by spreading my tray and coat. Then I hurried to summon the others, laden with their full trays. By the time we returned, an old grey-haired *tricoteuse* was solemnly tucking into a tomato stew.

Myrtle Kellet, betraying the aristocracy with her most care-fully enunciated English accent, said, 'We're awfully sorry, Madam, but we have taken this table. It's reserved.'

The old revolutionary frowned, looked up for a withering moment and barked, 'That's just *too* bad.'

She went on masticating. The proletariat had triumphed. Relegated to an adjoining table, Myrtle remarked pointedly on how unbecoming toughness was to the elderly. Her observation went for nought.

PAUL DRAPER

Paul Draper's dancing is a revelation. I remember him as a quietly uninteresting young man with a stutter. He performed at one of Osbert Sitwell's small parties some ten years ago, embar-rassing the guests by doing a clumsy Black Bottom. In the interim, his uniquely individual gift has found its own method of ex-pression.

Draper is like no other dancer. He does not even look like a dancer; he wears no false smile, invokes no artificial means of appealing to his audience. This is a creature from the woods—a gamekeeper or lean young groom, fond of animals and looking rather foxy himself.

Most touching is his quality of purity and youthfulness. He explains (still with a stutter) that he likes to dance. The encores, he maintains, are a pleasure to him; he never tires of dancing. Now he will execute a minuet written by Mr Haydn in 1765, next he becomes a woodpecker tap-dancing a minuet with elaborate rhythms.

Paul Draper is like a fencing master or ski instructor, wedded to a fantasy born in the age of Fred Astaire. He gives nobility to a hackneyed golliwog dance of Debussy, the taut grace of his body expressing muscular beauty without so much as a trace of decadence. His dancing is surely a work of contemporary art.

LOUIS EILSHEMIUS

I went with Bibi Dudensing and Henry McBride to visit Louis Eilshemius, the infirm and controversial American painter. We lunched beforehand at the Dudensing's Gallery, where they are now having another show by the Pittsburg miner, John Kane. Kane's pictures are primitive and strong, in the *genre* of the best America has yet produced. On display, among the self-portraits was one which showed his wife, who disapproved of Kane spending Sundays painting, appropriately depicted in the background as a cross-patch, while her husband makes the parlour untidy with his paints.

Henry McBride arrived unexpectedly, bringing with him the *Evening Sun*. 'I've written about your exhibition,' he tapped me with the paper. 'You are the Horace Walpole of your time!'

'I'm being showered with comparisons. This week's *Life* refers to me as the Byron of the camera.'

Louis Eilshemius is partly paralysed and lives with his aged brother entirely isolated from the world outside their rooms. Wrapped in shawls, he sits in a chair beside his bed, gesticulating wildly with bird-claw hands that have dried and pointed nails two inches long. His hair streams on to his shoulders. He reminds me of an old dog, and his eyes are the intensely human eyes of my father.

323

Eilshemius is a great personality, no more gaga than he has been for years. In spite of his infirmity, his vitality is enormous. He shouts frighteningly and is like a child because he only speaks of what is on his mind. Hence manners do not exist and he is apt to offend people. 'Who are you? Bibi Dudensing? You look different. McBride, thank you for writing about me in the paper. And you, Beaton, never heard of you!'

McBride sat blinking like an owl. Bibi's eyes popped from her head with intensity.

Later Eilshemius said, 'Well, you look good, McBride. How old are you, seventy-one? You don't look more than sixty-nine.' To our embarrassment, McBride refused to recognise that he was being addressed. Pretending Eilshemius was talking to me, Henry added, 'Yes, it is known that Englishmen age very quickly.'

The dark house has no electricity. Today its gloom seemed all pervading, intensified by a grey and snowy atmosphere outside. Photography proved impossible, though I tried to take a few exposures—of necessity against the light, as Eilshemius's chair could not be moved and his back was to the window.

Louis went on to complain that no one wrote to him; he never received so much as a single letter. His friends had written successful books but made no mention of him, in spite of the fact that no one could paint oceans as well as he, that his trees and forests were as good as Courbet's. Critics and public alike were dumbbells not to accept his greatness.

In the dark, overcrowded room, hundreds of his pictures (painted on canvas, cardboard and letter-writing block) had been stacked in hysterical profusion. It is many years since Louis Eilshemius stopped painting, but his output was enormous. All about us, bevies of pompadoured nudes splashed in mountain streams and waterfalls, backed by chutney-coloured arbours. More than one detractor had complained that he made his nudes wooden. 'To HELL with the critics!' Louis shouted. On and on he raved. He had no use for the present day; he was great, and his pictures should be acclaimed. Not only was he a great painter, but a poet and composer too. He compared himself to Beethoven. 'You know Beethoven, don't you? Well, I'm that great.' Oddly, these paeans of self-praise could not have been dismissed as mere paranoia. His mind was too alert for that. And in spite of the

squalor of the scene itself, there was a certain grandeur about this
old man's fanatic arrogance.

On our way out, we met Louis's elder brother, aged eight-five.
He looks younger than the painter, but is hard of hearing. As we
peeped into the drawing-room, which stands intact and doubtless
unchanged from what it was fifty years ago, we could hear the
two old cronies upstairs shouting at one another. 'Dudensing,
Dudensing?, McBride, McBride? Beaton, Beaton?'

The German domestic, looking like one of Eilshemius's painted
figures, winked sympathetically and hoped we would return.

Outside, the familiar pavement looked strange for a moment. I
thought of what we had just left—the stuffed birds, framed
photographs, stacks of strange pictures, and the invalid barking
and thumping in his bedside chair. Our visit had seemed like some
incident from a book. Certainly, Eilshemius's world had none of
the reality of the present day—which, I realised with a start, was
the last day of the year 1937.

MRS PATRICK CAMPBELL

New York, 1938

Mrs Pat is a great woman, triumphing over the sordid difficulties
of poverty and age by a resolute sense of beauty and poetry. For
today's sitting she wore black velvet and artificial pearls. She
brought with her the white Pekinese dog to which she is so in-
ordinately devoted that she will not return to England (dogs
must remain in quarantine for a year before entering the British
Isles).

In appearance, Mrs Pat seems a prototype of a stage duchess.
But after the hot lights had played on her for a while, she began to
disintegrate. There was something ghastly about her dirty white
gloves, her fallen chins and the tragic impedimenta of age. She
bellowed like a sick cow, throwing her hands to the skies, 'Oh,
why must I look like a burst paper bag? Why must I have all
these dewlaps? Why can't I be a beauty?'

I took Mrs Pat to lunch at Voisin's. She was in good form
castigating Orson Welles' production of *Julius Caesar*: 'They have
no reverence, those boys. They speak the lines as if they had
written them themselves. You can't recite the *Song of David*
spontaneously. You must recite it as David. Mr Welles's Brutus

is like an obstretrician who very seriously visits a lady in order to placate her nerves.'

As only an artist can be, she is canny and clear in her observations about people: 'Lilian Gish may be a charming person, but she's not Ophelia. She comes on stage as if she'd been sent for to sew rings on the new curtains.'

Kirsten Flagstad 'walks meaninglessly around the stage, like a wardrobe at a séance.'

About Violet, Duchess of Rutland (whose recent death robbed us of a landmark) Mrs Pat said, 'She was the most beautiful thing I ever saw. In my day, beauties were poetic looking. They wore long, pre-Raphaelite tea gowns. They moved and spoke very slowly, giving the impression that they had just been possessed.'

At this point, our lunch was momentarily interrupted when Mrs Pat sailed over to join Noël Coward and another man at a wallside table. I watched her pantomime, and noticed that Noël seemed ill at ease. When Mrs Pat floated back she said, 'He wants to put me in his new play. I refused. I could never talk like a typewriter. I couldn't tap out, "Do you love me? Don't you love me? I don't love you".'

I laughed, but wondered how she could turn down a part on Broadway when she has not had an opportunity for years. I remembered someone saying about Mrs Pat and her present plight: 'She is like a sinking battleship firing on her rescuers.'

She quoted a line from Swift to Vanessa, 'You have taught me to distinguish and you leave me desolate.' This was on the street as we said goodbye. I turned for a last glimpse of her standing in the snow, a monument in black velvet.

In the corridor outside my room I could hear a booming voice coming nearer. '2645, 2645, 2645. . . . Ah! Here we are. Can I come in? Are you expecting me?'

Mrs Pat arrived, swathed in furs, wearing a feathered hat and the usual black velvet dress with train. She brought with her the proofs of the pictures I had taken; also, for my inspection, a selection of old photographs of herself as she used to be. These documents attested such beauty that it was almost frightening to compare them with what they have turned into. 'Look,' she moaned, 'at the beauty of that neck, at that line of cheek. And look at me now, all wind and water.'

The early pictures depicted a magnolia beauty with dark hair and prune eyes, communicating an acute sensitiveness and delicacy. Mrs Pat inveighed: 'Oh God, how can You be so unkind as to do this to me? Why must we all become ugly? I don't know how some women stand it. Why don't they commit suicide?'

She was apparently comforted by my photographs. I didn't dare protest what I thought—that they were really quite ordinary. To Mrs Pat, they seemed the distillation of magic. 'Oh, that shadow under the jaw! You're a genius to put in that shadow. And no one has taken such a photograph of gloved hands. Those gloves are alive. Look at the depth between the thumb and first finger. That's what everyone wants to have!'

She was likewise delighted with the photogenic qualities of Moonbeam, who, according to my spy, David Herbert, had been the cause of trouble a day or two ago. David, having taken Mrs Pat out to dinner brought her back to her hotel in a taxi. When the driver discovered that Moonbeam had wetted the floor of the vehicle he remonstrated vehemently with Mrs Pat. To placate him, she held Moonbeam high and wagged a finger at the culprit, cooing, 'Who would have thought the old dog to have so much pee in him?'

Abruptly, Mrs Pat broached the irrelevant subject of money. 'Now I've brought you forty dollars for these pictures.'

I remonstrated with her. I had no intention of her *buying* any photographs. They were meant as a tribute.

Mrs Pat insisted on paying. She said, 'It's rather affected of you to go on like this, you know. I shall give you *thirty* dollars, then. I can afford it. I have a rich pupil now.'

Everything she does or says is touched with Shakespearean grandeur. When she named the price I must accept for the photographs, the word dollar became something as beautiful as a gold coin. She took away from it the stigma of commercialism and invested it with dignity.

'Now tell me about your life at the moment,' I asked.

'I am poor but I'm not afraid of being poor. I could easily have been rich if I'd been just a bit vulgar or broken a little dog's heart. You can understand my giving up a career for Moonbeam, can't you? I couldn't go back to England and let that little dog die! Anyway, I live in an old-fashioned hotel, a red brick building full of old people who adore me. They look after me so kindly;

327

they adore Moonbeam. I have two rooms with French windows and a high ceiling. And I don't have to hear other people's bath water!'

It was in her present hotel that John Gielgud visited her. He felt so sorry for her poverty that he offered to lend her money, then sent fruit and all sorts of food she couldn't eat. He wept for her, which she thought silly. She had no wish to be pitied. She said, 'Get along with you. Pull yourself together. You're too hysterical on and off the stage.' Wiping his eyes, Gielgud replied, 'Those are Terry tears.'

Mrs Pat turned now to discussing her pupils. 'Oh, how they read! I have one woman who teaches at a school and has forty pupils a day. But no matter, she reads Milton so badly! She can't keep her voice up, just crashes right on without hearing the sound of the music. She is incapable of understanding a half beat. She never pauses before a He with a capital H, says He as if God were the butcher boy! Fancy not being able to give the reverence of a half-pause before talking of our Maker. She gabbles on as if it were our Dressmaker!'

Mrs Pat, a mountainous stage duchess, sat draped in her fur coat with a history. 'Isn't it a beauty! It was left me by my greatest woman friend, Brigit Guinness. She wore it for six years and I have worn it for six. Yet it's just as luxurious as ever! You see, Brigit left three coats. Tanis[1] took the mink, Meraud[2] got the sable. They gave this to me because they thought it was rabbit. But I knew it was flying squirrel: if you blow on it the fur is soft and blue-grey all the way down. It hasn't been dyed. It wears so well, whereas the girls haven't got an inch of their coats left. I wrap myself in it and I am as comfortable as in a house.'

Mrs Pat on love: 'Oh, I was loved once. But it didn't work. The French have a proverb, "Become like honey and the flies eat you".'

Mrs Pat said she was having an anxious time trying to find someone who could write the necessary explanation about herself and Shaw, for the publication after their deaths of Shaw's letters to her. Gaps in the correspondence must be filled in; it must be understood that this was not just the gaga drivellings of a writer to any actress. The editing had to be done with understanding, reverence and taste. 'It's difficult to find someone who will not

[1] and [2] Tanis and Meraud, Mrs Guinness' daughters.

throw these letters to the ground so that you have to stoop to see them. We want them on a pedestal just at eye level! I believe we have got hold of an Irishman; and, you know, Irishmen are never vulgar!'

She talked about her difficulties in the theatre. Only today she had had such a bad snub. Someone had asked her to take the part of a drivelling old woman of a hundred and two. 'It is very difficult to be a hundred and two convincingly. Even at my age I can hardly move. But to be a hundred and two and drool at the mouth is too horrifying. It is surely better that I remain a legend!'

The legend went on to talk of her big opportunity, when she played Mrs Tanqueray. 'I never got my chance until I had two children. Then, straightaway, I went right to the top. It's a question of taste and not experience. Alexander[1] knew I had had no training, but he always listened to me. He told me to lose my temper in one scene and brush all the photographs from the piano on to the floor. But I replied that I could never lose my temper or do ugly things with my hands. In the play, I was supposed to be a musician: no musician would put frames on the piano! And again, at rehearsal, he told me to strum the piano. I said, 'I *never* strum. My mother locked the keyboard and only let us open it if we were going to *play*.' Alexander then said to me, 'Well, *play* then.' But it so happened that my teacher had discovered the third finger of my right hand was weak. I must rest it a while. In the interim, he'd been teaching me an arrangement by Bach, for left hand only. Thus, in front of Alexander, I held a book high in my right hand, adopted an expression of complete disdain, and played the piano with my left hand until the poor man was eventually able to gasp, "That's enough, Mrs Campbell!" '

By now, Mrs Pat was in a reminiscing mood. She began to tell many stories of sorrow and heartbreak on the stage. Magic names of dead actors and actresses were evoked once more— Cyril Maude, Herbert Tree, and Maude Millet, whose eyes shone as though she had just seen a little piece of heaven.

Ivan Moffatt suggested that conversations at Ashcombe, Rhinebeck and Kammer should be recorded on a hidden dictaphone, then collected in a book to be called *A Year's Conversation*.

No sooner had the suggestion been made than we left for

[1] Sir George Alexander.

Rhinebeck to find Raimund with a new toy—a recording machine. Rather self-conscious conversation was recorded. A few people did special stunts for the occasion, such as imitations and anecdotes. Certain voices sounded better than others. My own seemed nauseating and smug. I minded the nasal twang less than the overtones of meticulous self-assurance.

Something must be done about it. I telephoned to Ruth Ford. Did she think, as a result of her recent studies, that it was possible to alter the register of one's voice? 'Oh dearre, no. Don't alter your voice. It's a bee-utiful voice.'

Unconvinced, I telephoned to Mrs Pat for advice. She was correctively enthusiastic, 'Yes, yes, come along to me. You must be taught not to place your voice up there. We can easily get it down. Oh, *do* try. *Do* come along.'

On the afternoon arranged for the first lesson, I arrived promptly at her gloomy, overheated hotel. It seemed very unlike New York in its antiquated atmosphere. Everyone knew everyone else in the lobby; idlers gossiped about their pet dogs.

'Would you wait? Mrs Campbell is engaged.' (She hadn't written down the appointment.)

After a few minutes, the summons came for me to go up to Mrs Pat's rooms. A wiry old fox was being shoved out as politely as possible. It turned out that Mrs Pat had been trying to get him to offer four thousand dollars for her correspondence with Shaw. The letters, done up in large white envelopes, lay in the pigeon-hole shelves of her desk. 'Oh, if only he would buy them and see that they were treated properly. But it's all so difficult.'

My lesson proved a revelation. Mrs Pat recited a poem of Tennyson: 'Come not when I am dead, to drop thy foolish tears about my head. . . .' She had chosen the passage as being impossible to recite in an offhand, fashionable, nasal twang. I listened, amazed by the turtle-dove richness of her cooing. I tried, but only after remonstrance did I realise how light and murderous was my own interpretation.

An improvement set in at the second attempt. She lowed enthusiastically, 'You've done it! You've altered the pitch of your voice. You can hear. Now you must learn to give variety.' Her own register possesses infinite variety, though I had never before been conscious of it.

The two rooms in which Mrs Pat lives cost her a hundred

dollars a month. Her Pekinese lies in a basket. Every piece of furniture has been covered with remnants of brocade. There are a number of photographs and water colour sketches, bags of all sorts hang from lamps and corners, the radiator is covered in a snood of red brocatelle. For art she has a living Degas: opposite her window, pupils of the American ballet practise incessantly in white *tutus*. The titles of various strewn books indicate Mrs Pat's passion for the classics—Shakespeare, the Works of Milton, *La Dame aux Camellias, Pelleas et Mélisande*.

'But my dear,' she continued warmly, 'you've *got* it! You *must* go on the stage. You have practically all the advantages. You have grace, looks, youth and a lovely voice which you must learn how to use. You have an appealing quality and (though better looking) are like Leslie Howard. You must *do* it. I'll help you. Why, you should see the people that come in to me. One man, this morning, was tall and handsome, but his legs dangled like a marionette's. I sent him off to see a doctor. I said, "You can't be an actor with legs like that!" '

Mrs Pat demonstrated how she moves on the stage, a stylised technique in which the foot precedes any other part of the body. Thus, if she but turn to look out of a window, the foot turns first.

Arm movements, too, were different from those which I would have executed. 'No, no, you cannot open your arms with elbows close to your sides. You are not a Jewish comedian. You must show the best part of your arm, the inside. Now, raise the palms of your hands and push outwards as if you were parting the winds!'

The head, as apotheosised by Mrs Pat, became a gracious appendage of one's body. 'In moments of anxiety, you must never throw your head from side to side. It is foolish and restless Raise the head and clasp it still; no, not with your hands, with your spirit! Now you're learning all my tricks!'

Finest of all Mrs Pat's techniques is her development of the spontaneous: saying exactly whatever comes into her head, she endows every word with freshness and spontaneity. Today she looked like an Italian housekeeper in the inevitable black velvet, as seated at her typewriter, very badly pecking out the Tennyson poem and spoke her mind. 'Oh, you are so pale today. "There let the mind sigh." You have suffered so unfairly and these people are so vindictive. "And the plover cry." You mustn't pitch your voice up, like a wife who hates her husband. "Child if it were thine error or thy crime." You know the way they nag, "Darling-be-an-angel-and-get-me-another-piece-of-toast!" But you'll do it, I'm sure.'

Mrs Pat has also made a study of being absent-minded. When the telephone bell rings, she calls, 'Come in.'

As a teacher she is excellent. Her criticisms are cannily apt, and one relishes her cruelty.

It was Mrs Pat's seventy-third birthday. Some gardenias and a cablegram from England paid homage to her great character, to an actress who had been loved by Shaw, who had brought a new influence to the theatre and was now a waning one. The young ballerinas across the street were doing their arm exercises now. Moonbeam, who would never be in quarantine, snoozed contentedly in his basket.

Part XX

Summer Abroad

1938

*The late thirties were the great 'holiday' time. Sometimes monthe
would be spent motoring about the pleasant places of Europe with eass
and nonchalance. Yet fortunately, my work could be continued wherever
I happened to be, and eventually I would return with the task of editing
notebooks, sketch-pads and exposed films, which had accumulated.*

*Some of the holidays were spent enjoying the godlike sensation of
flying on water skis over the sapphire sea of the Cote d'Azur, to be
followed by a pilgrimage in William Odom's Hispano Suiza to the
birthplaces of the painters of the Italian Renaissance. With Peter I was
initiated into the Rococo marvels of Austria and Bavaria.*

*A visit to Russia under Intourist conditions was a saga of frustration.
Because of their imcompetence I was thrown off the train in the middle
of a snowy night in Poland and sent all the way back to Berlin for a one
and ninepenny transit visa.*

*In Moscow I had to fight my indoctrinated guide, Miss Polak, to be
allowed to see the relics and remnants of the degenerate days of the
Czars rather than be suitably impressed by the underground station,*

the science museum, or the reformed (but nevertheless sullen) prostitutes working in a laundry.

The first sight of a typical citizen of the Soviet, a bloodlessly pale and drawn woman, with the expression in her eyes of a whipped dog, was a shock, the effect of which will remain with me always. In fact, the general unhappiness and ugly squalor gave me my first stirrings of a social conscience. Before, the lot of the working classes had been the concern of my more intelligent and civic-minded contemporaries, who

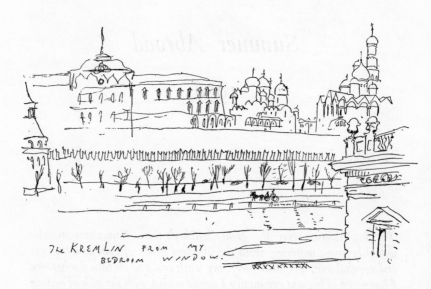

THE KREMLIN FROM MY
BEDROOM WINDOW.

had even gone to Spain to fight for their convictions: now for many nights on end I could not sleep for thinking of the abject misery of the people. My shut eyes were filled with pictures of their unhappy colour-less faces which showed the beaten acceptance of a life only a degree above that of animals.

Not all the journeys were of a luxurious nature, for instance, my first glimpse of Spain: this was in the company of Tchelitchew. For reasons of economy we travelled by cattle train, put up at the cheapest hotels and savoured the full ardours of Seville in the heat of August. The following cruise, however, could be described as the apex of luxury.

ON BOARD SS SISTER ANNE

August 1st 1938, Monte Carlo

The *Sister Anne*, like a white toy boat in a child's bath, awaited our arrival in a blue bay. Our bags were put in a dinghy and, with as little fuss as if we were going to Salisbury for another weekend, David Herbert and I boarded the boat that would take us on a cruise to Constantinople. In mileage, it was to be a trip as far as from Europe to America.

The party on board consisted of our hostess Daisy, with an Edwardian coiffure of curls high on her head, her daughter Rosamund, who should have been a Tahitian model for Gauguin, Lord Aylwin and Armand de la Rochefoucauld.

The *Sister Anne* looked bright and shining. Her brass fittings gleamed from perpetual polishing; her cabins were spruce. A few items, such as cushions embroidered with maps of our itinerary and a parrot in a Maltese cage, gave the Stevensonian note of adventure to the expedition.

We sailed, waving goodbye to the pine trees in Daisy's garden; and, after an unexpectedly calm voyage over a colourless lake, we arrived to take part in the night-time gaieties at Calvi in Corsica.

Remnants of daylight made it possible still to see the contours of the town. Soon lights at Calvi's windows and in the restaurants offered glimpses into the private activities of the inhabitants— vignettes that the day denied us. The layers of flat, flanked houses looked like homes made of wafers or some sort of pastry, flaking down one on top of the other from the height of the hillside to the strip of brilliantly lit port where the world paraded up and down. Dogs barked in the distance, orchestras played in the cafés and people sat in windows, a part of the illuminated picture of their room. We could see scarlet wallpaper and china plates hung as pictures on the wall. Palm trees stood silhouetted against the lighted houses. Lanterns created dappled effects as they shone through complicated trellises.

As we neared shore, wafts of musk and herbal scents were thrown down on to us from the groves of maquis trees. We trekked down the ship's gangplank to an evening of surprises. In the half light, every object assumed an added mystery. Indeed, since the boat was to leave at daybreak next morning, there would be no opportunity to destroy our illusions.

335

The proprietor of the restaurant supplied us with an excellent meal made by throwing, with unerring instinct, any old scraps into a pot of eggs or beans.

We ate under an awning of pepper trees. Acacia gleamed about us in phosphorescent bouquets. The tree that blossomed with poufs of thistles was to be avoided, for anyone who smelled it at once got a swollen nose. We did see a woman who had obviously made this mistake, and she looked like a figure Breughel painted quite often.

Our mood became gayer, perhaps on account of the red wines we drank. Soon everything seemed and *was* funny. We explored the citadel in the dark with the aid of a torch lamp that only worked when it was least needed. Under the enormous walls, more like a Gordon Craig setting than anything he could have invented, or like the bows of a stone *Queen Mary* ship, we climbed in circles until in the dark an unexpected step asserted its presence and Daisy's ankle was painfully turned over.

The tropic heat made sleep impossible. I took advantage of my wakefulness to muse idly on subjects that day does not encourage —morbid thoughts of death, accidents and love.

BONIFACIO

It seemed to be the end of the world. The last light was fading from the sky. A pink cloud reflected the sun that had already disappeared below the horizon. The whiteness of buildings and earth alike created an emptiness that is fashionable among painters of today. Near the barracks, built around a quadrangle, groups of Arab soldiers in fez and khaki squatted on the ground. They were the only coloured inhabitants of our otherwise un-inhabited and colourless world. They seemed bored to a stupor, longing for anything to happen but not minding the fact that nothing would. Diana Cooper, who takes her special brand of wit along with her wherever she goes, would have said, 'They have no plans.'

MARSALA

Lord Aylwin looks to sea through a telescope and, though he speaks but little, his age-seared face makes one speculate about what must have been an adventurous youth. Armand's humour becomes more definite in its elusive way. He is an unexpected and subtle comic. David's enthusiasm is unquenchable.

Daisy shows her most delightful and primitive side. This cruise is her holiday of complete relaxation. She is no longer the lady who holds *conférences* while wearing clothes that are not only indicative of the fashions to come, but reflect the great French

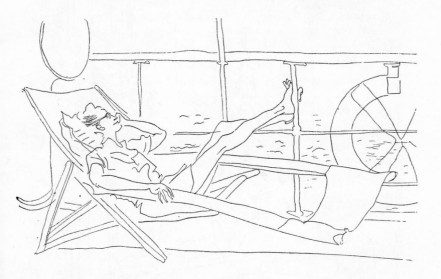

tradition as well. Here she talks like a child to her child, observing how nice it is to walk on cobblestones, with the round stones fitting into the curve of one's instep. Or she extols the satisfactory feeling of walking up the stairs and touching the edge of each step with one's instep. She screams with amusement when a playing card flies off a table. With her toes she plays 'Ten Little Nigger Boys.'

Daisy is a remarkable woman, but never more so than as mother to a child who becomes part of the family party, and for whom conversation is never needlessly tempered. There is no question of playing down to Rosamund. Rosamund takes everything in her stride, and unlike most girls of her age, is without shyness, precocity or inhibition.

MALTA

It was after dark when we approached, but the moon was bright and the port sufficiently illuminated to give a clear, if too romantic view of the island. The activity of so many boats made a sharp contrast to the day's solitude. One or two battleships in the harbour added to an impression of great organisation and power.

As we manoeuvred to our berth a small official boat drew alongside. The sailor shouted his ritual questionnaire, one that has been employed for thousands of years. In his foreign accent, he called, 'Where are you from?'

The Captain yelled back, 'Marsala.'

Silence. Then, 'Is that in Italy? Is all well? Are there any passengers in transit?' And the boat was off again into the night.

A young English officer, with red face and gold bands on his starched white uniform, paid us the honour of greeting us. In so doing, he gave us our first glimpse of the official Englishman stationed abroad. He spoke as if with a plum in his mouth, most awfully hearty with jerking knees and head swinging from side to side. 'Oh, it's a *hell* of a place to be for two years. I'm still looking for someone to play squash with me. Anyone here care for a game? Or perhaps you'd all like to come and have a drink with me?' He was kind in facilitating our progress through the Customs House. Only Armand was called aside, thereby furnishing copy for many jokes. 'Where's the Frenchman? You've got a Frenchman aboard, haven't you?'

The portholes were shut at six in the morning. As we left Malta a choppy sea sent the *Sister Anne* rolling from side to side. Great bangs and crashes now became usual occurrences. Shipboard life took on an utterly different aspect. Everyone sprawled horizontally; no one dressed. Hair looked untidy, the men went unshaven, the women greased their faces.

Meals were served as we lolled in various parts of the boat. The boat rocked and lurched. Some of the sailors were sick, but none of our group became actively ill. At most, my stomach felt weak from time to time.

Malta now seemed far distant as we read the guide-books and history of the Knights. I regretted not having gone with the others to see the *Citta Fecchia* by moonlight. Here old Maltese families still inhabit palaces that have been their homes for four or five hundred years. There are no shops to disturb the elegance or the residential quarter, only avenues of coloured saints lining the streets. The Maltese thus confused the invading Turks by making one street identical with another.

MILOS SILHOUETTES

At ten o'clock we rowed ashore to see the marionette (really silhouette) show. It took place at the one and only café, where a stage has been semi-permanently rigged up.

Against a sheet of stretched white muslin, lit from the back, the silhouette figures, jewelled with cut-out triangles of coloured gelatine, are brought to life by means of implements resembling fire tongs or toasting forks. These little cardboard personages, half fly and half Persian prince, resemble those seen in Balinese drawings. Their antecedents are, however, Turkish: they are identical to those figures (perhaps a thousand years old) that were brought to Greece in the Turkish invasion of five hundred years ago. The play ritual remains unchanged; like the Turkish music it has been appropriated as a part of Greek national life.

The moonlit audience sat at coffee tables, hilariously receiving this traditional drama. I remember seeing such a performance during the Ramadan in Tunis. The plot was undoubtedly the same: a young man is counselled as to how to win the favours of a lady. Not knowing one word of Greek, it was difficult for us to appreciate fully the humour of the evening. David and I wandered around to the back of the stage and were allowed to watch the performance from behind the transparent curtain. Every character in the play was being enacted by one wildly gesticulating, adroitly manoeuvering Greek. He had the wiry intensity, the black curls, moustache, striped baggy trousers and tragi-comic quality of Charlie Chaplin, and the tired, sweet face of an artist.

This performer—Aleko Mavromati is his name—has for sixteen years been touring the Greek islands with his marionettes. In the confines of his miniature world he is God Almighty. While running a gamut of emotions, he simultaneously manipulates rods, twists his arms to allow personages to cross one

Queen Elizabeth the Queen Mother in the Blue Drawing Room at
Buckingham Palace

My Mother photographed with her children in her garden

another, whispers asides to his helpless assistants, and also prepares the next effects—the figures about to appear, the sounds to be employed.

Assisting Mavromati on this rickety, shaking box-stage were three or four grown assistants, including a flautist, plus half a dozen children whose job it was to hold the rods of temporarily unmoving characters, while the maestro expertly caused a fight to take place in another corner of the stage. Though incompetent

and apt to giggle, these wild-eyed children yet seemed fully conscious of their responsibility to the unseen audience that could be heard reacting somewhere beyond the proscenium. Loud laughter gratified the leading performer. It allowed him a moment—between singing an oriental song, crowing like a cock or slapping his thighs with resounding fierceness to find a certain character that had been removed from its rightful position in readiness for its immediate appearance. With flaming eyes, the marionette God swore, slapped the laughing children, and in time brilliantly assumed the convulsive sobs of hysteria.

There could be no doubt we were witnessing a supreme mastery of technique. Stage actors always have a few lines with which to work themselves into a necessary mood. Cinema

M

artists can prepare the proper emotion before the cameras grind. But here was a succession of quick-fire effects, all equally demanding—a woman screaming, a Moor roaring lustfully, a youth pleading pitifully, dogs barking, songs sung by drunkards. With machine-gun succession and perfection, the one responsible man accomplished everything. If, by chance, one hand was free, he would gesticulate in the manner of the most flamboyant orator.

Mavromati tinkled a small hand bell as a sign that another act had come to an end. Then, although apparently exhausted, he went out front to take an offertory plate around to the island folk and Greek sailors from a naval ship offshore.

When the performance was over, we had drinks with Mavromati at the café. He sat wrapped in scarves and overcoat, as his vest had become soaking wet in the course of the evening. He smoked a cigarette with the simplicity of a child and the dignity of a king. His wife sat next to him, holding their newborn baby. He asked us about Mickey Mouse. Would we send him a marionette magazine from England?

The Greek sailors were very friendly and loth to let us go home. After we returned to the *Sister Anne*, a little rowboat filled with these white figures in white plate caps kept circling around the boat to give the ladies a moonlight serenade.

David's enthusiasm was too much for me as I lay trying to wake up. 'Good morning, Cess. Nice thing's happened: the steering wire has broken. Didn't you hear it? The engines have stopped. We'll have to remain here in Milos for three weeks. If it'd happened in mid-ocean or a rough sea, the rudder would have fallen to bits. We would have sunk, indubitably. That's a bit of news, isn't it? I was first on the scene. I upped myself out of bed, put a towel around my loins and, curiosity getting the best of me, was on the spot before you could say "knife"! Daisy doesn't want you to ask any questions. She's delegated me to tell you all. Well, goodbye.'

The day was the hottest we have so far encountered. The sun stung our flesh with waspish violence. But the poor crew must work on their repairing job with no protection from afternoon scorching. It made us feel guilty to lie about in idleness. As a sort of penance, I elected to work at my diary and write some letters.

There were six splicings to be made. It took the entire crew the whole day to do the job. When the wire broke, the steering mechanism received such a resounding jerk that something vital was dislocated in the fore part of the ship. This meant that

'Monopoly' on board

343

Daisy's cabin had to be dismantled and the panels taken out for necessary adjustments.

Daisy didn't seem in the best of humours. I believe the game of 'Monopoly' wasn't very enjoyable this morning. David, in reply to Daisy's, 'That's not a gentlemanly thing to do,' snapped 'All's fair in love and war.'

Armand, most balanced of all persons, was put out by these clashes of temperament. He said, 'When we are on a cruise like this, the strain is so great one must pinch oneself all the time not to be annoyed or annoying.'

In the hottest hour of the day, I went up to the sun deck, lying naked with a towel over my head. I could stand half an hour of gruelling. Soon my body was a pouring torrent of sweat.

When the heat went out of the sun, David and I started ashore, bent on doing some water colours in the square opposite the marionette theatre.

We watched a number of men answering a roll call in the square. It turned out they were prisoners. Most had been sent here for a three year sentence in punishment for white slave trafficking. They are not allowed to work, and must live on an allowance of three drachmas a day—barely enough for bread. So they eat and sleep as best as they can. Some become ill and wasted. Others strike up a friendship with the peasants.

We felt acquainted with half the population. We had re-christened most of them. There was the 'sandwich man' (a fisherman to whom we gave black currant sandwiches from the boat); the 'fish boy' (who sold us red mullet); 'the 'angel' (a boy aged seven who helped with the marionettes and served *ouzos*); and the 'Egyptian', one of the nastiest young boys imaginable.

As a subject for painting, David and I chose a house in the process of demolition. Strange, how anything which is being destroyed assumes a mysterious quality. The Paris exhibition, I remember, only became beautiful in the last days when it was being torn down; even the houses near us in Knightsbridge seem beautiful when they are razed to make room for new apartment blocks.

The marionette show started again, with a different play from last night's. But Mavromati showed no sign of flagging spirits. If possible, his performance was even more astonishing.

We stood once more behind the scenes, discovering new

aspects of the maestro's talent. His technique includes more than
the mere imitation of many different voices expressing every
conceivable emotion or singing all sorts of songs. He makes
descriptive and suggestive noises that belong to this puppet
world alone—noises that one recognises as an index of human
emotions, and yet cannot translate into speech or song. These

Puppet Show

indefinable sounds suggest moods of hunger, appreciation,
expectation or satisfaction. There are noises having an affinity
with the animal world, or that very creative world of infancy.

It is quite possible that Aleko Mavromati could invent an
entire pantomime employing these noises—an elaboration of the
language used by Charlie Chaplin in his all-language song in
City Lights. Charlie's song sounded like any tongue of which one
understood nothing. But Mavromati conveys, by clucking,
gurgling, gasping, kissing and clicking noises, many feelings that
are universally understood. To capture the oblique traits of
humanity is a rare art. Sometimes, on the stage, I have loved an
actor merely for his presentation of some particular facet of human
life, his understanding and knowledge of a special foible. The
marionette master seemed in this respect the richest actor I have
ever seen.

345

Mavromati stood with hunched shoulders, protruding stomach and backward-tilted head. He stamped on the floor boards of his impermanent stage; he took a hasty sip from a chipped cup of coffee strategically placed behind the footlights, then back to the most inhuman grimaces. His mouth opened wide, stretching so far back that the flesh on his cheeks formed crescents into his neck.

We asked Mavromati about the unusual range of his acoustics. Last night, we had observed that a whisper carried to the farthest table at the café; while when he chose to thunder, even the crew back on the yacht had heard it.

Mavromati explained that he knew his confines well, and thus was able to judge his effects precisely. If he lowered his head, his frenzied asides would not reach the audience. But if he raised his head towards the sounding board of the plaster wall, he could make his cries heard throughout the bay.

Perhaps the maestro has inherited the acoustical acumen of his early Greek ancestors, who planned their open-air theatres so that a coin dropped on the central stage could be heard by someone sitting in the furthest circle of stone seats. Now this science has been lost. Music pavilions are built, found wanting in the essentials of sound transmission and then abandoned. Yet Aleko Mavromati, in his improvised theatre of cardboard, could be heard for miles around.

News arrived that the splicing of the steering wires had been finished. We must leave our genius declaiming against the back wall of this table-sized theatre to an appreciative rustic audience. They were fortunate but unaware of the measure of an itinerant artist, poor but great, someone to be ranked with Garrick, Grimaldi and Coquelin.

The ship mended, we were on our way early. The day was spent cruising. Shipboard life has now settled down to a routine seldom broken. Bright talk at breakfast, then a general scattering and reunion at midday for 'Monopoly'. Lunch. Sleep. Cold drinks. 'Monopoly' again. Perfunctory chatter and a last minute dash for a guide book as we arrive at our next port of call. Land is inevitably first spotted by Eric Aylwin, an old salt of thirty years standing and very efficient with long distance glasses. (One of the jokes of our trip was my initial gambit of conversation with him, when I handed him a telescope and asked, 'Can you use this?'

Daisy was in a mood to please. To this end, she wore a dazzling native costume of gold and many colours she had bought in Bali; with its broad obi-like sash and draped skirt it showed an affinity with Japanese clothes. The apparition was a ravishment.

DELOS

Arrival at Delos was our first glimpse of the real Greece. Whereas Milos had nothing of antiquity, here we found a whole town of ancient arcades, shops, cisterns, wells, temples and theatres ruinous but still impressive.

The mosaics on the floors of courtyards and roofless houses are still in perfect condition. Near the theatre is a small house built for an actor, with a design of masks on the dining-room floor. Other dwellings have elaborate mosaics of urns intertwined with olive branches, circles of sea horses, medallions of dolphins. Most beautiful and delicate in work was a design of a goddess in yellow skirts riding a spotted panther, both garlanded with leaves. Our guide upturned a pot of water over it, in order to make the colours sing with brilliance.

For us, who are neither archaeologists nor art historians, Delos was thrilling simply because the remains of ancient Greece create, paradoxically, a living atmosphere. It is elusive, this atmosphere—mysterious, classical, primitive yet highly civilised. It is all of these things and more. Its impact is violently strong, not unlike that of a drug or a potent new drink. In fact, as we bounded about among these fallen columns and wandered through the labyrinths of deserted arcades, we all of us felt an elation that made our eyes brighten, that stirred a great longing to merge with the beauty of the place until we became a natural part of it.

Today was our first whole day on land since the cruise began. We suddenly took stock of our boat existence—roaring and grumbling through vibrating waters, and holding desultory conversations at meals while Rosamund stuck the labels upside down on the Evian bottles. We'd spent long nights of sleep and long days of doing nothing.

At lunch, when Daisy was absent, the rest of us agreed that it

347

was a pity to spend so much time cruising by day, arriving at some town by dusk and then sailing again by breakfast time. Also, David and I must leave before the cruise is over, as Juliet[1] will be furious waiting for us in her *palazzo* in Venice.

Other matters have affected our intentions as well. We were sitting at a café table this evening when David came up with serious news. The wireless officer had had an unofficial message saying that Hitler has mobilised a great force on the Czechoslovakian borders. France and England sent an inquiry, to which Hitler replied that 'manoeuvres' were in progress. Nothing more, but enough to scare.

War seems imminent. Being the last person to take things optimistically, I was suddenly sunk in gloom. All our private jokes, all our activities fell into perspective. My remorse at having missed some Greek island or other couldn't matter less now. What did it signify if we didn't get to Constantinople? What did anything matter if there was a war? I took to my bunk as a dog scurries off to hide during a thunderstorm.

The others continued to discuss politics after I left. Their voices could be heard on deck. Hitler may be bluffing. France and England may be calling his bluff. If he invades Czechoslovakia, England and France may still not go to war. Perhaps the news was complete fabrication. But the world is so prepared for war, and wars generally start in August. It is not in Hitler's character to retreat, to play his hand with restraint.

I lay sleepless, wishing I had taken the opportunity to 'put my house in order', so that my mother could enjoy a certain security she does not now possess.

No more war news from the wireless. Though much talk continued over late breakfast of air raids, precautions and strategic tactics during the next war, we sailed on towards Constantinople. The morning passed eventlessly. I talked with David as if we hadn't met for weeks.

David has an admirable knack of leaping on to the funny things that other people say, repeating them almost simultaneously. Often a witty remark is unheard except by him. Quick of hearing, he takes it up and makes it win appreciation and applause.

[1] Lady Juliet Duff.

ISTANBUL: ST SOPHIA

Still half-asleep, with eyes that hardly register, we hurry up on deck to catch an early dawn glimpse of the old city of Stamboul. It is now only six o'clock. In the pre-daylight morning, the minarets and domes glimmer with an added opalescence. The still, dull waters of the Marmora Sea seem to be motionless, while the Blue Mosque and Santa Sophia float by. Gradually, our eyes accept this kaleidoscopic mirage as a reality.

Few people have yet stirred themselves; business has not been embarked upon. Several dead animals float by, as inflated as the domes of the mosques.

Our first indelible impressions now rain thick and fast upon us as the official steamboat draws alongside to conduct us to our place of harbour. Past the old town we glide, past the Bay of Galata and the Galata Bridge, towards the new, shining, hideous white Palace of the President.

We had heard that Constantinople was now a large modern city, where the fez had been replaced by the bowler hat. But we had not expected to find the colour of the Orient so entirely banished. The town surprised us by its monochrome. All the buildings are greyish, even the mosques dun-coloured or biscuit. All day long we waited in vain for an effect of colour.

On our first morning of sightseeing, we picked up a guide in a ridiculous panama hat. Achmed was never to leave us for the rest of our stay. First, of course he conducted us to Santa Sophia. It is not its jewel-like quality of gold further encrusted with gold, but rather, the proportion, the grandeur and the size of the architectural achievement by which one is most impressed. Only by a careful and studious inspection of the various details of its component parts does one fully appreciate Santa Sophia's richness, greatness and beauty. Achmed asked if we would like to go up the scaffolding and see the work the Trust was doing above the high altar. Here we met Mr Whittemore, the American responsible for the discovery of the mosaics which have been uncovered within the last seven years. Mr W. was anaemic and stringy, dressed like an old Lesbian. But he soon showed the force and appreciation of a dedicated artist, a specialist in his field.

It was explained to us that, under Turkey's new presidency the Mosque has been turned into a museum. Hitherto, the ruling

349

of the Moslem religion forbade revealing Christian scripture figures made at the time of Justinian and Theodora. But we are now permitted to see the crowning achievement of mosaic art. The decorations here are considered infinitely more refined and splendid than those at Ravenna.

Mr Whittemore now led us higher up the scaffolding, our giddiness overcome by a zest to see the work that has justified his loftiest hopes. At an altitude at which an aeroplane might fly above the altar, we finally arrived at a platform where a native workman held back with a long rod a canvas curtain to reveal a large head of Christ, dazzling in the transcendency of its colours, subtle and sensitive beyond all imagining in the drawing of the face. The eye furthest from us had been placed lower and, as the head was slightly turned, made smaller than the eye nearest us— tricks of perspective that are stressed in modern painting. In fact, these fifth century mosaics have a great affinity with Modigliani or Rouault.

Other decorations uncovered have revealed family portraits of many Emperors wearing state robes and all their jewels, grouped with their wives and sons. One of the Empresses, a Hungarian, is shown to have been a very painted lady. The way in which her pink and white enamelled face has been differentiated from the unmade-up complexions of the others is miraculously subtle. Mr Whittemore observed that she was like Queen Alexandra, preserved in a perpetual state of youthful artifice.

We poked about upon the scaffolding, peering at fragments— a border made of fruit, flowers and cones, or an angel's wing like a waterfall.

Our sightseeing expeditions are generally made *en club*. None of us being specialists, these tours prove cursory, with few or no observations to help one appreciate things. Seldom is there more than, 'What a pretty pink!' Or, 'What a charming place, etc.'

Fortunately I was able to see Santa Sophia again in the company of Mr Whittemore. He pointed out many felicities I had not noticed before: that the porphyry and marble columns (some from Baalbec) supporting the bubble domes of the mosque are often of varying lengths so that the capitals, carved in an exquisite design of leaves, must be of different proportions.

Mr W. also went into a technical discussion of the subtlety that this art of mosaic had attained here, a pitch never again to be reached. For example, these mosaics exemplify the lost art of playing with light in the placing of each cube of stone. Here, over a main door leading into the church, is a decoration upon which strong daylight plays. But, in order to give the impression that the decoration is shining out from within the church, the cubes in the gold background have been placed to reflect the light at a different angle from these cubes which make up the representational figures. In effect a new dimension has been brought into play. In another panel, the cubes have been so angled as to shine only when seen from a low vantage point. These mosaic cubes are made of every sort of stone and glass. The luminous effect of shadows is created by the glass cubes.

THE CEMETERY AT SCUTARI

The cemetery was the focal point of our visit to Scutari. After taking a ferry across the Bosphorus we had ridden part of the way in one of the bobble-curtained horse carriages that are painted with flowers and landscapes. But since the hills were so steep, out of consideration for the horse and to the astonishment of the driver, we walked in the scorching sun. But the effort was worthwhile.

The cemetery proved a haunting sight with its thousands of carved marble tombstones; turbans and fezzes for men, with flowers for girls and children. Cypress trees were stripped bare by the winds or bent low. The earth was dry and impoverished; only flaky grasses and thistle grew. A venerable gardener, who had worked here for sixty years looked like someone out of an ancient myth.

The foundations of many headstones had given way. Down they fell from their erect positions, toppling in all directions.

Half-hidden in the long grass lay a skeleton, its bones strong and white and baked by the sun. I felt no compunction about taking these remains and photographing them in all sorts of arrangements against tombstones lying in the grass.

The others in our party were conscious of a strong smell of death. And, indeed, more than one grave gaped wide. Vandalism is a frequent occurrence here, as the thieves can cart away the slabs of marble to be cut up, recarved and sold again for further tombs.

BROUSSA

Broussa ('the green') lived up to its name for fertility and lush vegetation. The only flowers we saw in Turkey grew here: the fountains were oases of refreshing coolness. The olive groves, dotted with cypress spikes, stretched in a pale carpet for miles below us. Olympian, we commanded a huge world; and, to make it even more airy, we climbed a minaret to become part of the sky.

We bought gaudy silks in the bazaars, wandering about the open air markets overhung with vines, choosing shoes and belts. We visited (as sightseers) the whores' quarters where the reception rooms were furnished with brass beds and yellow lace curtains.

We motored down from the heights through fields of olives and green peppers. Daylight faded. A few Biblical figures, shrouded, moved away on donkeys. The road-menders ate their evening meal, preparatory to sleeping in small Boy Scout tents. And soon it was dark.

LESBOS AND LEMNOS

A frustration known to all who own yachts is to plan a visit to certain places only to discover that owing to a caprice of nature they are unable to land. So it was with us. Here we were in the midst of so many historical wonders, and missing so much. Some of us had hoped to arrive on the morrow at Santorin, but the captain informed us the winds are wrong. So we anchor at some other, and completely uninteresting island. An ill wind took us to Lesbos. What is there to see here? Nothing; but Daisy, waving her fingertips in the air, says, 'I thought it would be amusing to send postcards from Lesbos.'

After a few days of this island-hopping, everyone's nerves were frayed. The setting was for pleasure, but I am certain no one fully enjoyed his day on Lemnos. Why hadn't we gone to an island where the sponge divers are; where, because of their hazardous profession, none live long and it has become an island of the young? Or we might have landed at Mykonos, an oriental island, with the houses all domed and white-washed, with dove-cotes on the roofs. Or what about an island where they still wear

Greek national costumes, with gold necklaces and full skirts?
No, we had to come to a rather barren little bay of oily waters,
with a few modern houses dotted on the undulating slopes.

In the harsh sunlight, Lemnos proved to be a bleak island. The
evening walk inland provided our only pleasure.

There is no more transcending moment than twilight. This
evening it melted our hard hearts, beautifying even these surroundings. Venice is at its best when the light fades; Nimes and
Arles show their souls in the gloaming. But it seemed a positive
miracle that the dusk could transform ugly-duckling Lemnos into
this crepuscular swan.

The village children clustered around in growing numbers,
making Pied Pipers of those of us with cameras. They beckoned
us to further alleyways to show the childs' brick church, their
parents' home, to point out the pump, the goat or the geese. The
women hurried out of hovels, their latest born held high. Each
snapshot was taken amid clapping, cheers and hilarious laughter.

The sky, now pink and yellow, showed a horizon of purple
mountains. A short distance from the mainland, a small green
island bore an entirely different look. It was like a chip of another
world, with spinach-green trees and fresh, juicy grass.

So persuasive was the sunset from our seats under the trees of the
little café, that we decided to have here a picnic dinner to be sent
from the boat.

As we eat, under trees hung with lanterns a few villagers and
soldiers watched, like children at a Punch and Judy Show.

ATHENS

A five-hour run and we arrived at the port of Piraeus.

While cruising in Greece last year, the Sister Anne was shot at
for being in forbidden waters. The ensuing fracas was appalling.
It seemed rather unnecessary that, again this year, we should run
into trouble. But owing to the captain not having the latest
charts or instructions, he had cruised home on the wrong side of
some fortified island. Police arrived the moment we docked, to
take the captain off to jail.

Daisy had a face of steel. Eric looked harrassed. But for David
and me the cruise was now over. Armand said, 'Your high spirits
are rudely obvious.'

We rushed off to get our tickets to Venice, at the Hotel Grande Bretagne. After such long confinement on the yacht, we found that a large hotel had the same effect on us as an Arab finding himself in an oasis. We drank our *ouzos* heartily, shouting as more and more French and English acquaintances appeared.

At last I dragged David away to go to the Acropolis. A world on top of a world, a great bone-white city high about its counterpart of tramways and concrete below, the ruins seems part of a lunar landscape. Everywhere broken columns and pediments and decorated remains which, as Cocteau put it, give the effect of the aftermath of a picnic by the gods.

My predeliction for ruins makes me wonder whether this temple is not more dramatic now than when it was new and complete. But on closer examination of the sublimity of proportion of the Parthenon and Erectheum with the vase-shaped spaces between the tapering columns, one mourned for such desecration, and inveighed against Doge Morosini, wishing he might burn in perpetual torment. Like all great things on earth, these temples are without nationality. Like trees, stars or the sky, they are part of the universe and cannot be considered as belonging to any country or date. They have nothing to do with the 'Classical Period', represented in the theatre by women holding pots and walking sideways in a room empty but for a few slender pieces of uncomfortable furniture.

Later we returned to see the Acropolis at sunset. Unfortunately a great many other people had the same notion. We arrived simultaneously with hundreds of English visitors off cruise boats, puffing, staggering, mopping themselves; they then would sit down plomp to put up their feet sensibly shod in golf shoes. They wore sun hats, garden hats, veils.

Freckled young men in khaki shorts offered sweets from a crumpled paper bag to over-ripe girl friends. After weeks cooped on board they swarmed energetically over the broken columns. They sweated, wiped their necks and under-arms, and formed a resolute cloud of locusts as they swept into the small museum where perhaps the most dynamic of all archaic figures are housed.

Even this mob could not damage the dignity of the greatest eruption of grandeur the world has ever known. As the sky slowly turned to apricot the marble assumed an incandescence.

We went back to say goodbye to Daisy. She was sad to see us go. She offered Rosamund a pound note if the child could induce us to stay.

'We couldn't, Daisy. Think of poor Juliet waiting in that rented *palazzo*.'

Daisy turned dewy, love-in-the-mist eyes upon us and smiled. 'No matter! you've done very well to last as long as this. Most of my friends send themselves urgent telegrams after ten days of a cruise!'

JOURNEY TO TAMARIS

Arrived in Venice to a cloudburst. The deluge continued for a week, and my longing for the sun drove me towards the South of France. So on to Genoa, only to be hailed by more storms. William Odom[1] had sent his Dusenberg from Cannes, and I motored six hours through heavy rain to join him there.

Cannes is bad enough at the beginning of summer; now, at the end of the season, it seemed even more odious in the ubiquitous rain.

The decadent cronies of the Carlton Hotel made the downpour an occasion for an extra little drinkie, sitting around more foolishly than ever and stewed to the gills. With money to burn, they insist upon doing just that.

One of the species, a fat slut encased in tight blue trousers, wore

[1] William Odom, an American, a gentleman jockey until a horse rolled on him after which he inherited a fortune and became interested in the Arts.

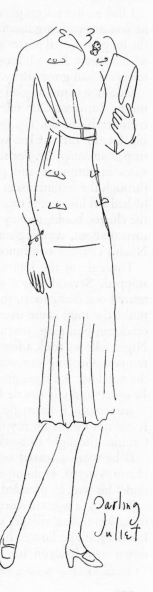

Darling
Juliet

gladioli in her dyed blonde hair. She was telling the hotel manager and clerks at the reception desk how she had been so badly fitted under the arms for her new suit that she had refused to pay.

I had earlier telegraphed Bébé at Tamaris to find out whether he was in a painting mood; if so, I would like to come and sit for the long promised portrait. No reply. Now, in Cannes, I was able to telephone him. I found Bébé awaiting me—his answering telegram had gone astray.

Odom was just as glad to leave Cannes, and suggested driving me to Tamaris. Our release from the hotel, however, entailed considerable to-do. The storm still raged, the baggage seemed too big for the car. At last we were under way, but Odom had to stop at an *antiquaire*. For sixty pounds he bought a pair of opaline vases in turquoise and gold. Then, after an hour of forging through the mountains in a torrent of rain, it was discovered that he had left his attaché case in the shop. Since the case contained all the cheque books, money and papers necessary to his holiday, we turned about, winding our way again through the gorges while Noah's cascades continued with renewed energy.

Throughout the journey to Tamaris, the deluge never once stopped. Several times we took the wrong road. When we neared our destination, the car stuck in the mud. We got out to push; the mud came over our ankles. The car lurched forward, cracking, bumping, roaring and swerving over mud and stones. Night fell; we took a few more wrong turns, at last arriving in a tempest. Groping our way through the dark, we stumbled into the hotel bar and were greeted by the welcoming voices of Denise Bourdet[1] and Charles de Noailles.

After such a dramatic arrival, the evening meal was balm. It did not even ruin my composure when Odom felt ill, rushed out into the night to be sick and came back looking gangrenous.

Bébé wore a scarlet sweater that contrasted sharply with his chestnut beard. Holding a once-white and now filthy little dog under his arm, he presided at the huge table of twenty-odd diners.

Tamaris is a small encampment on the water's edge—something less than a village, with a hotel and no more than a dozen Louis Phillippe houses built on bright-green slopes that stretch down to a halcyon bay. The houses have been developed by

[1] Madame Edouard Bourdet, wife of the playwright.

Michel Pascha, whose Turkish tastes are much in evidence. For many years now, a collection of original individuals and characters—painters, poets, writers, authors and ladies of the *monde*—have come to this spot. In a medieval tower on the water's edge live Maria (Gramont) and Francis Hugo. Denise Bourdet cossets her friends in her white and blue house, which is perched high on a green rock with a view on three sides, including the twinkling lights of distant Toulon by night. Nearby, too, is Antoinette d'Harcourt, considered by Eluard to be the greatest French woman poet alive. Also on top is Georges Auric, the composer, and his painter wife, Tony Gandarillas and his daughter and Frosca Munster.[1]

Our hotel swells the strange populace. Bébé would be intrinsically exotic anywhere. But his friend Boris, ordinarily a great eccentric, here seems almost conventional. Then there is Felix,[2] teetering on the edge of a nervous breakdown and growing more fantastic each day with his real or invented maladies. Most people, if they ever got into anything resembling his recent scrape, would hide away in shame. Not Felix: delighted, he spends the entire night telling even strangers of his idiosyncracies, in such a loud voice that he keeps half the hotel awake. Francis Rose, whom Felix has only known a few days, was up for three nights running, and once received an invitation to inspect a certain portion of Felix's anatomy with a magnifying glass! Felix had the notion that a romantic disease was about to punish him.

Sir Francis himself is someone not to be found every day. Though barely twenty-seven, he gathers laurels from several eminent art connoisseurs who consider him a great painter. Since childhood, he has been friends with people like Cocteau and Bébé, was Kit Wood's[3] bosom companion. Though English, he has never lived in England, spending his time in China and the South of France. Once Francis was rich. Then he became involved with an American crook, who not only relieved him of two million pounds but managed to have all Francis's possessions—furniture, *objets d'art* and even the pet Chihuahua—

[1] Madame Munster, a Russian lady, and one of Bébé's closest and most intimate friends.

[2] Felix Rollo, a rich young Egyptian.

[3] Christopher Wood, the English painter who died tragically at the age of twenty-nine.

N

made over in his name. As a result, Francis found himself stranded in New York earlier this year. Now he will live on a small sum of money forthcoming from the sale of his house in Cannes—enough perhaps to last him another year.

Looking like an otter already, Francis increases the resemblance by cutting his hair en brosse and a bristly moustache which accentuates a rush of teeth.

His exaggerated manners are of Horace Walpole's epoch, his speech that of a nineteenth-century squire. He has extremely refined tastes and a broad diversity of knowledge. If his life is a waste, it is all the more tragic for being a waste of so much excellent material.

Bébé tells stories of Francis's youth. When his mother was alive and the fortune intact, she dressed her otter-like prodigy in roses and lace. A man at the Hotel Negresco in Nice supposedly saw an apparition wearing Chinese silks, jewels and a rose in his buttonhole. The spectator was roused to such fury that he threw an apple tart the length of the hall. Since the man was a first rate sportsman and shot, his missile found its mark, spattering full on Francis's face.

Undated, Tamaris

It continued to rain for thirty-six hours after our arrival in Tamaris. The first evening we ignored the storm, gathering at the little casino where sailors and fishermen came to gamble and dance. Down poured the skies; lightning flashed through the shutters, thunder cracked overhead. Next day the storm persisted, flooding roads and gardens, making us resign ourselves to life indoors.

When at last the third day brought sunshine, we all felt as if we could embrace the world with gratitude. Everything was re-created in the brilliant light; the nebulous landscape of yesterday now revealed an almost uncanny succulence. Variations of light and shade impose never-ending changes on the salad greens and blues of the landscape at hand, as well as on the distant panorama. Though the coast further along towards Cannes is ugly and impossible to paint, here everything seems congenial to the eye.

Every sort of artistic activity is going on at the moment. John

Sutro, who suddenly appeared with Marc Allegret to confer with Bébé about doing a film, dubs Tamaris 'the artist's Locarno'. Certainly, the number of conferences that take place here is remarkable. Someone came from the *Comédie Française* to discuss *Cyrano de Bergerac*; and each day is so full that appointments have to be made in advance for these high-powered talks. Bébé paints me all afternoon. When John and I, having seen one another only at a distance for two days, decided we must plan a playwriting project together, we were obliged to make a date for lunch two days ahead, as if we had been in London, New York or Paris. Living as we do *en masse*, it is practically impossible to discuss anything *à deux*.

Tonight Hitler makes his decisive speech at Nuremberg. Meanwhile, everyone waits breathlessly to hear if this civilisation is at an end.

I keep feeling, quite absurdly perhaps, that the chances of war might be diminished if we stopped having a good time. Yet inevitably, we find ourselves fiddling while homes and families may tomorrow burn.

As a result of this grim possibility, however, every unimportant detail of existence looms with sudden significance. I live each day as if it were part of future annals, as if this very diary in which I write were already being read by some idle post-war stranger. Thus this morning's *petit dejeuner* became a historical event. I noticed with new eyes the *croissants* and the paper napkin beneath them, sprigged with modernistic roses. My coffee cup seemed a curious object, decorated with brown and yellow futurist designs. Perhaps that stranger, reading through these pages, will say, 'My God! Why didn't those artists at Tamaris *do* something instead of being such irresponsible idiots?'

I have written this with sea water, as the ink has almost given out.

The night after Hitler's speech found our whole community sunk in gloom. News came through from journalist friends at *Paris Soir*, that an ultimatum had been presented to the Czechs: either they must accept a plebiscite or the country would be invaded within six hours. This sudden threat allowed no time for any political readjustments by the French, in the event of an unavoidable war.

Conversation centred solely about the pros and cons of whether there would be a war. With nerves strained, it proved difficult to condone stupid remarks which, at any other time, might have gone unnoticed. Francis Rose gabbled on about his friends and about China. Denise's silent gloom seemed preferable. Francis's American friend became suddenly unbearable. And we all could have scragged Lesseps for being so coy, indulging in a ridiculous pantomime while he helped himself to sweets from a box.

CHRISTIAN BÉRARD

Bébé has an elementary quality. It is one of his many virtues. No one could be more highly civilised and, to use a word I hate, *sophisticated*; yet his instincts, reactions and gestures are those of someone utterly primitive. When he is in his room and thirsty, it is unnatural for him to pour mineral water from the Vittel bottle into a tumbler—he drinks straight from the bottle. Instead of spreading butter on bread with a knife, he will dip his bread into the butter dish.

For his work, Bébé is without paraphernalia. Here in the hotel, the bed has been taken from the room he uses as a studio. On the bedside table lies his paint palette; on the mantelpiece his canvas perches, somewhat rickety. But Bébé finds this emptiness full, making me aware of how an unfurnished room can stir the imagination.

Bébé's preparations are animal. He smears the paints with his hands, never bothering to screw the tops back on paint tubes. Colours are squeezed directly on to ever thickening mountains of paint. He recognizes and justifies a sloppiness that, in others would be inexcusable: 'If I am careless and dirty and drop everything, it is all right. I can spatter filth about the floor, and it will not be repulsive. But when Francis Rose leaves a pair of bedroom slippers lying about, it seems as unprepossessing as a dirty comb.' This paradox is true enough. Bébé seldom washes; he never sleeps *in*, but *on*, his bed. His clothes are filthy. Yet he is never revolting, never unpleasant. His personality and temperament outweigh all disadvantages.

When he works on my portrait, I notice that Bébé's every stroke of the brush, every daub, is the result of intense concentration. After each bout of work, lasting perhaps fifteen minutes, he sinks exhausted on his bed. There must then be an intermission, time to smoke an opium pipe.

In spite of lassitude, the amount of work he was able to do, at least at our first sitting, surprised me. And the results could not have been more felicitous if I had *willed* him to paint me just as I wanted myself to look. However, it is difficult to nurture Bébé's persistence: after many months away from painting, he has a dread of returning to his canvas. The least thing—a strange arrival, the door banging, the dog being sick, some private disaster of Felix Rollo's—is quite enough to prevent him from working, to excuse a postponement.

This morning I had to wake Bébé. His snores were interrupted by the dirty little dog barking. He came to consciousness, suffering so much that he groaned and moaned aloud. He lay in a heap on his bed, incapable of action, abandoning himself to despair. He was convinced of war. His imagination fed him with gruesome details.

I spoke about leaving, 'Yes, you must go,' Bébé concurred. 'I can't take the responsibility of your being here, so far from home. If there *should* be war, you'll have a nightmare journey.'

Odom, too, had begun to feel responsible for the art students at his Paris school, and decided he must leave today. It confirmed my own half-hearted impetus. Regretfully, I began to dismantle my room. I packed the rows of Alinari photographs, reproductions of the museum pictures I had liked best in Venice. I pulled down the impromptu curtains made from the poisonous rose material bought in Constantinople. Francis, who had wandered into my room, kept gabbling away about an epergne that Queen Victoria had given his grandmother; he spluttered on about Mrs Wellington Koo, about the green paper umbrellas which were the only defence the Chinese could put up against English bullets during our attacks in the Chinese war.

Everything was now ready. The trunks had been taken downstairs; and I telephoned my goodbyes to Denise while Odom, quietly businesslike, saw to the stowing of the luggage into the car. 'Are you ready?' he asked.

'Yes, but I thought we'd go after lunch.'

'Oh, er—no. I thought we'd lunch in Toulon. We'd—er—get a better meal.'

I hated the thought of lunching so near and yet so far from Bébé, Denise, etc. I ventured, 'What news from the school when you telephoned this morning?'

Odom, very grave, said, 'Oh—er—everything's—er—very calm.'

I shouted up to Bébé's room: '*Si je reste, peut-on travailler aujourdhui?*'

'*Mais oui!*'

'*Alors, je reste.*'

Odom was gone in a flash. And suddenly, everything changed. Our mood became gay; everyone laughed. Bébé's despair left him; Denise showed her gums. Frosca beamed. Maria Hugo waved. John Sutro made an upward, frustrated and indeterminate gesture with his arms—his particular way of expressing himself when he cannot find words.

Bébé burbled, 'Since you've packed you must move over and stay with Denise.'

'Fine.'

All was calm now. There would be no war. Hurray, hurray! The sitting to Bébé was the most fruitful of all.

One of the reasons Bébé has been so aghast at the thought of war is that he realises he must be disintoxicated before being called up. Otherwise his long-drawn-out death would be one of the greatest suffering. He showed me his registration card: '*Bérard—numéro such-and-such—soldat. In the event of war report immediately. . . .*'

It seems to me that Bébé has been smoking more and more. He rationalises, maintaining the stuff he now has is extremely weak. But frankly, I doubt if he can ever be disintoxicated.

Today he seemed especially anxious for a fresh supply of opium to be prepared. At all costs, if he goes to war in a hurry, it will be with his little pot and pipe! Raw opium had already been mixed with earth. Now the mess would be boiled in water, producing a leach which must filter through a cloth several times over. After this, the clarified liquid had to boil down to a final residue, the consistency of treacle or maple syrup.

Bébé's bedroom looked like the scene of an alchemist's nightmare. Casseroles had been brought out; spirit lamps flickered. A shirt was sacrificed and torn in shreds. Two lady friends now appeared, volunteering to do the cooking for him, while he worked on my portrait in the adjoining room. Strange odours of earth and opium wafted in to us—Picasso says opium is the cleverest smell. Soon every piece of furniture was covered with steaming casseroles of brown liquid. This would be passed through the sieve of the torn shirt. The residue left in the cloth was squeezed dry and set aside for future leaching, while the filtrate was boiled down.

One can buy opium in the final form; but glycerine, morphine and heaven-knows-what are often added as adulterants, so that it is only safe to prepare the product oneself. I wondered why the very process did not put Bébé off the stuff forever—the smells were sickening, the brown liquids looked extremely unpleasant.

Busily the two cooks fidgeted, giggled and fluttered. Bent double over their witches' brew, they reminded me of Nancy and Baba as children, making fudge on rainy days. And when, in extremis, the *pot de chambre* was whisked from its little wooden home to provide another receptable for the slimy liquid, my imagination could not be curbed.

Undated

Today's war news seemed less acute. Mr Chamberlain, aged sixty-nine, has taken an aeroplane for the first time and flown to confer personally with Hitler. While these conferences are on, war can not be started.

After the anxiety and gloom of last night, our present happy mood continued. The pendulum had swung violently back to gaiety, the evening became a bacchanalia.

After dinner at Denise's John Sutro released his pent-up emotions, bursting forth with a spontaneous programme of improvisations, recitations, mock-Alexandrine peace orations, Restoration plays, folk songs and what you will. His plays in rhymed couplets were inspired; his impromptu Shakespearean scene proved the best I had ever known him to do. Bébé entertained by executing a ballet imitation of a butterfly fluttering over flowers; or could it have been a moth in a wood? He skipped about on minute feet, a fantastic sprite with red beard and twinkling almond eyes. John provided the score, whistling like an inspired bird. Challenged, I danced with Denise to Brahms waltzes and Liszt.

Oliver Messel arrived with Peter Glenville. Bébé said, 'Now Oliver, do some new imitations. You've done the same ones for ten years, and you must get something new in your repertoire.' Oliver looked astonished.

Towards the end of the evening, our entertainment became more ribald. We resorted to a number of *Folies Bergéres* spectaculars: *Les Folies Nues, Les Pays, Les Fleurs, Les Vices*, etc.

Some French political journalists arrived unexpectedly. God knows what they thought as they witnessed the scene in Denise's drawing-room, with the company dressed in anything to be found in the hallway—umbrella stands, garden chairs, a globe of the world, tennis nets, rugs and cacti.

Undated

This afternoon we went to Revest, a village built around a Saracen tower on the top of a mountain eight kilometres from Toulon, which supplies water to all the surrounding towns. It is a small and entirely complete world in itself, exuding such an atmosphere of serenity that just to visit the place for a few moments is as refreshing as drinking from a running brook. Winding alleys mount to the crest of a hill; the bar of the local hotel was in medieval times a falconer's lodge. A rectangle of plane trees surrounds the village square, where an eighteenth-century fountain stands ornamented with carved heads.

We arrived just as day was about to fade (I seem always to discover places by twilight). We compared it to the moment when a formerly young and beautiful face is on the brink of waning; Bébé said, '*la dernière heure de Greta.*' During this hour, people seem to have fewer occupations than at any other time of day. They sit with their children on a wall; they watch from a window. Others sort grains of corn from the husks, or play bowls, or sit on the green iron chairs of the café and exchange news.

Revest is a silver-toned village, rock-like strata continuing the design of its walls into a landscape of Leonardo-esque mountains, dotted with silver-grey and fish-green olive trees and a reservoir of blues appropriated from one of Patinir's paintings.

Everywhere we looked, the composition gave the impression

of having been arranged by a master hand. Strewn on thistles to dry lay garments that ranged from white to purple. Some wild flowers growing against a stone wall appeared more softly lavender than the breast of any dove. In a buff alleyway, a black cat sat in front of a fragment of looking-glass that reflected a correspondingly black image in an otherwise dun-coloured world. We could see beautiful faces leaning from the windows above. Then, abruptly, a sunburned young man came out of a doorway. He was wearing a virulent green sweater, making his appearance as dramatic as if he had been the hero materialising at some crucial moment in a melodrama.

Bébé walked with flashing eyes, never looking twice but seeing more quickly than anyone else. 'Look at that door,' as if for our benefit, a door had been painted with crimson paint which, weathered now, ran through a gamut of red shades like a ripening strawberry. Over the door hung a vermilion curtain.

A man ringing a tinkling bell hurried along, with dozens of small children behind him. 'Tonight at nine o'clock,' he announced, 'a great presentation. A play, not marionettes! A theatre with five *décors* and twenty-five costumes. Seats, one franc to five francs. See the great presentation of *Le Fou Rire.*' And he hurried off to make his announcement elsewhere, followed by his excited retinue.

In the village square, the theatre was being erected against a high stone wall. Atop ladders, boys stood balancing canvas draperies, preparing to tie them to the boughs of the plane trees (most theatrical of all trees, with their mottled bark looking perpetually sun-dappled). The children, at a given command, hurried off to the local school and returned on the double, carrying light wooden trestle benches from the classrooms. Some balanced these benches on their heads; smaller urchins carried them like trays.

We sat in the café, contemplating all this. Bébé said he would like to paint a huge picture of the scene. It is what he likes best— life as expressed by people beautiful in their simplicity, integrity and good manners.

Undated

This morning Bébé painted like someone in the throes of

N*

mediaeval torture. He did not talk during the sitting. He groaned, whispered, sighed, whimpered, stamped his feet, jerked backwards and forwards, lunged with noisy intakes of breath. 'You don't *know* how difficult it is! Oh God, oh God! Ah, *je vois. Non, ce n'est pas ça! O, Dieu!*'

It was both a revelation and a lesson to me. Bébé's work is the result of acute concentration, making even so lightly painted a portrait as mine a tribute to agony.

After a long bout, he rested to smoke a pipe. I said, 'I'm so sorry you have suffered as you did today.'

He replied, 'It's all I like in the world!'

He then went on to concentrate for half an hour over a thumb that finally looked as if it had been wished on to the canvas. But the result still did not please him. Every portion of the head too, had been treated with such loving care you would think the portrait were a living thing.

In the evening we dined at the Sablettes, about twelve of us— the inevitable group. It was an interesting dinner, with Bébé in a ferocious mood I had never seen before. He seemed to be possessed of a devil. As a matter of fact, when we discussed strange occurrences, ghosts and spirits, he averred that the devil was the one thing in which he believed. Bébé seemed to direct his fury against Frosca, who laughed healthily at his sallies.

At some meals we talk about food, at others about painters, the theatre, books or personalities. Tonight's conversation centred about the deadly struggles between serpent and mongoose. This led Frosca to tell how Jean Pierre delights in watching all sorts of combat in the animal and insect worlds. It seems that he collects natural enemies and puts them in the same cage, then joyfully seeks the sacrificial remains the next morning—a broken wing, a lizard skeleton. This is the kind of thing that makes me hate Jean Pierre.

After dinner we played the 'Tower Game'. Three people are left in the world, two of your greatest friends and yourself. Only one of these friends can survive. Which one would you throw from the heights? It is an unfair game, assuming such surprising reality. Also the participants are seldom able to play with superficial tact. Friends can be lost in a minute; people frequently burst into tears. I refused to choose between Bébé and Denise.

September 22nd

I see by the newspaper that yesterday was Wednesday, September 21st. The days of the month have meant nothing to me of late. And now, on the 24th, I must be back in London to sign some books which the publisher wants to ship to America.

A lot of the portrait remains unaccomplished. Portions that at first were considered successful have now altered in relationship to the whole, thus requiring further work. The progress is a lengthy and slow one, as Bébé refuses to be slip-shod.

Today I sat both morning and afternoon, while Bébé smoked his interminable pipes. It takes a long time for him to get into the right mood for painting. The opium interruptions are, alas, continuous now. He admittedly smokes more than any addict he knows of—at least fifty pipes a day. The preparation for smoking is a long and elaborate process—rather like having to cook one's own meals, yet meals that must be prepared every half hour or so throughout the day and night. 'You can see what an agony I am in? I can't escape this terrible business.'

We were interrupted by Francis Rose, who appeared for the first time in two or three days. He has been to Cannes, arranging the disposition of his house, the last vestige of former affluence. All that remains is a coffer filled with forgotten treasures. He has brought it with him; he opens it, producing two gold snuff boxes, one dated 1720, the other more recent with a jewelled cross implanted in the lid. He tells us these things belonged to Horace Walpole. Why, this was the very box Hogarth had painted! When Bébé contradicts him, Francis complains of feeling ill and accuses Felix of having put opium in his drinking water. Bébé shouts 'Go away! Work at your painting and don't talk nonsense'.

This afternoon Bébé was anxious to work automatically and not concentrate too hard on his painting. Thus he sang a lot; he also talked a great deal.

Frosca afforded enough material for a novelette. Bébé related how she had escaped from Russia, how rich she used to be; how clever she was to manage without money, living elegantly on nothing at all.

Frosca's taste, Bébé confessed, had exerted great influence on him. Lacking the means to buy beautiful furniture, she sparsely arranged her apartment with the most simple and elegant pieces, finding them for practically nothing at the *marché aux puces*. The apartment itself was always swept and garnished, clean and orderly, smelling of the most luxurious Floris perfumes. Copper was brightly polished. Frosca always had good soap, good cheese and iced milk in the frigidaire, was a first-rate cook. (And an inventive genius to boot: once, when Bébé had no pipe to smoke, she blew an egg hollow, attaching it to a length of rubber taken from a douche bag!)

Bébé described a typical Frosca strategy. Someone telephoned from Fourques and asked her to retrieve her husband, who was indulging in an exaggerated bout of drunkenness. She arrived to find him beside himself with drink—shouting, breaking glasses. Frosca, neat as a pin and cool as a cucumber, sat down beside the raging bull and ordered a whole bottle of Pernod which she handed to him. Within minutes he dropped his head on the table and meek, as a lamb, was quietly conducted to a sanatorium.

Another time, in Normandy, she saved Bébé when he had no money to pay for damages in his room. Stains and burns had made a shambles of the parquet. But, just before the landlady arrived to make her tour of inspection, Frosca soused the entire floor with a bucket of water. The wood turned dark, showing no blemishes until it dried after Bébé's precipitate departure.

Having exhausted the topic of Frosca, Bébé fell silent for a few minutes, darting to and from the canvas with burning eyes. Then he began to talk about Diaghilev. It was only after Diaghilev's death that Boris and Bébé became friends and decided to share an apartment. For years previously, Boris had travelled with Diaghilev.

Though the ballet was Diaghilev's job, music remained his greatest passion. Nothing could rival the singing of Caruso, nor the works of Stravinsky and Tschaikovsky. Yet in spite of D.'s inordinate love for this most abstract of all the arts, he preferred his ballet old-fashioned and with a definite story. It was only on the surface that his aesthetic seemed to become harder and colder, his taste more abstract with the passing of years. As each new season called for new dance creations, ballets such as *Ode* would be produced. But such works had little direct appeal for him, were considered merely a part of the job, an attempt to fuse the best of modern genius into a contemporary dance expression.

Diaghilev hated success. When the cheers of the audience had died down after the *premiére* of *Le Chat*, he hissed to the composer, 'How *pleased* I would have been if it had failed.' When a dancer received great applause, you could be sure that he or she would be placed in the back row of the *corps de ballet* at the next performance. These humiliating tricks extended to composers as well. On one occasion, after he had asked a composer to come and play his music, D. summoned the hotel orchestra upstairs and had them substitute their own palm-court selections.

In the main, Diaghilev liked the ballet because it created a kingdom for himself—a kingdom filled with youth. His sentiments inclined, above all, to young creatures with lithe figures, dark hair and long eyelashes. The older and fatter he became, the younger and thinner he liked his minions to be. He had, of course, admired Nijinsky, but Massine became an even greater source of inspiration. Later, ballets were created around Lifar. And Markevitch, as a musical prodigy, received the master's final accolades.

Apart from his recognition of true talent, D. was often taken in by adventurers or place-seekers, who inevitably treated him abominably. The worse they treated him, the more he was titillated. Once, towards the end of an evening at the Savoy Grill, Bébé had seen a reigning beauty helping Diaghilev on with his coat. The myrmidon saw Bébé, winked and let the coat drop, while the old man fumbled clumsily with arms stabbing the air.

Like Proust, D. remained, in spite of his great culture, sensitivity and intelligence, the most sentimental and doting of persons, suffering wild seizures of jealous anxiety. Often he would wake in the middle of the night and wander into the neighbouring room to see if his favourite was sleeping soundly. More often than not, the object of affection had skipped off on a nocturnal expedition to Nice, taking the precaution of arranging bolsters and pillows to look like a sleeping form. When Diaghilev eventually discovered the ruse, there would be a terrible row ending the expeditions.

Some time later, D. might become suspicious on another score. And though the young deceiver went to great lengths of secrecy, it would be discovered that a friendship had been struck up with one of the scene carpenters at the theatre. Promptly, D. set about having this workman removed to another theatre, and thought nothing of spending two hundred pounds to accomplish his object.

Sometimes Diaghilev could be seen at his window, scrutinising the beach through a pair of binoculars: it was a way of keeping watch on the behaviour of his current favourite. Afterwards he would hide these glasses, oblivious of the fact that his enormous form could be seen even at a distance, as he peered jealously towards the sands.

Though his predilections were common knowledge, D. disliked to think people should notice him expressing an interest in some enticing young man who might pass by in the Bois. But age and fat made him unable to turn his head without also having slowly to swivel his entire body.

Bébé observed that all the young men who became friends of Diaghilev would be influenced by his courtly manners and mannerisms, his way of dressing and his hypochondria—he spent a great deal of time lying down, carrying on his life of books and music from his bed. Each friend in turn started to bother about his own health, imagining all sorts of germs and impossible illnesses. Each adopted the same way of dressing—very formally, like a mannequin, with tight, tall collar, buttonhole, tie-pin and specially shaped Homburg hat. All Diaghilev's friends could be recognised by their dress; indeed, most of them still wear that sort of hat.

Throughout this bout of gossip, Bébé continued to paint. And at length I discovered he had added a second figure to my portrait: a small boy who, by contrast, throws my likeness into dramatic relief.

September 23rd

What a congenial last evening we spent in Tamaris—Denise, Bébé and myself. We looked at back numbers of the *Théâtre* magazine, then went upstairs to Edouard's little library. Cushions were spread on the floor, and Bébé and I lay down and smoked opium.

I had had no sensation whatsoever on two previous occasions, nor did I this time, though Bébé prepared three pipes in all for me. The smoke has a fresh, vernal taste, like the juice of a blade of grass. I became strangely unsleepy yet restful, capable of understanding more quickly than before. But I could not honestly pretend to feel anything else.

Tonight Bébé seemed excited because I was smoking with him. His enthusiasm, both touching and funny, made him want to share with me the things he loves. He produced Freud's book on Leonardo, an illuminating discovery. He read the poems of Rimbaud aloud and told of the poet's life.

Bébé glowed with unparalleled inspiration, behaving like what he is—one of the few grand characters of our epoch. He smacked the dirty white dog (as dirty as himself); he snorted while he inhaled pipe after pipe of the most adulterous opium.

We ended the evening by raiding Denise's kitchen together. And I slept as soundly as usual, with no ill effects from my three whiffs of illusion.

Today, our departure day, was a sad end of holidays. With the news so ominous, it may well be my last vacation before the debacle. Bébé had slept in Denise's upstairs library, fully intending to start off early for Hyères and buy some extra baggage, as he was returning to Paris with me. But the smoking habit prevents him ever being punctual. Two hours late, he put in an appearance downstairs. Later, I noticed that the comb in my bathroom was very dirty: Bébé's toilet reduces itself to the simplest methods.

Somehow he got to Hyères, reappearing with a smart bag and many nickel-plated kitchen utensils for packing his smoking products and paraphernalia, also a few magnum bottles of Guerlain scents. He put on his town suit and threw away all other garments.

I am writing this in the train that takes us to Paris. Perhaps Bébé will want a few more sittings, though I expect the light will have changed or his mood will be less reposeful. More than likely, the picture will have to stand on its unfinished merits.

Part XXI

The Last Summer

1939

The following extract might be said to record the climax to date of my photographic career. Publication of the results of this session was held up by the outbreak of the Second World War. Their delayed appearance provided a refreshing contrast to the grim pictures that then filled the newspapers.

THE QUEEN

July 1939, London

The telephone rang. 'This is the lady-in-waiting speaking. The Queen wants to know if you will photograph her tomorrow afternoon.'

At first, I thought it might be a practical joke—the sort of thing Oliver might do. But it was no joke. My pleasure and excitement were overwhelming. In choosing me to take her photographs, the Queen made a daring innovation. It is inconceivable that her predecessor would have summoned me—my work was still considered revolutionary and unconventional.

A rush of organisation had to start forthwith. Telegrams were sent off summoning electricians and operators.

I arrived at the Palace soon after ten o'clock the following morning, to choose the rooms in which the photographs would be taken.

Following a scarlet-liveried page down miles of the dark-red carpeted corridors of the Palace, hung with petunia-crimson cut-velvets, I was in the clouds. We passed rows of family portraits, busts on columns, and gilt chairs. Housemaids, busy with their dusters, hurried through baize doors. Groups of grey-haired, be-medalled servants stood in posses at the end of an enfilade. Through the door of a small dining-room, I saw crumbs on a white linen table cloth.

The superintendent made himself congenial, and showed me the Rembrandts, Le Nain, Vermeer, and other pictures in the long and ugly railway-station gallery; also the Boucher tapestries, French furniture, and objects of art that during the past twenty years Queen Mary has collected to replace the Victorian stuff gradually being weeded out.

The Palace is now a happy combination of Regency and Edwardian. I admired a certain Louis Quinze desk, as it proved to be one of the treasures of the Palace. Moss Harris, the antiquary, had offered Queen Mary fifteen thousand pounds any time she wished to sell it.

The superintendent opened the double doors to various drawing-rooms, the throne room, the small sitting-rooms. He explained that workmen and artisans, non-stop throughout the year, are making repairs or renovating some aspect of this huge ensemble—the superintendent has forty men under him.

He confessed, 'We have a lot to do matching the silk on the walls. Do you see how it has faded behind these pictures? We have a great deal of the material, but it must be the same tone as where it has faded. Look at these sofas: also upholstered in the same material. Look at this patch. We've had that bit of silk out in the garden to fade it in the sun; but even so, it looks different from the rest. These repairs go on all the time. After every party we find someone has slashed a sofa with his sword.'

Through the windows, I could hear the changing of the guard. The commands of the officers, shouting to their men, sounded like someone retching. Throughout the Palace, I

373

noticed, one has no feeling of remoteness from the people. The garden, though enormous, hums with the distant burr of traffic. Through the windows of many rooms, one can see the curious crowds waiting beyond the railings.

The Deputy Master of the Household suddenly appeared. He cleared his throat, seeming like so many courtiers, who enjoy communicating their nervousness to suitably terrified 'outsiders', and explained, 'Uh-huh-Her Majesty wanted to see you-uh-huh—about—uh-huh—choosing the dresses for this afternoon's pictures. I'll try and get you in quickly, because as a matter of fact I know the Queen—uh-huh—has got the—uh-huh—hairdresser at eleven.' By the time we had waited outside the Royal apartment and I was at last bidden into the presence, any self-confidence I might possibly have assumed had been knocked out of me. My mouth was dry. When the mahogany doors were opened, I felt I was being precipitated on to a stage without knowing any of my lines.

The Queen was in the act of moving towards a desk. All about her, a blue haze emanated from the French silk walls embroidered in bouquets of silver. The room seemed a pointillist bower of flowers—hydrangeas, sweet peas, carnations.

The Queen wore a pale grey dress with long, fur-edged sleeves.

She greeted me, smiling and easy. Nevertheless, I felt myself standing stiff, my knees shaking. 'It is a great happiness for me, Ma'am.'

'It is very exciting for me.'

We discussed dresses. 'You know, perhaps the embroidered one I wore—in Canada . . . ?' A slight hesitation prevented the remark from being conceited, for the Queen must have known I was aware of what she wore on her Canadian tour.

The Queen made other tentative suggestions: 'And I thought, perhaps, another evening dress of—tulle? And a—tiara?' All this wistfully said, with a smile, and raised eyebrows. The charm of manner was so infectious that, no doubt to the Queen's astonishment, I found myself subconsciously imitating her somewhat jerky flow of speech, and using the same gentle, staccato expressions. I wrinkled my forehead in imitation of her look of inquiry as I asked if—perhaps—as much jewellery as possible could—be worn? The Queen smiled apologetically—'The choice isn't very great you know!'

374

I went away in high spirits and full of hopes for the afternoon.

In a corner of the semi-circular music room, with its lapis columns, a great group of men were preparing the lights. Others had already set up a platform, and a screen with my backgrounds hung on it.

The superintendent had told me that I wouldn't be allowed much time with the Queen. In fact, he explained, not since the late King George's reign had any photographer been allowed to take pictures for more then twenty minutes.

Thus, at last, when a rush of pages and a hustle in the corridor preceded Her Majesty's entrance in ruby encrusted crinoline of gold and silver, I began to photograph with monkey-like frenzy. This seemed to amuse my sitter.

We photographed now from room to room. The electricians and the camera assistants could hardly keep up with us. Nevertheless, the sitting went with such ease and rapidity that I beamed even as I sweated with the effort. The Queen smiled as freshly as ever. In fact, she said, 'It is so hard to know when *not* to smile.' She tidied her shoulder straps meticulously and placed her fan just so. She was gamely prepared for another picture to be taken.

It was only when the plates had to be reloaded that I could possibly allow Her Majesty to change into another dress. I apologised for my over-enthusiasm and expressed the hope that the results would justify this behaviour.

The Queen disappeared, then reappeared in spangled tulle like a fairy doll. She admitted with a smile, 'I changed the tiara. And these diamonds—are they all right?' They had been given as a coronation present by the King: two rows of diamonds almost as big as walnuts.

Then, after the diamonds, the Queen produced three rows of enormous pearls. 'Are three rows too much?' I protested. But a little later Her Majesty removed all but one row, saying with a chuckle, 'I think three *are* too much!'

The camera devoured plates with gluttonous rapidity. The Rolleiflex did service whenever the big camera was not ready. Pictures were taken of the Queen against my old Piranesi and Fragonard backgrounds, with flowers from her rooms padding the sides of her chair. We also took shots against the pillars of the drawing-rooms, in doorways, on sofas and against the precious Louis Quinze desk.

The sun now came out, encouraging the hope that I might be able to take photographs outside. What about—a garden party dress—on the terrace? The Queen assented. In ten or fifteen minutes we would meet downstairs.

While I waited, a tea tray was brought to me in the lapis drawing-room. My superintendent friend came in and said, 'Do you realise you are the most fortunate young man I've ever known? Why, you've had three hours of the Queen's time already. Do you mean to say she's gone off to change once more? Why, she hasn't had her tea yet, has she? Well, it means the poor King will have to have his tea alone!'

Never has tea tasted better. The bread and butter was like angel cake. Yes, I was a fortunate young man. I smiled to myself, recalling the little comments the Queen had made during our indoor sessions. When I ran out of Rolleiflex films, someone was sent to Heppels for more. The films arrived very soon. Her Majesty exclaimed, 'Never have I known such celerity.' Again, when we tried consciously to arrange her hands on her lap, they became self-conscious. Abandoning all efforts to put one hand on top of the other, the Queen said, 'I'm afraid your instructions were too rigid.'

I waited on the terrace. The Queen appeared, smiling and laughing in a sudden gust of wind. She was wearing a champagne-coloured lace dress and hat. She carried a parasol.

She walked down a flight of steps while I ran about with my small camera.

The lawns of the Palace were fitfully strewn with sunlight; the atmosphere seemed strange and timeless. I felt that our expedition to the lake, to photograph by the water's edge was something outside reality.

The Queen talked gaily. 'I am interested in your photography. You have such a high standard. Can you do a lot afterwards? Can you take out a whole table?'

'A table is a bit much, Ma'am. But I can slice people in half.'

'How the King will laugh when I tell him you photographed me directly against the sun. We have to spend our time running round to face the sun for the King's snapshots.'

Her Majesty halted suddenly on the lawn. 'Do you realise we are in the Sacred Circle?' On the grass a white circle had been painted. 'This is where all the Bishops assemble at the Garden

Party and wait to be received.' How disappointing for ten thous-
and people that yesterday the rain had wrought havoc! The Queen
commented that for ten days they had listened to the hammering
of the tents being erected. Now they would listen for nearly as
long while the tents were being pulled down.

Photography continued beneath a giant stone vase, in a summer
house of tridents that came, it seems, from the Admiralty. We
then took pictures from under the trees against the water, with
the Palace in the distance.

'Will my parasol obliterate the Palace?'

'It is a very big Palace.'

'That central part is the original Buckingham House.'

In the filtered light, it looked as though it were made of opals.
We stood for a moment listening to the distant roar of traffic.
The evening sun was beginning to lose its power. Soon the sky
would become rose-coloured; as if, as the Queen said, 'Piccadilly were on fire every night.'

We walked back to the Palace, where tired and baffled officials
clustered by the door.

Downstairs, in the circular hall, I took my leave. As mementoes
of the honour, there would be a hundred negatives. But in my
pocket was hidden, scented with tuberoses and gardenias, a
handkerchief that the Queen had tucked behind the cushion of a
chair away from the onslaught of the camera. I had stolen it. It
was my particular prize, one which would have more romance
and reality than any of the photographs.

STAYING WITH GERTRUDE STEIN AND ALICE TOKLAS

August: Billigoin, Bellay, Ain

This house has an atmosphere that every artist must respond to.
It is an invitation to work in ideal conditions. Colours, sounds and
smells combine to produce an impression of complete simplicity
and harmony. Here everything necessary is at hand, nothing more.
The whole day may be spent idling or working, as one pleases.

The house was built *circa* 1649 when domestic architecture in
France was good. It is solid, boldly proportioned. Each room is as
satisfying as the solution of a mathematical problem.

Throughout the house, there are few objects. But each object
is of merit. There is nothing to offend the eye. A polished

perfection dominates this rusticity. The cakes of soap in the bathroom are placed in rigid, sharp-edged precision. The food is the best food, for Alice has not only a *cordon bleu* but watches her cook with a rapier eye. The plates and the goblets are bold and beautiful.

In the terrace garden, frail China-pink roses bloom between the borders of box hedges. Wisps of ivy climb over the gnarled stone parapet. At intervals along it are three small pavilions as simple as a Noah's ark house, but with the proportions and textures and colours of the best relics of the fifteenth century. The distant mountains and poplared valley are constantly changing throughout the day, as clouds gather or the sun shines.

Gertrude is delighted here. 'Yes, it *is* nice. Yes, it is *very* lovely.' She beams with enjoyment as she snatches a handful of weeds from the rose bush.

Alice wakes at five each morning. She puts on a cretonne smock, then sets about the task of collecting vegetables from the garden, planning the meals for the day and arranging the flowers. By eight, she is wandering with a large basket over her arm and a cigarette wobbling between her lips. By nine o'clock, the vases have become the most esoterically arranged still-lifes. I know no one who arranges flowers better than Alice. They have an architectural quality.

We passed by a fair where the roundabouts were hung with chandelier teardrops. I shot for roses, missing only one bull's eye out of twenty. To the great excitement of Gertrude and Alice and the entire village, we left with an enormous bouquet of puce, waxen-paper flowers—roses, carnations and dahlias.

'She wasn't a servant. She had never been trained. She was only good at making a bed. She was the best maker of beds we have ever had.'

I had not realised there could be such difference in the way a bed was made. But then, I am English. The French have a ritual of bed-making. The mattress is thrown one way one day, another way the next. The sheets are drawn tight as a board over this newly aired mattress, then tucked in by half the length of the whole sheet. Gertrude and Alice, when they come to England, have great difficulty sleeping in beds made by the servants in even so well ordered a house as Gerald Berners's. And Francis

Rose's mother used to weep tears of rage when she came to England, as she could get no one to make the bed properly.

There is no one more alarming than an optimist. Gertrude Stein is a great general and a great optimist. She will not hear of war talk. It is almost a breach of etiquette to mention the fact that events look black or the prospect horrifying. 'Oh, no, no. War isn't logical, no one wants a war. Yes, of course Hitler is making a speech tomorrow. He's always making a speech. Of course, Roosevelt's going to talk. Ha, ha, he's always talking. No, no, things aren't serious. Last year they were serious, yes. But last year, the postman had been called up by this time. He hasn't been called this year, and they're perfectly calm down at the village.'

I didn't want to contradict these *obiter dicta*. But the truth is, they *are* becoming anxious down at the village. One by one, the men have been mobilised. On the walls, the *affiches* or *rappels* have been posted. We go off in the car on expeditions to neighbouring towns, to Aix or Annecy, and almost in defiance of the 'General', we buy newspapers with portentous headlines: '*Situation plus grave.*' By degrees, the peaceful existence we've enjoyed these last weeks has been shattered. And there is nothing to be done about it. For the time being, at any rate, all thoughts of peace are at an end.

The 'General' faced reality when at last the butcher telephoned this morning, to say that the soldiers had requisitioned all the meat and he could not supply the joint that had been ordered. The household became panic stricken. Gertrude now felt she could no longer take the responsibility of our being there. Francis Rose, with nowhere to go, has tried to influence me to join him at Jean Hugo's in the Dordogne. But there is an unwelcome taste in my mouth at the thought of the future. I do not wish to get further away.

Tonight my nerves were awry. I had seen too much of even these delightful people. I'd been closeted in this small house, or in the small car overrun with dogs, all day. I decided to go for a walk by myself for half an hour before dinner. I followed the tracks that Gertrude had taken me on, then went further. I walked fast and long. Night came upon me, while I hastened to complete what I thought was a circle.

379

Rain came down, as heavily as it does in mountain country. I ran. By continuing further I must surely reach the village, even if it should be less quickly than I had imagined. At any rate, I mustn't retrace my steps now. So I continued for miles, running and walking.

If I cut through this wood, perhaps it would lead me to the village. But the neighbourhood was unrecognisable. I realised I was seriously lost. I laughed a little to ward off panic. I must already have been walking nearly two hours!

At length I spotted a house I had seen on the *last* lap of my walk out! The landmarks on the way back were like memories of middle age.

My calves ached. Running only made them ache more. Then they no longer ached, but my feet were sore and the skin rubbed off my toes. To lose time sitting on a fence would be little help. I imagined the panic back at the General's. What were they saying? Dinner must have been announced long ago. Every ten minutes that passed they would be talking of my disappearance. Soon they'd become really frightened.

The night was black, the rain fierce. This was a living nightmare. I could prove its reality to myself, but it had all the sensations of a nightmare. Eventually I met a man under an umbrella. He told me the way back. I had come too far, and must retrace my steps.

The last part of the adventure was almost the most unpleasant. Although I felt within reach of home at last, I had no idea of the cross-country routes. Small lanes forked in every direction. I became lost again in a maze of quagmired paths. At last I saw a light! I made a beeline for an isolated cottage. I banged on the door. A woman shrieked inside; a dog barked. The door opened to reveal a group of peasants staring in terror and amazement. They were listening in on their radio as their President made a fateful pronouncement.

Bolstered by fresh instructions, I started to run again. Then I was blinded by some car lights. I heard Gertrude shouting. The nightmare was over.

Never have I enjoyed a hot bath and fish more. The household had been overwhelmed. The Chinese boy and the French cook had gone out to reconnoitre; Francis was beside himself. But we were all gay again. Gertrude felt relieved to have forgotten the prospect of war for three hours! A friend had telephoned to ask, 'Have you heard the latest war news?'

'War?' replied Gertrude. 'Who cares about war? We've lost Cecil Beaton!'

War was now imminent. The journey home was precarious. But Francis Rose and I managed to make an earlier departure than we expected, as all trains were late. For hours we travelled in the dark, stopped at each small station where more and more people bundled into the little space available. The people were optimistic or else resigned, and they behaved with a dignity and courage that was very pleasant. The English more probably would have hidden their alarms under gales of raucous laughter, or community singing.

The atmosphere of Paris was gloomy and quietly panic-stricken; and the days dragged on in a dislocated fashion. One could not enjoy the company of friends: museums were shut.

In England some people were still saying that there must be a way out. Others felt they would rather face the issue now.

Randolph Churchill, with eyes blazing and voice hoarse with pro-longed enthusiasm, banged the table and exclaimed that he was enjoying to the full the last lap of gaiety. Life, in fact, did continue in much the usual way; the same friends would meet together, and the same food was eaten; but for most people the threat of war had already dimmed the lustre of existence. The desire for pleasure had gone.

There was already a movement to find available jobs should war break out; and suspecting how useless I should be in any of the fighting services, I made efforts to get into 'camouflage'. I was told to return home and cultivate my garden.

At Ashcombe, in fact, I worked while listening to the Radio News bulletins—on designs for a film. Korda's intended production of 'Manon Lescaut' should have been my initial foray into the world of the cinema. But, the film was never made, and the costumes mouldered away in packing cases.

The lease of an old-fashioned flat in Rutland Gate, in which my parents and I had for the last couple of years existed rather than lived, was now given up. My father had died in that small dull bedroom. My mother and I left without regret those impersonal rooms and the superannuated clanging lift. My mother, with only a few of her most loved possessions around her, temporarily lived with her sister

Cada. I was offered a room in Gerald Berners' house in Belgravia.

But whereas at an earlier period, this house, with its birds-of-paradise on the half-landing, and the Corots on the wall of the drawing-room, had been the scene of much festivity and gaiety—no chef could surpass the artistry of Gerald's Mrs Nelson—now a change had taken place. The house had suddenly become shabby and sad—and saddest of all was to see the change that had taken place in my host. Appalled at the prospect of war, Gerald, already prone to fits of melancholia, became convinced that he was going insane. Although even to his intimates he had seemed so aloof from human suffering, now he became only too keenly aware of what misery another war would bring. Overnight Gerald became old.

It was while I was about to step into the olive green bath that one morning, Nelson, the deaf butler, came upstairs and shouted, 'The war's started.' I felt as if a strong electric current had run through me. When recovering from the shock I telephoned to Kaetchen Kommer to ask this most sanguine of friends if such tragic news could be true. Sadly he replied, 'Yes, the Germans have started the war on a lie: they pretend their offer of negotiation has been rejected, but the offer has never been received by the Poles. Without declaring war, they have invaded the country, and bombed Warsaw.'

But I am skipping too far forward. There were still a few days left to us of peace, Meanwhile, a dentist's appointment, and a journey into the past.

Visiting my former home, it was strange to notice that only the unimportant events were brought to mind, not the moments of decision, the memories of unconscious fears and anxieties and all the half-truths of youth.

TEMPLE COURT

September, 1939

I usually find time to pay the dentist a long-standing visit before the summer holidays, 'just in case'. This year it had to wait for my return from Gertrude's. Mr Tattersall, our dentist, has been filling family teeth for years, is considered without peer by the Beatons. He still lives in Hampstead where we were brought up; so back to the scene of my childhood I went, dutifully entering the little red brick house in Finchley Road.

The necessary tooth drilling took up less time than I had allowed for, and I was out in the street with an hour to spare before lunch —a situation in which I practically never find myself. Rather than hurry back to my secretary and unending business, I decided to enjoy my leisure.

Nor did I feel guilty in doing so. After all, I'd been promising myself a sightseeing day in London for a long time. At best, I seemed only to glimpse my city through the windows of hurrying car or cab. It looked more romantic and beautiful than ever now at the end of the summer. When would I find that free day to walk in the parks, visit the City churches and perhaps even go to Greenwich? The day might never arrive; but anyhow, here was an hour suddenly offered to me on a platter. What better place to spend it in than Hampstead—two minutes away from the road I was born in, five minutes from those haunts where most of my early years had been spent?

I remember so well that, as I grew older, my chief desire in life was to quit suburbia and 'come down' to London. When I reached adolescence, postal address marks and the names of telephone exchanges loomed as things of vital interest. I considered there was all the difference in the world between plums bought on Avenue Road, N.W. or South Street, Park Lane; or between someone living in W.1 or W.2. When we eventually moved to Hyde Park Street, I even induced my poor father to write to the telephone authorities and inquire whether our number could not be altered to a Mayfair exchange instead of the inevitable Paddington one.

Today, having passed on to higher forms of snobbishness, I remembered, with a certain sly patronage only, the pleasanter aspects of living in a bourgeois community like Hampstead. I noticed wistfully how fine the flowers were in all these little gardens. It now seemed very agreeable to breathe the atmosphere of an arcadia where, only twenty minutes from the West End, families enjoyed country pleasures. Hedges were being trimmed by gardeners; flower borders were being watered, and oak trees flourished in back gardens.

As inevitably happens when one visits the scene of one's childhood, things seemed ridiculously small. Every landmark, however familiar, had shrunk to Lilliputian scale. The long walk up Heath Drive could no longer be reckoned the dragging climb it once was. Even the width of the pavement had diminished.

This was where we used to walk to Miss Dale's school. I conjured up the water-colour class. Clean, wet paints were prepared for each lesson, the necessary colours already squeezed out on to an individual saucer. How exciting that class had been, how full of promise were three daubs of paint! Once I glorified a spray of ivy in a very bold way, making glutinous use of prussian blue and raw sienna.

We had been allowed, Reggie and I, to walk to school unaccompanied. This always rather surprised me, for it was quite an adventure. Yet today I noticed that the distance from the door of our home to the front door of Miss Dale's school was less than a few hundred yards, even with two corners to turn.

By now the car had stopped outside Temple Court, the house that more than any other could be called our home. Here I spent all my remembered childhood; and I had almost grown up when we left. Here Nancy and Baba were born. Daddy's business affairs had flourished in those days. And there was a lot to keep him interested, with his four children, billiards, cricket, riding on the Heath.

Today, the familiar house stood deserted. A board had been erected with the inscription 'Property for Sale, Caretaker Within.'

Cautiously, I walked up the drive to the porch I knew so well. With a heart that had stopped beating, I rang the bell for perhaps the ten thousandth time. It still had the same ring, though twenty years must have elapsed since I last rang at this door.

The door itself seemed unchanged; the wood had not acquired an appearance of greater age. Even the letter slot, as in the old days, still wore a new and rather fashionable look.

Near to the door, gusts of wind blew through the creeper I had so often studied as I waited for the door to open, scrutinising the delicate, immature quality of new tendrils. How was it that, after the plant settled down to thrive, as so obviously it had done, it did not grow more sturdily? Today, at last, the old creeper had managed to climb higher. The leaves in the centre of the wall seemed larger; but the tendrils framing the door lintel were still weak and delicate, pale yellow in colour, sticky and shiny-looking as though cut from a yellow oilskin southwester.

No one answered the doorbell. And I dared not bang the knocker, though I suddenly remembered exactly the sound it would make. There was no caretaker, no one at home. As I peeped through the letter slot, I could see the hall floor littered with letters and circulars that had been plopped in by the postman and now lay unheeded on the parquet we had laid down so proudly.

Nothing can be more haunting and tragic than an abandoned house. Since we deserted it two separate families had lived here, each adding their own little touches in the way of alteration or decoration. But it was us the house remembered; it was our irrevocable memories that vibrated there. These walls still gave forth the vivid atmosphere of my childhood; these rooms echoed a past whose least detail, whose very smell, I could once more savour. There was the 'cloak room' by the front door, with hanging rows of riding crops and an interesting assortment of caps, hats, riding coats. This was where Daddy's cricket bats had been oiled; there the sticking plaster had been kept for mending the bats. Just off the 'cloak room' was a lavatory with bright red-tiled floor. Down the main hall ran a long path of Turkish carpet, and on it stood a table that was as much of a focal point in the house as Piccadilly Circus is to London. It was, I remember a Kentishly carved table, said to be Irish eighteenth century, with a tray of calling cards on it. Leading off from the hall were the library with never a book in it; the drawing-room, whose apple-green taffeta curtains had been embroidered in Paris and whose occasional tables held enamel and silver *objets d'art* which had once been stolen by a burglar; lastly, the dining-room, with a strip of material under the floating bowl on the dining table. From the dining-room, one could enter the garden.

As I peered through the bolted windows at these changed but familiar rooms, nostalgia was suddenly dispersed by the feeling of being unwanted, a stranger. Again the telescope was reversed, making everything seem minutely proportioned in comparison with the memory of it.

Yet I felt impelled to complete my tour. Since the house was so obviously deserted, what prevented my exploring the garden? At worst a policeman or stranger might appear, in which case I could always offer the excuse, 'I've come back to see where I once lived.'

But no one interrupted my sentimental musings. Through the side garden I walked around to the back. The main garden seemed much smaller now. Weeds flourished, and everything was so overgrown that the lawn had become a field. Yet I recognised the traces of happy days. Here were the London pride and other rock plants I knew so well, from which cuttings had been made for our window-boxes when we moved into town. What a vast expanse this lawn had once seemed, when Reggie practised cricket in his cage of netting, when we had learned to putt. Untended now, the grass grew so thick and long that hay could be made from it. Here I took my first snapshots; here we played Catch-as-catch-can, and Nancy and Baba wheeled their dolls' prams.

The old oak tree remained unchanged. The day of the storm it had lost an arm and never recovered its symmetry. As I walked towards this amputated relic, two startled blue pigeons flapped out of the branches with a throaty squawk, causing dead leaves and twigs to fall.

My mother's garden seemed especially small. Long ago, it was quite a promenade to walk from the rose garden to the bed where lilies of the valley grew. Yet now these two gardens appeared to be part of the same bed. The standard roses my mother had planted used to grow in rich profusion. A few still bloomed, rather undernourished and poor-looking compared to the large pink and red and salmony-yellow blooms that once filled the house.

It was no good to linger too long. I felt choked and mawkish. However much I still thought of myself as a boy, I was a grown man now, with an unlived life stretching before me. It could never be healthy to regret the past, to cast a haunted eye on a house and garden 'as fugitive, alas, as the years'. I tore at a few of these roses for my mother, then fled from the memory-filled spot like a thief.

I motored home with the handful of flowers lying on the seat beside me. I was thrilled with anticipation at the prospect of being able to surprise my mother.

When at last I arrived, my mother was in a busy mood. But she stopped, alert to hear my news. 'You'll never guess where I got these!' I held up the bunch of now rather drooping roses. 'They're from Temple Court. I've just picked them!'

A wild look came into her pale blue eyes. For a terrible moment she remembered the rose trees she had planted, resurrecting the garden of Temple Court, the happiest days of her life when all was going well with Daddy and the children were blithely growing up. Pitted against those lost days came the inevitable events of later years—the breakup of the home, Reggie's fatal accident, Daddy's death two years ago, and now the war.

She became like an animal. She snatched the roses from my hands, crying in anguish, 'They're mine! They're mine!' Then she hurried into her bedroom, placing the wilting remnants of a lifetime in her favourite vase—a little blue china vase with a painted design of mixed flowers on it.